C000279999

Fashionability

MANCHESTER
1824

Manchester University Press

Fashionability

Abraham Moon and the creation of British cloth for the global market

Regina Lee Blaszczyk

Manchester University Press

Copyright © Regina Lee Blaszczyk 2017

The right of Regina Lee Blaszczyk to be identified as the author of this work has been asserted by her in accordance with the Copyright, Designs and Patents Act 1988.

Published by Manchester University Press
Altrincham Street, Manchester M1 7JA

www.manchesteruniversitypress.co.uk

British Library Cataloguing-in-Publication Data
A catalogue record for this book is available from the British Library

ISBN 978 1 5261 1931 5 paperback

First published 2017

The publisher has no responsibility for the persistence or accuracy of URLs for any external or third-party internet websites referred to in this book, and does not guarantee that any content on such websites is, or will remain, accurate or appropriate.

Typeset by
Servis Filmsetting Ltd, Stockport, Cheshire
Printed in Great Britain by
Bell & Bain Ltd, Glasgow

Contents

Foreword

From time to time, our receptionist will take a call asking, 'Could I speak to Abraham Moon please?' Abraham passed away in 1877 so it's a tricky call to put through. For many, it is difficult to conceive of a company surviving 180 years over seven generations of two families.

I am often asked, 'So who is or was Abraham Moon?' Until very recently, I have had to reply, 'We don't really know.' Not much anyway. We knew that Abraham founded the company in 1837 and we knew where and how he had died as we had clippings from newspapers of the time. Similarly, we knew that his son Isaac Moon was taken ill at Headingly watching a test match between England and Australia in 1906. But that was more or less all we knew. We have few business records preceding 1920—although our archive has a large collection of original design books.

I wanted to discover more about the Moon dynasty but also the story of how the mill came to be sold to Charles Walsh and how the company had survived through the decades that had decimated the Yorkshire wool textile industry. I wanted to know more about the fascinating tale of how Abraham Moon and Sons had managed to keep reinventing itself through the years of constantly evolving fashion and changing consumer demand. Charles Walsh, my great-grandfather, bought the mill from the Moon family in 1920. What fascinated me was that Charles was not a wealthy man. He was a hired hand, a trained designer and mill manager but not a man of great financial means. Here was an early twentieth-century entrepreneur who found an early twentieth-century venture capitalist and an accommodating lender to back his acquisition.

Some years ago, I decided we must have a history book written because so much of our company history was interesting but anecdotal. What we really needed was a forensic historian. I consider myself extremely fortunate to have 'found' Reggie, the perfect author for this book. Regina Lee Blaszczyk is Professor of the History of Business and Society at the University of Leeds, a brilliant historian and an author of books not dissimilar to the one I wanted written. Reggie (or Miss Marple, as I now know her) has not only uncovered a myriad of facts and stories through the generations but has been able to set them in the context of the evolution, and sometimes revolution, in the world of fashion.

The rest, as they say, is history.

John P. T. Walsh
Chairman and Managing Director,
Abraham Moon and Sons Ltd

Preface

The history of the Yorkshire woollen industry is entwined with the history of clothing, fashion and global trade. This microhistory of Abraham Moon and Sons Ltd opens the doors to the interlocking worlds of textiles, fashion and international commerce, encouraging further historical research on the fashion system in its entirety, from fibre makers to fashion retailers.

This book traces the history of a single mill from the Industrial Revolution to the era of globalisation in our own time. It reveals the hidden history of creativity, innovation and entrepreneurship in an industry long associated with utilitarian fabric rather than with fashion. It is the story of entrepreneurs such as the first Abraham Moon, who went from weaving shawls in a cottage to building a factory next to a new railway line that transported his cloth to Leeds, Liverpool and the wider world, and John P. T. Walsh, who understood that the game had changed and globalisation was going to be bigger than ever in the twenty-first century. It is also the story of the woollen merchants, clothing makers and trade fairs that have been left out of fashion studies, as if beautiful dresses and handsome suits were sewn from thin air rather than carefully designed cloth that found its way to market through layers of intermediaries.

The British woollen industry has a deep past—and at various times, its history has been a liability. For much of the late twentieth century, the Yorkshire mills fought a losing battle against man-made and synthetic fibres and the youthful easy-going styles that rendered tartans and tweeds nearly obsolete. One of the great ironies of our time is that globalisation has created consumers in some market segments with an interest in clothing and other products that are anchored to faraway times and places. The digital consumer is free to imagine the past as he or she sees fit and 'vintage' is cutting-edge fashion. The design sensibilities that had pushed British tweeds into the margins are now an invaluable asset to firms like Abraham Moon and Sons, which has learned to harness the past for the present.

Regina Lee Blaszczyk
University of Leeds
7 February 2017

Introduction

From 15 to 17 September 2015, the British woollen mill Abraham Moon and Sons Ltd exhibited at Première Vision Paris, the prestigious juried trade fair for apparel fabrics. The mill was one of 1,924 exhibitors from fifty-seven countries that made their new ranges for Autumn/Winter 2016 available to some 62,000 visitors, three-quarters of whom were international. Held at the Parc des Expositions de Paris-Nord Villepint, a convention centre near the Charles de Gaulle Airport, Première Vision Paris is a biannual trade show for the six major industries that supply the global fashion industry with ingredients and services: yarns, fabrics, leather, designs, accessories and manufacturing. Launched as a modest silk exhibition in Lyon in 1973 to give the customers a 'first look' at the new luxury fabrics, over the past forty years Première Vision, nicknamed 'PV', has become Europe's most important textile trade show for apparel.[1]

In many trade shows, exhibitors have wide-open booths that advertise the products to the passers-by, but at PV, the vendors and their fabrics are all hidden behind tall white barriers. The idea is to keep the samples away from the prying eyes of competitors. Admission to a particular stand is limited to the customers, and people from rival mills are not allowed in. The customers—the fabric merchandisers, fabric buyers, apparel designers and other creative staff from retailers and brands—are identified by their badges. Besides the manufacturers' stalls, the exhibition halls have public spaces with curated exhibitions, including a major display that forecasts the upcoming season's trends in colour, style and texture.

Abraham Moon and Sons was one of a dozen English and Scottish manufacturers of tailoring cloth to exhibit in the PV Fabrics Hall. Italian mills dominated the tailoring fabrics section with more than sixty booths; there were smaller numbers of exhibitors from China, France, Japan, Mexico, Portugal, Spain, Turkey and a few other countries. Visitors could find the stand of Abraham Moon and Sons by looking through the exhibition map and directory, but they were also alerted to the booth by the Union Jack judiciously draped over the entrance. Over the three days, a stream of customers from apparel brands in Europe, North America and Japan dropped in to meet with the staff from the mill. The managing director, John P. T. Walsh, and agents such as Trevor Brann, who handles the home trade

I.1 Peeking into the mill's stand at Première Vision, September 2016. © Première Vision.

from London, wandered in and out. The sales team was a constant presence, as was typical at the stands of other woollen and worsted manufacturers and distributors such as Dormeuil of Paris.

But something unusual was happening on the stand of Abraham Moon and Sons. Five of the mill's six woollen designers—Martin Aveyard, Pam Birchenall, Judith Coates, Amanda Dougill and Claire Pearson—were a major presence. The designers were busy throughout each day, sitting at small tables and interacting with the customers (figure I.1). One such customer was Ivan Green, president of Canabrogue Inc., a fabric-sourcing company that serves private label menswear manufacturers from offices in Montreal, Canada, and factories in Hangzhou, China. Green, who spoke with a thick Irish brogue, was browsing through Moon samples in search of heritage fabrics for some vintage-inspired brands he was planning for North America.[2] Other customers included the president and the designer from Boden, an up-market British brand with a strong mail-order business and a sprinkling of high-street stores; representatives from the London couture house Alexander McQueen; selectors from the British high-street retailer Marks and Spencer (M&S); and fabric buyers from the children's division of Polo Ralph Lauren in New York.[3]

There was a respectful exchange of ideas between the woollen manufacturer and the customer, as the mill's designers interacted with the fabric buyers from all around the world. The designers watched the customers flip through the mill's sample cards and compare them to their own swatches, sketches and notes. Sometimes two buyers from a brand talked quietly among themselves as the mill staff listened. They were poised to offer technical advice or trend opinions, sometimes fielding a steady stream of questions: does Moon have this herringbone in a darker grey? Can you make a slightly smaller check? Could Moon match this heather bouclé? Here in a nutshell was the creative process of the global fashion system in action.

Abraham Moon and Sons has been exhibiting at PV since spring 1981, when it first participated in a showing of British woollens and worsteds coordinated by the National Wool Textile Export Corporation (NWTEC). Established during the early part of the Second World War to promote British wool cloth and yarn abroad, during its heyday and before its cessation in 2009 NWTEC helped dozens of British mills display British fabrics and yarns at PV and other trade fairs in Europe, North America and Asia. Today, the mills independently arrange for their own space at international textile trade shows from New York to Shanghai. The British woollen industry, which boasted 3,000 mills and employed 180,000 blue-collar workers in the years after the Second World War, is now a slim shadow of its former self. Abraham Moon and Sons is one of the rare survivors.

Past and present

This book uses the history of Abraham Moon and Sons to examine design and innovation in the British woollen industry from the 1830s to the 2010s. It is a history of a single firm—a business that originated in 1837 with two clothiers, Abraham Moon and his likely half-brother, William Moon—that reaches out from microhistory to macrohistory, from the local and the regional to the national and the global. It starts in a Yorkshire village called Guiseley and ends up on the stage of international commerce that connects a small mill in greater Leeds to the creative economies of major global fashion cities such as London, New York, Paris and Tokyo. This book is a narrative history, and narrative is about storytelling. The stories told here are about a mill, a town, a region, an industry and a nation whose fate for the past two hundred years has been inexorably linked to the international political economy and the global fashion system.

For many years, historical research on the British textile industry focused on dark satanic mills, management–labour conflict and industrial decline. With a few exceptions, very little historical research on the British textile industry of the nineteenth and twentieth centuries examines the design process or connects cloth production and distribution to the fashion system.[4] This curious disconnect between the history of fabrics and the history of fashion is rooted in disciplinary biases and fragmentation. For many years, the mainstream academic history profession considered fashion to be feminine, frivolous and generally unworthy of study. New fields such as design history, material culture studies and fashion studies emerged as alternative disciplines for researchers who value the material world and understand its place in history.

Yet for all of its accomplishments over the last quarter century, fashion studies remain mainly cultural in emphasis. Researchers primarily focus on the meaning of dress, the materiality of objects, debates on class and gender, or celebrity designers and luxury brands. The cultural and the economic have yet to meet in fashion studies, as they have in one of my fields, the new business history. The reality is that global brands like Alexander McQueen, Burberry, Chanel, Dolce & Gabbana, Gant, Hugo Boss, Paul Smith, Polo Ralph Lauren and Tommy Hilfiger cannot create luxury lines or lifestyle apparel without high-quality textiles. The same goes for up-market national brands and retailers such as Boden, L. K. Bennett and Hobbs in the United Kingdom; Brooks Brothers and J. Crew in the United States; and Beams, Ships, Tomorrowland and United Arrows in Japan.

The interface between the textile manufacturer and the fashion marketplace is centuries old. The historian John Smail has explained how Yorkshire woollen merchants served as intermediaries between weavers and the market in the eighteenth century. The merchant showed cuttings of fashionable fabrics to the weaver and asked him to adjust his patterns accordingly—so as to sell more fabric.[5] In the nineteenth and early twentieth centuries, the interface between the manufacturer and market became more complex as large wholesalers, often involved in foreign trade, assumed a central role. The wholesale woollen warehouses of Bradford, Leeds and London served as mediating zones wherein merchants, textile manufacturers and garment makers could interact. The conversations often focused on quantity, price and delivery, but before they got down to brass tacks, the men talked about which patterns were selling and which were not. Over the course of time, major high-street chains such as M&S and Jaeger and mail-order houses such as Littlewoods and the Great Universal Stores came to exert a good deal of control over everyday fashion, and their selectors and technicians came to dictate the quality and the look of the textiles (figure I. 2). The design and sales staff at mills like James Ives & Company in Yeadon, another town that is part of greater Leeds, mainly worked to accommodate the demanding specifications of large retailers, especially M&S, which was their major customer for several decades after the Second World War.[6]

In recent years, heritage-minded companies like Abraham Moon and Sons and Johnstons of Elgin, a cashmere mill in Scotland, have turned back the clock and adapted some of the older ways to contemporary practice. Developing a keener awareness of the market has been essential to the reinvention of the industry. The UK's remaining woollen and worsted mills have several common features. They are 1) family firms with 2) a penchant for refurbishing the physical plant

Young

JAEGER

is a shop-within-a-shop at Robbs

Which means your
Jaeger choice is wide and wonderful.
The three coats shown here are:
    Left. In all wool face cloth.
Sizes: 10, 12, 14.
    Centre. In herringbone tweed.
The colour is paprika with grey braided
edging. Detachable bolero.
Sizes: 8½, 10, 12, 14.
    Below. In all wool gaberdine.
Black, taupe or stone. Sizes: 10, 12, 14.

it's Robbs!

Robbs

Robb Brothers Ltd.
Grange Road,
Birkenhead. Tel: 647 7711

I.2 Jaeger put high-fashion woollens on the high street with stand-alone stores and the shop-in-shop, as indicated in this advertisement for their boutique within Robb Brothers in Birkenhead, near Liverpool. Courtesy of Jaeger Ltd and Westminster City Archives: 1327, Jaeger Archives.

and 3) a strong commitment to design. These private companies have no need to increase shareholder value, can hunker down during an economic downturn and can plough their profits back into the business, investing in new equipment—and even retail shops. Thirty years ago, Johnstons was a small tweed mill with a modest turnover. Several tactical moves generated successes that enabled the firm to see that 'making big and selling small was profitable'. The company diversified into scarves in the 1980s and into knitwear in the early 1990s, and established retail shops to market its distinctive range of Scottish cashmere and woollen accessories. By 1997,

Johnstons was no longer shackled to the fickle ready-to-wear industry; apparel cloths accounted for a mere 20 per cent of the firm's annual turnover. Inch by inch, the firm discovered ways to get closer to the ultimate consumer, either in retail shops or through the internet, thereby increasing its profit margins. With 'patience and slog', the mill reinvented itself as a brand with a three-pronged product portfolio in apparel fabrics, scarves and knitwear.[7]

Creativity has been crucial to the reinvention of the industry. Historically, the British system of technical education and practical experience had produced outstanding textile designers, particularly in Scotland. But many mills put design on the back burner during the postwar era, when they could sell almost anything to the makers-up and when powerful retailers called the shots on large orders. 'Designers were tucked away in a little office in the back of the mill and didn't see the light of day', explained James Sugden, who managed Johnstons for more than thirty years. Those who believed they could 'sell anything' received a rude awakening with the rise of youth culture and Carnaby Street styles, the synthetics revolution and competition from Italy. The British woollen and worsted industries were forced to undertake some serious soul searching and, ultimately, had to relearn the benefits of linking design and sales. 'The designer came out of the shadows', Sugden said. 'You can't underestimate the power of design.'[8]

The revival of traditional patterns—tartans and tweeds—is the public face of this design renaissance. Far more interesting, however, is the process of innovation that is hidden behind the scenes. As we saw in the discussion of PV, the fabric buyers for major brands meet with the designers from Abraham Moon and Sons to their mutual benefit as a matter of routine during the procurement process. The woollen designers share their technical knowledge of the cloth, which often helps the fabric merchandisers, fabric buyers and apparel designers with their deliberations. These interactions are part and parcel of what John Walsh calls 'design-led' sales.[9] International textile trade fairs like PV are just one interactive zone. The Sales and Design Showroom at the mill in Guiseley, the customer's headquarters in New York or London, and the agent's offices in Milan or Barcelona are other spaces for collaboration.

The marriage of cloth and clothing sustains the global fashion system, whether the apparel is retailed on Oxford Street in London or avenue Montaigne in Paris. Fashion itself is an all-encompassing cultural *and* commercial phenomenon that knows no boundaries. There are fashions in interior design, pottery and porcelain, automobiles and architecture.[10] In recent years, Abraham Moon and Sons has acknowledged fashion's all-inclusive nature, and besides diversifying into scarves and throws, has ventured to make furnishings fabrics for interior décor—and happily watched Johnstons and other mills follow suit. In academia, there is a similar imperative for fashion history and design history to connect the dots: the coat and the cloth, the fashion producer and the fabric designer, the history of clothing and the history of interiors, the cultural and the economic. As a narrative story about one British mill and its customers around the world over two centuries, this book is an attempt to nudge fashion history and design history in this new direction.

Tweeds and cultural identity

Ever since the traders of the North Sea connected London woollen merchants to European markets, wool has been equated with British identity. The somewhat stereotypical example of British wool fabric is tartan, which has been associated with Scottish nationalism and Highland pride since the romantic era of the early nineteenth century. In the twentieth century, tartans found their way to consumers through retailers such as the Scotch House, which sold merchandise in traditional British styles at several London locations, and the souvenir shops along the Royal Mile in Edinburgh and in other Scottish tourist destinations. More recently, celebrities such as Rod Stewart and Madonna and superstar fashion designers such as Alexander McQueen and Vivienne Westwood have used Scottish tartans and plaids with irreverence.[11] But tourist shops filled to the brim with tartan throws and kilts, and rock stars strutting across stage in oversized tartan scarves to the sound of bagpipes, mask the real history of British woollens.

Over the past two hundred years, a variety of woven woollen fabrics made in various places in the British Isles—England (the West of England and West Yorkshire) Ireland, Scotland and Wales—have been sold globally under the rubric of British tweed. Historically, tweed was a type of hand-made Scottish fabric with a twill (diagonal) weave, but over time, the term came to describe woollen fabrics in either a twill or a plain weave with a check, twill or herringbone pattern.[12] The photographic evidence says it all. We only need look at *carte de visite* portraits from the 1880s (figure 2.4) or street photography from the 1930s (figure 4.5) to see North Americans and Europeans of all ages and income groups wearing everyday clothing sewn from 'British tweeds' or copies of it. The 1945 film noir *Brief Encounter*, a Noel Coward drama about Laura Jesson, a suburban housewife who falls in love with a married doctor named Alec Harvey, depicts the star-crossed pair in typical British tweeds.[13] In our own time, we can thank Rosalind Ebbutt, Joan Wadge and, primarily, Maria Price—the careful costume designers for the 2002–15 ITV series *Foyle's War*— for thoughtfully dressing nearly everyone in the reimagined wartime Hastings and postwar London in a jacket, overcoat or suit made from warm British woollens.

Despite the historic ubiquity of tweeds, little is known about the web of connections that linked the British woollen industry to the fashion system and the wider world. In my other work on design and development in the creative industries,

I have highlighted nodes in the 'fashion-industrial complex'—the intricate web of people, companies and organisations that produce fibres, design textiles, make garments, forecast trends and sell fashion—and have urged historians to look beyond the canon of 'great designers' to develop an understanding of the 'fashion intermediaries' who labour behind the scenes to make the system work: managers, designers, forecasters, stylists, agents, merchandisers and distributors.[14] The history of design, production and distribution in textiles should not be isolated from the history of retailing, fashion and consumer culture, as it so often is. The beauty of a case study is that it allows the author to explore the many cultural, social and economic interactions within the fashion-industrial complex.

Exactly why has one hand been clapping, silently? The first generations of historians who studied British manufacturing were preoccupied with the technological achievements of the Industrial Revolution, and focused their research on landmark inventions, the division of labour and the rise of factories. In the early twentieth century, historians of the Yorkshire wool textile industry looked back to the advent of mechanisation and documented the transition from craft to industry. Yet all about them—everywhere in Birmingham, Bradford, Huddersfield, Leeds, London, Manchester and Glasgow—were the signs of seismic shifts in the textile and clothing industries. The ready-to-wear manufacturers had started to buy fabric directly from the mills and were pushing the powerful woollen merchants out of business, and the mills themselves scrambled to find more foreign customers as the home market was flooded with cheap imported fabrics. In the mid- to late twentieth century, the rise and triumph of high-street multiples wreaked havoc with the supply chain and, in the relentless drive to offer lower prices, laid the groundwork for the offshoring of textile production. In the midst of these changes, the wheels of fashion whirred away, generating the constant need for new patterns and colours. In mills all around Yorkshire, pattern designers laboured over their point papers and weavers watched over their looms, while salesmen crossed the English Channel to chase after Continental customers. Squirrelled away in libraries, archives and universities, early historians of the Yorkshire textile industry fixed their eyes on the distant past and averted their gaze away from the significant, if unsettling, transitions of the moment.[15]

The silences of the past can be a powerful testimony to the most important realities of the past. Few people took the time to write down what everybody knew; there was no reason—and no time—to document the commonplace. The textile collections in museums and historical archives hold countless textile-range books that were created by mills as a permanent record of their output and as reference tools for the design staff.[16] Technical schools assembled similar pattern books for teaching. Everyone knew what types of fabrics each mill made, so no one bothered to label the swatches in the books. Today, nobody knows which mill made which piece of cloth, or if it was a bestseller or not. Historians are a bit like Agatha Christie's detective, Miss Marple. The fictional sleuth lurks in the background and watches, knowingly, as the protagonists reveal their true character. Historians have learned to work with limited evidence to peek into the lives of the dead and to construct a reasonable facsimile of what may have happened. Artefacts and documents provide the clues.

An artefact can open the door to the alien world of the past, where people looked like us but did things differently. A pattern book dated 1889 from the Yorkshire College of Science—the precursor to the University of Leeds—sheds light on the marvellous creative world of Victorian woollen design (figure I.3). Established in 1874 during the heyday of the British wool fabrics industry, Yorkshire College was a school for training designers, dye chemists and mill managers for the woollen and worsted mills in Bradford, Huddersfield and Leeds; the surrounding valleys of the West Riding; and faraway places like Germany, Japan and the United States. Yorkshire was home to the world's most advanced wool textile industry, which exported wool, yarns, woollens and worsteds to the four corners of the earth. The pattern book contains the

I.3 Pattern book, 'Class C. Woollen & Worsted Dress Fabrics, Autumn 1889', Yorkshire College of Science. Courtesy of ULITA: 1999.361; photo by Tracey Welch Photography.

finest woollen dress fabric—the 'high-tech' products of a high-technology industry. The motifs are intricate and the colours brilliant, most likely made with the new modern dyes from the rapidly industrialising synthetic organic chemicals industry in England, France, Switzerland and, especially, Germany.[17] Young men such as Charles Herbert Walsh, born in Guiseley in 1860, studied dyeing and weaving at Yorkshire College. Talented students applied what they learned at the college to jobs in design and management in mills around the world. As a local man, Charles Walsh went to work at Abraham Moon and Sons, where he laid the foundation for the firm's twenty-first-century commitment to design-led sales.

A document can help break uncomfortable silences on topics like sales and merchandising. The interactions between mill and customer were so routine—and so confidential—that no one wrote about them in history books. We see hints of these endless private exchanges in account books like those found in the archive of Abraham Moon and Sons (figure I.4). To break the silence of these records, we can look to the archives of another mill for letters sent to England by a Yorkshireman travelling abroad. In April 1934, Rueben Gaunt Hainsworth of

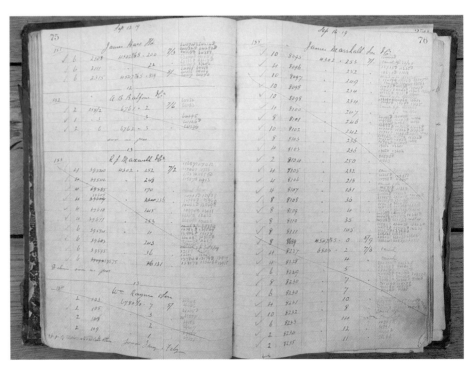

I.4 Ledger showing sales to the Leeds merchants James Hare Ltd, James Marshall Son & Company and other customers, 1919. Courtesy of Abraham Moon and Sons.

A. W. Hainsworth & Sons Ltd wrote home from Milan, Italy, where he was meeting customers and studying the market:

> I spent all the morning with Mr. Carlo Imperiali … Enclosed is a pattern of Herringbone shewn by Dormeuil Frères … The enclosed patterns were bought from Garnetts last season @ 9/– per yd. He intended them for coats but sold mostly in trousers. Something after this type of colour in various makes would interest him. I mentioned herringbones,—this is a rather popular design in Italy—The Bedford cord might also be of interest. It appears just under 300 grammes is the best weight to make—Over this weight pay 15% extra duty. *It's a very important dividing line* … I don't think there is *much* business to be done in Italy but a little in specialities … When it comes to cheapness we're simply not in it.[18]

Here we glimpse the reconnaissance mission of one British mill seeking new business from the Italians. There was an air of sophistication, an awareness of which fabrics were in fashion and a knowledge that economics and trade policies mattered. If the cloth was over a certain weight, it would incur extra customs duties at the border and all profits would be lost. Then, as now, the British mills had higher labour and production costs than manufacturers in a low-wage economy. Back then it was Italy, today it is China.

In a world connected by free trade, instant communications and container ships, we seldom think twice about the continuous flow of raw materials, ingredients and finished goods from Australia to Europe, Europe to China, and China back to Europe. The phrases 'supply chain' and 'supply chain management' are part of our daily lexicon. But the supply chain is a relatively new concept, dating back to the closing decades of the twentieth century. For much of their history, British textile mills sold fabrics to wholesale merchants or garment manufacturers with little thought of the end user. Today, a mill like Abraham Moon and Sons is necessarily fixated on the needs and expectations of the apparel brand that will sew up its cloth into a heritage tweed jacket, and that brand is concerned to know more about the fabric's place of origin. The fast fashion sold in Primark and Zara is underpinned by anonymity, but heritage apparel brands such as Boden, Brook Taverner and Paul Smith appreciate and tout the identity of their suppliers. At the upper end of the market, there is value in unpacking the supply chain and in being able to point to the British mill that made the fabric. Heritage mills like Abraham Moon and Sons, in the words of Peter Ackroyd, a long-time executive at the NWTEC, 'tick off the boxes that people want to have at the upper end of the market'.[19] Those mills that survived the dramatic changes that transformed the woollen and worsted industries in the 1980s and 1990s did so by focusing on three elements: the history, the product and the design.

Fashionability

This book traces the history of Abraham Moon and Sons from its beginnings in 1837, through the heady days of the Victorian craze for tweeds; two global wars that saw unprecedented demand for military cloth; the postwar rise of consumer culture and the boom in man-made fibres; the transformation of the British high street with the triumph of multiples and chain stores; to the rise of a new global fashion system in our own time. It discusses the history of design, innovation and entrepreneurship through a series of stories about one tweed mill and its major customers: woollen merchants in Leeds and London, ready-to-wear manufacturers, high-street retailers such as Jaeger, M&S, C&A Modes and Next, and global brands such as Polo Ralph Lauren and Dolce & Gabbana.

The stories in this book focus on the creative processes and the marketing innovations that made British tweeds the most desirable woollens in the world. The text interrogates the silences of the past and poses a stream of small questions about design, continuity and innovation within the fashion system. Who decided what types of patterns to make? When did the designer first appear in the Yorkshire woollen industry? How much say did the customer have in the look of the fabric? When did trade fairs like PV come to be major sites for knowledge exchange between the mill and its customers? When did brands and branding become part of the picture? These small questions are building blocks for the book's larger query: what constitutes *fashionability*, and how do entrepreneurs, firms and industries create fashionable products? To explore this greater question, we can pull back the curtain on the global fashion system and turn to the history of Abraham Moon and Sons.

1 The case of the grey tweed

Between the years 1860 and 1870, Guiseley enjoyed a prosperous trade, the Guiseley Waterproof Tweeds being noted for their superiority of make and finish. (*History of the Ancient Parish of Guiseley*, 1880)[1]

On the afternoon of Saturday, 27 January 1866, clothiers from the Yorkshire villages of Pudsey and Guiseley flocked to the city of Leeds and crowded into the Town Hall, an impressive edifice on Victoria Square, now part of the Headrow. The Town Hall housed the Leeds Borough Court, which was hearing a case about the clothier Abraham Moon of Guiseley. Over the past two months, several pieces of Abraham Moon's dark grey tweed had been stolen from the Coloured Cloth Hall, the large commercial market where local clothiers—or cloth makers—laid out their 'coloured cloth', or 'mixed cloth', for inspection by the customers (figure 1.1). The stolen pieces had been traced to the premises of Law Atkinson, a cloth finisher at Harcourt Mill, on the western edge of Leeds, and to the warehouse of Joseph Padgett & Ephraim Benjamin & Company, which operated a tweed mill on the outskirts of Leeds and a merchant house on Park Row in the city's main business district. In his capacity as a merchant, Padgett had purchased the grey tweed below market value from the Pudsey clothier, who was known as a maker of white and heavily napped melton cloth. Everyone in the courtroom knew that Pudsey clothiers did not make tweeds. This type of cloth was a speciality of Guiseley.[2]

Industrial espionage

Abraham Moon testified in court, along with his sons, Abraham Junior and Isaac, and two employees. For the past few years, Abraham Senior had turned out 'grey tweed cloth of various qualities', producing about ten undressed pieces, each fifty-one yards in length, every week. In keeping with tradition, the elder Abraham tracked his output in one of those pocket-sized stock books that clothiers guarded with their lives. Flipping through his notebook, he explained that his Leeds agent sold some of his fabric to a Glasgow merchant and that he offered the rest to the shipping merchants who frequented the Coloured Cloth Hall.[3] Most of the cloth

7.—COLOURED-CLOTH HALL, EXTERIOR.

1.1 Exterior of the Coloured Cloth Hall, Leeds, 1850. Author's collection: *The Land We Live In*, vol. 3 (London: Charles Knight, 1850), 116.

made in Guiseley—two-thirds of the output—was exported to the German states and to France.[4]

Completed in 1757, the Coloured Cloth Hall sat opposite Wellington Station, the passenger depot for the Midland Railway. Also known as the Mixed Cloth Hall, it was an assemblage of red brick buildings that housed nearly 1,800 clothiers' stalls, each marked with the owner's name, arranged around six 'streets' or pedestrian walkways with names such as 'Change Alley' and 'Cheapside', the latter thus called after the main thoroughfare in London where merchant warehouses sold cloth (figure 1.2). On Tuesday and Saturday, the Coloured Cloth Hall was open for business for a mere hour and fifteen minutes, from 9:30 a.m. to 10:45 a.m. Merchants walked down the corridors, looking over the counters to find the pieces they needed. According to the *Penny Magazine*, everyone knew everyone else, and sellers tried to tempt passing buyers with new designs and colours. "'Mr. N., just look at these olives!' 'How much?' 'Six-and-eight.' 'Too high.'" Sometimes, a merchant would select £40,000 worth of woollens during one of these brief visits. The merchant settled up with the clothier at his warehouse and then arranged for the fabric to be

1.— COLOURED-CLOTH HALL, INTERIOR.

1.2 Interior of the Coloured Cloth Hall, Leeds, 1850. Author's collection: *The Land We Live In*, vol. 3 (London: Charles Knight, 1850), 92.

taken to a local finisher, who 'dressed' or prepared the wool cloth for market through processes that made it soft and fuzzy.[5]

Local clothiers paid carriers to take their woollens from the countryside to the Coloured Cloth Hall, mainly in horse-drawn carts.[6] Shortly after the New Year in 1866, Abraham Moon had sent his carrier to Leeds with 'three pieces of dark grey tweed cloth' for display on his tables. When the Moons came to Leeds on 16 January, they were surprised not to find these pieces and others that had been sent to market in December. A few days later, rumours directed them to Joseph Padgett's warehouse and to Law Atkinson's finishing mill where they found the purloined goods.[7]

In keeping with stamping laws passed by Parliament to prevent fraud in the woollen trade, the selvedge of the cloth was identified with two signatures: 'A. Moon, Gy.' for the clothier Abraham Moon, and 'H.F.' for the weaver Henry Foggitt.[8] The thief had tried to remove these marks and added new initials. But a maker could readily identify his own work. Henry, who had married Abraham's daughter Hannah in 1860, had been employed by his father-in-law for the past five years. On the witness stand, Henry identified the dark grey tweed as a piece of his weaving from October, judging the cloth from 'its general appearance and by the colour and arrangement of the lists'. Some irregularities on the selvedge were the mistake of a young apprentice whom Henry had scolded. 'The boy who wove the cloth tied all the ends of the thread together at that place into a knot, and when he finished the cloth he cut off the knot, leaving the white spot.' The next witness was William Pawson, a 'cloth tenterer' employed by Abraham. William swore under oath that he had stretched and dried the piece-dyed cloth and pencilled each selvedge with the number '51', which was still visible.[9]

Why would someone steal Abraham's tweed from the Coloured Cloth Hall? We can speculate that industrial espionage may have been at play. The clothiers who crowded into the Leeds Borough Court knew there was something special about his fabric. 'The staple trade' of Guiseley 'is the manufacture of woollen cloths,' noted one 1866 business directory, 'but principally tweeds, for which this place is famous'.[10] The merchant Padgett, who purchased some of the stolen cloth, lived in Guiseley. The Padgetts and the Moons had known each other for decades, but the Padgetts were more upwardly mobile.[11] By 1866, Padgett lived in Tranfield Lodge, a rambling house on the village outskirts, while Abraham was a man of modest means who worked out of a stone cottage. However, Abraham appears to have had the better eye for design. When questioned in court on how and why he acquired the stolen cloth, Padgett was evasive. We can imagine an envious Padgett, holed up in the back of his Park Row warehouse, carefully unpicking the dark grey tweed to learn how his home-town rival achieved his distinctive look.

Historians will never know if Padgett secretly masterminded the tweed heist, or if the Pudsey clothier came up with the idea to earn some quick cash. Regardless, the theft of another man's cloth was a serious crime, and the court charged the Pudsey man with 'stealing property exposed in the Cloth Hall'.[12] The gravity of the offence was reflected in the hefty bail and fines imposed on the thief and by the extensive press coverage in the *Leeds Mercury* and the *Leeds Times*. As was customary, newspapers around the country reprinted the story. The theft made news in Sheffield and Manchester and in distant Dundee, Scotland.[13]

Leeds and the West Riding

Today, Leeds is known for its service industries, shopping arcades and universities. But at the time of the theft, Leeds was the capital of a vast woollen empire that made fabrics used across the globe. This empire, the West Riding area of Yorkshire, was the largest producer of worsted and woollen textiles in Britain, which in turn was the largest global exporter of these fabrics.[14] The central business district of Leeds was dominated by the cloth trade and ancillary businesses. The astute commercial traveller, in town for a few days to buy or sell goods, could readily size up the scene, noting the large number of enterprises with wool in their lifeblood. Besides the cloth halls and the merchant warehouses, Leeds centre was packed with shops, banks, shipping houses and insurance brokers; train depots for passengers and freight; and public houses where clothiers and merchants met to close deals. On market days, thoroughfares such as Boar Lane were thronged with shoppers, merchants darting between meetings and clothiers trucking pieces on their heads (figure 1.3). All Leeds seemed to live and breathe woollens.[15]

Located on the River Aire, Leeds in medieval times had been home to an agricultural manor and a Cistercian monastery. By the thirteenth century, the wool clip of Kirkstall Abbey, combined with the softness of the local water, led to the growth of the wool cloth industry.[16] In the sixteenth century, Leeds surpassed York and Beverley in woollen production. The town received a charter of incorporation from King Charles I in 1626, and the first local governing body was established. During the eighteenth century, the local coalfield was developed and the economy diversified to include forges, potteries and soap makers. But the most powerful citizens of Leeds were the woollen merchants who had grown wealthy from the shipping trade. Built in stages between 1770 and 1816, the Leeds and Liverpool Canal connected Leeds to Manchester and to the port of Liverpool.[17]

By the early 1840s, West Riding and Leeds especially were known as Great Britain's 'clothing district'.[18] As woollen manufacturing declined in importance in Leeds and became a major industry in the valleys of the West Riding, the

1.3 'Leeds on a Market Day, A Sketch in Boar Lane and Briggate'. Author's collection: *The Graphic* (21 September 1872).

town ventured into clothing production and distribution, among other things. Leeds became known for its tailoring workshops, shawl warehouses, drapers' shops or haberdasheries and garment manufactories. The Leeds ready-made garment industry started to modernise in the 1850s, following the adoption of sewing-machine technology from the United States.[19] As living standards improved, consumers in Europe and North America began to covet stylish wool clothing. Men, women and children all wore the new wool garments, made more affordable by scale economies in Yorkshire. Wars and military skirmishes created a demand for durable wool cloth for uniforms and blankets to cover men and horses. Trade policies also affected woollen production. Over the course of the 1860s and 1870s, several major Western economies—France, the German Zollverein or customs union, and the United States—lowered tariffs on imported fabrics, which opened these important markets to British cloth. There were still plenty of woollen merchants in Leeds, and they all clamoured for distinctive fabrics to sell abroad.

By 1870, Leeds was home to about 140,000 people who earned their livelihoods from commerce and industry, working in offices, shops, warehouses, woollen mills, iron foundries, potteries and garment factories.[20] Money was being made and impressive new buildings testified to the city's achievements and ambitions. Several new edifices by the prominent architect Cuthbert Brodrick—the Town Hall opened in 1858 by Queen Victoria, the Corn Exchange of 1862 and the Mechanics Institute of 1868—appeared on the fringes of the old medieval core. Under construction was the General Infirmary, a Gothic Revival building by the London architect George Gilbert Scott, who is today renowned for the Albert Memorial and for the former Midland Grand Hotel at St Pancras railway station in London.[21] In the centre of Leeds stood older structures that spoke to the city's heritage. There were ecclesiastical buildings like Holy Trinity Church on the ancient Boar Lane and the nonconformist Mill Hill Chapel, whose eighteenth-century parishioners had been ministered to by Joseph Priestley, a polymath who later discovered oxygen. At the foot of Briggate (the main shopping street), Leeds Bridge, a cast-iron structure built in 1871–73, spanned the River Aire, replacing a series of bridges that had housed the wool cloth market in earlier times. Also notable were two large commercial structures for the buoyant woollen trade: the Coloured Cloth Hall where Abraham Moon sold his grey tweed and the adjacent White Cloth Hall of 1868, the fourth such structure in the history of Leeds.[22]

In 1874, a *Handbook for Travellers in Yorkshire* noted that the 'great *Manufactories* of Leeds are … the chief sights of the place'. Running northwest out of the city, Kirkstall Road connected Leeds to the ruins of Kirkstall Abbey and eventually meandered past the villages of Horsforth, Yeadon and Guiseley. Between the bustling city centre and the medieval abbey, the mills and factories of Leeds were a sight to behold, particularly 'at night, when the light streams from innumerable windows, rising tier above tier'. Bean Ing Mills, the impressive woollen manufactory run by the Gott family, used steam power throughout, 'even for packing the bales of cloth'. The *Handbook* noted that 'Leeds and its immediate neighbourhood' was home to 'between 800 and 900 manufacturers of woollen cloth, some of them representing firms of great wealth and importance'.[23]

Leeds was connected to surrounding towns and villages, the national market and major ports by an expanding railway network. The Midland Railway provided a regular service to nearby manufacturing and farming communities. By mid-century, one Midland route stretched fifteen miles northwest from Leeds to the picturesque town of Ilkley on the River Wharfe. Ilkley was a favourite residence for prosperous Yorkshire businessmen, including mill owners, and a major tourist attraction. Well-heeled residents and visitors appreciated the hydropathic spas, the ancient Roman and Saxon ruins, and the scenic walks across Rombald's Moor. In 1865, a new station opened on the Ilkley line at Guiseley, a 'large village' some nine miles out of Leeds known for a stately Norman church called St Oswald's and 'some worsted-mills'. A 'pretentious modern town hall' was built in 1867, as testimony to the town's ambitions.[24] St Oswald's Church served the Anglican parish. In 1812, Patrick Brontë and Maria Branwell, the parents of the Brontë sisters of Victorian literary fame—Charlotte, Emily and Anne—had married there.[25] Guiseley was situated in a valley between the River Aire and the

River Wharfe in a region known as Wharfedale. Like their neighbours in the nearby villages, the cloth manufacturers in Guiseley produced worsteds, but woollens were their forte.[26]

Abraham Moon, clothier

Clothiers like Abraham Moon, some of whom became mill owners, were the backbone of the Yorkshire woollen industry. Abraham was born in Guiseley on 30 October 1805. His mother Ann may have died in childbirth; the records for the baptism of baby Abraham on 4 April 1806 show him living with his father, John Moon, and another Abraham Moon, perhaps his grandfather.[27] As Steven Caunce's study of cloth making in one West Yorkshire parish has shown, clothiers inhabited a rural commercial network that encouraged business activity and fostered entrepreneurship. They interacted as a matter of course with merchants, who provided them with market information that was used to develop new products. Over time, these complex interactions led to the emergence of regional manufacturing clusters, or districts, specialised in different types of cloth for different types of markets.[28] Abraham was born and raised in a district that came to be known for inexpensive tweeds.

At the time of his birth, Guiseley was a market town on the fringes of the Yorkshire Dales whose population lived off farming and woollen manufacturing. In 1795, Guiseley was home to 771 people who farmed 286 acres, growing wheat, barley, potatoes, oats, beans and turnips. Life in nearby Carlton and Yeadon—one with a smaller population than Guiseley, the other twice as large—was much the same.[29] In the 1820s, Guiseley had a population of 1,200 people, including numerous *Woollen Manufacturers* with the names Baldwin, Barrett, Binns, Brown, Clapham, Earle, Hardwick, Holmes, Hudson, Ive[s], Marshall, Padgett, Pollard, Preston, Rhodes, Riley, Robinson, Shepherd, Smith, Unthank and Waite.[30] No one knows how Abraham became a weaver, but it is likely that he was apprenticed to one of his neighbours or learned the trade from his father John.[31] In 1829, a man named John Moon rented a cottage from Thomas Waite, living in proximity to other households with 'woollen' surnames.[32] Also in 1834, one John Moon was among the Guiseley woollen manufacturers who displayed their pieces at the Coloured Cloth Hall in Leeds.[33]

In 1832, the 'clothier' Abraham married Susannah Waite of Guiseley and in the next year, their daughter Hannah was born.[34] The Waites, the Moons and the Claphams were neighbours, all renting three-storey stone terraced houses on New Row (figure 1.4), just north of St Oswald's Church and the remains of a Norman cross at the village centre.[35] The men all worked as clothiers, overseeing the spinning

1.4 New Row, Guiseley, shortly before demolition in the 1950s; Abraham Moon lived and worked in one of these terraced houses when he was a clothier. Courtesy of Aireborough Historical Society: G126.

of yarn and the weaving of cloth in the cottages. Following Susannah Moon's death, Abraham remarried in 1835, this time to Elizabeth Clapham, with William Moon, likely his older half-brother, as a witness.[36] A year later, this same William married a Hannah from the Clapham clan.[37]

By 1837, Abraham Moon and William Moon were in partnership as clothiers. The half-brothers may have decided to pool their technical know-how and financial resources to develop new products or to reach new markets. Unfortunately, the Moon brothers established their partnership at a difficult moment for West Riding clothiers: the start of a seven-year depression for the woollen and worsted industries. The troubles began when American merchants, who purchased substantial quantities of British wool fabrics, failed to meet their obligations during the Panic of 1837.[38] A chronicle of the worsted industry published in 1857 discussed the effects of the financial crisis in the West Riding. Looking back, the author of the *History of the Worsted Manufacture in England* described 1837 as one of

the most unfortunate in the modern annals of [the] worsted industry. From the beginning of the year symptoms prevailed of the panic, which afterwards spread over the country, and affected every branch of trade and commerce ... During the month of April, the stuff markets were very much depressed; many manufacturers failed in May, but the grand convulsion was witnessed at the commencement of June, when several of these great American houses went down with a crash, and involved in ruin a multitude of manufacturers, especially those of Bradford.[39]

These unfortunate conditions resulted in fewer orders for Yorkshire fabrics. The depressed market for cloth, combined with a rise in wool prices, put pressure on manufacturers. The partnership of Abraham and William fits into this story. Notices of the failure of the Moons' partnership were published in the *Leeds Mercury* and the *London Gazette* in early June 1837. The Moons were unable to pay their bills and, as was the law, were imprisoned for debt.[40] In September 1838, their partnership was dissolved.[41] The trade depression lingered. In December 1839, the *Leeds Mercury* reported on the continued distress at Yeadon, Guiseley and adjacent places 'in consequence of the stagnation in trade'.[42] There was nothing unusual about the Moon brothers' failure. Nineteenth-century entrepreneurs understood that partnerships involved risk and that all business ventures were susceptible to recessions, depressions and international trade winds.

Abraham returned to work as a clothier, spinning wool and weaving it into shawls in his cottage. Fashion historians have documented the Victorian fad for imported Kashmir shawls and Anglicised 'cashmere' spin-offs, but just as important was the fact that shawls were a practical necessity for the damp British climate (figure 1.5). Women wrapped themselves in shawls to stay warm in an era when houses, schools, churches, factories and other buildings were not well heated. British weavers offered a range of shawl designs, from paisley to plaid.[43] Around 1839, a Parliamentary committee concerned about impact of power looms on handloom weavers surveyed the wool cloth-making districts. The investigator who visited Guiseley described Abraham Moon as 'a sober, steady and industrious workman' and documented their conversation. 'My wife and I do the whole', Abraham said of his weekly work routine. 'I can weave about two and a half shawls a day, and I work more than 11 hours.' Together, Abraham and his wife Elizabeth made about fifteen shawls per week, earning approximately one shilling and sixpence per shawl. Abraham owned a loom that he had purchased for six pounds; he preferred the up-front investment to renting a loom at one shilling per week, which was the convention. The Moons' gross weekly wages totalled about twenty shillings: thirteen shillings for Abraham's labour and seven for Elizabeth's. Their net weekly wages, after deducting expenses for materials, totalled eleven shillings. Other handloom weavers in Guiseley earned different amounts. Men in their peak years, such as Timothy Waite, age forty-two, netted just over nine shillings per week, while older

1.5 The shawl was essential for warmth in the days before central heating, but also as an indication of social standing; this woman's striped woollen shawl is simple but of good quality. Author's collection.

men like J. Hewitt, age seventy-four, netted a mere six shillings.[44] Although the trade recession lingered, industrious weavers kept working, often by combining handicraft with agriculture to earn a living.

Shortly after the Parliamentary report, Abraham appeared in the 1841 census of England, the first year when detailed information was recorded about each household. He was described as a cloth manufacturer, aged around thirty. The Moon household included his wife Elizabeth, three small children—Hannah from his first marriage, Emma and baby Abraham—and Grace Clapham, a thirteen-year-old girl probably related to Elizabeth.[45] William Moon, also a cloth manufacturer, lived nearby.[46]

The census is mute on the seasonal routines of Abraham as a clothier, but the diary of another handloom weaver, Reuben Gaunt of Pudsey, provides insight into a Yorkshireman's everyday experience. Gaunt belonged to a family of spinners and weavers who combined cloth making with agriculture. His diary documented daily life in his village, including births, marriages and deaths; horse injuries and carriage accidents; the Methodist chapel and the temperance movement; buying cows, slaughtering pigs and planting turnips; and a summer holiday at the fair in Scarborough on the North Sea coast. The diary also sheds light on the inner workings of the cloth trade itself. By the 1840s, more than half of the fine merino wool used by the British textile industry was grown abroad, mainly in Australia, South Africa and Germany. Before Bradford became a major centre for wool imports, Yorkshiremen went to London or Liverpool to purchase their supplies. Several times per year, the Gaunt men visited the port cities to stock up—and to see the sights. 'Father left home about ½ past 8 o'clock in order to go to Liverpool, to the wool sales, which commence tomorrow.' 'I went to Liverpool from Leeds with Uncle Daniel. At Liverpool we went to Easthanic's Picture Gallery, New Market, Mechanic's Exhibition, Races, and the Zoological Gardens. Bought 11 Bales of Wool 2 at 1/4½, 4 at 1/5½ and 5 at 1/6. Returned on Saturday.' Trips to Leeds to sell woollens at the cloth hall were routine, if not always fruitful. 'Went to Leeds but sold nothing and was much annoyed with walking the ground being covered with snow.' 'Brother Isaac went the first time to Leeds cloth market but did not sell anything. I sold 14 ends of my own to Mr. Sykes.' 'I went to Leeds on Bess today and sold 8 ends at 5/- to Mr. Sykes.'[47]

By this time, the West Riding of Yorkshire was second only to Lancashire in significance as a British manufacturing district. The West Riding encompassed an area of nearly 800 square miles, including the hardware industry of Sheffield and the cloth industry of Leeds. As one authority noted in 1847, the

> mixed cloth manufacturers reside partly in the villages belonging to the parish of Leeds, but chiefly at Morley, Gildersome, Adwalton, Driglington, Pudsey, Farsley, Calverley, Eccleshill, Idle, Baildon, Yeadon, Guiseley, Rawdon, and Horsforth, in or bordering upon

the vale of the Aire, principally to the west of Leeds; and at Batley, Dewsbury, Osset, Horbury, and Kirkburton, west of Wakefield, in or near the valley of the Calder.[48]

Within these woollen towns and villages, clusters of specialisation were starting to become evident. The neighbourhood of Batley and Dewsbury, for example, was known for its shoddy mills, which spun yarn from old woollen rags and refuse, often imported in quantity. Shoddy cloth—an economical blend of recycled wool and new or 'virgin' wool—was used for blankets, carpets, greatcoats, table covers, padding and other applications in the clothing trade.[49] In 1845, the *Leeds Times* praised the manufacturers in 'Batley and that neighbourhood' for reworking discarded material into 'elegant and comfortable clothing'. The same observer documented the nascent speciality of woollen makers in Yeadon, Guiseley and Rawdon. These manufacturers were building the market for 'fancy-cloakings', a 'branch of the business ... only just in its infancy'.[50]

Spring Head Mill

By 1845 when the economy picked up, the Moon brothers were back in business together. Perhaps a little prickly from their failure, they were among a group of around twenty clothiers who were partners in Spring Head Mill, a public mill or 'company mill' built in 1842 by Pawson, Hudson & Company.[51] The first British ordnance survey, conducted in 1847–48 and published as a series of maps in 1851, shows Spring Head Mill in Guiseley centre, a mere five-minute walk from Abraham's cottage on New Row.[52] The mill was sited on the town springs and on a tributary of the River Aire with the quaint name Guiseley Beck, so there was plenty of fresh water for industrial processes.[53] The spring water from the Yorkshire limestone region was ideal for woollen production, as it gave the cloth a desirable softness to the touch, or 'handle'. The *Bradford Observer* wrote that the Spring Head Mill 'was not a trading company, and the members had only facilities for "scribbling and fulling"'.[54]

The organisational form known as the 'company mill' was not unique to the West Riding, but it was more widely used there than in the other woollen districts. These mills processed raw wool for clothiers who spun yarn and wove fabric in their homes, and then finished the fabric on behalf of the clothiers so they could take it to market. The clothier James Ives from nearby Yeadon recorded that, commencing in 1848, he used a company mill to advance his business.[55] Ives bought the raw wool, engaged local weavers to make cloth in their own lofts and then used the equipment at the mill to finish the fabric.[56] Even though company mills were also called 'Joint Stock Company Woollen Mills', they were not incorporated. Many of them predated the liberalisation of incorporation laws in the 1840s. Sometimes they had legal partnership deeds, but many of them were informal arrangements built on trust. A group of clothiers would 'put their heads together, and subsequently their purses' to overcome the difficulties associated with carting raw materials and pieces of cloth to distant facilities for processing and back again.[57]

Company mills were an ideal proving ground for clothiers who aspired to expand their business and perhaps one day run their own mills. Each clothier invested a small amount of personal capital in the enterprise to become a shareholder. The manager at the company mill used this money to purchase equipment for processing raw wool (scribbling, slubbing and carding) and for finishing the woven cloth (fulling). In exchange for his investment, the clothier was given access to costly textile-processing equipment, which was housed under a single roof not far from his cottage. The company mills of the West Riding were unusual enough to attract the attention of Parliament, which researched them while planning the legal reforms that led to the Joint Stock Companies Registration and Regulation Act of 1844. The prominent woollen manufacturer John Nussey from Leeds helped lawmakers understand how the clothiers made use of company mills:

> The wool is generally bought sorted of the woolstapler, and is sent to the mill to be scribbled and slubbed, for which process a small sum is paid per lb. weight, in the same manner as a load of corn is sent to the country corn-mill to be ground into flour; it is then returned to the clothier, who spins, weaves, and looks after the processes of manufacture at his own home; it is again sent to the mill to be fulled, and the clothier afterwards prepares it for the market. It is sold in the cloth halls in the balk or unfinished state to the merchant, who finally dyes and finishes it ready for use.[58]

Company mills were part of a manufacturing system that was making the transition from handcraft to industry. The widespread use of company mills spoke to the entrepreneurial spirit of the Yorkshire clothiers. These facilities allowed the clothiers to do what they did best—spin and weave in their cottages—while relegating some of the heavy work to expensive machinery. John Nussey elaborated on the financial arrangements:

> From the first introduction of machinery, the clothiers united to build mills in shares … The numerous woollen mills scattered throughout the populous clothing villages of the West Riding are principally owned and occupied by clothiers in shares. When the shareholders are numerous, say forty (they seldom exceed, but often amount to that number), they will subscribe £.50 per share in the first instance; they then buy the land, and proceed with the building; they next borrow on mortgage the largest amount they can gain credit for, which will generally pay for the building and steam-engine; the machinery is obtained on credit.[59]

In a letter to government officials, another Yorkshireman wrote of the ubiquity of company mills: 'These mills are not the exception, but the rule.'[60]

Initially, Abraham probably used Spring Head Mill to process raw wool and the cloth made by his family in New Row. In 1845, fellow investors in the mill included the clothiers John Barrett, Lister Bradley, Thomas Chaffer, Matthew Clapham, William Cooper, John Dickenson, John Harrison, William Hewitt, Henry Hudson, Samuel Ibbitson, Benjamin Pollard, James Pollard, Samuel Pollard, James Preston, William Preston, John Smith, two men called John Waite, Joseph Waite, Joseph White and Joseph Winterburn.[61] Guiseley clothiers supported a number of company mills. Besides Spring Head Mill, the village had the Low Mill and the Green Bottom Mill.

The costly machinery at Spring Head Mill allowed the clothiers to achieve economies of scale in processing, which in turn encouraged them to weave more fabric. Eventually, Abraham began to employ people from outside his family to spin and weave. In nineteenth-century parlance, this marked his transition from 'clothier' to 'cloth manufacturer'. The 1851 census described Abraham as a 44-year-old 'Cloth Manufacturer Woollen' in New Row, employing eight men. By this time, his daughter Hannah, aged seventeen, was working as a woollen spinner, while three of his other children—Isaac, Mary and Abraham the younger—were learning to read and write at the local school.[62] William Moon lived nearby and along with his son, Matthew, worked as a woollen handloom weaver.[63]

By the 1850s, Guiseley township, a tract of about 1600 acres, was home to some 2,500 people. Thirty-seven per cent of the population was engaged in woollen textile production and related occupations. There were four scribbling and fulling mills, plus an assortment of professionals, farmers, butchers, joiners, maltsters, stonemasons and tailors. The packhorse was becoming a relic of the past. Local wagon carriers transported goods on behalf of manufacturers and farmers to Leeds, Otley and Bradford and offered door-to-door service for people who needed to do business in the city. An omnibus took people to Bradford on Thursdays and to Leeds on Tuesdays and Saturdays.[64]

No one in little Guiseley knew that the Yorkshire woollen industry was on the brink of a major boom. A staunch supporter of free trade, Prime Minister Robert Peel had orchestrated the repeal in 1846 of the price-hiking tariffs on imported grain, known as Corn Laws, which was followed by the abolition of the restrictive Navigation Acts between 1849 and 1854. These measures, which had been vigorously championed by Richard Cobden and the Anti-Corn Law League, laid the foundation for Britain's free trade era.[65] Still in the future was the Cobden-Chevalier Treaty of 1860, which would open the French market to British wool fabrics. In the meantime, the Crimean War (1853–56), wherein Britain and its allies fought Russia in a continuation of the Ottoman Wars, created a large demand for blankets and uniform cloth.

In 1857, Abraham and William were among some forty-five cloth manufacturers listed in the *Post Office Directory* for Guiseley. In keeping with tradition, these clothiers combined agriculture with manufacturing in a dual economy. Most of them raised cattle, horses, pigs, pigeons, poultry and sheep for personal consumption or commercial sale, competing for prizes in the annual autumn show of the Guiseley Agricultural Society. In one year, Abraham, for example, took second place for his 'pen of five ewes'.[66] But all signs pointed to the demise of agrarianism. In its heyday as a market centre, Guiseley had hosted two horse fairs every year, but the last of these equestrian showcases took place in 1859.[67] The demand for lightweight woollens kept the clothiers busy. The *Manchester Guardian* summed it up: 'Yeadon, Guiseley, and Rawdon are all partaking in the advantages resulting from the brisk demand for the light cloths, to which the attention of those places is mainly directed.'[68] Although the men loved their horses, they preferred the money brought in by the cloth.

In 1860, the Abraham and William still owned shares in Spring Head Mill, but by the end of the decade, they would be out of that enterprise. With characteristic honesty, John Nussey commented on the pros and cons of company mills. When in top form, these mills served to advance shareholders' interests. They provided clothiers with the chance to learn something about machinery and to learn how to run a mill. In this respect, these operations served as training grounds for future factory owners. But as an organisational form, company mills were not firm enough to mitigate harsh circumstances. 'If the times are good, they will generally succeed not only in working off their incumbrances, but in raising the condition of the clothiers themselves', John Nussey wrote. 'But when the speculation is soon followed by bad harvests and consequent bad times, they not unfrequently get into great difficulties.'[69]

The disadvantages of company mills stemmed from problems inherent in partnership agreements. Nussey elaborated:

> They are subject to all the inconveniences arising from the law of partnership, in common with other Joint Stock Companies: in particular, from not being able to sue or to be sued by one of their number, and from not having the power to proceed at law against a member of their partnership, these two points form their chief difficulty. There is the difficulty of getting rid of a partner compounding with his creditors, with many unpleasant circumstances arising from that source. The act of one binding the whole ought also to be mentioned, but as being a less frequent source of trouble.[70]

Another Yorkshireman explained that the absence of a partnership deed could encourage fraud and theft among the members or the bookkeepers.[71] The Spring Head Mill was not without its share of headaches. At a later date, some of the thirty-six members appeared in the Bradford Borough Court to testify against one of their own who had forged bills of exchange under the company's name.[72]

By the 1860s, the Spring Head Mill had outlived its usefulness to Abraham and William. As the Moons got older, they may have thought it wise to invest their skills and capital in setting up the next generation in the family business. In 1861, Abraham, 'Woollen Cloth Manufacturer', was secure enough to have moved from his rented cottage on New Row to a freehold dwelling on Town Street. William was a mill owner (but we have no evidence as to which mill). By this time, Abraham's eldest daughter, Hannah, had married the weaver Henry Foggitt, but five of her siblings still lived at home. Four of them worked in the family woollen business. Emma was a spinner, the younger Abraham and Isaac were weavers and young Mary had the job of 'burler', or wool cleaner. Now in his mid-fifties, the robust Abraham was on his third wife, Grace, who at the age of thirty-two had recently delivered a baby daughter, Ann.[73]

Abraham Moon and other Guiseley clothiers began to imagine a brilliant future for themselves as the owners of vertically integrated woollen mills. For one, the American Civil War (1861–65) had created a large export market for British cloth (figure 1.6). The heavy woollen makers in and around Dewsbury filled much of this demand, but manufacturers elsewhere in Yorkshire also responded.[74] More important was a major development in international trade policy. In 1860, the British government, in part under pressure from the Bradford Chamber of Commerce, signed a landmark treaty with France. The Cobden-Chevalier Treaty of 1860, also known as the Anglo-French Treaty of Commerce, was a triumph for free-market liberalism. Influential members of the Bradford Chamber of Commerce, who were at Richard Cobden's side during the Paris negotiations, secured important concessions for the British woollen and worsted industries. The French *ad valorem* duty for most British textiles was reduced to a mere 10 per cent by 1864.[75]

In the words of one historian, the Cobden-Chevalier Treaty led to a 'swift break with centuries of protectionism' and ushered in a free-trade era.[76] This bilateral treaty had a most-favoured nation clause stating that France and Britain would extend to each other the benefits they granted to third parties. This meant that the advantages France extended to Italy, for example, applied to Britain.[77] There was a snowball effect as other European nations, swept up in industrialisation and hungry for markets, signed bilateral preferential trade agreements that liberalised trade to an extent not seen again until the late twentieth century.[78] By the late 1860s, commerce was freely flowing among the major European trading partners.

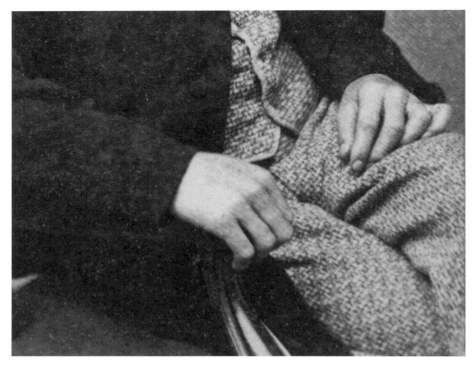

1.6 During the second half of the nineteenth century, tweeds for suiting were often highly textured, as seen in this detail from a *carte de visite*, Providence, Rhode Island. Author's collection.

Abraham saw great promise in the unrestricted flow of trade between European nations and between Europe and North America. In 1867, he joined forces with his two older sons, Isaac and Abraham Junior, in a partnership called Abraham Moon and Sons, with an eye to capitalising on opportunities at home and abroad.[79] Armies, navies, police forces and transportation systems around the world needed durable warm cloth for uniforms. The expanding ready-to-wear industry in the United States, Germany and Great Britain, especially in Leeds, was ripe for Yorkshire woollens. Even when sales of other types of wool cloth languished, Guiseley tweeds held their own. In February 1867, the *Leeds Mercury* wrote that the 'mills in the neighbourhood of Yeadon, Guiseley, and those districts where the manufacture of tweeds, meltons, and other light fabrics suitable for the spring trade mostly prevails, are kept in tolerably good work, and are running full time'.[80] The upward trend continued in early 1868: 'Tweeds continue to keep their position, and manufacturers are very busy, the Guiseley makers being able to employ not only their own mills, but a considerable amount of machinery elsewhere.'[81]

Netherfield Mill

On Saturday, 25 July 1868, Abraham watched his youngest son Arthur, aged eleven, lay the foundation stone of a new mill, to be called 'Netherfield' and adjacent to the tracks of the Leeds–Ilkley line of the Midland Railway, not far from Guiseley station. The architect, contractors, workmen, friends and several 'Leeds merchants' attended the ceremony. Two business associates—'Mr Hewett, of Leeds, and Mr Taylor, of Bradford'—made speeches. The first speaker was probably the 'Hewitt' in Bishop, Son, & Hewitt, a firm of Leeds woollen merchants, while it's likely the second was James Somerville Taylor, a Bradford wool-stapler who was a close associate of Abraham Senior. Like other Guiseley woollen manufacturers, Abraham Moon looked to Leeds to sell his cloth and to Bradford for the materials to make it. The little celebration spoke to the vitality of the local woollen industry. 'Guiseley continues to be well employed throughout', the *Yorkshire Post* explained, 'especially in the manufacture of excellent tweeds.'[82]

Abraham's success as a clothier, combined with his experience with Spring Head Mill, seem to have whetted his appetite for entrepreneurship and fuelled his desire to see his sons succeed as cloth manufacturers. Evidence on the financing for Abraham Moon and Sons shows how some Victorian clothiers used local social networks to establish themselves as capitalists. Netherfield Mill and its cottages were constructed on a parcel of land purchased from William Wells, a gentleman from Bradford, and Thomas Holmes, a worsted spinner and worsted manufacturer from Otley.[83] The parcel had been 'measured out and fenced or staked off from three several closes of land called Turner Stiles Broad Ing and Nether Moor', which may have previously been the property of the local gentry, Francis Hawkesworth Fawkes (1797–1871) and his nephew Ayscough Fawkes (1831–99) of Farnley Hall in Otley.[84] Like other wealthy landowners, the Fawkeses were art lovers who assembled large picture collections and befriended their favourite artists. In earlier decades, Farnley Hall was often graced by the presence of the renowned landscape painter J. M. W. Turner (1775–1851), who depicted the Wharfedale landscape in watercolour sketches that embodied the Romantic style in art.[85]

A small parcel of the inspirational Yorkshire landscape landed in Abraham's lap through a circuitous route. The Fawkes family owned one of the 363 great estates of England, covering 11,000 acres of farmland and 2,000 acres of moor and woodland in Wharfedale. The tenants raised cattle and sheep, generating income for the extended Fawkes family.[86] Land sales were strictly prohibited by law with the exception of projects that benefited the public good. According to one local historian, in 1847–56 and 1861, land from the Fawkes Trust Estate was sold to the North Eastern Railway and the Midland Railway. Eventually, the Midland built

the line from Leeds to Ilkley.[87] After the railway was completed, a long triangular
piece of land near Guiseley station ended up in the hands of Wells and Holmes,
who may have planned to construct a worsted spinning mill there but never did.
Abraham acquired the land and put up Netherfield Mill. The Fawkes family had
a vested interest in the Wharfedale economy. In a small way, they facilitated the
industrialisation of the region by providing Abraham Moon and Sons with access
to the resources needed to buy the land, build the mill and eventually improve the
property.[88]

Netherfield Mill—named after the 'Nether Moor' property—was about half a
mile west-northwest of Spring Head Mill and St Oswald's Church.[89] A few years
earlier in 1860, another woollen factory, Ing's Mill Company, had opened on a
greenfield site a bit further north along the railway tracks. By 1864, workers at Ing's
Mill and Spring Head Mill had cricket teams that enjoyed a friendly rivalry.[90] In
another part of town in 1868, Peate Brothers was building a woollen factory called
Nunroyd Mills, which opened in 1869.[91] With several new mills, a stop on the
Midland Railway and an impressive Town Hall, all signs pointed to Guiseley as a
Victorian town on the rise.[92]

Abraham built Netherfield Mill at a fortuitous moment. As one local historian
noted, the town of Guiseley 'enjoyed a prosperous trade' in the manufacture of
waterproof or water-resistant tweeds.[93] Wool was naturally resistant to moisture
because of its lanolin, but tweed makers further waterproofed the cloth by
impregnating it with oxide of alumina. One process involved soaking the material in
a large vat filled with the waterproofing solution and then hanging the cloth for six
days in drying rooms heated to 65 degrees Celsius (149 degrees Fahrenheit).[94] Since
waterproofing took a week or so, cloth manufacturers sometimes sent their fabrics to
finishing mills that offered 'proofing' services.[95]

Waterproof tweeds, or showerproof tweeds, were the ideal cloth for everyday
life in Victorian times (figure 1.7). They provided warmth in the days before central
heating and were excellent for retaining body heat in the cold damp weather. Tweed
outerwear was worn for walking around town; riding in carriages, carts and horse
cars; participating in country pursuits such as riding, hunting and fishing; and
for visiting the seaside.[96] Tailors all around Britain bought tweeds from wholesale
merchants and offered to clothe the local clientele in made-to-measure warmth.
In a typical newspaper advertisement, one Bedfordshire tailor beckoned the public
to his shop with descriptions of riding habits, hunting coats, liveries, uniforms
and 'Ladies' Waterproof Tweed Cloaks'.[97] The *Bradford Daily Telegraph* reported
on the mad rush for Guiseley cloth in the Leeds market. 'The greatest actual demand
is for tweeds, and some of the producers of these goods in the Guiseley district are
running their mills overtime … Tweeds are greatly used for female as well as male

PLATE IV.

Supplement to THE TAILOR AND CUTTER,
October 9, 1874, No. 418.

LADIES' FASHIONABLE WATERPROOF.

1.7 Ladies' fashionable waterproof cloak, 1874. © The British Library Board: *Tailor and Cutter*, 10 (9 October 1874), Plate IV.

attire; and hence, in some degree, the increase in their manufacture.'[98] The demand for Guiseley cloth was just as great overseas. It was often noted that Guiseley and Yeadon depended heavily on the North American market for their livelihood.

Government reports tell us something about Netherfield Mill. In 1868, Parliament created the Rivers Pollution Commission to determine how to rid British waterways of industrial effluents. Investigators collected information from the industrial districts, including the West Riding. The River Aire was foul with noxious waste from slaughterhouses, gasworks, clothworks and other manufactories that used its tributaries as drains. This was long before the advent of chemical engineering, which took responsibility for cleaning up industrial discharge. In the woollen mills, the jobs of washing and milling the cloth were especially foul. To remove lanolin from the cloth, the mills used a mixture of urine, manure and pig's blood, which, along with the grease, was discharged into nearby waterways.[99] The Rivers Pollution Commission published six reports from Guiseley; two reports were from scribbling, spinning and fulling mills, and four were from woollen mills. The four woollen manufacturers were Robinson-Smiths', Reilly & Company; the Low Mill of Smiths', Riley & Company; Pullan, Gill and Pinder; and Netherfield Mill run by Abraham Moon and Sons.[100]

Shortly after its completion in 1869, Netherfield Mill was comprised of a cluster of buildings: 'Mill Engine House Dyehouse Boiler House and Willey House messuages [houses] cottages and other buildings'.[101] A few years later when the Rivers Pollution Commission surveyed Guiseley, the mill employed fifty hands to produce an annual output of 100,000 lb. of cloth valued at £11,000. The materials used to make this cloth included 42,000 lb. of dyestuffs, notably logwood, an extract from a tree native to Central America that was commonly used to produce dyes in dark blue, grey, violet and black. The mill also used 9 tons of olive oil to prepare the wool for spinning, 5 tons of soap for washing the wool, 9 tons of alkali to adjust the water quality for scouring and softening the wool, and 20,000 gallons of urine for cleaning and dyeing the wool. The pure spring water found on site was used to process the wool, as is still done today. Although the mill was near a creek, it was not a water-powered facility. It was run by a twenty-horsepower steam engine that used 700 tons of coal each year. Netherfield Mill was one of two larger woollen manufacturers in Guiseley. Measured by the size of the workforce, Netherfield Mill was similar to the operation of Robinson-Smiths', Reilly & Company, which employed sixty hands to produce 492,000 lb. of cloth annually, worth £60,000.[102] The difference in the output for comparable manpower suggests that Abraham Moon and Sons may have been producing higher-quality cloth.

Netherfield Mill grew quickly, as did the social standing of Abraham and his immediate family in the local community. The Franco-Prussian War (1870–71) and the Russo-Turkish War (1877–78) created a large demand for military cloth and added to the export boom.[103] The impact of the war was reflected in the growth of the Moon business. The census of 1871 described Abraham as a 'Woollen Manufacturer & Mill Owner' who employed '110 work people'. His two oldest sons (and business partners) had established their own households. Abraham Junior was a 'Woollen Manufacturer' who lived near his father on Town Street. The second son, Isaac, lived in the Netherfield section of town, side by side with families whose breadwinners probably worked at the mill: an 'Over Looker Woollen Mill' and a 'Power Loom Turner (Woollen Mill)'. By this time, Abraham's half-brother and former business partner, William, was a 72-year old widower and the 'Beerhouse Keeper' at Ing's Inn in Menston. One of his sons, also named William, carried on as a weaver.[104] In 1875, the town of Guiseley benefited from the addition of a new railway connection to Bradford.[105] In later years, old timers in the Yorkshire woollen industry remembered the large export trade of the 1870s and thought of that decade as a golden age.

With his rising fortunes, Abraham increased his visibility in the community and built his social network through public service. Poor relief was a major concern of the Victorian middle classes, particularly after the Reform Acts increased the tax burden of newly enfranchised voters. Back in the early 1830s, a Royal Commission had reassessed the Old Poor Law, initiated during the reign of Elizabeth I and subsequently refined, which had empowered the parishes of the Church of England to raise money to aid the poor, the aged and the infirm. The Poor Law Amendment Act of 1834 had established a new relief system to be administered at the local level by clusters of parishes called Poor Law Unions. Each Poor Law Union was run by an elected Board of Guardians that held weekly meetings to discuss and plan the 'maintenance, clothing, lodging, employment, or relief of the poor' at the local workhouse. In 1861, a bureaucratic reshuffling of the West Riding administrative district led to the establishment of the Wharfedale Poor-Law Union in Otley, not far from Guiseley.[106] In 1865, the clothier Abraham was nominated to represent Guiseley on Wharfedale Board of Guardians, but his bid was unsuccessful.[107] In 1871, the mill owner Abraham had better luck and was elected as a Guardian of the Wharfedale Poor-Law Union.[108] In this capacity, Abraham probably participated in planning the new Wharfedale Union Workhouse, which provided shelter for a hundred paupers and an infirmary for forty patients (figure 1.8). He networked with like-minded local businessmen and again interacted with the Fawkes family. The Fawkes Trust Estate sold the land on which the workhouse was built and Ayscough Fawkes was involved in the construction project.[109]

The Moons' commitment to the community extended to St Oswald's Church and to the Guiseley schools. Abraham Senior had been involved in parish affairs for most of his life and his sons Abraham Junior and Isaac helped to raise funds

WHARFEDALE UNION WORKHOUSE, NEWALL.

13. 4. 02

1.8 Abraham Moon participated in civic culture as a guardian of the Wharfedale Poor-Law Union, which built the Wharfedale Union Workhouse shown in this postcard. Author's collection.

for a modern parochial school in Guiseley. The campaign was a joint project between the Wesleyan Methodists and the Anglican parishioners at St Oswald's, where the younger Abraham was a warden. The cornerstone for the school was laid in September 1874, with a celebratory parade. The usual assortment of woollen manufacturers—the Moons, the Ives, the Waites, the Padgetts, the Peates and others—partook of the festivities. Funded entirely by subscriptions, the school had classrooms for 400 children. It was located near St Oswald's Church and opened with great fanfare in August 1875.[110]

The tweed boom continued into the early 1870s, rewarding mill owners who invested in technology and design—the subject of Chapter 2. Entrepreneurial managers could secure enormous orders from the wholesale merchants engaged in overseas trade. 'In the out-townships the mills are fully occupied with orders', wrote the *Leeds Mercury* in January 1873. 'At Guiseley there is an active demand for tweeds, and one Manchester firm has this week purchased 2,000 pieces, 1,200 of which were delivered to-day.'[111] If we read between the lines, we can speculate that the 'Manchester firm' was engaged in the shipping trade and that the large order would soon find its way to the docks of Liverpool and then the warehouses of the dry-goods importers of New York, Baltimore and Philadelphia.

Just as the West Riding woollen mills benefited from global demand, so too did they suffer when the international economy turned sour. The end of the

Franco-Prussian War left France burdened with large reparations payments to Germany. The investment boom of the Second Industrial Revolution came to an abrupt halt when panic hit the European and American exchanges in 1873. Britain, the United States and other major Western economies sank into a long deflationary period that contemporaries called the Great Depression. The effects trickled down to the little boomtown of Guiseley. In 1874, the Green Bottom Mill went up for sale after having been privatised and converted to tweed production. Power looms, bobbins, oil and tweeds, all hit the auction block.[112] An entrepreneurial attempt to jumpstart the Green Bottom Mill was a failure. In 1875, auctioneers again announced the disposal of the assets. The looms, raw materials, mill shares and other 'manufacturing property' were again up for grabs, along with shares in the Spring Head Mill and the Green Bottom Mill.[113] In June 1874, Abraham Moon and Sons extended its loan on the Netherfield Mill property, perhaps to channel resources into an expansion of the plant or to purchase new machinery.[114] Given the economic realities, the money was more likely used to ward off creditors.

A fatal carriage accident

On the evening of Monday, 20 August 1877, Abraham Moon died after a carriage accident at Yeadon. He was driving his phaeton, accompanied by his grandson and one of the Waite clan from Guiseley. The third week of August was a busy time in Yeadon. The mills were closed for a summer holiday and the annual Yeadon Feast was on. The carnival atmosphere excited the horse, which had to be led by walking. Soon afterwards, the Yeadon Band started to play and the agitated horse was further startled by the music. The frightened animal set off at great speed down the steep hill on Henshaw Lane. Waite grabbed the boy and dropped him out of the carriage and, in doing so, unbalanced the load and fell out. Both of them sustained a few minor bruises. Waite walked home and the boy was carried away on an observer's shoulders.[115]

Abraham stayed in the phaeton and attempted to calm the horse. They proceeded downhill on Henshaw Lane and when the horse saw a familiar turn known as Back of the Wool Pack (now called Gill Lane) that led to the Wool Pack pub, it leaned to turn right. The animal was trotting too fast for the sharp turn. At around 6:15 p.m., the horse ran directly into the wall at the corner schoolhouse, taking down several yards of the short protective wall. Two witnesses rushed to the scene, finding the horse and the phaeton in a heap across the broken stone. Abraham was lying on his back on the road, senseless. There was a wound on the temple and another on the side of the head; blood streamed down his face. The men propped Abraham up in a chair and gave him water and brandy. He swallowed small amounts of the liquid, but in about ten minutes, he died. The horse, although severely injured, was able to walk to a nearby stable.

Abraham was buried in the graveyard of St Oswald's Church on 23 August 1877.[116] His will was probated on 7 March 1878 at the county courthouse in Wakefield. The will was proved by his three sons—Abraham Junior and Isaac (both 'Cloth Manufacturers') and the young Arthur—and by James Somerville Taylor, the Bradford 'Woolstapler' who had delivered a speech at the ground-breaking ceremony for Netherfield Mill. The trustees were charged with investing funds from the estate, worth around £18,000, to generate life incomes for Abraham's daughters and their minor children.[117]

To put Abraham Senior's legacy in perspective, we can compare his estate with that of John Gott, heir to the firm of Benjamin Gott and Sons, the merchant-manufacturing dynasty that operated two large textile mills, Bean Ing Mills and Armley Mills, in Leeds. At Gott's death at age seventy-five in 1867, his estate was worth £350,000. This level of wealth supported a lifestyle fitting to a gentleman of the Leeds commercial elite. Gott had lived at Armley House, a country mansion near Armley Mills built in 1820 by his father, Benjamin Gott, and enjoyed a second estate at Woodhall in Calverley. He had been a generous benefactor to the General Infirmary, the Mechanics Institute and other local charities.[118] In contrast, the former clothier Abraham had moved from humble artisan to mill owner and at the time of his death, enjoyed a level of comfort that was fitting to the middle ranks of the business class.

Grey tweed reconsidered

Abraham Moon lived through a transformative period in the West Riding woollen industry. At the start of the nineteenth century, Leeds was pre-eminent in woollen production, the jewel in the crown of the Yorkshire industrial district. But by the third quarter of that century, woollen manufacturing had mainly, but not exclusively, shifted from Leeds to the surrounding towns and villages. As its economy diversified, Leeds became a major player in the British ready-made clothing industry. By the twentieth century, the city was famous as the home of 'wholesale bespoke tailors' such as Montague Burton Ltd and Fifty Shilling Tailors, which had shops on the British high street that measured customers for suits and workshops in Leeds that made them.[119] Another branch of the Leeds clothing industry served the wholesale trade, producing ready-to-wear for men, women and children. These makers-up became especially well known for the 'tailor made' ladies' costumes—coats, jackets and suits—that would become synonymous with British fashion in the years between the First World War and the Second World War. However, woollen distribution remained important to the city's economy. Merchants from Glasgow, Liverpool, London and Manchester, and importers from Canada, Germany and the United States who wanted the best British woollens, travelled to Leeds to shop at the warehouses. Eventually, woollens from all around Britain—from Scotland, the West Country and West Yorkshire—were channelled through the Leeds merchants. Two key Leeds businesses—woollen merchant and garment manufacturer—would be important to Abraham Moon and Sons in the years ahead.

The tweed boom that led Abraham to build Netherfield Mill was prompted by favourable conditions in international trade and the fashion system. Aggressive Leeds merchants promoted tweeds to exporters, tailors, retail drapers and garment manufacturers, who in turn promoted the British woollen look to their customers and to the ultimate consumer (figure 1.9). The new modus operandi was evident all around Leeds. Established in 1868, the auctioneers Hepper & Sons on East Parade, specialists in 'Leeds Cloth Sales', catered to shippers, merchants, wholesale clothiers, woollen drapers and cap and hat manufacturers who wanted all kinds of tweeds: Cheviot, Derby, Herringbone, West of England and Waterproof.[120] The woollen merchant Bishop, Son, & Hewitt—likely to be the 'Mr Hewett' at the Netherfield Mill ceremony—sold waterproof tweeds from their warehouse on Wellington Street. The merchant's prize-winning display at the Yorkshire Exhibition of 1875, an effort to boost civic pride and promote products made in the region, included 'waterproof tweeds of all shades and colours'.[121] The makers-up in Leeds, London and Manchester were hungry for Yorkshire cloth, particularly the tweeds that came to be emblematic of British style.[122]

The village of Abraham's birth was vastly different from the industrial town of his maturity. Over the course of his lifetime, progressive West Riding clothiers had turned away from spinning and weaving in stone cottages to test their mettle as the proprietors of vertically integrated woollen mills. The most nimble were able to adapt to the turbulent new business environment, while others failed. Vertical integration proved efficient and became the preferred way of organising production among the family firms in Guiseley and elsewhere in the Yorkshire woollen industry.

On the occasion of the Yorkshire Exhibition, the *Leeds Mercury* recorded the great progress of woollen manufacturing over the past thirty years, noting that the plain all-wool broadcloth, once the mainstay of Leeds producers, had been replaced by 'mixed tweeds and coatings' in a variety of colours and designs.[123] Product differentiation helped the Guiseley tweed makers distinguish themselves from other Yorkshire manufacturers. Specialisation came to define each of the manufacturing hubs in the West Riding. Bradford became a worsted manufacturing centre and the world's greatest distribution centre for wool. Dewsbury made heavy woollen goods

1.9 *Carte de visite* showing William Gladstone in tweeds, c.1868. Author's collection.

such as blankets. Huddersfield produced fancy woollens and worsteds. Choosing the style option, the mills of Guiseley and Yeadon focused on inexpensive Yorkshire tweeds. By no coincidence had the Pudsey weaver pinched Abraham's fabric from the Coloured Cloth Hall back in 1866. There was something special about those purloined pieces of grey tweed cloth. Yorkshire tweeds were the mass-market fabric of the future and Abraham Moon was among those who had led the way.

2 Looking good

The great demand for fancy woollens of late years has afforded full employment both to pattern designers and to dyers, and the discovery of Aniline has led to vast improvements both in the patterns and colours of the better classes of woollens. (Worshipful Company of Clothworkers of the City of London, 1873)[1]

The Victorian tweed boom that brought glory days to the mills in Guiseley and Yeadon was linked to changes in the fashion-industrial complex. From the start, firms such as Abraham Moon and Sons pegged their prospects on the global demand for British woollens. Much of the fabric made in Guiseley and Yeadon was sold to the shipping trade and exported to France, Germany, Italy, the Levant, North America, South America and the British colonies.[2] The merchants also served as intermediaries between British mills and unfamiliar markets in Asia, helping firms like Abraham Moon and Sons to understand customer needs in faraway places such as Tokyo.[3] The cloth that was not sent overseas was channelled into the domestic market. Whether abroad or at home, Guiseley tweeds ultimately found their way to tailors, retail drapers and garment manufacturers in the expanding ready-to-wear industry.

Tweed mania dates from Scotland in the mid-nineteenth century, when warm woollen outfits in 'traditional' patterns were marketed to well-heeled British tourists who went on shooting holidays in the Highlands. Fashionable London tailors promoted Scottish tweeds as suitable for men's attire whether worn in the country or the city.[4] The fad for tartans and tweeds spread, publicised by tailors, drapery shops, ready-made clothing manufacturers and the press. On both sides of the Atlantic Ocean, women's magazines showcased the new feminine vogue for tweeds: cloaks in waterproof woollens, walking suits or 'costumes' in colourful patterns and juvenile outfits in tartans (figure 2.1).[5] Extreme styles appeared on the backs of London dandies, including the dashing young clerks of the Strand and Fleet Street. These 'glasses of city fashion' wore 'scarves and shawls of wondrous pattern and texture despatched from distant Manchester and Paisley' and trousers that were 'unrivalled, patented, and warranted'.[6] Woollen fashions made from British tweeds were in vogue.

2.1 Plaid dresses were a favourite choice for small children; this girl in a tartan dress lived in Hettstedt, Germany. Author's collection.

As the demand for tweeds grew, the market bifurcated into high and low. The Scottish mills made expensive, heavy fabrics that went into men's coats, jackets and sporting outfits. The Yorkshire mills made cloth that was sold at lower price points, capturing the trade in woollens for ladies' wear and children's wear. By the 1860s, two places in the West Riding were known for tweeds. Huddersfield, a large town at the confluence of the River Colne and the River Holme some twenty miles southwest of Leeds, was the headquarters for fancy goods, while three towns near the River Aire—Guiseley, Rawdon and Yeadon—focused on inexpensive tweeds for the mass market. The famed Guiseley Waterproof Tweeds were used in outerwear for men and women, while the district's lighter weight tweeds went into ladies' costumes and children's clothing.

Design was an important factor in Victorian tweed mills. Tweediness depended on the skilful manipulation of different types of wool that were carded, dyed and spun into yarns of different weights, textures and colours. Someone had to decide how the yarns could be combined into a pattern that might look good as a form-fitting jacket or a skirt with a bustle (Colour Plate 1). As tweeds became even more fashionable, manufacturers had to exert discernment in pattern design. The Scottish mills competed on quality, masculinity and heritage, whereas the Yorkshire mills offered a wide selection of patterns, colours and textures at affordable prices. Variety became the hallmark of Abraham Moon and Sons, which understood that choice mattered to customers in the mass market.

The woollen designer in Yorkshire

Who was responsible for 'the look' of fashionable tweeds? In the eighteenth century, woollen merchants had watched the market with an eye to new product development, gathering samples that might be adapted to their particular trade. The merchant would take fabric samples to the clothier, asking him to copy or modify the designs. By mediating between the market and the manufacturer, the merchant secured the best possible cloth for his particular set of customers.[7]

Clothiers were technical experts in spinning, weaving and dyeing, but some of them also had a talent for the manipulation of colour, texture and pattern. The more imaginative clothier took pride in the creation of original patterns; 'at home, and under their own superintendence', the clothiers made 'their fancy goods' and 'articles of a newer, more costly, or more delicate quality', to which they applied 'a much larger proportion of their capital'.[8] If these samples, or idea fabrics, went into production and sold well, both the clothier and the merchant benefited. But sometimes an inventive clothier found himself subject to unscrupulous merchants and manufacturers, who were known to pirate attractive patterns. Nothing could prevent an unsavoury mill owner from buying an eye-catching piece in the cloth hall, taking it to his factory and asking his weavers to copy the pattern.

Yorkshire clothiers remained active in product development throughout the nineteenth century, particularly if they became capitalists. The clothier who became a mill owner often created the new designs himself. That way, he could play his cards close to his chest, ensuring that no one saw his designs before they went to market. But product design could become a chore to the mill proprietor who was burdened with matters of finance, labour relations, production, sales and technology. The responsibility for 'the look' was channelled to a new technical specialist called a 'pattern designer', or simply, a 'designer'.

One of the great historical mysteries about the Yorkshire wool cloth industry is when designing first became a separate job from weaving or running the business.[9] Early newspaper accounts offer some clues that point to Huddersfield and the surrounding villages in the Colne Valley as a hotbed of design innovation.[10] In 1829, the *Leeds Mercury* reported a spike in the Huddersfield 'fancy trade' due to 'the introduction of a machine called a *Witch*, which enables the weaver to beautify the cloth with a great variety of flowers' and to produce a new 'species of goods' that was 'in considerable demand'.[11] One designer's reminiscence about fancy vestings provides further guidance. In 1857, Thomas Etchells, a designer at T. Hinchcliffe and Sons in Huddersfield, traced the advent of 'woollen designing into this district … to the commencement of the manufacture of Bolton quilts in the neighbourhood of Dalton'.[12] 'Bolton quilting' was a patterned fabric used in women's petticoats and men's waistcoats, and Dalton was a forward-looking place with a penchant for new technology.[13] There, some thirty years earlier, two men at the firm of George Senior and Sons had perfected the 'Engine' or 'Dobbie', a type of handloom that could produce small figured patterns, as did the Witch or Drum Witch. The foreman at this mill, Thomas Brooke, doubled as the pattern designer.[14] Once looms could create complex figured motifs, the industry needed designers to create the patterns.

Advertisements for 'pattern designers', 'pattern weavers' and 'designers' appeared in Yorkshire newspapers during the 1830s and 1840s.[15] Not surprisingly, many of these job openings were with Huddersfield fancy manufacturers who produced intricate patterns for men's waistcoats. As masters of the Witch and the Engine, the Huddersfield mills were slow to adopt the French mechanism that had been developed by Joseph Marie Jacquard to help silk weavers produce complex figured motifs. Operational by 1801, the Jacquard mechanism was only gradually adapted for large patterns and thus adopted by French weavers. By the early to mid-1820s, the silk weavers of London and Coventry were using the Jacquard device, which found its way north to Halifax and Bradford over the next few years. By the 1830s, the Huddersfield makers of fancy vestings started to use the Jacquard.[16] In late 1841, one such mill advertised for a designer 'who must understand both Designing and Weaving, and who is expected to make himself generally useful in the Pattern Department'.[17] The skilled artisan who could plan complex floral patterns for the Jacquard and help set up this mechanism was highly valued.

While Huddersfield developed a reputation for design, the cottages of the Guiseley woollen district also hummed with activity. In 1845, the Guiseley clothiers produced 'fancy cloakings' and shawls that were praised by the *Leeds Times*—with one caveat. The cloth was well made, but lacked the latest look coveted by fashion-conscious consumers. The newspaper thought that Guiseley could learn from Huddersfield:

> It would be for the interests of the manufacturers in these parts, if they would employ a first-rate pattern-designer, as is done in the fancy-waistcoatings about Huddersfield, and the shawl-trade in Paisley. There wants something fresh every season, to keep the trade in motion. These articles in the moist atmosphere of Britain cannot well be dispensed with, and the clothiers ought to endeavour by all means to keep pace with other branches, and never come out, year after year, with the same everlasting patterns. The outlay caused by the wages of a first-rate designer, would be nothing to the spur the business would experience; and if one person should think the risk too great, three or four more could join, and a good workman with a fertile brain would do for the whole district at first, and then, if the business called for more, there would soon be plenty to supply all wants. The shawl-trade is much in the same way. Any quantity might be sold, if there was something new about them, and then those useful and comfortable appendages to the ladies, would, as in times of old, become a first-rate article of consumption.[18]

The Huddersfield fancy woollen manufacturers set the pace with design and the infant industry of Guiseley needed to catch up.

John Beaumont, superstar designer

The experience of John Beaumont illustrates how design knowledge was developed in the fancy woollen trade and, in turn, how it shaped product innovation in Yorkshire. Beaumont was a native son of Huddersfield who became an eminent textile designer and a tutor at the Yorkshire College of Science, the first advanced educational institution in Britain for weaving, dyeing and textile design. His work experience is important to our story because his talent for innovation would influence design practice at Abraham Moon and Sons. This knowledge transfer would occur in Leeds in the 1880s, when a young 'Woollen Manuft' named Charles Herbert Walsh of Guiseley became a Beaumont protégé at Yorkshire College.[19] But here, as a backdrop to our discussion of Charles's later work as a woollen designer for Moons, we examine his tutor's early career.

Born in Lepton near Huddersfield in 1820 to a family of handloom weavers, Beaumont inherited his father's proclivity for fancy textile production and his mother's refined taste. His earliest recollection was seeing in motion 'a loom constructed on the drum witch principle employed to some extent to lift and depress the warp yarns'. By age eight or ten, the weaving wunderkind had demonstrated an aptitude for working with pattern and colour, and was soon creating distinctive designs that delighted the Huddersfield merchants. His cloth with a 'figured hairline' pattern, made on his own Witch or Dobbie, impressed local artisans and merchants. At eighteen, he went to work as a 'Designer of Vestings for Machine Patterns' at a local mill. Next came a series of jobs in designing and dyeing at Huddersfield and at Leeds followed by an entrepreneurial venture as a 'fancy textile manufacturer' in partnership with one Mr Tolson at Lodge Mill near Lepton, his home town. As a mill owner, Beaumont made an effort to connect the Yorkshire woollen industry with the London market, where fashion mattered to consumers. He was reported to be one of the first Yorkshire textile manufacturers 'to submit patterns to London merchants, travelling frequently up to town for this purpose and being well known and highly respected by many of the best London houses'.[20]

Some time around 1850 after Lodge Mill was destroyed by fire, Beaumont leveraged his reputation a textile design pioneer to secure a series of positions with highly respected woollen manufacturers. At James Tolson & Sons in Dalton, he applied his skill in designing figured textiles to various types of weaving. His patterns helped Tolson & Sons win a Gold Medal for Fancy Woollens at the Great Exhibition of the Works of Industry of All Nations, held at the Crystal Palace in London from May to October 1851. With this feather under his cap, Beaumont moved to Scotland, where the tweed industry was operating at full throttle. He spent five years at a tweed mill operated by the Scott family in Dumfries, where he purchased the raw materials, superintended the design and production departments, and sold the fabrics. Upon his return to Huddersfield, he adapted the colour and design sensibilities of Scottish tweeds to worsteds. In 1870 as a director at William Learoyds & Sons' mills, he introduced colour-weave effects to worsteds and helped to launch the 'Fancy Worsted Trade' that brought fame and fortune to Huddersfield. Up until then, most worsteds had been piece dyed and fancy yarns had been confined to vestings with small spots and figured patterns made on the Witch and Dobbie.[21] The introduction of fancy woollen yarns into worsteds allowed for the creation of the fine cloth with subtle colour details that are now a classic

2.2 A British lawn bowling team wearing every imaginable variety of woollens and worsteds, 1892. Author's collection.

feature in men's suiting. Today's *GQ* cover model owes much to Yorkshire and to John Beaumont (figure 2.2).

Like other designers, Beaumont was bound to strict rules of confidentiality that protected the commercial interests of his employers. For much of the nineteenth century, secrecy dominated the Yorkshire textile industry. Most woollen designers assembled a record of their work in pocket notebooks or on sample cards that they carried with them or took home for safekeeping. Some masters were 'very jealous about any of their pattern-weavers taking patterns home with them', but a mill owner seeking to hire a new designer would expect to see examples of his best sellers.[22] In 1864, 'An Old Designer' described the practice: 'Ever since designers were installed into manufactures they have always had the privilege of having a small bit if they thought proper, from any or every range they thought of consequence for their future guidance; and as a library wherein they could read the history and changes of styles which had taken place in their respective lives.'[23]

Secrecy protected the interests of the manufacturers, but it discouraged the free flow of ideas that was essential to creative thinking. By the 1850s, rising competition from continental European woollen mills vexed the British industry. The Germans were seen as technological wizards, the French as creative geniuses. If Yorkshire designers could learn from each other, perhaps British mills could better compete.

West Riding woollen designers undertook an effort to pry open sealed lips. In 1857, the Huddersfield and Holmfirth Fancy Woollen Designers' Association convened for the first time, attracting twenty members. One mill foreman lauded the association as 'possibly the first united meeting of designers in the world'. Previously, woollen designers had been 'so very jealous that they could scarcely speak to each other, for fear they should steal each other's ideas'.[24]

Mill owners were adamant that designers safeguard the factory's patterns against competitors' eyes, stating their desire to 'keep new patterns to themselves'. In 1861 near Huddersfield, a pattern designer signed a five-year contract with a fancy woollen manufacturer. The contract stipulated that the designer would 'keep secret from all other persons whosoever, the designs, patterns, or other trade secrets, which are now in his knowledge or possession, or which shall at any time hereafter, be devised by him'. A lawsuit ensued in 1864 when it was discovered that the designer had taken some fabric samples home.[25] The court considered how the designer's professional concerns as a technician with marketable skills clashed with his employer's need to protect trade secrets.

Nobody used the terms 'work for hire' or 'intellectual property' in Victorian Britain. But in the deliberations about the scope of the designer in the woollen industry, we can delineate the faint outlines of concerns that now preoccupy the global creative industries. By the time of the Paris Universal Exposition in 1867, the woollen designers of Yorkshire were not only highly paid, but they were valued enough to be acknowledged in the official British report: 'The great demand for fancy woollens of late years has afforded full employment both to pattern designers and to dyers.'[26] Everything pointed to a growing awareness of design as a factor in competitive strategy.

Registered designs

The first evidence of the rising importance of fashion, design and intellectual property rights for Abraham Moon and Sons comes from an obscure source in The National Archives at Kew in Greater London. Deposited there are the surviving records for product designs and textile designs registered for copyright protection with the British government from 1839 to 1991.

The need for a system of copyright protection for decorative designs emerged during the Industrial Revolution of the eighteenth century. Design piracy was rampant in the cotton textile industry and, in response, Parliament passed the Calico Printers' Act 1787, the first copyright law that explicitly provided protection for designs. During the 1830s, there was a growing concern that British industries were not keeping up with foreign competitors, notably in France, which had strict anti-piracy laws. Britain led the world in terms of manufacturing output, but British products needed more of a style element to meet the rising expectations of middle-class consumers around the world.[27]

Parliament appointed a Select Committee on Arts and Manufactures to research the status of British design. In 1836, the committee recommended three initiatives to improve British design practice: 1) the establishment of design schools; 2) the opening of museums for public edification; and 3) the creation of a copyright system for decorative designs. The first two recommendations inspired commercial centres such as Manchester, Leeds and Huddersfield to establish design schools for training a new creative class for industry. Public exhibitions of applied arts were mounted to benefit students and consumers alike, following the Continental model. The popularity of these local displays in turn inspired the Crystal Palace exhibition of 1851, where John Beaumont's designs for fancy woollens had won a gold medal, and which laid the foundation for the extensive arts and museum complex in South Kensington, London.[28]

The third outcome of the 1836 report was the creation of a Design Registry at the Public Record Office, now held in the National Archives. The registry was established by an Act of Parliament in 1839, which was followed by a series of refinements in Acts from 1842 to 1907. The early Acts provided design copyright for thirteen classes of goods, six of which related to textiles: 1) printed shawls; 2) woven shawls (not printed); 3) printed warps, threads and yarns; 4) printed fabrics with small patterns; 5) woven and printed fabrics with large patterns for furnishings; and 6) other woven fabrics. Depending on the class of goods, designs were protected for a period of nine months to three years.

Designs were registered with the Public Record Office by the companies who owned the intellectual property, rather than by the individuals who designed the goods. The Design Registry thus recorded the work of countless designers who, like John Beaumont, worked anonymously for British industry. Little is known about these designers, but we can glimpse their work through the sketches, samples and fabric swatches that have been preserved at Kew.

Yorkshire woollen manufacturers invested in copyright protection through the Design Registry. Evidence from a small group of digitised records from the 1840s to the 1880s give some indication of the scope of their investment. Between 1843 and 1883 alone, the fancy woollen manufacturers in Huddersfield registered 866 designs for woven cloth. From 1844 to 1868, the woollen makers of Leeds registered forty-eight designs. In the 1870s, two woollen manufacturers from the Guiseley district—Abraham Moon and Sons and J., J. L., and C. Peate—registered four designs.[29] Huddersfield led the way as design centre and little Guiseley toddled along.

Abraham Moon and Sons at the Design Registry

We know little about the early products of Abraham Moon, but the cloth-hall theft of 1866 and the Kew archives help us in our investigations. The fact that Abraham Moon and Sons submitted some of their fabrics to the Design Registry suggests that the company was trying to hook its star onto the worlds of fashion and consumer culture. On 1 February 1872, the mill copyrighted a grey tweed fabric, Registered Design 260178. On 28 December 1875, it copyrighted two examples of striped fabric, Registered Design 297231 and Registered Design 297232.

Registered Design 260178 looks quite plain, leading us to ask why the mill claimed this fabric was unique. We know that grey piece-dyed fabric had been a signature product of Abraham during his days as a clothier, but the Kew fabric is woven from a combination of grey and white yarns. Later company records indicate that Netherfield Mill created 'union cloth', blending wool and cotton yarns to achieve the depth of colour and the textured appearance that are characteristic of tweeds. Copyright protection may have been seen as a mechanism for differentiating the mill's union cloth from piece-dyed fabric. Further musings might lead us to speculate that this mystery swatch could be an example of the celebrated Guiseley Waterproof Tweeds.[30]

The two 1875 designs by Abraham Moon and Sons—Registered Design 297231 and Registered Design 297232—are a bit more flamboyant (Colour Plate 2). The designer of these lightweight dress fabrics used black, grey and white threads to create contrasting black and grey vertical stripes that were accented by thin orange-red stripes and thin yellow stripes. These tweeds may have appealed to the makers-up that produced ladies' costumes or men's trousers. The vertical stripes would make a bold statement on a jacket, skirt or trousers. The documentation for these items gave two addresses for Abraham Moon and Sons: Guiseley, and 99 Queen Victoria Street, London. The address for an agent in the City of London near St Paul's Cathedral, where the wholesale drapers were clustered, suggests that Netherfield Mill was catering to the shipping trade or targeting the style-conscious metropolitan market of retail drapery shops, tailors and makers-up.[31]

Trade reports on Guiseley tweeds shed some light on why the mill wanted to protect these striped designs. Around this time, observers remarked on the innovative use of brightly coloured warp yarns by the Guiseley mills. In 1867, the *London Evening Standard* wrote of the Leeds market: 'The home trade was mostly of a hand-to-mouth character ... More business, however, was done in waterproof tweeds in orange and other coloured warps.'[32] The American commercial attaché in Britain corroborated this observation in his annual report to the United States

Congress. In discussing the 'manufacturers at Yeadon, Guiseley, and those districts where tweeds are generally produced', he reported:

> Fancy tweeds began to be inquired after for the fall trade, and, as in the former part
> of the year, great difficulties again appeared as to the procuring a perfect color in the
> warp. However, many experiments were tried in dyeing the warp after the goods were
> woven, but so bright a color could not be obtained as by dyeing the warps separately.
> Consequently, the original practice of yarn dyeing had to be resorted to … The orange
> warp tweeds were more in favor than any other of the fancy colors which have been
> introduced, and a tolerably good trade was done. The demand for a time was in advance
> of the supply.[33]

Thus, two seemingly ordinary fabric cuttings may be evidence of a remarkable technical experiment by a small Victorian tweed mill.

The official report on the British woollens displayed at the Paris Universal Exposition of 1867 provides further clues to the mystery of the striped dress fabrics: 'The discovery of aniline has led to vast improvement both in the patterns and colours of the better class of woollens.'[34] Synthetic dyes were developed from the mid-nineteenth century onwards, following experiments in England, France and Germany. The 'eureka moment' occurred in the East End of London in 1856 when the teenaged chemist William Henry Perkin discovered how to synthesise the colour mauve from coal-tar, a by-product of the carbonisation of coal used to make gas for lighting. The commercialisation of synthetic dyes followed, notably in Germany. In 1868, the year when Abraham Moon laid the cornerstone for Netherfield Mill, the precursor to the German chemical giant Badische Anilin- und Soda Fabrik (BASF) issued the world's first known colour handbook for marketing the new synthetic dyes. Textile mills around the world could use this book of yarn samples to order these dyes, which produced bright hues including some that were fade-proof or colourfast. The new blacks were truly black, and it was finally possible to dye wool yarns in distinctive shades of green, blue, fuchsia, orange and yellow. Maybe someone at Netherfield Mill got the technology bug, tried out the new dyes and created the striped fabric as an experiment.[35] Today, bright colourfast synthetic hues are so ubiquitous that we take them for granted, but in 1875 when Abraham Moon and Sons submitted the striped samples to the Design Registry, the look was novel.

By registering its designs, Abraham Moon and Sons hoped to protect its intellectual property against the design piracy that was rampant in the woollen industry. But the mill may have had another motivation. Back in 1866, the clothier Abraham had labelled the selvedge of his grey tweed with the signature 'A. Moon, Gy.' Parliament had passed the stamping act in an effort to circumvent industrial espionage, but the practice of identifying fabric with the maker's initials may have evolved into an early form of business-to-business marketing. Branding was still in an early stage of development and no one associated brands with experiences as we do today. There were no stories to go with the name, no logos to convey a sense of time and place and no emotive music to suggest how the audience should feel. But there was cultural value in a Registered Design that had passed muster with the copyright authorities in London. Registered designs provided salesmen with talking points when they were with potential customers. Abraham Moon and Sons showed itself to be a Yorkshire mill in the know, a modern enterprise that was in step with the latest marketing techniques.

Challenges to free trade

After the accidental death of Abraham Moon in 1877, the family business passed into the hands of his three sons, Abraham Junior, Isaac and Arthur. By the early 1880s, the Moon brothers sat squarely in the middle class, as typified Victorian mill owners. Described as 'Woollen Manufacturer' or 'Cloth Manufacturer' in the census, each of the brothers lived with his family in a modern house maintained by servants. Isaac stayed in the Netherfield section of town, close to the mill (figure 2.3). Abraham Junior lived at Upcroft House, a farm some distance from the mill with bucolic views over pastureland. Arthur had a house in Wharfedale View

2.3 Guiseley station looking north with the chimney of Netherfield Mill in the background, 1907. Courtesy of John Alsop Collection.

in the nearby village of Menston, surrounded by middle-class neighbours in white-collar occupations.[36]

At the age of thirty-seven, Abraham Junior became the new senior partner in the firm. Soon after he took the reins, the golden age of Guiseley tweeds collapsed in the wake of major changes to international trade policy. The French Third Republic, founded in 1870, took a protectionist stance that led to the repeal of the Cobden-Chevalier Treaty in 1875. After German unification in 1871, Chancellor Otto von Bismarck took measures to protect industry and agriculture against foreign competition. Bismarck's famous Tariff Act of 1879 ended Europe's low-tariff era and virtually barred British woollens from Germany.[37] The Yorkshire mills first tried to make up for the loss of German orders by taking contracts for army cloths.[38] Next, they increased exports to France, but in 1881, the French again raised their duties. In 1881–82, the Austrians joined the hike-the-tariff game.[39] 'Machinery in the district is well employed', reported the *Leeds Mercury* in January 1883, 'with the exception of the Guiseley and Yeadon districts, which suffer somewhat from the alteration of the French tariff.'[40] Foreign protectionism wiped out the good times for Yorkshire mills.

By this time, Abraham Moon and Sons operated a sales office at 44 York Place in the centre of Leeds. As the West Riding woollen industry matured, the old-time cloth halls, with their open stalls and strict regulations, were becoming outmoded. Woollen manufacturers distributed their goods through wholesale merchants who had offices in Leeds, London, Manchester and Glasgow. Some also maintained their own offices and showrooms in major commercial centres. By the 1880s, several sections of the Leeds central business district were dominated by the woollen trade. One woollen cluster sat just north of the main passenger railway station and the freight depot close to the cloth halls. Streets such as York Place, Park Place, Britannia Street, Queen Street and Wellington Street were lined with woollen warehouses. The York Place warehouse of Abraham Moon and Sons provided customers with a private space where they could study samples and submit orders. Queries about the availability of a certain tweed pattern or a rush delivery date could be directed to Netherfield Mill using the new communications tool: the telephone.[41]

The export situation had an adverse effect on Abraham Moon and Sons. In keeping with his commitment to free trade, Abraham Junior supported the Conservative Party and was an outspoken critic of the Liberal government.[42] In 1882, he became the founding president of the Conservative Club in Guiseley and was a familiar figure at Conservative soirées in Leeds and Otley.[43] But the public demonstration of confidence masked troubles at the mill. By the late 1880s, the Moons were heavily indebted to their brother-in-law Henry Foggitt. Under the second generation of Moons, Henry no longer worked as a weaver but was the bookkeeper at Netherfield Mill. He was a man who watched his purse strings. In down times, Henry lent numerous sums to his brothers-in-law, including £5,500 in 1887. The money may have been used to improve the mill, but given the trade conditions, it was more likely used to ward off creditors.[44]

By 1888, orders for Guiseley woollens nearly stopped. A deadly cocktail was to blame: the tariff wars and a paucity of new designs. The *Leeds Mercury* accused manufacturers of resting on their laurels and recycling old patterns. In 'the Guiseley district the shipping trade is nearly at a standstill. The makers will have to change their makes entirely to come in again for shipping, as the article "curls," which has had so long a run, is now entirely dead, and although a few stripe effects have been sold to replace them, the quantity shipped is a mere trifle' (figure 2.4).[45] Guiseley faced a major threat in its secondary market, the domestic clothing industry. The threat came from Huddersfield, which by now was the 'head of the fancy woollen trade'.[46] When the market for fancy tweeds took a beating, the Huddersfield mills looked to less expensive goods. They began to make 'cheap tweeds of all kinds' for the 'large London and other wholesale clothing houses'.[47] Guiseley was sideswiped. Netherfield Mill tried to fight back with better designs. In 1889, Isaac Moon and Arthur Moon obtained a patent for 'an improved cloth' that combined woollen yarns, knotted yarns and mohair yarns to create a distinctive pattern of raised stripes that had a 'flakey appearance' (figure 2.5).[48] Other Guiseley mills limped along by weaving 'mantle goods' in 'low qualities' for the ladies' trade.[49]

Nothing about the Moons' lifestyle suggested that trade was doing poorly and that debt was piling up. The Moons knew how to spend money, and they put on a good show. By 1889, Abraham Junior had moved to Ilkley, the nearby spa town that was a favourite upscale retreat for mill owners. Arthur had upgraded his accommodations to Laurel Bank, a detached house in Guiseley centre.[50] The middle brother, Isaac, lived at Crooklands, a rambling stone villa atop the hill just east of Netherfield Mill (figure 2.6). Built by a clothier in the 1830s, Crooklands originally was a modest two-storey dwelling to which Isaac added a substantial three-storey wing in the Aesthetic style. The renovation was designed to impress visitors with modern features such as polychrome floor tiles, stained-glass windows, indoor plumbing, large bay windows, tin ceilings, imitation wooden wainscoting and willow-patterned wallpaper by William Morris.[51] Crooklands commanded a view downhill through open fields, allowing Isaac to watch over Netherfield Mill like a medieval lord presiding over his manor. For pleasure, he enjoyed hunting on the moor with his hounds or playing 'ye ancient game' of lawn bowling. The Guiseley bowling club, established under his auspices, had a bowling green on Isaac's property just across from the mill. As second-generation industrialists, the Moons had distanced themselves from the terraced cottages of the early clothiers. Spacious

2.4 This fashionable American girl from Beverly, Massachusetts, wears a dress of wool made fancy with the addition of mohair or another curly fibre. Author's collection.

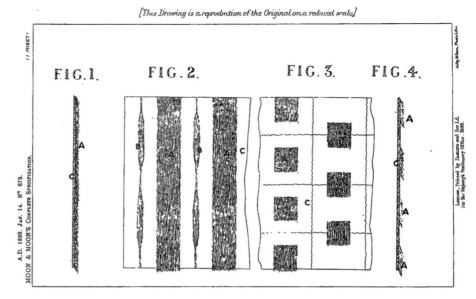

2.5 Patent for 'An Improved Cloth', A.D. 1889, no. 679, filed by Isaac Moon and Arthur Moon on 14 January 1889 and assigned on 2 March 1889. © The British Library Board.

2.6 Crooklands after its expansion by Isaac Moon. Courtesy of Jane Blake.

homes and leisure pursuits helped the men to define themselves as members of the new business class forged by the Industrial Revolution.

Isaac, like his brother Abraham Junior, embraced Conservative values and championed them through the Yeadon District Chamber of Commerce.[52] The Chamber of Commerce gave a voice to mill owners who were concerned about the effects of protectionism. In the United States on 1 October 1890, the McKinley Tariff became law, raising duties on some imported goods by up to 50 per cent.[53] The French were proposing higher duties that 'would destroy the little trade that was done by such districts as Yeadon and Guiseley'. This view was expressed when the tweed men convened to discuss these new realities. All the district's power brokers were present: Isaac Moon, Jonathan Peate, William Murgatroyd and J. W. Denison of Yeaton's Moorfield Mills and Crompton Mills respectively. Chairman Peate, who had co-founded Nunroyd Mills in 1868, painted a grim picture of the recent past:

> It was a most remarkable fact that since the French and German tariffs were brought into force there had been no development in the manufacturing industry of Yeadon and Guiseley, and since that period there was not one solitary man, who was not established before, that had been successful. Mills had been stopped, if not altogether, at least partially, and mill property had depreciated in value.[54]

Isaac Moon was silent, but he joined his friend Jonathan Peate in a delegation to the West Riding Chambers of Commerce in Leeds the next day to further deliberate the tariff menace.

Tariffed out

Foreign protectionism devastated the Yorkshire wool cloth industry. In terms of the American trade, the 1890s were a roller coaster, with high duties under the McKinley Tariff of 1890, reductions under the Wilson-Gorman Tariff of 1894 and a reversion to high duties under the Dingley Tariff of 1897.[55] The impact on the Guiseley mills was horrendous. 'The American market is a very valuable one for the manufacturers of Yeadon and Guiseley', explained the *Leeds Mercury*, 'being worth more to them than any other foreign market in the world.'[56] By the end of 1892, the district was 'badly off' because the French trade had been '"tariffed" out of existence'.[57] The slump in exports coincided with a European depression that began in France in 1889 and spread to England in 1890.[58] According to the *Bradford Chamber of Commerce Annual Report*, the year 1894 was 'one full of disappointments for the wool trade generally'.[59] Over the course of five years between 1890 and 1894, the volume of wool textile exports declined by 40 per cent.

This economic climate exposed the vulnerability of the Moons. After Abraham Junior died in March 1891 at age fifty-one, Isaac and Arthur purchased his share of the business.[60] In October 1891, they assumed the £7,400 mortgage on Netherfield Mill and nearby properties.[61] In December 1893, the brothers admitted their nephew Charles Moon into the firm. Profits were to be shared as follows: 50 per cent to Isaac, 40 per cent to Arthur and 10 per cent to Charles. The new partnership was meant to be temporary, lasting for three years. Perhaps the plan was to help Charles, who had recently married into the Murgatroyd family of Moorfield Mills in Yeadon, learn the woollen trade.[62]

The ambitions of the new owners were soon thwarted. In July 1895, the newspapers commented on the buoyant trade in the Leeds woollen district, with one exception: the 'ladies' goods made in the districts of Yeadon and Guiseley, where not only is trade bad, but all the weavers are out on strike'.[63] Business was at a standstill.[64] 'Hostile tariffs, change of fashion, all are against the productions of these large villages,' wrote the *Leeds Mercury*, 'and they will have year by year to count less upon the shipping trade to relieve them of their productions.'[65]

The Moons' house of cards came tumbling down. In October 1895, Arthur declared personal bankruptcy and the partnership agreement was terminated.[66] In November, the newspapers posted notice of the dissolution of Abraham Moon and Sons.[67] As the patriarch, Isaac was left to pick up the pieces, assisted by his nephew Charles.[68] Isaac chased down Arthur for his brother's portion of the business. In 1898, Leeds bankruptcy officials transferred the whole of Arthur's interest in the firm to Isaac, preserving the firm's name as Abraham Moon and Sons.[69]

In 1896, the *Leeds Mercury* had reassessed conditions in the Guiseley district. 'Taking the year altogether, a considerable quantity of machinery has been more or less standing idle, and employment has been very uncertain and irregular.' The tariff loomed large, but the topic of design resurfaced. 'Unfortunately, the goods made in this district have not been to the front to the same extent as in former years', the paper noted. 'There has been no marked departure during the year as regards new styles to take the public taste.'[70] The new cloth with the 'flakey' striped design patented by Isaac and Arthur Moon back in 1889 may not have met with favour in the market. Besides their design shortcomings, the Guiseley mills continued to feel the effects of the global downturn. Although the European economies had started to rebound by 1895, the full recovery took several years.[71] In the British wool industry, the recession lasted until 1901–2.[72]

In this period, the Moons tried to maintain a prosperous public image even though internal conflict undermined blood ties and debt burned a hole in their pockets. Large houses, showy carriages and holidays in fashionable destinations were funded with income from the mill—even when sales were in a slump and the business was mortgaged to the hilt. The clothier Abraham Senior had been sober and industrious, but some of his descendants appear to have been spendthrifts. The second generation believed they had 'made it' and kept up appearances, thinking it necessary to display the trappings of middle-class respectability. Although trade winds were a shaping force, imprudence seems also to have contributed to the decline of the Moons' fortunes.

Abraham Moon and Sons grappled with financial difficulties into the new century. In 1900, Isaac negotiated with the firm's creditors, leaving behind legal documents that reveal the extent of the firm's obligations. He and his nephew Charles were unable to pay the firm's creditors and the company was encumbered with a number of mortgages. As was the convention in British law, a committee of creditors was appointed to assist the trustee in the resolution of debts and the reorganisation of the business. The committee consisted of a Leeds banker and several of the mill's important suppliers, including wool merchant Peter William Musgrave from Bradford. With support from the trustee and the creditors, Isaac Moon gained full control of the business, purchasing the mill and some of the family's personal property for £10,600.[73]

The stoic Isaac—a devout parishioner at St Oswald's Church and a stalwart member of the Conservative Club—was the family's salvation in this difficult period (figure 2.7). Perhaps the patriarch hoped that the younger men in the family would grow enthusiastic about woollens. By 1901, his nephew Charles was a manager at the mill, whilst his only surviving son, Walter Smith Moon, was learning the ropes on the shop floor.[74] The disgraced Arthur and his immediate family had retreated from

2.7 Isaac Moon, 1909. Courtesy of Abraham Moon and Sons.

wool. The 1901 census described Arthur as a 'Commercial Traveller', residing at Laurel Bank with his family. He appeared in the 1911 census as an unemployed 'Widower', 'Formerly a Woollen Cloth Manufacturer'. His sons did not work in woollens.[75] The tweed dynasty begat by Abraham Moon was falling apart.

As Isaac struggled to keep the dynasty intact, Abraham Moon and Sons suffered another blow. By 1902, business had picked up and Netherfield Mill was 'exceedingly busy' and 'running overtime'. But in the early morning hours of Tuesday, 12 August 1902, a fire destroyed the mill, causing damages of £12,000. The fire started in 'some raw material stored in the yard between the scribbling and spinning department and the weaving shed'. By the time the fire brigades from Guiseley, Shipley and Otley arrived, the conflagration had spread through the scribbling and spinning departments, 'in which there were ten sets of carding machines and ten sets of spinning mules'. The building was completely gutted and only the stone walls were left standing. The gable end of the structure had collapsed onto the tracks of the Midland Railway, completely severing the telegraph wires and blocking the line.[76] Most West Riding mills were multi-storeyed buildings with stone walls, a wooden roof and wooden floors, but from the early nineteenth century, some weaving sheds were single-storeyed structures with an open floor plan.[77] The fire was a blessing in disguise. Netherfield Mill was rebuilt as a modern factory with a one-storey weaving shed, which allowed for natural overhead lighting, ease of movement and greater efficiencies in production.

Ultimately, the opening of new markets brought a degree of prosperity to the Yorkshire woollen industry. A series of military conflicts around the world—the First Sino-Japanese War (1894–95), the Second Boer War (1899–1902) and the Russo-Japanese War (1904–5)—stimulated the demand for woollens. British soldiers first wore khaki uniforms made from wool during the Boer conflict and the new camouflage colour soon became standard issue. In addition, the ready-made clothing industry of Leeds and London expanded, clamouring for cheap tweeds suited to mass-market tastes. These factories also needed large quantities of grey and blue cloth to make uniforms for every constable, inspector and mounted policeman in Britain.[78] Although protectionism kept older foreign markets out of reach, new sales opportunities emerged in the Far East, Latin America and the British colonies.[79]

For a time, Isaac was the sole owner and manager of Abraham Moon and Sons. The return of prosperity brought him sufficient fortune to pay off a good deal of debt by December 1906.[80] Eventually, the firm was reorganised with 'Walter S. Moon (his only surviving son) and others being admitted into partnership'.[81] The rising fortunes of the business should have pleased Isaac, but his satisfaction was dampened by the death of his brother-in-law Henry Foggitt. For more than half a century, Henry had seen the Moon family business through thick and thin, and his passing in April 1906 symbolised the end of the nineteenth-century world of the clothier Abraham Moon.[82]

On 16 August 1909, the 64-year old Isaac died at his hilltop mansion, Crooklands. Signs of failing health appeared in the late spring, prompting him to draw up a new will. In June, a trust fund was created to benefit his wife Hannah and his children, with the exception of his son Walter, who was 'well provided for by his interest as partner in my said business' as a woollen manufacturer.[83] A month later on 2 July 1909, Isaac attended a cricket match at Headingley, a suburban section of Leeds, with his two daughters, but he had to be helped out of the carriage when they got home. He was forced to abandon his plans for a sightseeing trip around the world with his friends Jonathan Peate of Nunroyd Mills and John Harry Ives, whose family owned Leafield Mills in Yeadon. Instead, a three-week trip to Germany, perhaps to enjoy the waters at one of the famous spa towns, only served to weaken the frail entrepreneur. In keeping with family tradition, he was interred in the graveyard at St Oswald's Church.[84] (Colour Plate 3.) His legacy totalled a modest £37,200, a sum that paled next to the estate of one contemporary worsted manufacturer from Huddersfield.[85]

New blood

Besides the Moon family, the mourners at the funeral of Isaac included Charles Herbert Walsh and his wife Hester. The inclusion of the Walshes among the intimate circle at the funeral speaks to the fact that Charles, a trained woollen designer, had been a confidant of Isaac's and a key employee at Abraham Moon and Sons, perhaps even a partner.

Like the Moons, the Walshes had a long history in the Guiseley woollen industry. Here again, genealogical research opens the doors on to kinship and social networks. In 1837, the clothier James Walsh was a partner in a firm of millwrights called Riley, Walsh, Robinson and Company, formed to construct a scribbling mill at Guiseley. Like the partnership of Abraham and William Moon, this business dissolved during the trade depression caused by the Panic of 1837 and no mill was ever built.[86] James, however, was soon back on his feet. In 1851, he was a 'Cloth Manufacturer Woollen Master' who employed twenty men. A decade later, he employed eighty men at the Top Mill in a place called the Gill, on the border between Otley and Menston.[87]

James Walsh had two sons who also had a passion for woollens: Thomas and John Unthank Walsh. The 1861 census described Thomas as a 'Woollen Cloth Manufacturer' who lived on Town Street with his wife Mary, a housemaid and two small children, including an infant son named Charles Herbert Walsh.[88] John

Unthank was a grocer who worked in woollens as a sideline. In 1860, he married Martha Waite, the daughter of Thomas Waite, a 'commission agent' at 10 Old Jewry, just off Cheapside in the City of London.[89] This fortuitous marriage into the London branch of the Waite family, who also made woollens locally, may have provided the Walshes with connections to the fashionable metropolitan market and the export trade. The Walshes also had links to the Moons. James was the warden at St Oswald's Church, where he interacted with Abraham Senior.[90] Further ties between the two families came through the Guiseley Mill Company. This public mill (possibly an iteration of Spring Head Mill) had wool processing equipment that was used by the Clapham, Waite, Ives and Moon families, among them 'Abraham Moon the elder' and 'Abraham Moon the younger'.[91]

Charles Walsh was born into a town whose every breath involved woollens.[92] In 1865, when Charles was five years old, his father Thomas died.[93] Although his uncle continued the family's cloth manufacturing business, woollens were no longer the main topic of conversation at Mary Walsh's dinner table.[94] Charles spent his childhood in a household of a genteel persuasion. His mother came from a modest branch of the Tempest clan, an extended family of Yorkshire gentry whose wealthiest members enjoyed a baronetcy, seated at Broughton Hall in Craven, near Skipton. The widow Mary kept face by working as a schoolmistress to support her small children. Charles himself grew up in the care of Ellen Tempest, a spinster aunt who lived with the family and helped with childcare and housekeeping.[95] Woollens ran through the Walsh blood in his veins, but so too did the Tempest appreciation of good table manners, church music, proper spelling and white-collar work.

The Yorkshire College of Science

At some point in the 1870s, Charles Walsh went to work in the Guiseley woollen industry. It was the height of the export boom, when Guiseley Waterproof Tweeds were popular at home and abroad. Everything was new and exciting: the vertically integrated mills, the aniline dyes and the fashion element. With innovation swirling around him, Charles imagined a bright future in the woollen business. His practical mill experience, tempered by the middle-class sensibilities fostered by his mother and aunt, led the twenty-year-old Charles to look beyond Guiseley for training. Aware of the growing need for technical expertise in the mills, he turned to the Yorkshire College of Science in Leeds.

Established in 1874, Yorkshire College of Science was a private endeavour launched by Leeds woollen manufacturers concerned about foreign competition.[96] Members of the Nussey family, who made and sold woollens in Leeds as the firm Hargreave & Nussey, devised a plan for the college after a disappointing tour of the

British woollen displays at the Paris Universal Exposition of 1867. In his report for the British government, Thomas Nussey wrote:

> There can be no doubt that the French, Belgian and Prussian manufacturers are greatly indebted for their progress … to the very superior technical education which their manufacturers and workmen obtain, by means of the schools instituted for special instruction, not only in design, but in everything which has any relation to each particular manufacture … The adoption of similar schools in Britain will before long become a necessity, and the sooner they are established the better.[97]

Two other men in the Nussey clan, George Henry and Arthur, were among the Leeds textile elite who pushed for technical education in the city.[98] With the expansion of the woollen industry, there was 'an urgent and recognised want, viz., instruction in those sciences which are applicable to the Industrial Arts' for 'the use of persons who will afterwards be engaged in those trades as foremen, managers, or employers'.[99] The Nusseys supported the idea, espoused by reformer-educators such as Walter Smith, master of the School of Art in Leeds, of establishing a central design school connected with the South Kensington Museum in London and with satellite technical institutes in the manufacturing districts. As a great woollen centre, Leeds should have a 'School of Weaving and Designing' situated in beautiful surroundings to inspire students and refine their tastes.[100] The Nusseys joined forces with other prominent citizens to create a plan for the Yorkshire College of Science. The group included several Members of Parliament and leading industrialists such as Titus Salt, who had built the model industrial village of Saltaire near Bradford, and John Barran, the father of the mechanised ready-made clothing industry in Leeds.[101]

The fledgling Yorkshire College of Science benefited from the largess of the Worshipful Company of Clothworkers of the City of London, a guild or livery company founded in 1528 as a private association to advance and guard the interests of 'the Fullers and the Sheermen' and later expanded to include other branches of the wool cloth industry and trade.[102] By the Victorian era, the Clothworkers' Company functioned mainly as a charity whose remit included providing financial support to schools, universities and mechanics' institutes. In May 1873, Thomas Nussey and John Barran visited the Clothworkers' Company with a request for a 'Professorial Chair for instruction in the art of designing and in the details of the manufacture of textile fabrics similar to that given in the Continental Technical Schools'.[103] Nussey told the guild about the 'Weaving School' in the Prussian industrial town of Elberfeld (now part of Wuppertal, Germany), which taught young men 'the manufacture of Textile Fabrics, more especially for Woollens and Cottons;—to form, design, and to assist them to arrange and draw patterns, classify and mix the colours used in the manufacturer of Woollens, Worsteds and other Fabrics'.[104] The story was the same in 'nearly all the principal Towns of Germany', including Brünn, Munich, Nuremberg, Darmstadt, Karlsruhe, Stuttgardt and Hanover.[105] The Weaving School at Brünn opened in 1860 and was awarded a silver medal for its students' work at the Paris Universal Exposition in 1867.[106] The Clothworkers' Company got the message that Britain led the world in textile production but was behind in technical education. It agreed to *'appoint a Professor in connection with the Yorkshire College of Science, when, and if, it shall be regularly established, with especial reference to the Manufacture of Textile Fabrics and Designs*, who shall assist pupils to arrange and design new patterns: classify and mingle colours with taste and judgment and otherwise to give instruction to students in connection with the Cloth Trade'.[107]

Further gifts from the Clothworkers' Company permitted the Yorkshire College to move in 1880 from makeshift quarters on Cookridge Street in the centre of Leeds to a purpose-built campus in a leafy part of the city. Located on the site of the former Beech Grove Hall estate, the new Gothic Revival complex was designed by the architect Alfred Waterhouse, who is today best remembered for Manchester Town Hall and the Natural History Museum in South Kensington, London. Two connected buildings— the Clothworkers' Building (1879–80) and the Baines Wing (1881–85)—housed the Textile Industries Department and the Dyeing Department (figure 2.8). Built at a cost

YORKSHIRE COLLEGE AND PORTRAIT OF SIR EDWARD BAINES.

2.8 The Yorkshire College of Science and one of its founding fathers, Edward Baines, the editor-owner of the *Leeds Mercury* and the Liberal MP for Leeds from 1859 to 1874. Author's collection: *Our Own Country: Descriptive, historical, pictorial* (London: Cassell & Company, 1898).

of £15,000, the Clothworkers' Court had a lecture hall, a room full of pattern looms, a large weaving shed and a well-equipped dye house.[108]

The establishment of Yorkshire College coincided with a growing national concern over the dismal state of technical education. The Clothworkers' Company supported fledgling technical institutes in Batley, Bradford, Bristol, Glasgow, Halifax, Huddersfield and Keighley, but those gifts paled next to Yorkshire College. The guild also played a seminal role in establishing national standards for technical education.[109] In 1878, the Clothworkers' Company and other London guilds met with the Corporation of London to discuss this pressing need. In 1879, the association known as the City and Guilds of London Institute for the Advancement of Technical Education was created to advance technological training. Its showcase was the Central Institution, which from 1881—in a new building in South Kensington—offered 'technical education of a high character to intending teachers in technical schools, to manufacturers, to managers, to foremen, and to leading workmen' from all around the country.[110] The City and Guilds of London Institute established branch trade schools in London and the provinces, and created a national system of standardised biannual 'Technological Examinations' for various trades, including textiles.[111] Many students at Yorkshire College elected to take the City and Guilds exams in dyeing, textile design and textile mill management to further their qualifications.

Rising star

Yorkshire College was established to prepare young men for technical and managerial positions in the textile industry, such as dye chemist, works manager and fabric designer. Many students, including Charles Walsh, already had experience in the woollen and worsted industries. An 1880 report to the Clothworkers' Company noted that a 'fair number of these young men are engaged in mills in the district during the day, and some of them have been carrying out at the mills where they are employed, the knowledge they have acquired at the College'.[112]

Charles attended Yorkshire College from 1880 to 1884. He spent two years in the Dyeing Department and then moved to the Textile Industries Department.[113] The Clothworkers' Company awarded scholarships to textile students who scored highly on the entrance exam. With his background in woollen manufacturing, the test in Textile Industries was a breeze for Charles; it required knowledge of 'Simple Weaves, and the various processes through which wool passes from the fleece to the finished cloth, both in the woollen and worsted trades'. In 1882–83, he received a Clothworkers' Company Entrance Scholarship, worth £25 per annum to cover his course fees and living expenses.[114] In 1883–84, he was awarded a Clothworkers' Company Advanced Scholarship to complete his studies.[115]

2.9 Yorkshire College of Science, interior of the dye house. Author's collection: *The Graphic* (18 December 1880), 613.

Charles was one of the first students in the new Dyeing Department, founded in 1880 by John James Hummel (figure 2.9). A practical authority in dye chemistry, Hummel was a product of the international textile industry and the university system. His family had been dyers for generations and he had studied with two renowned chemists: Professor Pompejus Bolley at the Polytecknikum in Zürich (now ETH Zürich) and Professor Frederick Crace Calvert at the Manchester Royal Institution. Typical for the time, Hummel did not have a graduate degree but taught based on his practical experience in British dyehouses and calico printworks.[116] The assignments given to students in the Dyeing Department were highly technical.

Charles completed the two-year dyeing course, but his interests lay elsewhere. In 1881 at age twenty-one, he had married Hester Busfield, a young woman from a Guiseley textile family.[117] Charles worked as a 'Clerk' while studying at

Yorkshire College.[118] Hester kept house in Guiseley and started to have children. In the summer of 1882, a dark cloud descended on the household. Charles's grandfather James Walsh, who had launched the family woollen business, had passed away two years before.[119] Within the space of a few short months in 1882, his elderly grandmother died and the couple had to bury their infant son.[120] Personal tragedy may have led Charles to reflect on his life goals. Even though he had good marks in chemistry, he seems to have realised that dyeing was not his forte. With his numerical talent and his artistic eye, Charles was drawn to textile design.

In the autumn of 1882, Charles found his calling in the Textile Industries Department, headed by John Beaumont, who we met earlier in our discussion of the first Yorkshire woollen designers (figure 2.10). Given John Beaumont's long career

2.10 Yorkshire College of Science, interior of the weaving shed. Author's collection: *The Graphic* (18 December 1880), 613.

in the fancy woollen and worsted industries, there was no better role model for an aspiring young designer. Beaumont was one of eight candidates who responded to an advertisement for the textile industries job at the Yorkshire College and was appointed as an instructor from 1 July 1875.[121] A long-time critic of trade secrecy, Beaumont relished the chance to groom the next generation to be open-minded and scientific. It was under his watchful eye that Charles developed his competence in textile design and laid the foundation for his life's work.

Beaumont drew on decades of practical experience in woollens and worsteds to build a textiles curriculum that combined theory and practice. 'The true object of technical colleges is not to teach so much the mechanical art of weaving as the theory of designing', reported the *Textile Recorder*, 'and hence the endeavour has always been at the Yorkshire College to make the mechanical subservient and at the same time suggestive to the higher art of designing.'[122] Beaumont filled the Textile Industries Department with the mill equipment needed for proper student experimentation. There was a loom 'for weaving worsted, woollen, and other shawls' and a 'small Twisting Frame, suitable for producing not only all kinds of twist yarn effects, but also knopped, cloud, and variegated yarns in a large diversity of patterns'. But he was delighted when the Clothworkers' Company sent funds to buy 'a large assortment of fancy yarns'. As a specialist in fancy woollens and worsteds, he recognised the creative opportunity for his students. With a greater choice of yarns, they could better apply colour and design theory to 'produce new designs of merit'.[123]

During Charles's first year in Textile Industries, the department had 112 students, mostly male: forty-four in day classes and sixty-eight in evening classes.[124] In the first-year course, Charles received instruction on the nature of raw materials, including the various fibres, and on processes such as scouring, fulling and finishing. He learned practical weaving on small handlooms, studied drawing as applied to textile fabrics and worked on the drafting, designing and colouring of different weaves of cloth. In the second-year course, he learned about 'Practical Weaving on large Hand Looms; Free-hand Drawing, as applied to textile fabrics; Designing Original Patterns on Point Paper, and Colouring them to indicate the Woven Fabric in Figured Twill-Cloths; Figured Double Plain Cloths; Triple-make Figured Cloths, &c.' He also did 'Practical calculations of Woollen, Worsted, and Cotton fabrics, and Analysis of Patterns' and studied colour theory. The Textile Industries track was geared to students engaged in the various branches of manufacturing, such as 'Trouserings, Coatings, Ladies' Dress Goods, Mantle Cloths, &c.'[125]

Charles blossomed as a designer and produced 'new designs of merit', just as his teacher Beaumont had predicted. In 1883, the proud professor highlighted the work of his protégés in his annual report to the Clothworkers' Company. Beaumont described the student designs for double cloths, mohair mantles, matelassé goods, woollen coatings and woollen trouserings that showed 'careful workmanship and ingenuity'. The skilfully executed 'designs of Mr. Walsh, a day student (in milled woollens and worsted coatings)', were among those 'worthy of mention'. [126]

In 1884, designs by Charles were the high point of a student exhibition at the Textile Museum, a study collection operated by the Yorkshire College. Students in the advanced day class dominated the space with 'excellent work for ladies' dress goods, mantle and double cloths, and worsted coatings'. 'The designs of Mr. C. H. Walsh are of a superior kind', reported the *Leeds Mercury*, 'and will compare well with those produced by most professional designers. He has been awarded both the class prize and the competitive prize among day students.'[127] In May of that year, Charles finished his programme at Yorkshire College with various awards to his credit (figure 2.11). In the Dyeing Department, Charles had received a first in

2.11 John Beaumont (centre rear), his son Roberts Beaumont (next to the right) and their students from the Textile Industries Department, Yorkshire College of Science, session 1884–85. Charles finished his studies 1883–4, so does not appear in this, the earliest surviving, picture of textile students at Yorkshire College. Courtesy of ULITA; photo by Tracey Welch Photography.

dye-house practice, a first in wool dyeing and a special achievement award from the Clothworkers' Company.[128] But he hit the jackpot when it came to his bailiwick, textile design, taking three prizes in his first year and again in his second year.[129] In May 1884, he passed the City and Guilds of London Institute Examination in Cloth Manufacture with an 'Honours Grade'.[130] The newly credentialed designer was poised to begin his life's work in the West Riding woollen industry.

Back in Guiseley

Charles Walsh immediately put his Leeds education to use in the Guiseley mills. The oral tradition in the Walsh family is that he had always worked for Abraham Moon and Sons. But memory is selective and, in this case, it does not take into account the fact that the Walshes were woollen manufacturers. When Charles finished his studies at Yorkshire College, the Guiseley mills were struggling due to the hiatus in international trade. As a protégé of Beaumont, he could have secured a position at any mill that wanted fresh eyes. But Charles looked for a position close to home because he and Hester were trying to start a family (figure 2.12). Between 1884 and 1891, four healthy babies, including Frank Tempest and Arthur Cyril (who were to play a part in the mill), were born.[131] Little else is certain, except for the fact that Charles took pride in his new profession and that he interacted with the Moons at St. Oswald's Church and at the Guiseley Conservative Club.[132] By 1887, he was identified as a 'designer' in the West Riding business directory.[133] The 1891 census reported that he was 'Employed' as a 'Woollen Designer' and lived in a modest terraced house at 25 Station Road (now Oxford Road).[134] The house was short walk from Netherfield Mill, so we can let our historical imaginations roam.

    The late Victorian era witnessed major changes in the West Riding woollen industry. The traditions of the clothiers had not yet disappeared, but they were fast being rendered obsolete. In Leeds, there was no greater evidence of modernisation than the demolition of the Coloured Cloth Hall in 1890 and the White Cloth Hall in 1895.[135] In the transition to the factory system, the old company mills experienced a similar fate. The Spring Head Mill ceased operations as a public mill, was privatised in 1879 and was eventually acquired by Jonathan Peate, who created another private enterprise, the Springhead Mill Company.[136] The Yorkshire mills continued to employ a small number of handloom weavers, mainly in the high end of the trade where they were needed to trial patterns and make sample lengths. The few old clothiers who worked in their cottages—some two or three hundred of them—created rugs, fancy waistcoats and one-of-a-kind pieces.[137] But the new order of the day—family-operated mills, designers trained in technical schools and weavers who

2.12 Charles Herbert Walsh and his wife Hester Walsh, 1906. Courtesy of Jane Blake.

learned their trade in factories—made the clothiers, the apprenticeship system, the cloth halls and the public mills into relics of a bygone era.

The Yorkshire woollen industry was a family affair. The complicated Victorian genealogies of the Clapham, Moon, Nussey, Waite and Walsh clans can make heads spin, but the interconnectedness was typical of British industrial districts or manufacturing clusters. In the West Riding woollen industry as elsewhere, families intermarried and shared financial resources, expertise and confidences. For business purposes, marriages provided assurances beyond the formal partnership agreements. All of the vertically integrated mills in the Guiseley district were owned and operated by families: Netherfield Mill of Abraham Moon and Sons; Nunroyd Mills co-founded by the brothers Jonathan Peate, Joseph Long Peate and Caleb Peate in Guiseley; and Leafield Mills run by the second generation Ives family in Yeadon.

Whenever it was that Charles had begun working for Abraham Moon and Sons, he was well enough established in the firm to assume a larger role in its management after Isaac Moon died in 1909. A talent for design was emerging as a Walsh hallmark. Charles had a designer nephew named Thomas Walsh, who had studied textiles at Yorkshire College under Professor Roberts Beaumont, the son of John Beaumont. In 1894, Tom, as he was called, passed the City and Guilds of London Institute's Examination in Weaving and, by 1901 was living in Guiseley, playing the organ for St Oswald's Church and working as a 'Designer' in a 'Woollen Mill'.[138] Frank Tempest Walsh, the older son of Charles, had worked as a 'Chemical Dyers' Assistant' at Netherfield Mill since at least 1901.[139] From 1907, he took night classes from Roberts Beaumont at the University of Leeds, as Yorkshire College was called after 1904. Frank pursued two courses of study: Designing and Weaving, and Woollen Yarn Manufacture.[140] We can imagine the three Walsh men—Charles, Frank and Tom—working side by side on new tweed designs at Netherfield Mill.

For generations in West Yorkshire as elsewhere in England, the knowledge of a particular trade was passed down from father to son. Charles, Tom and Frank Walsh were among the new breed of designer who augmented practical experience with advanced technical education. The decision to obtain technical training earmarked the Walshes as forward-looking. Emulating his mentor John Beaumont, Charles saw that closely guarded trade secrets were no match for systematic study and scientific expertise. With this open-mindedness, the Walsh family was poised to take Abraham Moon and Sons into the twentieth century.

3 The wider world

There is … enormous cost of production of the patterns made by all woollen and worsted manufacturers in this country—for, for many year, all our productions have been copied by the manufacturers of all countries. (John Shaw & Company, woollen and worsted manufacturers, Huddersfield, 1905)[1]

In 1911, *The Economist* published a special report on the woollen and worsted trades of the West Riding and its twin cities, Bradford and Leeds. By this time, Bradford was a major centre for worsted cloth production and the world's largest market for raw wool. The city was 'never more prosperous than it is to-day', wrote *The Economist*, 'more machinery was never running and the weekly output of tops, yarns and pieces was never larger'. Leeds was the 'most important city in Great Britain producing ready-made suits, many firms being devoted to the wholesale clothing industry' (figure 3.1). This great Northern manufacturing powerhouse was in the vanguard of 'producing garments for the million', using wool cloth made locally.[2]

The Economist also reported on the towns and villages around the West Riding, each specialising in different types and grades of wool cloth. Just north of Leeds were the towns of Guiseley and Yeadon with 'some important mills which are largely devoted to the production of ladies' dress goods and fabrics for men's caps'. Here, significant quantities of 'very pretty cloths' were 'turned out for very little money'. The mills kept down costs by using recycled fabric and other inexpensive materials. 'No big weight of wool is consumed in this district, but great quantities of noils, wool waste, mungo and cotton are used.' The output was 'shipped to all quarters of the world' by merchants in Bradford, Manchester and London.[3]

The cloth makers of Guiseley and Yeadon had spent decades learning to make inexpensive woollens, including waterproof tweeds, for international markets (Colour Plate 4). Adaptability in design and production was essential to their survival, but their international success was circumscribed by factors beyond their control. In the first decades of the twentieth century, the Guiseley tweed makers faced unfavourable trade policies, labour unrest and the First World War. But one major development bears close scrutiny for its relevance to the evolution of the

6094—Superior French Cloth Coat, in various colors.
Scolloped cape, trimmed fancy braid ; collar and cuffs
with white or colored silk inserted. Sacque or swing
back   Length 27 inches.   All Black 15/6.

3313—Norfolk Coat and Skirt, lined throughout.   Shaped yoke and
strapped.   Fancy cuffs with buckles.   Skirt with 8 gores.
Made in smart collection of Tweeds.   Prices from 29/6.

3.1 Fashionable ladies' ensembles as illustrated in a Herbert E. Coleman catalogue, *Spring 1906* (London: Herbert E. Coleman, 1908). Courtesy of West Yorkshire Archive Service, Leeds: WYL1008, Records of Heatons of Leeds Ltd.

supply chain in the fashion system. The rise of consumer society and the increased demand for fashionable attire fuelled the expansion of two major types of businesses: the garment manufacturer, or maker-up, and the mass retailer. Their growth, in turn, led to major changes in textile distribution. As ready-made clothing factories and large retailers looked for ways to reduce costs, they began to 'ignore the middleman' and 'deal more and more every year directly with the manufacturers'.[4] The new modus operandi brought greater profits to the textile mills—and challenged their capacities in design, production, sales and delivery. This chapter considers how Abraham Moon and Sons and other Yorkshire woollen mills adapted to these circumstances.

Tariffs and taste

The prosperity documented by *The Economist* in 1911 was a much-welcomed respite from the protracted doom and gloom in the West Riding textile industry. As we saw in Chapter 2, the British woollen trade had been in a slump for decades due to the contraction of export markets. 'This branch of British manufacturing industry is peculiarly sensitive to the state of business throughout the world', reported the *Financial Times* in 1898, 'and is, moreover, the favourite butt of tariff-mongers in America and other countries where it is desired to encourage the domestic product at the expense of the imported article and also incidentally of the consumer.'[5] During the golden era of free trade between 1862 and 1878, the Guiseley-Yeadon district had been home to twenty-five mills, all working at full stretch and serving export markets. Some of the mills had housed multiple enterprises, so that there were forty-four firms in 1895.[6] By 1904, however, only eleven mills and fourteen enterprises were still in operation, limping along at best.[7]

From the perspective of the woollen manufacturers, there was a major disjuncture between the British commitment to open markets and the protectionist policies of the nation's major trading partners. British politicians deliberated over tariffs as these related to industry, agriculture, income and empire. One stalwart reformer was Joseph Chamberlain, a retired Birmingham industrialist, the former Colonial Secretary and the father of future Prime Minister Neville Chamberlain. His ideas for tariff reform pivoted on the implementation of a system of 'colonial preference' or 'imperial preference', whereby members of the British Empire would grant favourable import duties to the mother country. In part, this policy was seen to be an effective tool for maintaining control in the wake of rising nationalism. The imperial preference would also give the home industries a competitive advantage in markets within the Empire. During a flurry of imperial pride spurred by Queen Victoria's Diamond Jubilee in 1897, Canada took steps to implement the preference. Within a short period, British manufacturers began to see a spike in Canadian demand.[8]

The Edwardian era was a period of great social reform and, on both sides of the Atlantic Ocean, middle and upper-middle-class activists organised themselves into voluntary associations to get the job done. Typically, a reform group might undertake a scientific study to gain a deeper understanding of the problem at hand. Founded in 1903 by advocates of Joseph Chamberlain's position, the Tariff Reform League set up an expert Tariff Commission to gather information on the effects of foreign protectionism directly from British business. The commission's findings, published in 1905, included an entire volume on woollens with reports and first-person testimonies from merchants and mill owners.[9]

The woollen mills in and around Huddersfield painted a despondent picture to the Tariff Commission. Tweed makers in the towns of the Colne Valley had mastered the art of using recycled materials to create colourful, attractive patterns at low prices. They combined virgin wool, cotton and coloured rags into fabrics that rivalled the brightness of high-priced Scottish tweeds. The skill lay in the artful blending of waste materials such as old stockings and underclothes to achieve eye-catching chromatic effects. The Colne Valley mills exported large quantities of tweeds to Canada under the imperial preference, but it was almost impossible to enter protected markets such as the United States. Cheap tweeds had no status in the fashion world and would not sell at the higher prices necessitated by the substantial American import tax. In contrast, Scottish tweeds had considerable prestige and could bear the large customs duties. Anglophiles who relished the tweedy British look willingly paid more for suits tailored from Scottish cloth. Despite their inventive recycling and ingenious designs, the tweed makers of the Colne Valley suffered from a paucity of export markets.[10]

The trouble for tweeds extended to greater Leeds, where the Guiseley mills were in a precarious position due to the distinctive character of their cloth. 'The trade of Yeadon and Guiseley', explained the Tariff Commission, 'is "almost a trade to itself," consisting of medium tweeds considerably lower in price than the class which is made in Scotland.'[11] The district was also a victim of foreign protectionism.[12] James Ives & Company, which made inexpensive tweeds at Leafield Mills in Yeadon, explained: 'Our business was originally almost entirely a shipping trade to Germany, France, Italy and the American markets, all of which in turn have been closed to us by high tariffs, and in South American, Levant and Colonial markets (the only shipping markets open to us) we have keen competition from the Continental manufacturing countries.'[13] The Guiseley firm of J., J. L., and C. Peate of Nunroyd Mills had once exported some 80 to 90 per cent of its cloth to German and French markets, but this trade was 'absolutely killed' by tariff barriers.[14] William Murgatroyd, the principal in William Murgatroyd & Company at Moorfield Mills in Yeadon, looked back forty years to his youth when 'two-thirds of our factories' made goods 'for export to Germany and France'.[15] 'With the United States we were very busy at one time', 'Billy Murg' explained, 'before the duty was put up so high.'[16]

One of the hallmarks of the British tweed industry—the investment in high-quality design—was proving to be a double-edged sword in the competitive global marketplace. British woollen manufacturers were in the 'unique position of being the leaders of fashion in the world' because rival mills competed against each other to create the best patterns.[17] Mill owners disagreed on the best source of good designers. Forward-looking firms employed designers who had been trained in technical institutes, while some old-timers believed there was no substitute for hands-on mill experience.[18] 'The designers who take up certain parts, study all that they have to do, and they are always at it', Murgatroyd told the Tariff Commission in his colloquial Yorkshire manner. 'They can do what is wanted, and they can do it well.'[19] One thing was certain: the design race was expensive. One company paid

£4,000 in 'designing costs' to achieve sales of £72,000.[20] Moorfield Mills spent at least £2,000 per year on pattern making and designing. 'You must do that on a fancy article', Murgatroyd explained, 'because however nice it is, the same design is never wanted again.'[21]

British patterns were admired in foreign markets for their distinctiveness—and widely copied by mills in Austria, France, Germany, Spain and the United States. The year-long gap between cloth production and apparel consumption gave the pirates ample time for their machinations. 'We are obliged to expose our designs nearly 12 months before the goods are actually worn', one British manufacturer explained. Nothing could prevent a foreign mill from acquiring his samples and making copies.[22] It was impossible to prosecute design pirates due to shortcomings in the laws on intellectual property rights. An intricate woollen pattern made with 120 threads in the warp and 120 threads in the weft could be easily reproduced using fewer threads, with perhaps 119 or 118 ends. In the eyes of the law, the two cloths were not the same and no one's rights had been violated. 'I have myself seen goods of my own design pirated by a Spanish firm and being woven in a mill near Barcelona', one frustrated witness told the Tariff Commission. 'I have also seen my own patterns carried round to American merchants by American manufacturers and orders taken for them.'[23]

The American woollen industry, hidden behind a tariff wall, had made great technical strides and could now produce cloth that competed with the British in terms of quality. With a home match advantage, they could readily scout out and cater to the distinctive 'American taste' that was emerging among fashion-conscious consumers. The woollen manufacturer Norman Crowther, from H. Crowther & Sons in Huddersfield, explained the relationship of tariffs to taste—a relationship not readily apparent to anyone outside the wool textile industry. 'If a distinct taste can be established, then the market will be almost entirely captured' by the American manufacturers 'for, under the present tariff, there is no encouragement for the British manufacturers to study its requirements and adapt himself to them'.[24] Crowther thought it best to forget about the United States and focus on doing business within the British Empire. He was straight with the Tariff Commission: 'What still can be done—and we emphatically think should be done—is to secure for ourselves our home and colonial markets whilst there is yet time.'[25]

The Yorkshire tweed mills were thrown back into the domestic market, where clothing factories in the principal ready-made clothing centres, Leeds and London, clamoured for wool cloth. But the home trade had its own peculiar set of problems.[26] Cheap European textiles were permitted into Britain duty-free and they flooded the market. The Peate brothers of Guiseley explained: 'Mantle and costume cloth and Venetian cloths are imported from Germany, Holland and France below our cost price … Longer hours are worked in Germany and Holland, and the rate of wages is very much lower.'[27] German cloth was of such low quality that it would last only one season, but *The Economist* reported that this was 'good-enough' for British ready-to-wear since 'fashions change so rapidly'.[28] Yeadon mill owner Murgatroyd saw things differently. His temper flared when he discovered his London agent selling overstock German patterns at bargain prices. Murgatroyd hesitated to discount-sell his old patterns in Germany in return, because the import tax would wipe out his profit and eat into his investment. The unfairness of the situation clearly made him angry. 'I am not a protectionist—I am a free trader, but I want to tell you what free trade means', he said to the Tariff Commission. 'It means that we are to trade with people evenly.'[29]

In the short term, the tariff reformers of the Edwardian era did not succeed in reversing Great Britain's commitment to free trade—the about-face would come later, briefly during the First World War and mainly during the global protectionist backlash of the Great Depression. But the work of the Tariff Reform League amplified the growing discontent with the British commitment to free trade. Most important for our discussion, the Tariff Commission gave voice to Yorkshire woollen manufacturers who felt that Whitehall did not understand the realities facing British business. They vocalised their dissatisfaction with foreign protectionism and hoped the word would get to Parliament.

Timing is everything. The tariff hearings of 1904–5 took place just as the British tweed trade was about to experience a major turnaround. The demand for Yorkshire tweeds was on an upswing, thanks to fashion. In the home market, tweeds were trendy. 'Everybody you see is in tweeds, and that is why the mills are all well employed', one witness stated. 'You will hardly see a man in worsted.'[30] By the time the Tariff Commission published its report in November 1905, the long decline of the market for Yorkshire tweeds had run its course—at least for the short term. The British observer for the *Textile World Record*, a trade journal published in Philadelphia, America's largest textile city, commented on the 'good business done by the low tweed makers in the small towns encircling Huddersfield … Wholesale clothiers at home and abroad are the buyers of these fabrics.'[31] In 1907, the *American Wool and Cotton Reporter* noted that the 'Leeds, Dewsbury, Batley, Morley and Huddersfield districts, along with Yeadon and Guiseley, have all been unusually busy … Solid worsted fabrics, such as serges and coatings, cannot hold their own against cheap tweeds.'[32]

As far as tweed exports were concerned, it could be said that Joseph Chamberlain got it right. The revival of Yorkshire tweeds owed much to the new system of preferential tariffs adopted within the British Empire. While the mother country adhered to the doctrine of free trade, the colonies took measures to protect their own developing industries against foreign dumping and to secure adequate supplies of high-quality British goods. One by one, they started to implement the colonial or imperial preference, wherein a tariff rebate was granted to goods that were imported from within the British Empire. Between 1897 and 1900, Canada led the way by introducing and refining the imperial preference. Similar policies favourable to British imports were adopted by New Zealand in 1903, South Africa in 1904 and Australia in 1907.[33] By 1913, the imperial preference was in effect in practically the whole of the British Empire. That year, the Empire accounted for 34 per cent of textile exports from the United Kingdom.[34] For Yorkshire woollens mills, the imperial preference acted as a countervailing force against the exorbitant duties that kept the United States and the Continent out of reach. Canada, with a chilly climate and a penchant for British style, became one of the most important markets for Yorkshire tweeds.

Hobbling along

Although the year 1911 opened with bright prospects for the Guiseley tweed makers, the outlook soured by Christmas. Some of the bugbears were familiar: labour troubles, foreign wars and tariff uncertainties. But this time round, it was fashion, rather than free trade, that 'played an unusual and disastrous part' in the fortunes of Yorkshire tweeds.[35] The year before, the Paris couturier Paul Poiret had initiated a trend for a garment that came to be known as the 'hobble skirt'. These long skirts were narrow at the hem, thereby constricting the gait of the wearer and causing her to hobble along. The fad for the hobble skirt—the precursor to the shorter modern pencil skirt—had unintended consequences for the Yorkshire wool cloth industry. The slim, tight-fitting style required lighter fabric and less fabric than fuller conventional skirts. According to the *Yorkshire Post*, something like 25 to 30 per cent less yardage was needed to 'clothe a lady in this cramped and crippled style'. The tweed makers of Guiseley were among the mills that 'experienced only a fair trading period' during the hobble craze. 'The demand has run on a great variety of materials', explained the *Yorkshire Post*, 'though of late it has turned rather more towards goods of a smooth surface than to naps.' The fuzzy look of tweeds was incompatible with the sleek, sexy new style.[36]

By the time of the hobble craze, Abraham Moon and Sons was under new management. The five-year period after Isaac Moon's death in 1909 was a significant time for Netherfield Mill. Isaac had groomed his only surviving son to continue the business and the designer Charles Herbert Walsh appears to have been a trusted confidant for Walter Smith Moon. From the paper trail, albeit a thin one, we can extrapolate some facts. By 1910, Walter and Charles were joint owner-managers of

Abraham Moon and Sons. In November of that year, they signed a ten-year lease on Netherfield Mill, which was owned by the Isaac Moon estate.[37] Over the next few years, Charles emerged as the man who was better suited to run the mill and he lobbied for a larger stake in the business. Other men in the Walsh family were also involved in the mill. His son Frank had completed his evening studies in textiles at the University of Leeds and helped to manage the company, while his nephew, the designer-weaver Tom, lent a hand.[38]

As the grandson of the founder, Walter Smith Moon brought some degree of continuity to the firm. In keeping with family tradition, he lived at Crooklands with his mother, two sisters, a cook and a maid. Other men in the Moon family had distanced themselves from Netherfield Mill. Charles Moon lived in proximity to his in-laws, the Murgatroyds of Moorfield Mills in Yeadon. He worked as a manager at the mill and then was a 'Traveller' in the 'Woollen Trade'. Each of his two teenaged sons was an 'Apprentice to Woollen cloth Manufacturing' at Moorfield Mills.[39] The relocation to Yeadon ensured the boys' future at William Murgatroyd & Company, while highlighting Charles's detachment from his roots in Guiseley. Walter was also growing psychologically distant from Abraham Moon and Sons; his thoughts were focused on sporting hounds and prize livestock. He was a frequent exhibitor at local agricultural fairs, showing his dogs at the Wharfedale and Airedale Canine Association and his shearlings at the Harrogate Agricultural Society.[40] Gentleman farming, rather than tweed making, seemed to be his forte.

The Moon indifference to the family business stood in contrast to the Walsh enthusiasm for all things woollen. Charles saw his future entwined in Netherfield Mill and the town of Guiseley. He was a man who was clearly going places in the woollen industry. The 1901 census had described him as a 'Woollen Designer' and a 'Worker'; ten years later, the census takers called him a 'Woollen Cloth Manufacturer' and an 'Employer'. The upward mobility of the Walsh family was reflected in their private lives. In 1910, Charles owned two terraced houses at 25–26 Oxford Road and, by 1911, he had a third dwelling in a new development called Park Gate Crescent.[41] Consistent with his deep religious values, he served as a warden at St Oswald's Church. In 1909–10, Charles and his wife Hester helped to organise a village fair to raise money to enlarge St Oswald's Church and buy a new organ.[42]

Ever-fickle fashion was always lurking around the corner, poised to turn the latest disastrous fad into the next fashion boon. Once ladies tired of hobbling around in their hobble skirts, the market for Guiseley tweeds picked up. By 1912, inexpensive woollens were again popular with customers and consumers throughout the British Empire (figure 3.2). 'The mills almost without exception are busy, those in the outlying districts of Yeadon, Guiseley, and Pudsey are especially so on lower

Correct Styles
FOR
SCHOOL & COLLEGE
WEAR.

CHAS. BAKER & Co., Ltd., with their immense experience in Tailoring, make

THE BEST-FITTING SUITS FOR BOYS.

They recognise that the modern schoolboy needs suits both serviceable in wear and smart in appearance. Accordingly, they tailor them with the utmost care, paying great attention to finish and cut. **Only long-wearing, thoroughly good materials** are used, so that a **Chas. Baker & Co.'s Suit is extraordinary value.** The stock is of such variety in size and pattern that **every age and build of boy can be accurately and comfortably fitted from stock.**

Eton Jackets and Vests
In Black Vicunas & Worsteds
16/11 to 41/6
HAIR LINE TROUSERS
6/11 to 16/11

Young Gentlemen's Jackets and Vests
In Black Serges and Vicuna Cloths,
19/11 24/6 27/6 33/9
Youths' Trousers
6/11 8/11 10/9 12/11 14/11

New and Fully Illustrated Price List Post Free.

Norfolk Suits
In Tweeds, Serges, and Scotch Cheviots,
12/11 to 31/6

Rugby Suits
In Tweeds and Blue Serges,
17/9 to 35/6

Young Gentleman's Suit
Smartly Cut in New Patterns,
17/9 to 41/6

CHAS. BAKER
& CO.'S STORES, LTD.,

HEAD DEPÔT, Export and Letter Order Dept.:

271 to 274, HIGH HOLBORN, W.C.

Other Addresses: CITY BRANCH—41, 43, LUDGATE HILL; 137, 138, 139, 140, TOTTENHAM COURT ROAD; 256, EDGWARE ROAD; 27, 29, 31, 33, KING STREET, HAMMERSMITH, W.; 5, 7, & 9, SEVEN SISTERS ROAD, N.; and at WHITGIFT HOUSE, 38 & 40, NORTH END, CROYDON.

3.2 Charles Baker & Company's Stores Ltd advertisement for men's and boy's wear made from British woollens and worsteds, 1912. Author's collection: *Illustrated London News* (13 April 1912).

qualities chiefly', explained the *Manchester Guardian*. 'The Canadian and Australian demand still keeps very good in low and medium prices.'[43] Global weather patterns had an impact on cloth orders. The northern and southern hemispheres experienced cold damp seasons at opposite times of the year. Through the serendipitous combination of public policy and geography, the imperial preference created a steady year-round market for wool cloth. Orders from within the Empire—by this time, the imperial preference was in effect in the British colonies and in the newly formed Dominions (Canada, the Commonwealth of Australia, New Zealand, Newfoundland and the Union of South Africa)—came to Yorkshire when production for the home market was slow. The Guiseley tweed mills now had orders twelve months of the year.

The tide always turns against a manufacturing boom, whether the result of changes in tastes or trade policies. By 1913, Britain exported about 40 per cent of all woollen and worsted textiles made in the UK.[44] That April, all eyes in the Northern industrial belt that stretched from Leeds to Liverpool were fixed on the United States, where the new president, Woodrow Wilson, summoned Congress to discuss the perennial tariff question. President Wilson hoped to revamp the federal revenue stream by substituting an income tax for high import duties.[45] Around this time, Australia and Canada were both 'good customers for low goods' such as Guiseley tweeds, but for the Guiseley-Yeadon district, Wilson's proposal was a godsend.[46] At last, American consumer society, with its voracious appetite for 'good goods and plenty of them at fair prices', would be open to inexpensive Yorkshire tweeds.[47]

The enthusiasm among Guiseley mill owners for the Wilson-Underwood Tariff dampened when female operatives co-incidentally demanded a wage increase. By this time, the combined population of Yeadon and Guiseley was 14,000, of which around 3,000 employees and their families depended on the textile industry. The last major conflict within woollen mills in the district had occurred in the desperate 1890s, when weavers went on a six-week strike. In 1913, the mill owners dug in their heels, claiming that the women already earned 10 to 30 per cent more than their counterparts elsewhere in the West Riding. Further agitation precipitated a major lockout. More mills closed as workers in other occupations demanded higher wages.[48]

The American tariff debate and the Yorkshire lockout may have given the partners Walter Smith Moon and Charles Walsh pause. Over the years, members of the firm had been personally responsible for company debts under the rules of partnership. In the spring of 1913, uncertainty weighed heavily on their shoulders. There was no predicting the duration of the lockout or whether orders would be forthcoming from the United States. The partners looked to incorporation as a legal mechanism that would protect their personal finances and make the business more secure.[49]

Many British firms were abandoning the traditional partnership for the joint-stock company. To facilitate economic growth, Parliament, commencing in 1844, had enacted a series of laws that reduced the burden of setting up a joint-stock company. The Companies Acts regulated the formation of corporations and provided for the monitoring of how the directors managed the affairs of the firm. Modifications to the rules under the Companies (Consolidation) Act 1908 made incorporation even more attractive. In the West Riding as elsewhere in the United Kingdom, the joint-stock company came to be preferred over the partnership because incorporation provided continuity and limited liability.[50]

One firm in the Guiseley-Yeadon district had already incorporated. In July 1909, Jonathan Peate reorganised his major firm as a private joint-stock company under the Companies (Consolidation) Act 1908. Back in 1868, Peate and his two brothers had built the first iteration of Nunroyd Mills, but he was the only one of the original partners still alive. The ageing woollen manufacturer joined forces with a younger relative and a third investor to incorporate the firm of J., J. L., and C. Peate (Guiseley) Ltd. The company was capitalised at £90,000 to carry on the business of 'preparers and spinners of and dealers in wool, silk, cotton and other fibrous substances, weavers and manufacturers of worsted and woollen goods, &c.' The wealthy woollen maker had no heirs; he may have seen incorporation as a way to ensure the continuity of Nunroyd Mills, his great accomplishment.[51]

Historians are not able to read the minds of the dead, but we can weave threads of evidence into a fabric of motivation. On 28 May 1913, Abraham Moon and Sons Ltd was registered as a private joint-stock company and capitalised at £26,000 under the Companies Acts. Walter Smith Moon and Charles Walsh were the sole shareholders and governing directors. Each man owned the same number of ordinary shares, but Charles owned more preferred stock and served as chairman. For Walter, incorporation may have been a way to guard his personal funds for other pursuits. For Charles, the incorporation was a matter of dignity, control and longevity. The incorporation agreement gave him a majority, essentially taking the reins away from the founding family and paving the way for the Walsh family to run company.[52]

As the ink dried on the incorporation papers, the lockout stretched into the summer months. *The Economist* lamented that mill closures in Guiseley, Yeadon and Leeds were having a significant impact on the production of cloth used to make the famous British flat cap.[53] The dispute affected 8,000 residents of Yeadon and Guiseley, if one counted the strikers' families.[54] In June, some 500 of unemployed workers in Yeadon undertook a series of hunger marches to Bradford and Leeds to publicise their plight and beg food along the way.[55] In late July, mill owners and operatives finally reached an agreement on wages, the length of the workday and overtime. The conflict ended on 26 July 1913.[56]

Once the labour dispute ceased, Charles and Walter each found solace in their favourite pastimes. Charles had no greater pleasure then when he was advancing parish matters or celebrating local heritage. On Feast Saturday in August 1913, he was among the local dignitaries who assembled in Guiseley centre to celebrate the restoration of the Town Cross. The original Saxon market cross had been a ruin for nearly three centuries, reportedly the victim of smashing by Oliver Cromwell's army during the English Civil War. The Town Cross was repaired under the largess of the Anglican clergy and other local churches. On this overcast summer day, Charles stood alongside fellow mill owner Jonathan Peate to witness Viscount Lascelles, the Earl of Harewood, unveil the stone relic. As a devout Anglican, Charles must have glowed to hear of the Guiseley Town Cross called a 'Christian symbol of civil life'.[57]

Walter was noticeably absent from the unveiling of the restored Town Cross. Perhaps he was busy with the agricultural shows that ran from the summer through to late autumn. Walter had his satisfaction at the Leeds Smithfield Club Show in December 1913. The first prize for Highland heifers went to a magnificent animal of eleven stone from the Sandringham herd of King George V, but an animal belonging to Walter took second place. Being the runner up was not too shabby an accomplishment for an aspiring farmer who competed against royalty.[58]

Hunting down the customers

Historians live for the hunt and revel in old records. The archive at Netherfield Mill has several sales ledgers dating from 1913 to 1921 that list fabric sales to civilian and military customers.[59] Unfortunately, there are no surviving business letters or sales memoranda—the documents that yield informative titbits about local tastes and regional peculiarities. However, we can get an impression of Netherfield Mill, their customers and the Yorkshire woollen industry by using the sales accounts, other primary sources and our imaginations.

From the bits of evidence, we can discern some patterns that persist to this day. Netherfield Mill had more than a hundred customers, mainly British merchants and makers-up. A handful of regular customers generated a steady flow of bulk orders, while dozens of other occasional customers ordered small quantities of cloth now and then. The mill had to balance the needs of the regular customers, who often wanted large runs of plain fabrics for export or for making up mass-market clothing, with the demands of small customers who sought more intricate designs or special patterns for niche markets. By 1913, British piece goods were exported to five major markets listed in order of importance: Continental Europe, the British Empire (mainly Canada), South America, the United States and the Far East (mainly Japan).[60] Despite this reality, there are few names of foreign customers or overseas destinations in the mill's sales ledgers. The cloth made by Abraham Moon and Sons, like that of other textile mills, found its way to overseas markets through shipping merchants in Bradford, Glasgow, Leeds, London and Manchester.

The old world of merchants

With the demise of the cloth halls, woollen mills relied on merchants to take their fabric to market. Bradford, Glasgow, Leeds and Manchester had major concentrations of merchants, but the City of London was the leader. Most of the large cloth merchants, known as wholesale drapers, had offices and warehouses in the City. Abraham Moon and Sons sold woollens to dozens of London wholesale drapers, including venerable firms such as Devas, Routledge and Company; J. & C. Boyd & Company Ltd; and Hitchcock, Williams & Company.[61]

The London wholesale drapers were the largest and most powerful players in the British textile industry.[62] These merchant houses grew in tandem with the national railway network and the concentration of capital in the City. According to the *Financial Times*, the wholesale drapery trade was nothing short of a 'barometer of national prosperity'.[63] Some wholesale drapers were so profitable that the newspaper urged the earnest investor to buy their stock rather than 'rushing to sink his money in a morass in Venezuela, or in a swamp in Yucatan'.[64] The wholesale drapers lorded over cloth Britannia from Cheapside, St Paul's Churchyard and surrounding streets, and from their own ready-made clothing factories in the City and the East End. Their warehouses were filled with samples and fabrics and staffed by clerks who spent their days scrutinising account books, bills of exchange and correspondence (figure 3.3).[65]

As London grew in significance as a textile distribution centre, merchants from other parts of Britain saw fit to establish a presence in the City. The leading Manchester merchant house, Rylands & Sons Ltd, opened a London warehouse in 1849 and charged its City branch with oversight for exports in 1874. With sights on the global domination of the cloth trade, Rylands also started offices in Paris, Montreal, Constantinople, Rio de Janeiro, Genoa, Lyon, Rouen, Alexandria, Barbados, Madras, Port Elizabeth, India and Japan. By the turn of the century, Rylands was the largest and most important dry goods house in England. In 1909, this large merchant-manufacturer employed 9,000 people in its textile mills, clothing factories, offices and warehouses. The firm made cotton fabrics in its Lancashire factories, bought other types of cloth from British and Continental mills, made

3.3 Interior of the woollen warehouse of S. Addington & Company, 4–6 Charing Cross Road, London, showing the scale of the operations in the 1920s. Courtesy of Westminster City Archives: 2268, S. Addington & Company Ltd, Business Records.

up some of the fabric into apparel in its own factories, and distributed cloth and clothing around the world.[66] Abraham Moon and Sons—and its competitor James Ives & Company of Leafield Mills in Yeadon—sold woollens to Rylands.[67]

The merchant houses in the City suffered terrible bomb damage during the Blitz in the Second World War and significant historical archives were destroyed.[68] The dearth of business records makes it difficult to examine the daily operations of the London wholesale drapers, but as the historian Stanley Chapman explains, the biography of a comparable New York commission merchant who learned his trade in Britain gives a glimpse of business practices. When purchasing cloth, the American merchant advanced 50 per cent of the fair selling price to the mill, charging annual interest and commission fees that totalled 11 per cent. He then sold the cloth to countless small retailers, invoicing them at 30, 90 or 120 days. Textile mills benefited from the steady income from the advances while avoiding the credit risk. Mills used the advances from the commission merchants to purchase materials and pay their workers.[69]

The British wholesale drapers sold cloth in the home market through travelling salesman. By 1889, some 40,000 commercial travellers competed for the business of 50,000 retail drapery stores around the country.[70] These travellers also drummed up business among tailors, makers-up and other types of textile customers. The salesman and his suitcase of cloth samples—a 'travellers' set' assembled by the merchant—was a familiar figure in the railway stations of Victorian and Edwardian Britain.[71] Following a successful visit to a tailor, the traveller arranged for the customer to receive 'bunches' from the merchant. A 'bunch' was a small collection of fabric samples assembled by the merchant as a sales aid for tailors. It was made of rectangular cuttings of fabrics—for coats, suits and trousers—that were clamped together at one end and sometimes placed in an embossed lambskin binder. There might be a bunch for medium weight tweeds, a bunch for certain types of worsteds and so on. As he contemplated a new suit, the consumer looked through an assortment of bunches and, with the help from the tailor, selected the cloth. The tailor ordered the length from the merchant for quick delivery and made the outfit. Initially, this method of fabric selection was popular at the lower end of the London tailoring trade, which the *Textile Recorder* said was frequented by 'the well-paid artisan employed in engineering and kindred occupations' whose tastes leaned 'towards showy and rather conspicuous types of cloth and design'. Upper-class tailors had more discerning customers who wanted to see the length of cloth.[72] However, the use of bunches eventually became standard practice for all market segments, including the bespoke tailors of the West End.[73]

Many of the wholesale drapers in the City carried inexpensive woollens that suited the flamboyant tastes of the large metropolitan menswear market. London was filled with men who wanted to look good on the cheap. It had a population of eight million people within a radius of fifteen miles, 'the larger proportion of which is composed of the middle and lower classes of society, who are not overburdened with wealth, but oftentimes in somewhat straitened circumstances, and must have presentable looking clothes at the lowest possible price'.[74] Dozens of new white-collar occupations and professions, ranging from bookkeeper to barrister, all required a certain degree of sartorial conformity. For business, the typical Edwardian middle-class man wore a suit that consisted of a matching jacket, waistcoat and trousers.[75] In contrast, a type of flashy 'fast' fashion dominated the lower end of the menswear market. The wholesale merchants to this trade selected their stock mainly for its 'smartness and attractiveness' because the 'ordinary citizen of the city' did not 'desire his suits to last more than a season'. The stylish Mr Everyman preferred trendiness to durability. 'Many of the suits on view in the large and multiple emporiums, though attractive to the eye, would not keep their shape and style longer than six months. Still they are what the majority of our populations desire and their wants are supplied by the enterprise of the city merchant.'[76]

Besides the large number of woollen merchants in the City, a small cluster was emerging in Golden Square, a West End neighbourhood sandwiched between Soho, Regent Street and Piccadilly. In the early nineteenth century, the area was a fashionable address for clergy, physicians, surgeons and solicitors, but by 1838, when Charles Dickens wrote about it in *Nicholas Nickleby*, many Golden Square properties had been converted to lodging houses for 'single gentlemen'. The square's fortunes reversed after 1863 with the arrival of the first woollen agents; the neighbourhood grew into a fabric hub during the Victorian tweed boom. By the mid-1880s, twenty-six woollen merchants, agents and manufacturers operated alongside lodging houses and hotels. By 1902, the number of woollen businesses—merchants, agents, warehousemen and makers-up—had grown to seventy-four.[77] Golden Square came be known as 'Woollen Square'.[78]

The wholesale drapers and woollen merchants in the City specialised in low-end and medium-quality fabrics for the home trade and the shipping trade, while those in Golden Square focused on the up-market home trade. The West End location was a business asset. Golden Square was in proximity to the bespoke tailors of Savile Row, the fashionable shops on Regent Street and the retail drapers of Oxford Street. More important, the West End was developing into a major market for fabrics and fashion. As was the case in the City, many of the West End's commercial buildings were filled with wholesale showrooms, foreign buying offices and other fashion-related businesses. During their semi-annual buying trips to London, retail buyers and shopkeepers from around the UK shopped the West End showrooms for fashion merchandise to sell in their stores. Golden Square was in the thick of all this fashion activity.[79]

By the early twentieth century, some London merchants who bought fabrics from Netherfield Mill recognised that Golden Square was the up-and-coming woollen distribution centre. The most prestigious of these was Dormeuil Frères, a French firm of 'woollen & silk merchants' with headquarters on 4, rue Vivienne in Paris and a branch in the West End. Dormeuil took pride in straddling the English Channel; it exported British fabrics to France and vice versa. During the early 1900s, Dormeuil had a shop at 10 New Burlington Street in the West End and a showroom-warehouse on Ironmongers Row in the East End. In 1926, the company built the 'House of Dormeuil', a stupendous London headquarters that straddled the space between 13–17 Warwick Street and Golden Square. The lower floors were dedicated to woollens and worsteds, while the top floor was a spacious apartment for the Dormeuil family.[80] The opening of the House of Dormeuil confirmed that Golden Square was *the* place for woollens—and the slow migration from the City picked up pace. In 1920, one customer, James Hare Ltd of Leeds, billed itself as 'dress goods manufacturers' with sales offices at 8 & 9 Trump Street in the City. By the end of the decade in 1929, this firm had joined the cluster of West End woollen merchants with new offices at 2 & 3 Golden Square.[81]

Another group of customers who bought tweeds from Abraham Moon and Sons was located closer to home in the industrial North. Leeds became a city in 1893 and its boundaries were extended by some 21,000 acres in 1912 to encompass some of the neighbouring towns and villages. The medieval core had been transformed into a thriving commercial centre. The principal shopping streets were Briggate, Boar Lane, Commercial Street, Bond Street, Vicar Lane and Duncan Street. The area north of Wellington Station, which served passenger trains, was packed with banks, insurance agencies and commercial offices, including woollen merchants.[82]

The Leeds woollen merchants gobbled up large quantities of inexpensive cloth for the shipping trade. The Bradford-based trade journal *Wool Record* reported that some Yorkshire mills operated full time by making 'the cheap grade of cotton warp cloths' that were exported by Leeds merchants to the Near East, the Far East and the Dominions, especially Canada.[83] Netherfield Mill had a number of important Leeds shipping merchants on the books. James Marshall, Son, & Company took the mill's products to London and abroad. Established in 1870, James Marshall was a manufacturer, merchant and exporter of 'Ladies' and Children's Cloths'.[84] By about 1915, another Leeds merchant customer, Ashworth, Brown & Company Ltd, proudly declared that it had been in business for nearly a century. The firm's offices and warehouses on St Paul's Street, West Street and Queen Street stocked 'woollens, worsteds, dress goods, costume cloths, linings, haberdashery and other goods for the wholesale trade' and shipped them 'to practically all the markets of the world'.[85]

Whether they were located in London or Leeds, wholesale merchants followed certain commercial conventions. The warehouses were open on market days, when customers could come in and browse through the samples. Foreign buyers, country merchants and agents poured into the woollen warehouses in Bradford, Glasgow, Leeds, London and Manchester on purchasing excursions. Correspondence was adequate for some transactions, but there was no substitute for handling the cloth to determine the quality. The fabric buyer browsed through the samples and, based on his familiarity with the market, placed large orders for the following season while he was sitting in the showroom (figure 3.4). After the First World War, there emerged a three-step practice of taking cuttings, following up with a request for sample lengths and then placing the bulk order.[86] The merchant had to know his customers and stock goods suited to his particular trade. The demand for cloth was subject to changes in the weather and in public taste. These realities forced the merchant to walk a tightrope. Warehouse supervisors had to ensure that fads and fashion did not override the good sense of his cloth buyers. 'It is obvious that

3.4 Pattern books at the woollen warehouse of S. Addington & Company, 4–6 Charing Cross Road, London, 1920s. Courtesy of Westminster City Archives: 2268, S. Addington & Company Ltd, Business Records.

warehousemen do suffer from the freaks of fashion,' noted the *Financial Times*, 'but after all, this resolves itself into a question of management and of judicious buying of stock.'[87]

A showroom brimming with the right merchandise would bring in orders—and impress journalists whose opinions influenced buyers. In 1905, a correspondent for the *Textile World Record* wandered through the woollen warehouses of Bradford and Manchester, where he saw what he called 'American shipping stuffs', describing them as of 'exceptionally good value, very stylish and very saleable'. In one warehouse, he flipped through sample books filled with swatches of woollen dress goods for the ready-to-wear industry. 'These fabrics look so well when made up into costumes, and the price is so reasonable, that a woman in moderate circumstances can buy a new costume any time.' One popular fabric was 'Guiseley tweed' in a subtle check pattern, 'made in five distinct shades of grey from light to dark, and a very tasty thing it is'. The clerks had set up displays to help the visitor envision how the fabric would look when made into a garment. This was a marvellous feat of woollen merchandising. The journalist walked out convinced that 'Tweeds "boss the show".'[88]

The new world of makers-up

The first salvo against the powerful wholesale merchants came from a certain type of independent-minded textile customer in the home market. These customers wanted to reduce costs and expedite deliveries and the best means to this end was to bypass the merchants. By the turn of the century, some large London retailers with drapery departments, including Harrods Ltd, on Brompton Road in Kensington, and Liberty & Company Ltd, on Regent Street, had started to source textiles straight from the mills. Costume and mantle makers such as Debenham & Freebody on Wigmore Street also preferred to buy fabrics directly from the manufacturers because they could specify the best textures and colours for their market and negotiate a better price.[89] In turn, textile mills welcomed the new type of customer who preferred to buy direct. For one thing, although merchants had access to a broad market, they were slow to pay. Those in the shipping trade were prompt, while those in the home trade dallied. It was not unusual for a merchant to place an order with a mill on 1 March, to demand delivery of the cloth by 1 April and to settle the account in December, less a discount.[90] Mills could get paid faster and make higher profits by selling to shipping merchants, large retailers with drapery or haberdashery departments, or clothing manufacturers.

Merchants coped with these new realities in a number of ways. Well-capitalised merchant houses such as Rylands & Sons realised that the domestic cloth trade was a lost cause and looked to increase their export business.[91] Rylands had been producing its own ready-made clothing for decades. As this market grew, other merchants also looked to enter into producing apparel for men, women and children. One example is Sparrow, Hardwick & Company in Manchester. Established in 1853, Sparrow handled a wide selection of woollen and cotton goods for domestic and foreign consumption. This merchant house had a 'large and growing Colonial connection, especially with Australia and New Zealand', but the bulk of its business was in the home trade.[92] The Manchester city directories described Sparrow as having three roles: stuff and woollen merchants, warehousemen and mantle manufacturers. In 1914, Abraham Moon and Sons was selling woollens to Sparrow's 'Fancy Dress Dept.' and to its 'Mantle Factory'.[93]

Like her male counterpart, the British woman who wanted to look smart without spending a lot of money started to buy ready-made clothing. More wholesale merchants diversified into clothing production. 'The wholesalers have become ladies' tailors, and it is now possible for any draper to stock costumes readymade for a customer, or to get one made at a few days' notice from any dress material that the wholesale house stocks', wrote the *Textile World Record*. 'This is a great convenience to many people because of the growing charges for dressmaking.'[94] Makers-up bowed to fashion and turned out new styles in quick time. Some wholesale clothiers—garment manufacturers who made clothing for sale to retailers—opened ladies' departments that could sew 'costumes at a few days' notice of elaborate finish, avoiding much delay to the consumer, which is always a desideratum', explained the *Textile Recorder*. 'Many of the costumes retailed ready-made in the large ladies' emporiums are manufactured in this system.'[95]

The diversification into clothing production by wholesale merchants was indicative of a trade in transition. The traditional system of clothing production—wherein the wholesale draper served as an intermediary between the textile mill and the local haberdasher, tailor and dressmaker—was crushed by the rise of a mechanised garment industry that made affordable apparel for the mass market. The importation of superior ready-made clothing from the United States inspired British makers-up to adopt American production methods and machinery.[96] Ready-to-wear factories cropped up in cities and towns around Britain, the most important clusters being in the East End of London, in major commercial centres such as Glasgow, Birmingham and Manchester, and in the heart of woollen territory in Leeds.

As shown in Chapter 1, by the mid-nineteenth century Leeds and the surrounding valleys were already recognised as Britain's 'clothing district'. The early investment in cloth halls, merchant houses, textile mills and clothing workshops laid the foundation for the city's complex modern garment industry. By the early twentieth century, Leeds was home to manufacturer-retailers such as Joseph Hepworth & Son and Montague Burton Ltd, whose menswear stores on the high street sold affordable ready-made suits and 'to measure' suits, respectively.[97] But Leeds was also a major production centre for ladies' clothing, children's wear and uniforms. At the start of the First World War in 1914, the city's factories produced £2 millions-worth of clothing annually, making Leeds the second most important British apparel centre after London.[98] The Leeds garment industry consumed large quantities of Yorkshire-made cloth.[99] Worsteds from Bradford and Huddersfield were perfect for men's suits, whereas tweeds from Guiseley, Yeadon and the Colne Valley were ideal for children's apparel, women's wear and lightweight outerwear such as caps, jackets and breeches.

No Leeds clothing manufacturer was too small or too large a customer for Netherfield Mill. At the higher end of the spectrum were customers such as James Corson, a Leeds retail draper (trained as a tailor in Scotland) who ventured into ladies' clothing production during the First World War. This small firm was a solid customer for several decades, using the mill's tweed fabrics in up-market ladies' ready-made clothing into the 1930s, notably for its Corsonia brand of 'tailor-mades'.[100] But more typically, Netherfield Mill catered to makers-up that produced affordable apparel for the mass market. The most prominent of these customers

3.5 John Barran & Sons' Moorish-style warehouse and clothing factory in Park Square, Leeds, 1877–78. Courtesy of West Yorkshire Archive Service, Leeds: WYL434, Records of John Barran & Sons Ltd.

was John Barran & Sons Ltd, a volume menswear manufacturer who also made ladies' wear, children's wear and school uniforms. You may recall Barran from our discussion of the Yorkshire College of Science. This early advocate of technical education in textiles is best known for his role in mechanising the Leeds ready-made clothing industry. In the 1850s, Barran established a series of garment factories, which used innovations such as the sewing machine, the band-knife for cutting through stacks of cloth and a subcontracting system wherein home workers did the more complex sewing off-site. In the ensuing decades, there were more inventions, new warehouses and bigger factories, including the dazzling Park Square facility of 1877–78, with Moorish-style polychrome tiles, horseshoe arches and minarets designed for Barran by the architect Thomas Ambler (figure 3.5). Incorporated in 1903, John Barran & Sons Ltd was one of the largest makers-up in Leeds, with assets of more than £440,000 in 1914.[101]

The relationship with John Barran & Sons may have helped Abraham Moon and Sons to hone its skill in the creation of wool fabric for children's wear. This speciality would be a hallmark of Netherfield Mill until the 1970s, when the market for children's woollen clothing disappeared due to the rise of synthetics. In Victorian and Edwardian times, mothers took pride in putting their little boys in fanciful suits with short jackets and knickerbockers, dressing them as Little Lord Fauntleroy, as one of the Kate Greenaway characters, or as a Gaelic warrior in a little skirt. The backbone of Barran's ready-made business was the production of these whimsies. The 'Little Boys' Tailors' range included amusing little sailor suits and fancy dress items such as a soldier's uniform and pirate's costume. Less theatrical everyday attire included countless variations of the tweed suit with a Norfolk jacket and knickerbockers. These outfits were widely exported to the Continent, to South America, and to British markets in Australia, Canada, New Zealand and South Africa. If we think creatively, we can envision the production line in a Barran factory sewing little Beefeater's uniforms or child-sized Hussar jackets using inexpensive woollens from Netherfield Mill.[102]

The proximity to the women's clothing manufacturers in Leeds was also an asset for Abraham Moon and Sons. With a large number of customers nearby, the designers at Netherfield Mill could develop an in-depth understanding of the nuances and needs of the ladies' clothing business. One of the most important ladies' wear customers was Thomas Marshall & Company, which operated out of Marshalls' Mills in the Holbeck section of Leeds from 1906. The firm made ladies' dresses and coats in plain tailored styles, including the 'tight-fitting coats with darted sleeve tops and long gored costume skirts' that were popular in the Edwardian period. The company expanded Marshalls' Mills during the First World War and relocated to larger quarters at Marlbeck House in the mid-1920s with the growing demand for tailored models.[103] By working with customers like Marshalls, Abraham Moon and Sons learned to make the types of woollens that were needed for affordable, well-cut women's dresses, jackets, suits and coats.

In the Victorian era, the Guiseley mills had established a reputation for their own brand of woven cloth, Guiseley Waterproof Tweeds. Like their grandparents, Edwardian Britons needed waterproof clothing to protect them from the damp North Atlantic climate. In 1909, the Leeds correspondent for *The Economist* noted that the West Riding 'makers of waterproofing materials, out of which capes, overall and macintoshes are made which contain not a particle of rubber' were 'all exceedingly busy' with repeat orders. The weavers combined fine merino warp yarns with small cotton weft yarns to create 'a very light, thin, compact, and tightly made fabric'. The material was waterproofed using traditional methods and the end result was a superior wet-weather cloth that was 'light, warm and yet porous'.[104] The records at Netherfield Mill do not describe the types of cloth that were sold, but some of the Leeds customers produced waterproof apparel. Hepton Brothers, for example, made ladies' garments, raincoats and other types of waterproof clothing.[105]

Heatons was famous for smart women's coats, walking suits and for the 'Alwetha' brand of waterproof rubberless raincoats (figure 3.6).[106] Perhaps Netherfield Mill produced an updated version of Guiseley Waterproof Tweeds for the 'Alwetha' line, whose name was a pun on 'all weather'.

All signs pointed to the triumph of ready-made garments and to a steady demand for inexpensive tweeds. The West Riding tweed makers continued to do what they did best; they blended wool, cotton and mungo to produce 'smart-looking' imitation Scotch tweeds for the middle and lower ends of the market.[107] The mills of Yeadon and Guiseley were among the most skilled producers of medium-grade cloth. Even when the Leeds woollen trade was 'of a hand-to-mouth character', the manufacturers 'catering for the million' were reported to be well employed, 'both for ladies' costume cloths and men's suitings in quiet styles'.[108] By 1914, the woollen and worsted mills of the West Riding stood unrivalled for 'clothing the world's multitudes with any kind of cloth at any price', using 'any fibre long enough to have two ends'.[109]

Bradford fleece and the khaki call

On 28 June 1914, the world was shocked by news of the assassination of the Archduke Franz Ferdinand, heir to the throne of Austria-Hungary. Within weeks, the major European powers were engaged in the First World War. In August, all of the West Riding sat on pins and needles as the lucrative trade with Germany came to a halt. Everyone wondered if there would be a repeat of 1872, when large military contracts for cloths, rugs and blankets helped to bring prosperity to the region.[110] As the British military prepared for conflict, large orders for khaki, blankets, rugs, puttees and shirting poured into the West Riding.[111] The production of civilian cloth such as tweeds, coatings and serges were put on hold as mills with government contracts operated into the early evenings to produce army and navy fabrics. Millions of yards were needed.[112] As a vertically integrated woollen mill, Abraham Moon and Sons was fully able to weave military cloth. But if it were to operate efficiently, Netherfield Mill would need trustworthy intelligence on developments in Bradford where the wool supply was controlled. For this, the firm looked to an experienced Bradford wool merchant.

The British wool industry was entwined in a global commodities system that connected woollen manufacturers to woolgrowers in the four corners of the earth. Great herds of merino and crossbred sheep were concentrated in the River Plate basin of Argentina and Uruguay in South America and, more importantly, in several British territories: Australia, the Cape of Good Hope (or the Cape Colony) and New Zealand. Australia was an especially wild and woolly place.[113] Traders in a few

Heaton's "ESIW" Winter Coats

A Striking Range of New Ideas for Ladies, Misses & Girls

EVERY buyer who has seen our Advance Show has expressed spontaneous approval of the efforts of our designing staff to create a series of unique and exclusive Coat Styles. For every age, from the schoolgirl of seven to the matron of mature age, there are appropriate creations.

The materials include Tweeds, Velours and Blanket Cloths in tasteful, attractive shades and designs.

Our representatives are now on the road, but the new range of ESIW Coats can be seen at any of our showrooms—will you honour us with a visit?

HEATONS
(LEEDS) LIMITED.
NORTH STREET. LEEDS

Represented also in South Africa, Australia, New Zealand, India, Holland and Denmark.

CANADA: Mr. E. Johnson, 2 Wheeler Avenue, Toronto.   U.S.A.: Mr. E. Johnson, 136 Liberty St., New York.

3.6 Heatons (Leeds) Ltd was an important Leeds maker-up that used tweeds, velours and blanket cloths to make ladies' coats, buying fabric from Netherfield Mill. © The British Library Board: Advertisement, *Drapers' Organiser* (3 July 1920), 28.

European commercial centres—Bradford and London, Antwerp in Belgium and Roubaix in France—controlled the global supply of fleece. Bradford, 'Worstedopolis', was the most important of these wool centres.

Bradford was surrounded by several Yorkshire manufacturing and trading centres: Dewsbury, Halifax, Huddersfield, Keighley, Leeds and Wakefield.[114] This accident of geography contributed to Bradford's rapid growth as a major player in the wool industry. Bradford initially made cloth, but after the 1824 repeal of laws forbidding the export of British wool, its entrepreneurs turned to the buying and selling of the fleece itself.[115] Its Wool Exchange, designed by the local architects Lockwood & Mawson in the Venetian Gothic style, was completed in 1867 (figure 3.7). Inside, the trading floor—an airy hall in wrought iron and pink granite—resembled the vaulted nave of a cathedral. With his characteristic loathing of all things commercial, the Victorian art critic John Ruskin had caustically described the building as a shrine to the 'Goddess of Getting-on' or to 'Britannia of the Market'.[116]An impressive medieval-style Town Hall by the same architects was opened in 1873. A year later in front of the Town Hall, a colossal Carrara marble statue of Sir Titus Salt, founder of the Saltaire model industrial village and a former mayor of Bradford, was unveiled by the Duke of Devonshire.[117]

The Bradford Wool Exchange was a powerful symbol of Bradford's commitment to wool and the wider world, but the global character of this trade was largely invisible to everyone except the auctioneers, merchants, warehousemen, brokers, shippers, spinners and weavers in the system. In the era of Abraham Moon the elder, the Bradford 'wool-stapler' purchased the fleece from growers or importers, sorted it into different grades and sold the lots to customers according to their needs. By the late nineteenth century, the wool-stapler had evolved into the wool merchant who imported fleece, sold some of it domestically and exported most of it to mills around the world.[118] One such merchant, P. W. Musgrave & Company, had supplied wool to Netherfield Mill since the days of Isaac Moon; the principal, Peter William Musgrave, was one of the creditors who had helped the mill to resolve its financial difficulties. By the early twentieth century, a large portion of the Australian and New Zealand clips were shipped to Yorkshire and distributed by the wool merchants of Bradford. The city's wool import-export business grew by leaps and bounds until Bradford became the world's foremost wool market. The wool came in, it was stored in warehouses, deals were made and the wool was shipped out. Sometimes the fleece was combed or carded, sometimes it was spun into yarn and sometimes not. Bradford wool merchants like P. W. Musgrave & Company knew this system inside out. The firm had modern facilities in Bradford and 'an old warehouse' in Cheapside, London.[119]

In December 1914, Thomas Musgrave of P. W. Musgrave & Company became a director at Abraham Moon and Sons.[120] This step formalised the mill's relationship

3.7 The Bradford Wool Exchange was an impressive Gothic Revival building dedicated to wool as a commodity. Author's collection: postcard, 1953.

with a wool merchant that had long been one of its major suppliers. In 1912, the Musgrave firm consisted of the ageing Peter and his sons, Charles and Thomas. When the father died in 1913, he left a sizeable estate and prosperous business.[121] The younger son, Thomas, was the heir apparent to the wool empire. If Charles Walsh needed business advice or financial backing, Thomas was a logical choice as a new board member.

Walter Moon continued to distance himself from Netherfield Mill. It was his willingness to sell some of his shares that permitted Thomas Musgrave to buy into the firm. Shortly after Thomas joined the board in December 1914, Walter took a modest pay cut and thus no longer earned the same governing director's salary as Charles.[122] These measures were largely symbolic, but they indicated the growing disengagement of the founding family. The Walsh family was taking the reins, bit by bit.

Men in uniform

Woollen fabrics made in the West Riding were ideally suited to military uniforms. For generations, Yorkshire woollen mills had made the cloth used for the red coats of British infantrymen. In the nineteenth century, the invention of smokeless powder and its widespread adoption by the military enhanced visibility on the battlefield. Soldiers no longer needed bright uniforms that allowed them to see each other through the smoke. They needed camouflage to blend into the background so they could hide from each other. The British military started to replace bright uniforms with gear in a drab yellow-brown shade, called 'khaki' after the word for soil in one of the native languages in India. In 1897, khaki was adopted as the universal dress for all British troops overseas and, in 1902, khaki service dress was adopted for general military wear.[123]

Yorkshire woollens went into uniforms for the British, French, Russian and other allied armies.[124] British uniform production was centred in the Leeds clothing district. Working under government contract, the makers-up used Yorkshire fabrics made from hard-wearing crossbred wools, as well those made from finer merino wool.[125] Each recruit was outfitted with khaki clothing that was in part made from woven woollens. The standard issue for each infantryman included two khaki service dress jackets, shirts, two pairs of service trousers, a cap and a greatcoat (figure 3.8).[126] British officers were expected to buy their own bespoke uniforms, fitted to them by bespoke tailors according to military specifications.[127] By the autumn of 1914, the looms of the West Riding were clacking away to make khaki, serge, blankets and rugs for the military. Most manufacturers had to skip their regular autumn trip to London for showing next year's patterns because so little had been done on the new

3.8 Military conflicts generated a large demand for woollens, which were used to clothe infantryman and officers; these men from the Cheshire Regiment wear uniforms from the First World War. Author's collection.

designs.[128] By March 1915, the 'ordinary trade', both foreign and domestic, was suspended due to the 'boom in war material'. According to the *Textile Recorder*, 'about three-fourths of the looms in the woollen trade and most of the factories in the tailoring trades have been requisitioned for military outfits'.[129] The boom times of the Franco-Prussian War had returned.[130]

The wool industry soon discovered that soldiers required about four times more wool fabric than civilians.[131] Not only was a complete kit required for each new soldier, but, as discussed below, uniforms worn by men on the front had to be replaced frequently. The British government took measures to control the wool supply, ensuring that a sufficient amount of raw material was available to produce enormous quantities of cloth. Between 1916 and 1919, the government requisitioned three British clips and contracted to obtain portions of the clips from Australia, New Zealand, India and South Africa.[132] The authorities also established a stringent system for controlling the wool supply. Based in Bradford, the Wool Control was managed by government officials with advisers from the wool industry. Stocks of wool were distributed under a rationing system, with military needs being given preference over civilian ones.[133] The services of merchants and brokers were dispensed with, as no wool could be bought or sold without a special permit.[134]

Abraham Moon and Sons received several contracts from the Royal Army Clothing Department for the production of military cloth, including flannel.[135] In his three decades at the mill, Charles Walsh had never been so busy nor seen such large orders. At a board meeting in July 1915, a 'general discussion took place as to the orders & Deliveries of Goods and the Chairman explained that 18,000 pieces were present on order for delivery to the approximate value of £90,000'.[136] In August 1915, the chairman 'informed the Board that the Company had received orders during the past week for 2000 pieces for delivery next Winter, and that our present output was about 350 pieces per week'.[137] The cloth made at Netherfield Mill eventually found its way to the Leeds garment factories and was sewn into uniforms for the British, Commonwealth, French and Russian armed services.

By December 1915, the mills in Guiseley and Yeadon were running at capacity, making cloth for both military and civilian needs. The *Textile Recorder* reported on the 'abundant signs of prosperity' and on the expansion of some factories in the district. During occasional lulls, the mills turned to 'the standard cloakings, cap, and costume cloths of the civilian classes, for which both merchants and retailers were anxiously waiting'.[138] That month, Netherfield Mill received larger-than-usual orders from James Hare, the Leeds merchant who doubled as a maker-up and who had probably converted to military production.[139] Regular customers waited anxiously as the mills met military needs, watching their cloth supplies dwindle and hoping for the moment when the weavers were permitted to respond to civilian orders.

In a time of crisis, the general manager of a textile mill would have turned to his main business partner or his heir apparent to make decisions. But Charles Walsh increasingly relied on wool merchant Thomas Musgrave. For one, Walter Moon seemed increasingly distracted after his mother died in 1915. He seemed to find greater solace in animal husbandry than in woollens.[140] At the annual show of the Wharfedale Agricultural Society in May 1916, Walter exhibited his best heifer against other calves that had not yet 'cut a tooth', and took first prize in the competition, which was 'Open to Farmers principally dependent on farming for their living'.[141] Walter, the farmer, was well on his way to severing the family's ties with Abraham Moon and Sons. Frank Walsh was next in line for the job of mill manager. He had a longstanding interest in military matters, having been a peacetime volunteer in the West Riding Regiment from 1905 to 1912. In early 1917, Frank joined the regular army and, within the year, had an officer's commission with the territorial forces. He was deployed to the Asian subcontinent to manage a textile mill for the Indian Munitions Board.[142] Meanwhile, Charles and Thomas took care of business at Netherfield Mill.

During the war, the British army ordered somewhere in the region of thirty to fifty times more cloth than in peacetime.[143] Modifications were made to the army uniform in 1916, streamlining the jacket design, but khaki and flannel, both made from wool, remained the fabrics of choice.[144] In the trenches, uniforms wore out and soldiers lucky enough to survive needed replacements.[145] The *Wool Record* estimated that the millions of soldiers in the British, French and Russian armies each wore 'perhaps a dozen suits, where perhaps they had only worn one before'.[146] In December 1916, the Leeds correspondent for *The Economist* marvelled at the volume of government orders of the previous four months: '13 million cap comforters, 23 million pairs of drawers, 8 million pairs of wool gloves, 57 million pairs of socks, 10 million vests, 20 million blankets, 80 million yards of uniform overcoating and trousering khaki, 110 million yards flannel'.[147]

Charles Walsh found himself going to and from the War Department's cloth office in Bradford to discuss Netherfield Mill's contracts with government officials. A board minute from February 1918 provides an insight into the scale of the orders:

> Mr. Walsh referred to an interview he had with Mr. Todd at the Flannel Office, G[reat].
> W[estern].Ry Hotel, Bradford, respecting a contract for 50,000 yards of Flannel.
> Mr. Walsh submitted the Government pattern, which he thought would be far better
> for the firm to produce than the Standard Cloth. He therefore suggested that we ask
> permission to cancel the contract for the Standard Cloth and accept instead a contract for
> 50,000 yds. of Natural Flannel which was very urgently needed by the War Office.[148]

Under new management

Like many Yorkshire textile mills, Abraham Moon and Sons was highly profitable during the First World War. Some of the mill staff, including Frank Walsh, had been away for the duration of the conflict, but others who had long been with the firm, such as Tom Walsh, worked at the mill during the war (figure 3.9). Shortly after Armistice Day in 1918, the controlling directors, Charles Walsh and Walter Moon, started to make plans to purchase Netherfield Mill from the estate of Isaac Moon.[149] A year later in November 1919, Walter decided to throw in the towel. The lure of country life seems to have been too strong for him to resist. Walter, who preferred cattle to the carding room, offered Charles his share of the business for £20,000.[150] According to Walsh family lore, Charles borrowed money to buy out Walter. But the reality may have been different. The business of making woollen cloth for the military was highly profitable. Financial data for the war period is scant, but we know that sales for 1918 had totalled £151,555 with a 13 per cent profit.[151] As the controlling director of Abraham Moon and Sons, Charles may have exited the war in a comfortable financial position. There is some greater clarity about other aspects of the transition to Walsh ownership. Back in 1913, Abraham Moon and Sons Ltd

3.9 The mill staff just before the start of the First World War; (left to right) seated: Herbert Proctor, Annie Baldwin, Jack Clapham, Tom Walsh, Tom Clapham, Frank Walsh; standing: Seth Robinson, Clifford Waite, Ned Clapham, Willie Wilson, [? unknown], William Brown, Harry Spence, Willie Knipe, Albert Lawrence. Courtesy of Abraham Moon and Sons.

had been capitalised at £26,000. The new joint-stock company of the same name, which was formed in February 1920 when Charles bought out Walter, was worth £90,000.[152] The firm's value had increased by 33 per cent over the course of seven years, adjusted for inflation.[153]

Isaac Moon had played his cards close, relying for support on family members like Henry Foggitt and bringing a few trusted employees like Charles Walsh into the fold. Under the control of the Walsh family, Abraham Moon and Sons broadened the scope of ownership and management. Charles was the chairman, while the wool merchant Thomas Musgrave was vice-chairman. Back from his assignment in India, Frank Walsh also sat on the board; he worked in the mill and was positioned to succeed his father as managing director. Charles was the majority shareholder and the remaining shares were divided between the vice-chairman, members of the Walsh family and key employees.[154] In 1921, the designer Tom Walsh, among others, became a shareholder.[155] That year, the board was expanded to include Thomas Clapham, who had been a salesman for Netherfield Mill since 1881. The Claphams were a fixture of the local woollen industry and founder Abraham Moon had married Elizabeth Clapham.[156] Tom Clapham brought to the board four decades of sales experience and a definitive understanding of the customers in the Leeds territory.[157]

The appointment of Thomas Musgrave as vice-chairman at Abraham Moon and Sons was indicative of a broader Yorkshire business pattern that had developed as a result of the war. The Bradford wool industries had long been divided into highly specialised firms in wool processing, worsted spinning, worsted weaving and so forth. As an unintended consequence of the Wool Control, wool merchants and top makers began to diversify their investments.[158] Much of 'their capital was liquidated by the control which the Government exercised over the wool supplies', the *Yorkshire Post* explained in 1919, 'and presumably, some of this liquidated capital has been employed in the purchase and running of other enterprises.' Some wool merchants invested in spinning and weaving mills. Most famously, Bradford men spent £2 million to acquire the giant worsted mills at Saltaire, a showpiece of the Yorkshire textile industry. Other notable acquisitions included those of William C. Gaunt, an entrepreneur who was known as far away as North America where he had textile investments. The New York based trade journal *Textile World Journal* described him as 'a man of destiny in the wool trade, with an enormous business in tops'. By 1920, this large, jovial self-made millionaire, who lived in posh surroundings in Apperley Bridge, owned or had controlling interests in seven Yorkshire firms—and his new spinning and weaving empire reached into Guiseley. In 1918, Gaunt and a co-investor had purchased Jonathan Peate's firm, J., J. L., and C. Peate (Guiseley) Ltd, and thereby gained control of Nunroyd Mills.[159] Peate himself spent his golden years in local politics, fighting a losing battle against a proposal to redraw the boundaries of the cities of Bradford and Leeds and to divide up and absorb the nearby countryside.[160] Vertical integration by the Bradford wool interests pointed to major changes in the West Riding—and Abraham Moon and Sons was swept up in the maelstrom.

Inside the mill

3.10 Spinning, 1912. Courtesy of Abraham Moon and Sons.

3.11 Sorting and blending raw wool, 1912. Courtesy of Abraham Moon and Sons.

3.12 The mill dye house, 1937. Courtesy of Abraham Moon and Sons.

3.13 Power weaving, 1930s. Courtesy of Abraham Moon and Sons.

3.14 The warping department, 1930s. Courtesy of Abraham Moon and Sons.

3.15 Burling and mending at the mill, 1912. Courtesy of Abraham Moon and Sons.

4 Moving up-market

Confirmation of the report that several Yorkshire woolen manufacturing concerns have in contemplation the elimination of cheaper woolen fabrics, and concentration on the production of higher-grade material is contained in the announcement that A. Moon & Sons, of Guiseley, near Bradford, are producing much finer goods than formerly. (*Women's Wear Daily*, New York, 1927)[1]

The wartime rationing of the wool supply had unintended consequences for followers of fashion and the fashion industry. The Wool Control inadvertently reshaped consumers' expectations of what types of fabric were comfortable, desirable and fashionable. Strong crossbred wool was reserved for military cloth and soft merino wool was used for civilian cloth. On the home front, workers who enjoyed high wartime wages purchased clothing made from the more expensive merino wool and became accustomed to its smoother touch to the hand. Returning servicemen, who had worn constricting khaki uniforms made from crossbred wool, looked to acquire civilian attire that was 'more suggestive of ease and freedom'. In 1920, the *Wool Record* reported that the 'public everywhere seem determined to have nothing but the best fabrics, and this would appear to be one of the direct results of the war'.[2]

The new appreciation for wool fabrics that were soft to the touch and appealing to the colour sense was the first of many taste shifts to hit the world of tweeds in the interwar period (Colour Plate 5). The influence of the new generation of Paris couturiers like Gabrielle 'Coco' Chanel is familiar in the annals of fashion history, but changes to the fabric scene are less well documented. The Yorkshire tweed industry is a case in point. The 1920s were an era of fierce competition when mills vied for scraps of the home trade and the overseas trade. A commitment to design and technology helped Abraham Moon and Sons stay ahead. The contraction of globalisation during the Great Depression sent the Yorkshire tweed makers back into the domestic market where they benefited from the steady evolution of the ready-to-wear industry and met up with the newly crowned kings of the high street, the multiples. Depression-era consumers shopped the high street for good-looking tweed garments that did not break the bank. As luxury mills struggled during the 1930s, mid-market firms like Abraham Moon and Sons continued to do what they did best. The firm combined a strong design sensibility with the best available technology to make tweeds that were attractive and affordable.

Efficiency rules

In 1920, Abraham Moon and Sons started its new life under the management of Thomas Musgrave and Charles Walsh by making union cloths for the low and mid-ranged tweed markets. The mill's designers—Charles, Frank and Tom Walsh—were experts in combining yarns spun from virgin wool and from shoddy to create attractive patterns. The colourful shoddy yarns were created from old rags processed at the Eller Ghyll Mill, a small facility in Otley, a nearby town.[3] The weaving shed at Netherfield Mill was equipped with more than eighty power looms by Yorkshire machine builders such as Lee & Crabtree, Leeming & Wilkinson and George Hodgson Ltd, of Bradford. Established in 1849, Hodgsons had been winning medals for engineering excellence at the world's fairs since the second Crystal Palace exhibition in London in 1862. Its power looms were used by textile factories in Germany, France, Italy, Spain, Russia and other countries around the world.[4] The triumvirate of design skill, recycled materials and high-tech machinery allowed Abraham Moon and Sons to make cloth that could be sold at competitive prices.

A penchant for technology was emerging as a hallmark of the firm. Charles knew the mill from the viewpoint of a designer-manager, but his son Frank was blessed with a mechanical bent that he honed while running a textile mill for the Indian Munitions Board during the war. The father-and-son team looked to technology as a tool for improving efficiency on the shop floor and the quality of the product. The men had been trained at the Yorkshire College and its successor, the University of Leeds, where the designer-weaver John Beaumont and his son Roberts Beaumont had pioneered textile education. As the younger Beaumont wrote,

> it is now a patent fact that the textile craftsman, carding engineer, comber, spinner, loom mechanician, designer and manager, seeking to attain distinction in factory life and organization, must possess technical knowledge gleaned from the best literature … Not to be in possession of textile literature is to lack the chief tools of equipment—the munitions of warfare—for the successful performance of one's duty in the factory; and, as a consequence, to be crippled and handicapped in the industrial race.[5]

We may never know if Charles and Frank read the latest technical journals, but they seem to have kept up with Roberts Beaumont. A photograph of the Leeds professor as a young man survives in the mill archive, testimony to some type of continued connection.[6]

Charles and Frank saw technology as the winning weapon in the battle for customers who wanted good-quality tweeds at a reasonable price. To this end, they established a policy of constantly reinvesting a portion of the mill profits in new equipment. The capacity of the weaving shed was enlarged with the addition of sixteen new looms from Yorkshire machine builders. An awareness of American theories on scientific management led to the installation of time clocks to keep track of the comings and goings of the mill workers. Students were welcomed into the mill to see the high-tech facility. In one instance, thirty-five members of the Bradford junior branch of the Society of Dyers and Colourists visited the works to see the 'complete manufacture of woollen goods, including dyeing'. A set of new iron gates proclaimed the firm's name in gold paint and let the world know that Abraham Moon and Sons was firmly committed to modernity (figure 9.4).[7]

The modernisation of Netherfield Mill was interrupted by a family tragedy that signalled the end of an era. After a two-month illness, Charles Walsh died on 19 November 1924 from a pulmonary haemorrhage caused by tuberculosis.[8] He had been a man of catholic interests, more of a Victorian generalist than a modern specialist, who identified with St Oswald's Church and projects such as the restoration of the Town Cross (figure 4.1). Fittingly, the flags of the Guiseley Conservative Club, the Guiseley Liberal Club and St Oswald's Church were all lowered to half-mast in his honour.[9] His death coincided with those of other local woollen men who came of age in the Victorian period. Over the course of the

4.1 Towngate in the centre of Guiseley, after 1921. Courtesy of Aireborough Historical Society: B281.

decade, the old guard passed on: William Murgatroyd in 1921; Jonathan Peate and Roberts Beaumont in 1924; Walter Smith Moon in 1926; and Charles Moon in 1927.[10] Following Isaac's death, the Moon family sold Crooklands in 1924 and the money went to support his spinster daughter, living in a Georgian house in Bedford Square, in the Bloomsbury section of London.[11] Amidst the turmoil, Thomas Musgrave and Frank Walsh pooled resources to purchase the firm of Abraham Moon and Sons.[12] Thomas was the new chairman; Frank, the 'Mill Manager'.[13] As they faced an uncertain future, the new owners of Netherfield Mill could not help notice the general feeling of melancholy, the sense that old times were slipping away.

Muddle at mid-decade

Thomas Musgrave and Frank Walsh took charge of Abraham Moon and Sons at a difficult moment in British industrial history. By the mid-1920s, the entire Yorkshire wool textile industry was in a muddle. Between 1920 and 1926, British woollen exports fell precipitously from 187 to 120 million square yards, mainly due to foreign tariff barriers and intensified global competition.[14] The tweeds makers in the Colne Valley and Guiseley held their ground by producing 'cheaper cloths which look smart'.[15] In 1924, the Chancellor of the Exchequer, Winston Churchill, announced his decision to return to the gold standard. This monetary policy, which went into effect in 1925, strengthened sterling but put British goods at a disadvantage in world markets. It was now even easier for low-wage economies to send their cloth to Britain and even more difficult for British mills to find markets abroad.

Panic gripped the West Riding mills as orders stagnated. In July 1925, desperate mill owners posted notice to workers of a wage reduction. Seventy-five per cent of the 6,000 textile workers in Yeadon and Guiseley were involved in lockouts and work stoppages. One morning, operatives turned up at Netherfield Mill and worked until breakfast, when the plant was shut down. Only Nunroyd Mills and Spring Head Mill were up and running.[16] The conflict surrounding woollen textiles, which coincided with a protracted coal strike, started to fizzle in the late summer, but the fierce competition on world markets did not disappear.[17] New competitors emerged. Everywhere in Europe, including Italy, textile mills were being built. 'Continental tweed manufacturers are progressing rapidly at the expense of the West Riding', *Women's Wear*, the daily newspaper for the New York fashion business, wrote in September 1925. 'Buyers who habitually dealt with Yorkshire are going to the Continent in increasing numbers to make their purchases.'[18] Some Yorkshiremen turned their backs on free trade to support the protectionist call of the Labour Party. In November 1925, a group of major trade associations for the wool textile industry implored the Board of Trade to implement duties on imported cloth.[19]

In May 1926, Britain felt the full effects of the gold standard when wage cuts in the coal mines led to the infamous General Strike. The country was at a complete standstill for nine days. In Bradford, the presses stopped at the *Wool Record*, the official organ of the woollen and worsted industries.[20] The merchants of Golden Square advised the Yorkshire mills 'not to send in their spring, 1927, lines' for fear the goods would pile up in the freight depots and American garment manufacturers wondered if they would receive the British cloth they had ordered for the new autumn styles.[21] Once the General Strike ended, fuel shortages forced Yorkshire spinners and weavers to adopt a three-day working week. Mills with repeat orders on the books had difficulty filling them, which was frustrating given the generally depressed state of trade.[22] In 1927, the president of the Bradford Chamber of Commerce, who had been in the wool business for forty-six years, claimed that he 'had never experienced times so bad as those of the past three years'.[23]

Looking to America

Some observers urged the Yorkshire mills to sidestep politics and stick to their strength: fashionability. Fashion was both their *raison d'être* and their *bête noire*. The revolutionary fashions coming out of Paris, London and New York presented a major challenge to traditional tailored clothing constructed from woven wool fabrics. The ladies' shops were filled with comfortable knitted costumes from Leicester, an East Midlands hosiery centre that had diversified into apparel. Another major worry was that the new leg-revealing styles simply required so little cloth. Yorkshiremen nervously watched the new trends from Paris and raised their eyebrows as hemlines inched up—and up. As couturiers like Coco Chanel showed short skirts in soft knitted fabrics, the tweed weavers shuddered. 'A few years ago women were wearing long coats and skirts of thick woolen tweed material', the London-based *Women's Wear* columnist wrote in 1925, and 'it was nothing for them to require anything from five to eight yards for a costume in 54-inch width … It is surprising what little length goes to make the coat frock today, and the weight is practically nothing.'[24] The Paris-inspired 'abbreviation in feminine garments' required fewer yards and softer fabrics, which ultimately meant less work for the Yorkshire tweed mills.[25]

Tweeds were the bread-and-butter for the mills in Guiseley, Yeadon and the Colne Valley, and those factories had to find a way of adapting the woven woolly look to modern times. The tweed and tartan aesthetic had evolved over many decades and depended on a well-established vocabulary of texture, colour and ornament. Cosy woollens were ideal for the tailored garments that many people still liked, but in the sensuous mid-1920s, consumers often relegated this warm durable style to casual weekend wear.[26] The Yorkshire mills had to do something to update their styling and turn tweeds into objects of desire. By 1925, there were signs that some factories were making a concerted effort to introduce distinctive patterns. 'While there is no difficulty in meeting buyers' wishes as regards quality,' the *Financial Times* wrote, 'there is some difficulty in coping with the demand for entirely new designs, and it is to that field that manufacturers are now turning their attention.'[27]

Abraham Moon and Sons was one of the Yorkshire woollen mills that led the way with novelty tweeds. No pattern books or customer correspondence from the 1920s survive in the mill archive, but we can extrapolate from other types of evidence. Back in the Isaac Moon era, Frank Walsh had worked as a cloth designer alongside his father and uncle.[28] As the new owner-manager, Frank combined his knowledge of design and his penchant for technology to gain advantage for Netherfield Mill. In late 1925, the board approved funds to electrify the weaving shed.[29] In March 1927, Frank replaced two of the mill's 'Plain Looms' with two new 'Fancy Looms' from George Hattersley & Sons, another prominent Yorkshire textile machinery builder.[30] The purchase of fancy looms suggests that Frank was either diversifying his fabric ranges or increasing his output of intricate patterns.

In September 1927, an important statement about Frank's intentions was published in *Women's Wear Daily* (formerly called *Women's Wear*), the trade paper for the New York fashion industry. Some Yorkshire mills were turning away from 'cheaper woolen fabrics' to focus on 'the production of higher-grade material'. One mill in particular—Abraham Moon and Sons—had decided to capitalise on its design skills to move up-market. 'The productions of this company now include all wool fabrics up to 7s 6d per yard and 54 inches, which is described as a big stride', the American paper reported, 'and it is believed with this initial effort, adjoining woolen manufacturing centers will follow the lead given.' Frank, it seems, was in the forefront of a movement to create Yorkshire fabrics that could compete against the Scottish tweeds that were so popular in the United States.[31]

The venture of Netherfield Mill into higher-end tweeds was a response to changes in the social and cultural milieu. Besides the trade recession, tariff barriers and the dictates of Paris fashion, the woollen manufacturers of Guiseley and Yeadon had to counter a certain level of faded glory. Tweeds constantly went in and out of fashion and the mills had learned to roll with the punches. But in the 1920s, new technologies reshaped daily life and the demand for certain types of cloth. Some people still needed heavy coats and motor rugs for riding in open cars (figure 4.2). But the advent of the closed car—the passenger automobile with a metal roof and plastic windows—portended the death knell for this important segment of the tweed market that had prospered since the days of horse-drawn vehicles. Writing about

4.2 Andersons' Rubber Company Ltd, *Motor Dust Overall Coats, Etc. for Ladies, Gentleman & Chauffeurs, Pattern Card No. 1216, Season 1930/31.* Courtesy of Museum of London: Costume Collection, 71.117/53.

Guiseley, the *Yorkshire Post* noted that fewer and fewer customers wanted 'the old waterproof woollen cloth for which the district was at one time famed—the heavy wool tweed'.[32]

Fashion also had an impact on waterproof tweeds. Since the war, a new type of weatherproof garment—the lightweight cotton raincoat that was treated or 'proofed' to be moisture resistant—had gained widespread popularity. The major trade journals for the wholesale and retail garment trade—*Drapers' Organiser, Drapers' Record* and *Tailor and Cutter*—were filled with advertisements for this stylish raingear. Given the shrinking market for classic waterproof tweeds, Frank Walsh had to figure out what Netherfield Mill should make and where to sell it. Flannels and double cloths kept the looms running while he developed a strategy.

Frank looked to enlarge the geographic reach of the mill by expanding the number of agents. In 1925, Abraham Moon and Sons had agreements with at least three agents in the home market: Fowler & Orr in the City (operated by L. Orr and J. W. Powell at 55 Knightrider Street, south of St Paul's Cathedral), J. H. Clay & Company in

Manchester and Thomas Laurie in Glasgow.[33] There was an agent in Leeds, and a Birmingham agent was added to improve coverage of the Midlands.[34] Experiments with a Paris agent never got much traction because it was difficult to find a French expert in British tweeds.[35] Foreign agents handled the trade in Germany, Sweden and Canada.[36] As we saw in Chapter 3, Canada had become an important market for Yorkshire tweeds following the implementation of the imperial preference in 1897 and this remained the case. Canadian imports of woven and worsted woollen piece goods from Britain increased from 11.4 million yards in 1922 to 18.8 million yards in 1929.[37] The bleak northern weather made Canada the ideal market for tweeds and tartans. Whether of French or British descent, people wore warm woollen clothing all year round, especially during the long snowy winters. And Canadians of British ancestry relished goods that reminded them of the mother country on the other side of the Atlantic Ocean.

British tweed makers also looked to make inroads into the United States, where consumer culture was flourishing. Many Yorkshire mills cannily eyed Edinburgh, from where the Scottish Woollen Trade Mark Association (established in 1917 to promote Lowland tweeds) had conquered the American market. In 1919, Scottish woollen exports to the United States were valued at a mere £5,700 (or $28,200), but by 1923, they totalled £675,000 (about $3.37 million). These figures were remarkable given the punitive duties that protected the American market from British woollens under the Fordney-McCumber Tariff of 1922. The Scottish Woollen Trade Mark Association attributed Scottish success in America to branding and advertising. Its twenty-seven member firms stamped their fabric with the association's trademark and, between 1921 and 1924, a group publicity campaign touted the quality of Scottish cloth in short films and magazine advertisements.[38] In 1925, the association boasted that the 'marking of their goods and three intensive press advertising campaigns convinced American people that they should buy Scottish tweeds, with the result that the "Scottish woollen trade is now producing hand over fist to meet the American demand"'.[39]

This type of collective effort did not appeal to Yorkshire's fiercely independent and highly secretive mill owners. Frank Walsh thought there had to be a way to broach foreign markets without sharing his ideas with the competition. One of the hurdles with the United States was figuring out what type of fabrics would sell there. 'The difficulty in this country is to get women's cloths made light enough in weight for the American summer market', wrote the journalist who covered Golden Square for *Women's Wear*, 'but our manufacturers are gradually being educated up to the requirements of American buyers.'[40]

Most American textile buying took place in the wholesale showrooms of New York City, which was the largest port, market and manufacturing hub in the

United States. Manhattan was the national centre for the design and production of ladies' ready-made clothing and an important producer of menswear. Women's wear manufacturers in the modern garment district around Seventh Avenue were always on the lookout for fashionable fabrics that might add distinction to their lines. Retail buyers from around the United States made biannual pilgrimages to New York to select piece goods, ready-to-wear and other fashion merchandise for their stores. The showrooms of Seventh Avenue were the great attraction, but the garment district spilled over into the surrounding neighbourhood. Within a mile radius of R. H. Macy & Company's colossal department store at Seventh Avenue and Thirty-Fourth Street, nearly every square foot of property was dedicated to clothing production, distribution and various support industries. The bustle of London's East End, the City and Golden Square paled in comparison.[41] A savvy agent with his feet on the ground in New York could help a British mill find its bearings in America.

In January 1928, Frank Walsh engaged Charles G. David & Company Inc. to act as the exclusive agent for Abraham Moon and Sons in New York.[42] The proprietor, Charles G. David, was a leading American importer of European fabrics. His swish Fifth Avenue showroom was filled to the brim with imported fabrics that had been selected to inspire the apparel designer from Seventh Avenue and the dry-goods buyer from the American hinterlands. David's firm specialised in quality, variety and European cultural cachet. In 1924, his stock included a group of women's wear coatings in Fair Isle fabrics from Scotland.[43] The next year, he pushed Jacquard patterns in pastel tones alongside mannish tweeds from Germany.[44] Shortly after David agreed to represent Netherfield Mill, *Women's Wear Daily* described his impressive stock of European fabrics: 'Novelty weaves and unusual effects in piece-dye coatings, discreet treatments of jacquards, bouclette and tufted constructions, wool plushes, tweeds and cashmeres'.[45]

Since the turn of the century, American retail buyers and wholesale merchants had been taking the steamship liners across the Atlantic Ocean once or twice a year on reconnaissance missions. Every summer, David crossed the pond to visit his favourite textile mills in Belgium, Czechoslovakia, England, France, Germany and Scotland.[46] We can just imagine the fast-talking New Yorker sauntering into gritty industrial Leeds or the smoky little factory town of Guiseley, where he convinced Frank that the Seventh Avenue ready-to-wear market was ripe for the picking. One can assume that Thomas Musgrave also saw promise in a New York venture. However, the arrangement with David lasted less than two years. Abraham Moon and Sons cancelled the contract in October 1929.[47]

Why was the New York venture so short-lived? Yorkshire tweeds may have failed to hold their own against Scottish cloth, but more likely Charles David violated one of the unspoken rules of the trade. In another context, one Yorkshireman explained how a travelling salesman could sabotage a mill's business. 'When these fellows take a very large collection of samples from so many manufacturers to a customer for his selection, the orders are apt to be very much split up, and no manufacturer really gets an order worthy of his collection.'[48] What was true for a traveller was true for an agent. Some time later, the directors of Abraham Moon and Sons discussed the difficulty of preventing an agent 'from representing competitive firms while acting for the Company'.[49] A conflict of interest on the part of David may have thwarted Frank's ambitions to sell up-market tweeds in the United States. The real issue with any sales representative boiled down to trust, particularly when mill and agent were an ocean apart.

'Tweed' … means 'British tweed'

In September 1929, the Paris couturiers declared, 'This … is a big tweed year.' The *Daily Mail* happily reported that '"Tweed," all over the world, usually means "British tweed," and manufacturers in Scotland, Yorkshire and Ireland are producing it in big quantities.'[50] But the timing of this particular Parisian tweed dictate could not have been worse. The Stock Market Crash on Wall Street in October 1929 had a ripple effect and the Great Depression that came on its heels exacerbated the troubles of the Yorkshire tweed makers. The wealthy entrepreneur Willie Gaunt, who had added Nunroyd Mills to his wool empire after the war, took measures to guard his interests in the wake of the crash by establishing the West Riding Worsted and Woollen Mills, a holding company, to manage his spinning and weaving businesses, including the old Peate facility, Nunroyd Mills, in Guiseley.[51] Companies without farsighted managers did not fare so well. The *Yorkshire Post* reported that more than 500 firms in the wool textile industry went out of business between 1923 and 1931.[52] Even though Parisian tastemakers smiled favourably on tweeds, many Yorkshire mills struggled to stay afloat.

Labour troubles resurfaced with the economic downturn. Relations among employers and operatives had been testy since the 1925 wage dispute.[53] In September 1929, the Yorkshire woollen makers, operating through a regional industrial council, announced a plan to reduce wages by more than 8 per cent. Operatives rejected the proposal by ballot vote.[54] In January 1930, the Minister of Labour, Margaret Bondfield, appointed a court of inquiry headed by the noted jurist, Lord Hugh Pattison Macmillan, to evaluate the situation.[55] The manufacturers claimed they were 'bleeding to death' and wage reductions were necessary to their survival. Lord Macmillan scoffed at the drama but concurred that wage cuts were inevitable given the 'dangerous position' of the industry.[56] Bucking the advice of union leaders who urged them to make the best of the situation, the rank and file voted to reject the 'Macmillan Report'. Efforts to negotiate a compromise went nowhere.[57]

As the looms lay idle, Yorkshire mill owners anxiously ticked the passing days off their calendars. They were worried about the paucity of patterns for the 1931 spring season. Normally between May and September, the cloth buyers for the ready-to-wear industry would flock to Golden Square to examine the textile ranges for the following spring trade. Before the First World War, the buyers had placed their woollen orders in person after they looked through the samples in the woollen warehouse. But since 1920, they had become more fastidious in response to the fashion-conscious consumer. They now took away cuttings of interesting fabrics, looked them over at their leisure, requested sample lengths by letter and studied those pieces before finally submitting an order. The mills sat on pins and needles as they waited for confirmation orders.[58] In the spring of 1930, their anxieties doubled because of the labour dispute. Without tempting new patterns in the London showrooms, there would be no orders from the makers-up and no work for the mills in the autumn. 'The pattern-showing season should by this time have been well advanced', the *Manchester Guardian* wrote in May, but 'owing to the stoppage, the patterns are either very much behind or are not in hand at all'.[59] One mill owner from the Guiseley-Yeadon district spoke about the business implications of the strike. 'The position now … is that we shall not get our patterns until October', he said. 'We have missed our autumn trade and the operatives themselves will be the biggest sufferers.'[60] Managers in the Huddersfield district were less worried. Because trade had been slow during 1929, they had a backlog of unused spring patterns they could put on the market.[61]

The towns of Yeadon and Guiseley had seven or eight mills that felt the effect of the work stoppage.[62] Leafield Mills and Manor Mill, run by James Ives & Company Ltd, in Yeadon, employed 700 people.[63] In Guiseley, Springhead Mills and Nunroyd Mills each had 400 to 500 employees (figure 4.3); Netherfield Mill had 200.[64] In May, workers in Guiseley agreed to the new rates and returned to the factories. Within a month or so, all the mills in the district were back in business and rushing to get out the samples.[65] But the production backlog caused by the stoppage ultimately led to the loss of orders. In early December, some of the Yorkshire mills were unable to deliver the spring patterns that were on order, and the buyers 'had to find an alternative in the foreign supply'.[66] The mill owners were not pleased—but they saw a light on the horizon.

All eyes in the woollen industry were fixed on the coalition government, which under Prime Minister Ramsey MacDonald grappled with the issue of protectionism. In the United States, the Smoot-Hawley Tariff Act of 1930 had raised import duties, so that the average tax on imported goods was around 40 per cent. This

4.3 Advertisement for the Springhead Mill Co. (Guiseley) Ltd, 1931. By kind permission of Leeds Library and Information Services: *Wool Record*, 40 (29 October 1931), 40.

ultra-high American tariff, combined with a series of banking crises in Europe and South America, led Britain to abandon the gold standard in September 1931. This measure resulted in the depreciation of sterling and triggered defensive responses from countries that retained the gold standard. To offset the depreciation of the pound, France, for one, imposed a 15 per cent surcharge on British imports and initiated restrictive quotas. Other countries followed suit. The MacDonald government saw the chance to put a knife in the heart of the free-trade policies of the Victorian era.[67]

The story of the effort to implement full protectionism is beyond the scope of this study, but there were two Acts of relevance to tweeds. In late 1931, Parliament enacted the Abnormal Importations (Customs Duties) Act, which empowered the Board of Trade to impose *ad valorem* duties of up to 100 per cent on foreign goods imported to Britain in unusually large quantities. Woollens fell into this category. In the following February, lawmakers replaced this temporary legislation with the Import Duties Act 1932, which imposed a minimum tariff of 10 per cent on most imports with exemptions for products that originated within the British Empire. The Chancellor of the Exchequer, Neville Chamberlain, the son of tariff zealot Joseph Chamberlain, helped push the Import Duties Act through Parliament.[68] After more than eighty years, Britain turned its back on free trade and embraced protectionism.

The entire British Empire was swept up in the protectionist tide. In 1932 in Ottawa, Canada, the Imperial Economic Conference—a summit of policymakers from the United Kingdom and its colonies and Dominions (Australia, Canada, India, Irish Free State, Newfoundland, New Zealand, Southern Rhodesia and South Africa)—convened to discuss the trade slump of the Great Depression. The resultant 'Ottawa agreement' set limited tariffs within the British Empire while raising them for imports from the rest of the world. Built around the concept of imperial preference, these bilateral trade deals lasted until 1937. Canada became an even more important market for British exports.[69]

Almost immediately, the new trade policies had an impact on the British woollen industry. Some woollen men were afraid that the new UK legislation would work against their interests, but those fears were unfounded.[70] The depreciation of sterling effectively imposed a 30 per cent surcharge on cloth imports, and the *ad valorem* duties of 1931 added another 50 per cent.[71] Imported fabrics, such as fine cashmeres from Italy, were more expensive than ever. The biggest losers were based mainly in London: the woollen importers, the agents for Continental mills and the bespoke tailors. Burdened with high taxes, wealthy Britons had to cut back on luxuries. Few gentlemen wanted to spend nearly twice the former price for a new suit from a West End tailor.[72] The situation was entirely different for the average Briton who wore ready-made clothing made from inexpensive Yorkshire woollens. Within

a few weeks of the Customs Duties Act of 1931, the *Wool Record* reported that
80 per cent of Yorkshire mills had new orders.[73]

One especially vigilant Yorkshire entrepreneur documented the turnaround of
the West Riding mills. Reuben Gaunt Hainsworth of A. W. Hainsworth & Company,
who ran Temperance Mills in Stanningley (midway between Leeds and Bradford),
had tracked the failures of more than fifty businesses in the woollen industry between
January 1932 and March 1933.[74] At the end of 1933, however, he noted improved
conditions in certain market segments. The trade in 'higher class' cloth was sluggish
'due to the restricted purchasing power of the wealthier classes in all civilized quarters
of the world where otherwise those who wish to be elegantly clad are ready to pay the
price for the fashionable English article'. But the lower end of the market was doing
well. Due to a brisk trade in cheaper fabrics for ladies' clothing, the mills in some of
the manufacturing districts near Leeds ran their 'looms night and day to cope with
the large urgent demands'. Although adding the caveat that exports 'are not yet equal
to 1930 and are very much below 1929', Hainsworth was pleased with the home
demand. 'The tariff of 20 per cent is fairly effective in restricting imports.'[75]

The tweed craze

With the slowdown of global trade, the Yorkshire tweed makers looked to exploit
the home market by adapting their export ranges to British tastes. They no longer
had to compete against low-priced cloth from Continental Europe. The Great
Depression was an especially creative time for these mills. The advance of knitwear
continued, but inexpensive woven tweeds got a second wind. Woollen designers
were given carte blanche to imagine, create and adapt. At the upper end of the
ladies' apparel market, the tailored British look was back in style, led by Lachasse,
a niche casualwear couture house in Berkeley Square, Mayfair, which catered to
the racing and golfing set with tweed costumes by designers such as Hardy Amies,
Digby Morton and Victor Stiebel.[76] Lachasse showed high society that tweed, the
unofficial national British fabric, could be used in new ways. In the mass market,
the popularity of tailored styles in tweeds and other types of wool fabrics owed
much to the wholesale clothiers of Leeds, London and Manchester who interpreted
traditional British styling for women who wore ready-made clothing (figure 4.4). The
'tailor-made'—a form-fitting two-piece suit or overcoat created in sizes for 'maids'
(teens and preteens), 'ladies' (adults) and 'matrons' (seniors)—came into vogue.
The woman who watched her wallet realised that, if she had limited money to spend
on clothes, it was best to spend it on investment pieces. Tweeds were warm, sturdy
and fashionable—just the thing for the penny-pinching depression decade.[77] Classic
British style, once the purview of the country-house set, was trickling down.

THE NEWEST COLOURS
THE SMARTEST WEAVES

CORONET BUNCHES

Costume, Coating & Dress Cloths Silks & Artificial Silk Linings for Day and Evening Wear

The new range of James Hare Ltd. materials shows a characteristic originality and variety of choice. Quality is the keynote throughout. Very striking use of the latest, most fashionable shades has produced many delightful effects.

There are many spirited new treatments of Costume and Coating materials (the smart shepherd's plaid check Saxony, illustrated, is an instance of novel charm secured by a slightly broken effect). The REK-A-VIK Coatings are still to the fore in popularity, for their graceful hang, and delightful woolly warmth without weight

Our silks are especially fascinating— sumptuous new Satins and Velvets, lovely Crepe de Chines, Marocains, Georgettes.

A marvellous new season's selection

Delightful new treatments

Appy for New Patterns now!

JAMES HARE LTD.

MILLS & WAREHOUSES : LEEDS. TELEPHONES : 31204, 31205, 31206, 31207. TELEGRAMS : HARE, LEEDS
London : Grafton House, Golden Sq., W.1. Telephones : Gerrard 3043, 3044, 3045. Telegrams : "Khareserge, Piccy, London"

SAY YOU SAW IT IN " THE TAILOR & CUTTER "

4.4 The Leeds merchant James Hare, a longstanding customer of Netherfield Mill, sold costume and coating fabrics to the makers-up who produced ladies'' tailor-mades'. © The British Library Board: *Tailor and Cutter*, 70 (10 August 1934), 769.

4.5 A British couple attired in wool, c. 1930. She wears a tweed check coat and a cloche hat; he wears a woollen overcoat and a classic tweed cap. Author's collection.

The tweed craze started in the late 1920s and was well underway by the early 1930s (figure 4.5), just as Parliament passed the Abnormal Importations (Customs Duties) Act.[78] Of course, the damp British weather did not disappear during the Great Depression and, after a few years, the average Briton's jacket and coat appeared threadbare and shabby. A cold spell before Christmas sent consumers who could afford a new overcoat to the shops to buy one. One menswear innovation shows how lightweight tweeds suited the economising mentality. Some of the wholesale clothiers designed a new model of men's raincoat that had a cotton gabardine shell and a detachable woollen lining and used quantity-production methods to introduce it to the mass market.[79] The tweed or tartan lining was worn for warmth in the autumn and winter and stored away in spring and summer. This type of raincoat is commonplace today, but few people know of its origins in the Great Depression. This garment was versatile, economical and just right for hard times.

Yorkshire tweed makers like Abraham Moon and Sons had long ago mastered the art of producing attractive low-cost designs in fabrics destined for ladies' wear and children's wear. The combination of novelty and value was ideal for the price-conscious market. Consumers had long associated tweeds with heavy fabrics: 'heavy, hairy-surfaced materials only fit for rainy weather and excessive hard-as-nails sportswear, "plus fours" and overcoats and uncompromising stolid wraps for "any sort of weather".'[80] But French textile mills had learned to use British yarns to make ultra-fine tweeds suited for dress fabrics. British manufacturers took note and soon were in the game. The London Fashions Exhibition in autumn 1930 showed garments produced from the new lightweight '"French" tweeds' made in Britain.[81] 'These new fabrics are as light as possible', wrote the *Daily Mail Atlantic Edition*, 'and yet cosy enough to wear on chilly days.'[82] Writing about the 'continued demand for tweeds', the *Wool Record* noted how the British mills had 'greatly improved their qualities, and even in the cheaper fabrics excellent values were obtainable'.[83]

In the warehouses of Golden Square, buyers browsed through the samples of ladies' tweeds for new colours that would delight the consumer. The *Wool Record* reported on one buyer in particular who 'has been enthusing over a shade of purple which has created a good deal of favourable comment among fashion houses, probably not because of any particular charm, but because it is different from the more popular colours'.[84] The proliferation of special effects, distinctive shades and pronounced weaves led one journalist to ask, 'When is a tweed not a tweed?'[85] But novelty thrilled the fabric buyers and brought in orders. In February 1931, the *Manchester Guardian* reported on the 'abnormally brisk' trade in Guiseley and Yeadon, where the mills were 'working day and night, and in some departments even on Saturday afternoons … The district is engaged in the heavy tweed trade which is peculiar to the area, and the demand for heavy woollens is the real reason for the "boom".'[86] More than ever, business went to the tweed mills that that offered distinctive designs at competitive prices.

Some textile men were circumspect about the recovery of the woollen business. The *Wool Record* thought the industry was overbuilt and should rid itself of extraneous production capacity given the shrinking global demand.[87] The growing popularity of man-made fibres such as rayon, promoted as an artificial silk but made from cellulose, contributed to the worries of woollen men because it was indicative of the consumer preference for lightweight garments.[88] One Yorkshire mill owner believed the Great Depression was a fitting time for thoughtful reflection and reassessment. 'We must inquire more closely into the trends of demand for yarn and cloth, the costing of our products, our buying policy and our selling policy, alternative outlets for our goods, and the character of the claims on people's incomes that reduce their demands for wool products', the yarn maker told his shareholders in 1931. 'Perpetual inquiry is the only way to get the gauge of our position.'[89]

At the same time, London tastemakers prodded Yorkshiremen to fret less and innovate more. The Halifax Textile Society reeled from a lecture by Edward Symonds, the managing director of Reville Ltd, dressmakers to Queen Mary and a bevvy of princesses, who suggested that textile makers direct their energies to creative pursuits. The protective tariff that had handed the home market over to the British mills was likely to breed complacency. 'Tariffs … do not affect the general appearance of the goods in the eyes of the consumer', Symonds said. 'They may safeguard production costs but they cannot safeguard distribution and consumption, because the final decision in the purchase of the goods rests with their appearance.' A woman was more likely to purchase ready-to-wear constructed from cheaper materials if the fabric had an attractive design. For the British woollen industry to succeed at home and abroad, managers needed to combine their business acumen and skilful workmanship with greater attention to 'fashion and showmanship'.[90]

The records of Abraham Moon and Sons are silent on Frank Walsh's position on fashion and fanfare (figure 4.6). We know that he was a technological enthusiast who believed that improvements to the physical plant would increase productivity and augment the quality of the cloth. The continued emphasis on lower and mid-range fabrics with a style element gave Netherfield Mill a competitive edge and allowed it to remain profitable for most of the Great Depression.[91] Frank and his cousin Tom

4.6 Frank Walsh in his office at Netherfield Mill, 1937. Courtesy of Abraham Moon and Sons.

Walsh designed the patterns, but the incessant demand for new styles created a mandate for new talent. Inspiration was needed and sometime around 1935, another designer was hired. Albert Holmes had studied textiles as an evening student at the University of Leeds in 1928–29 and then worked as a designer for Springhead Mills, the latest iteration of the old Spring Head Mill.[92] The parent firm, the Springhead Mill Company (Guiseley) Ltd, made velour, mantle and costume cloths, cap cloths, wool flannels, lightweight dress tweeds and showerproof tweeds, a variation on the classic water-resistant cloth on which the reputation of Guiseley had been built (figure 4.3).[93] Albert brought fresh eyes to Netherfield Mill at a moment when important new customers came knocking.

Fashion on the high street

The interwar period was a turning point for the relationship between Netherfield Mill and its customers. The demands apparent in everyday fashion boded well for the Yorkshire woollen mill that knew how to blend wool, cotton, rayon, shoddy and mungo into inexpensive eye-catching patterns. Tweed mania was a boon to Abraham Moon and Sons. The mill served customers all around the British Isles, from Belfast to Newcastle. Major London retailers such as Harrods were still on the books.[94] The factory also shipped cloth to foreign markets, including Australia, Austria, Canada, Germany, Ireland and the United States.

By the interwar years, increasing amounts of ladies' ready-made clothing were available on the British high street due in part to the simplification of styles that allowed for quantity production. The ready-made revolution underpinned the growth of British consumer society and the relentless drive for ever-cheaper production began to transform the supply chain within the fashion system. As discussed in Chapter 3, wholesale clothiers or ready-to-wear manufacturers competed for the custom of retailers on style and price and, to cut costs, they started to bypass the wholesale drapers and woollen merchants to source their textiles directly from the mills. Nevertheless, amid speculation about the likely 'extinction of the wholesaler', the *Drapers' Record* commended the merchant for his 'intermediary' role as a curator and tastemaker.[95] Indeed, the woollen warehouses of the City and Golden Square showcased the latest ranges and served as ad hoc idea laboratories. The identity of the buyer who had admired the striking purple tweed will never be known. Did he work for a drapery shop, an East End wholesale clothier, or a New York importer? One thing is certain. The exacting needs of the fashion industry forced the textile mills to think more carefully about market requirements. The hunger for creative designs encouraged producers like Abraham Moon and Sons to experiment even more.

Leeds—by now known as the 'Queen of the North'—was in the forefront of the ready-made revolution. By the mid-1920s, Leeds was the sixth largest metropolis in England and was celebrated as the 'world's greatest centre of the wholesale clothing trade'.[96] Ninety per cent of the cloth used in the Leeds garment factories was made within a twenty-five mile radius of the city centre.[97] Historians have studied the development of the menswear industry, but less is known about the major wholesale clothiers that made ladies' wear and children's wear using Yorkshire woollens. Firms such as James Corson & Company Ltd, John Barran & Sons, Heatons (Leeds) Ltd, Hepton Brothers and Thomas Marshall & Company Ltd had long purchased fabric from Netherfield Mill and continued to do so.[98] Many of these customers produced the 'tailor-mades' that exemplified British style.[99] Corsons, for example, manufactured ladies' coats and costumes with smart silhouettes and unusual tweed patterns under the trade name 'Corsonia Tailormades' (figure 4.7).[100]

In other British clothing centres—Glasgow, Manchester and London—the wholesale clothiers were also swept up in tweed mania. London is a case in point. In the East End, Dickson Millar & Company, a maker-up with factories in Aldersgate, used tweeds from Netherfield Mill to produce the 'Deemarco' brand of inexpensive ladies' coats for autumn and winter (Colour Plate 6).[101] In the City, the wholesale clothier Hitchcock, Williams & Company had an impressive building by St Paul's Churchyard and factories a short walk away in Warwick Lane, where mantles, coats and skirts for women and children were made from tweeds sourced from the mill.[102]

Most importantly, the ready-made revolution gave birth to a new type of business—based on branding—that purchased woollens from Netherfield Mill. By the 1930s, Burberry and Jaeger, two London-based manufacturer-retailers that evolved into iconic British brands over the course of the century, were on the books. These companies pioneered modern merchandising practices by educating consumers to associate their products with quality and, in turn, to expect a certain level of standardisation on the British high street. In the long run, these types of quality-driven brands and their dominance of the upper end of the high street, would be a game changer for Abraham Moon and Sons. But between the wars, the relationships were just getting started.

Known today for its luxury boutiques around the world, Burberry started as a tailoring shop and developed a speciality in high-performance outdoor clothing, mainly for men (figure 4.8). In the early twentieth century, British menswear was coming to be dominated by Leeds wholesale bespoke tailors such as Montague Burton, whose high-street stores offered suits at affordable prices. The clerk took the customer's measurements and sent them to the factory to be made up into a personalised garment within a short time.[103] Burberry operated on another model. It

4.7 James Corson & Company Ltd advertisement for Corsonia Tailormades, 1938. © The British Library Board: *Drapers' Organiser* (March 1938), 31.

4.8 A Burberry advertisement of 1925, showing British tweed coats that could be purchased at their Paris branch. Author's collection: *L'Illustration* (23 May 1925), 8.

sold ready-made outerwear of its own design from flagship stores in London, Paris, New York and Buenos Aires, and through provincial agents in towns and cities around Britain.[104] Burberry offered convenient shopping to the man who needed a new coat and did not have the time or money to make repeat visits to a tailor for fittings or come back to pick up the merchandise. The customer could try on a model, decide if it flattered him and, within a few minutes, leave the store with a coat in the latest cut, style and design—much like today.[105]

Like Abraham Moon and Sons, Burberry built its reputation on a technical innovation designed to combat the wet weather of the British Isles: waterproof clothing. Back in 1880, Thomas Burberry, a draper in Basingstoke, Hampshire, had invented a treatment for a cotton cloth called gabardine, which was specially 'proofed' to be breathable, durable, water resistant and wearable in all seasons. In 1891, the firm, trading as Thomas Burberry & Sons, had opened its first London shop at Haymarket in the West End of London and, in 1913, expanded to larger quarters. 'Burberry weatherproofs' became the favourite 'high-tech' gear for those who braved the elements: aviators, explorers, sportsmen, cyclists, skaters, motorcyclists and army officers. During the Boer War, Burberry had created the Tierlocken coat for British army officers; the design was modified to create the trench coat so widely used in the First World War. Burberry was one of many firms that helped to perfect, between 1910 and 1920, the everyday raincoat; the firm introduced the Burberry 'check', now trademarked, as a lining for its trench coats in the 1920s. Besides gabardine, Burberry needed woollens for the check lining and for other outdoor garments and accessories such as scarves and blankets.[106] Some of this merchandise was made with fabric from Netherfield Mill.[107]

Burberry mainly catered to men but also offered some women's wear. Jaeger was the reverse, focusing on women's wear with menswear as a secondary line. With the exception of the 'new woman' who needed stylish clothes for her job in an office or store but who had no time to sew and no money pay a seamstress, British women were slow to adapt to the practice of buying clothes in a shop. Modesty and decorum dictated that respectable women did not dress or undress in public, particularly in a store. Women from the middle and upper-middle classes had long relied on the privacy of the local dressmaker's atelier where clothing was custom-fitted to their bodies. Some of the large retail drapers that stocked ready-made clothing acknowledged feminine concerns about modesty and provided the ladies with private spaces for viewing apparel. Jaeger developed a new type of clothing store in response to these social conventions.

Jaeger understood the middle-class woman's concerns for quality, style and discretion. The company had been established in 1883–84 by British businessman Lewis R. S. Tomalin under a cumbersome name: Dr Jaeger's Sanitary Woollen

System Company Ltd. The London-based firm took inspiration from Gustav Jaeger, a zoologist and physiologist at Stuttgart University, whose theories on the health benefits of clothing made from animal fibres had inspired a Victorian fad for woollen undergarments. Initially, the firm made protective woollen clothing for outdoorsmen and contributed woollen blankets and sleeping bags to the national defence. After 1902, the founder's artistic son, H. F. Tomalin, revolutionised the product range and the retail shops, hiring the artist Charles E. Dawson to create a series of smart new stores having a similar identity. This novel approach to store design was a major break from the tradition of builder-driven commercial architecture. For the first time, a British clothing retailer used a purpose-built sales space that embodied its distinctive worldview. By the First World War, the newly renamed Jaeger Company Ltd had diversified its product line, so as to attract well-off women who wanted clothes that were practical, stylish and far less expensive than haute couture. The Jaeger line was enlarged to include sportswear and fashion accessories and the quality of the product was ensured by tests on fabrics and dyes conducted in a technical laboratory.[108]

Jaeger developed a holistic approach to product design and store merchandising that anticipated retailers such as Next, which was to become an important mill customer in the late twentieth century. Jaeger developed a '3-in-1 setup' that combined manufacturing, wholesaling and retailing, resulting in a high degree of control over the product and the merchandising. It was the first British retailer to create 'collections' of women's fashion and accessories that were coordinated by colour and style.

By 1930, a new generation of retail managers abandoned the 'wool for wool's sake only' philosophy and introduced a 'system' of dressing that emphasised 'style' and the 'toute ensemble'. An imagined consumer—'the Jaeger Girl'—was celebrated and targeted. The key players were Humphrey F. Tomalin and M. M. Gilbert, a protégé of the Oxford Street merchandising impresario, Gordon Selfridge. By this time, Jaeger stores were found in good-sized cities in English-speaking nations around the world, but the flagship store on Regent Street was the talk of London (figure 4.9). Designed by J. Duncan Miller, the store embodied Jaeger's policy that the look of the retail shop should be as modern as the look of the clothes. Jaeger interior designs, along with Jaeger clothing designs, set a new trend for shops and shopping. In 1935, Jaeger opened a chrome-fitted fashion boutique at Selfridges in Oxford Street, the first Jaeger 'shop within a store' in Britain. In 1936, the Jaeger brand was further updated when Francis Marshall, the well-known illustrator for British *Vogue*, created a new logo and advertising art.[109] Tailor-mades sewn from Yorkshire wool fabrics were part of Jaeger's signature style. By the 1930s, Netherfield Mill was sending woollens to Jaeger's production factories in London.[110]

4.9 Opened in 1935, the Jaeger store on Regent Street, London, was a smart shopping environment that was as modern as Jaeger clothing. Courtesy of Jaeger Ltd and Westminster City Archives: 1327, Jaeger Archives.

Some of mill's longstanding customers did not benefit from the ready-to-wear revolution. The wholesale merchants suffered the most. As more makers-up questioned the need for these intermediaries, woollen merchants retaliated by blacklisting the clothing factories who ordered fabric directly from the mills.[111] However, a few of the large merchant houses in the City, such as J. & C. Boyd & Company Ltd, and Devas, Routledge and Company, still bought cloth from Netherfield Mill to sell in their wool departments or to make up into clothing. John Rylands & Sons had the mill ship cloth to one of its facilities in Manchester[112] In addition, in 1924 one Manchester merchant—Sparrow, Hardwick & Company Ltd—had 5,000 accounts and boasted that its business was three times larger than before the First World War. Sparrow mostly served the home market, but its trade with the British Dominions, mainly Australia and New Zealand, was of growing importance.[113] By 1927, Sparrow advertised a range of 'Proprietary Lines', including 'Sparwick' coats made in its own factories, possibly from cloth by Netherfield Mill.[114] In Leeds, James Hare, another longstanding customer, not only sold fabrics to more than 20,000 accounts around the world, but also ran a 'C.M.T.' factory, established in 1933, to cut, make and trim men's tailored garments on a quantity-production basis (figure 4.4).[115] Sparrow and Hare, like Rylands & Sons, survived through diversification and globalisation, but they were the exceptions that proved the rule.

Traditional retailers were anxious about the rise of multiples and brands. Many of them suspiciously eyed the new stores, 'aware that the specialist house is becoming a power in the land'.[116] Now-forgotten London retailers such as William Hurlock and Company Ltd at Elephant and Castle, worried that national brands might bring an unsatisfying sameness to the high street. Brands threatened to undercut the shopkeeper's role as a cultural arbiter who selected the merchandise and shaped British taste.[117] Consumers did not seem to care. The old way of life with local dressmakers, private tailors, drapery shops and haberdasheries did not entirely disappear, but these types of businesses were deemed old-fashioned by consumers who appreciated the convenience, competitive pricing and less-intrusive shopping experiences offered by the multiples.

Khaki again

As the economy began to recover, there were signs that another global war was brewing. The Spanish Civil War (1936–39) was brutal and relentless. The Japanese invasion of China in July 1937 launched the Second Sino-Japanese War (1937–45), which had a major economic impact on the West Riding. When the conflict hit Shanghai, Bradford lost access to China, which was the city's second largest market for wool tops after Canada. The terrifying Japanese bombing raids of China foreshadowed the air war in Europe.[118] The mills in Guiseley and Yeadon carried on business as usual. In 1937, the towns of Carleton, Guiseley, Hawkesworth, Rawdon and Yeadon merged to form the Aireborough Urban District Council, and the mills began to think of themselves as part of the 'Aireborough district'.[119] But the international scene grew darker month by month. 'The international political situation', wrote the *Wool Record* shortly after the New Year in 1938, has 'played its part in disturbing the normal course of trade.'[120] The Yorkshire textile mills began to take precautions, appointing air-raid wardens and stockpiling gas masks.[121] In January 1938, Abraham Moon and Sons insured Netherfield Mills against bomb damage by aircraft.[122]

Two months later in March 1938, Adolph Hitler's troops marched into Vienna and Nazi Germany annexed Austria. Later that year, the Nazis threatened to occupy the Sudetenland, a German-speaking area of Czechoslovakia. Concerned to keep the peace, Britain and France bowed to conciliation with Germany and its ally, Italy, at Munich on 30 September 1938. Prime Minister Neville Chamberlain returned to the UK confident that the Munich Agreement meant 'peace with honour' and 'peace for our time'.[123] Secretly, some British government officials thought differently and braced for war. In anticipation of wool shortages, representatives from the British government struck a deal with authorities in Australia, arranging to buy the entire Australian clip for the duration of the war and twelve months thereafter, as in the First World War. When the Second World War broke out on 1 September 1939, British authorities were ready for the skyrocketing military demand for wool fabrics. The Ministry of Supply assigned the management of the wool supply to the Wool Control, a board headed by a representative from industry. Operations, not surprisingly, were based in Bradford, the Wool City.[124]

One source estimated that 50 per cent of Britain's industrial capacity in wool cloth manufacturing was needed to produce material for the armed services, as opposed to only 14 per cent of the capacity of the cotton industry. The demands on Britain's wool cloth manufacturers and garment makers increased as the conflict accelerated. Over the course of the Second World War, some 409 million garments were produced for the armed forces and other war personnel (Colour Plate 7). As in the First World War, Leeds was a centre of military clothing production; Montague Burton Ltd alone produced 13.5 million garments. In 1944–45, military orders began to decline, which freed up wool resources for the production of civilian cloth.[125]

One of the great wartime challenges was the shortage of labour.[126] As able-bodied men joined the armed services, the British government had to ensure that there were enough workers to run the factories that made essential war materiel, such as aircraft and ammunition. In 1941, the Board of Trade, headed by Oliver Lyttelton, 1st Viscount Chandos, implemented a scheme to 'concentrate' textile production in the most efficient mills and to shut down less efficient mills for the duration of the conflict. The 'concentration' scheme, also known as the 'Lyttelton plan', was initially applied to the Lancashire cotton industry. Yorkshire, however, had a greater need for the concentration of production because wool cloth was essential to soldiers on the front. Maximising efficiency in the woollen industry would generate the cloth needed for the government, civil defence, export and domestic use, while allowing the Ministry of Labour and the Factory Control to secure manpower and facilities essential for military production.[127]

In June 1941, representatives from the woollen mills formed a Wool Textile Delegation to decide how to cooperate with the government on the Wool Concentration Scheme.[128] By July, the Wool Textile Delegation had created a Central Concentration Association to plan and administer the concentration programme for the woollen industry and to help the government determine which mills would remain open and which would be shut down during the war.[129]

In July, Abraham Moon and Sons was accepted as a member in the Wool Textile Delegation's Central Concentration Association.[130] The company was required to submit a detailed list of its physical assets: the buildings, the power plant, the machinery and other effects.[131] The inventory demonstrated that Netherfield Mill had the equipment needed to produce woollen textiles efficiently. The mill was outfitted with 101 British power looms, durable workhorses built by Yorkshire firms such as George Hodgson, Lee & Crabtree, and George Hattersley & Sons between 1903 and 1936.[132] In the second half of 1941, the Board of Trade determined that all six of the woollen manufacturers in the Aireborough district—Abraham Moon and Sons, Edward Denison (Yeadon) Ltd, James Ives & Company, the Peate division of the West Riding Worsted and Woollen Mills, Springhead Mill Company (Guiseley) Ltd and William Murgatroyd & Company—should remain in operation during the war.[133] In January 1942, the Wool Textile Delegation's concentration experts recommended that the Board of Trade grant 'nucleus status' to Abraham Moon and Sons.[134]

What did 'nucleus status' mean? The Wool Concentration Scheme divided wool textile mills into three categories: 'closing' mills that were shut down during the war; 'nucleus' mills that continued production, operating at no less than 90 per cent capacity; and 'intermediate' mills that could be upgraded to nucleus status if the demand for cloth warranted it. As the *Manchester Guardian* explained, the closing firms remained 'in full and independent existence as commercial entities' and were assigned their rations of raw materials. Those raw materials were transferred to the nucleus mills, which undertook to fulfil orders at net cost, so that the products could be sold on the open market at no competitive disadvantage to other operating plants. Workers at all the mills were evaluated for their suitability for jobs in the textile and munitions sectors. Strong healthy workers were transferred to heavy industry. People with particular skills needed in the textile mills remained there, as did unskilled workers who were deemed unsuitable for heavy industry. For example, in October 1941, the Wool Textile Industry Concentration Committee advised firms to prepare to release 12,000 female mill workers, ages twenty to twenty-five, to work in munitions factories. Women who had left the workforce upon marriage were asked to do their patriotic duty by returning to work in the textile mills. The scheme was complicated, but it attempted to match the available labour with jobs that needed to be done.[135]

Efficient manufacturers like Abraham Moon and Sons benefited from the Wool Concentration Scheme. Nucleus mills had to be prepared to undertake production on behalf of closing firms if they wanted their factories to stay in commission. The nucleus mills were virtually guaranteed a full complement of orders during the war: from the government, from merchants for export and, to a lesser extent, from the makers-up of essential civilian clothing. These orders would keep the nucleus mills running at capacity, provided that there were enough factory operatives to get the job done.[136]

The Yorkshire woollen mills were also affected by measures implemented by the British government to conserve raw materials for the national defence. Food rationing is most often remembered, but austerity measures extended to necessities such as petrol, furnishings and clothing. Two government policies had a direct impact on woollen cloth manufacturers: the Consumer Rationing Scheme and the Utility Scheme.

Announced by Oliver Lyttelton on behalf of the Board of Trade on 1 June 1941, the Consumer Rationing Scheme for clothing was in effect until March 1949. Like other parts of the rationing scheme, it worked through a coupon programme, wherein each consumer was allotted a certain number of points that could be applied towards the purchase of necessities, or rations. The objectives were to safeguard supplies of raw materials and to channel workers and factories into production for the war effort. The problem with rationing is that it did nothing to combat rampant inflation or to counter the flood of poor-quality clothing.[137]

The Utility Scheme was initiated by the Board of Trade in 1942 and lasted until 1952. This government programme aimed to produce large quantities of durable consumer goods at affordable prices during a time of both scarce materials and rapidly rising prices. The Utility Scheme covered a range of consumer goods, including furniture, clothing and blankets. The clothing scheme had two major aims: to offer consumers well-designed garments at controlled prices as a countermeasure to wartime inflation and to standardise the production of materials, make factories more efficient and free up resources for the war effort. The textile mills that produced various types of Utility cloth (mainly made from wool, but also from cotton and rayon) were supplied with raw materials through a quota system. Like other types of manufacturers beholden to the Utility Scheme, woollen mills had to meet quality standards and production goals that were set by the Board of Trade.[138]

Utility regulations determined how Abraham Moon and Sons and other woollen mills produced civilian cloth for the duration. The Wool Control provided designated garment manufacturers with a limited number of Utility Category Ration Certificates, which controlled the amount and type of cloth they could purchase. In addition, to meet Utility standards, the amount of cloth (together with the number of buttons and other finishing touches) was defined for each garment type. The clothiers passed these certifications on to the textile mill, which in turn was supplied by the Wool Control with the raw materials needed to fill the orders. A ceiling price was assigned to each specification of cloth and each type of clothing. All parties in the supply chain, from mill to retailer, were forbidden to exceed a specified selling price. The price was based on what they paid for materials plus a predetermined mark-up.[139] Whether top couturiers such as Norman Hartnell or ready-made manufacturer-retailers such as Jaeger, all who could participated in the creation of Utility fashions (figure 4.10). In

4.10 Utility fashions for Spring/Summer 1943 as shown at Selfridges department store on Oxford Street under the auspices of the London designer Norman Hartnell; these included a Jaeger pair of slacks with a short coat and wool taffeta check blouse (second left) together with (left to right) garments by Frances Leopold, Harella and Koupy. Author's collection.

1943, Burberrys of London, a likely customer of Netherfield Mill given its interwar orders, reported that its civilian production was largely limited to Utility clothing that followed the design restrictions set by the government.[140]

Technological enthusiasm

At the start of Second World War, the West Riding was a study in contrasts. One Board of Trade official who toured the area was struck by the juxtaposition of the old and the new. Near Halifax, in a hamlet called Mount Tabor, he saw 'two small worsted spinning mills … driven by water power acting on a water wheel, the buildings dating back almost certainly for about 200 years'. In the city of Leeds, he marvelled at 'a large modern wholesale clothiers installed in a steel-framed building with maple flooring, air conditioning, special lighting arrangements to assist in the cutting of cloth and so on'.[141] By the end of the war, the difference between the two operations was probably even greater. The Wool Concentration Scheme valued efficiency and encouraged managers to take technology seriously.

As the war drew to a close, Abraham Moon and Sons looked to a bright technological future made possible by wartime profits. The machinery at Netherfield Mill was worn out due to the big push to make military cloth (figures 3.10 to 3.15). The mill had entered the war with some new equipment, but also had old workhorses such as a pair of self-acting spinning mules from 1903. After the death of Thomas Musgrave in December 1944, Frank Walsh became chairman.[142] With a penchant for improving the mill complex through the reinvestment of profits, he undertook a major renovation in anticipation of the large civilian demand for woollen cloth at home and abroad. In January 1945, the board of directors approved the first purchases of mill machinery since 1939, including two new spinning mules.[143] Over the next few years, a stream of purchases included spinning mules from William Whiteley and Sons in Huddersfield, power looms from George Hattersley & Sons, electrical equipment, some Belgian machinery and more.[144]

Around this time, the third generation of the Walsh family joined Abraham Moon and Sons. Arthur J. P. Walsh was the nephew of Frank Walsh and the son of the chemist Arthur 'Cyril' Walsh, who worked in Bradford. Arthur had spent his youth in Guiseley. As a teenager, he was frequently seen around Netherfield Mill, visiting his godfather, the dyer Alfred Dudbridge, who had been with the company since the days of Isaac Moon. After finishing school, Arthur enrolled in the textile science programme at the University of Leeds, but he was called to military service in the British armed forces in January 1943.[145] After his demobilisation in October 1946, he finished his studies at the University of Leeds and obtained a bachelor's degree in textiles in August 1948. While at university and after graduation, he worked for two Bradford concerns: Hopkinson & Shore, dyers and finishers, and Downs, Coulter & Company, worsted weavers. He joined the family firm on 10 August 1949 and worked directly under his uncle Frank.[146] For two years, Arthur was given a series of jobs in the mill, moving around the departments to learn the ins and outs of the business. He spent another two years travelling around the country, meeting the customers and developing a feeling for the trade. At this time, the major markets for the mill were London and Manchester. Arthur was a frequent visitor to the office of Fowler & Orr in the City, where he got to know the agent Alfred Chambers, who was to play a role in changes to come in subsequent years.[147]

The scarcities of the Second World War continued to shape the availability of products and the attitudes of consumers after the return to peace. Money was tight and pleasures were few and far between. The workers at Netherfield Mill eagerly looked forward to the company's annual outing to Blackpool, the famous Lancashire resort on the Irish Sea.[148] It was a treat for bus-loads of mill workers to put on their

Sunday best, take in sites such as the Blackpool Tower—a monument inspired by the Eiffel Tower in Paris—and have dinner at the Winter Gardens. These mill workers, basking in the glamour of a seaside resort, were not unlike the millions of UK consumers who yearned for even the smallest taste of luxury after years of deprivation. Everywhere in Britain, consumers watched their budgets and wistfully browsed through the shops afraid to ask, 'how much?' The International Wool Secretariat—an organisation established in 1937 by wool growers in Australia, New Zealand and South Africa to promote the use of wool—urged retailers to coax the penny-wise consumer, to tempt her with the

> 'come hither' look of Wool, irresistible; the glowing colours, the seasonable textures that graduate from cobweb fineness to the comforting blanket warmth of winter coatings … that from the equator to the poles women wear Wool, that the wardrobes of the world's fashion leaders reveal Wool—stylish tailor mades … glamorous form-fitting gowns.[149]

The Wool Concentration Scheme had kept the Yorkshire mills running for the duration of the war and the British woollen industry was well positioned to re-conquer the global market. In 1943, after the death of Willie Gaunt, a London investment trust had purchased his conglomerate, the West Riding Worsted and Woollen Mills. Five years later in 1948, the group reported that the immediate postwar era had been a 'world-wide sellers' market in wool textiles'.[150] Consumers around the world needed warm woollens and worsteds and the Yorkshire mills were prepared to make them in style. But terrible shortages of manpower and raw materials got in the way.[151] In particular, coal was in short supply and the mills sat idle as they awaited deliveries. The coal shortage affected all types of businesses. In February 1947, the *Wool Record*, along with other trade and technical publications, was forced to shut down the presses for two weeks in order to save fuel and power.[152]

One postwar development is particularly salient to our discussion of fashionability. The heavy demand for wool fabric led the Yorkshire mills to reduce the range of patterns in order to concentrate on long runs.[153] This strategy had an adverse impact on tweeds as a fashion item. 'Whereas there were 650 different colour schemes for cloth before the war', said the *Manchester Guardian* of the woollen industry, 'now their range was only 138.'[154] The circumscribed range was not broad enough to satisfy the postwar consumer's appetite for products with distinctive and novel designs. Frank Walsh and his nephew Arthur had to figure out how to steer Netherfield Mill through the new world order, wherein the lingering culture of scarcity stood at odds with the emerging culture of consumption.

5 From necessity to fashion

It wasn't really about fashion. It was about necessity. (Barbara Walsh, 2014)[1]

In the ITV series *Foyle's War*—a police drama set in the historic seaside town of Hastings on the English Channel during the Second World War—Samantha Stewart wears a khaki uniform for her job as the driver for Detective Chief Superintendent Christopher Foyle. Off duty, 'Sam' Stewart and other women are seen in tweed suits, jackets and coats. Tweeds were warm, serviceable and reflected the popular taste for tailored styling.[2] Real-life consumers who endured the Great Depression, the Second World War and the early Cold War appreciated the modicum of comfort offered by a new tweed ensemble (figure 5.1).

Barbara Sutcliffe was one such consumer. Born in Guiseley in 1931, she grew up in a middle-class household in a neighbourhood not far from Netherfield Mill and, as a teenager, pursued secretarial studies. In 1949, she secured a clerical job at Netherfield Mill, the same year that Arthur J. P. Walsh started working there. The young people first met in 1950 over coffee at the mill canteen on Netherfield Road; Barbara Sutcliffe would eventually become Mrs Arthur Walsh. Sixty years later, Barbara Walsh recalled the bleak postwar world. 'You must remember that houses weren't heated. There were no cars. The weather was bad and cold. You were lucky to get hot water.' Living standards 'only improved when new things started being imported from America like central heating, which was minimal'.[3]

British woollen manufacturers, like British consumers, endured a stark postwar existence. Barbara witnessed first-hand how shortages of raw materials and the need for serviceable goods shaped the ranges created by Netherfield Mill. 'We made things like double cloths. They were literally two cloths put together, just purely and simply for warmth.'[4] These cloths came in many forms, but a typical double cloth might have a plain design on one side and a colourful pattern on the other side to provide versatility and visual interest; as its name implies, it was often twice the thickness of many standard cloths by virtue of its two warps and two sets of wefts, each set interwoven often enough to bind together the two distinct sides. There is more to the smart styling of the check overcoats in *Foyle's War* than meets the eye. After the war, the fictional Sam Stewart becomes Mrs Adam Wainwright and lives in a

5.1 Known for children's wear, John Barran & Sons used woollens from Netherfield Mill to make stylish women's wear. Courtesy of West Yorkshire Archive Service, Leeds: WYL434, Records of John Barran & Sons Ltd, 'A Parade of Spring Fashions' at the firm's Ladies' Showroom, Leeds, 26 January 1954.

prefabricated house (a 'prefab') with her new husband, a Labour MP for Peckham in London. Although the TV newlyweds do not always have meat on the table, as middle-class professionals, they do not suffer too much want. In contrast, most of the population lived in damp old houses without central heating and kept warm by bundling up in clothes made from Yorkshire woollens.

Running the mill

The postwar culture of austerity stemmed from shortages of energy, raw materials and manpower. Wartime exigencies extended into peacetime as the government controlled the use of raw materials during the transition to a civilian economy. Two schemes initiated during the Second World War—clothes rationing and Utility—continued until 1949 and 1952 respectively. 'When the war finished, we went on to make whatever we could sell', Arthur Walsh said of Abraham Moon and Sons. 'But rationing governed the amount of stuff that people could buy. You could only buy one or two coats a year or something like that.'[5] The Utility scheme also had limited the type and amount of cloth that makers-up could use. They created imaginative designs within the parameters of the regulations: short jackets or 'toppers' in dogstooth and guncheck tweed, dresses with knitted wool bodices and woven tartan kilt skirts, and autumn-to-winter coats in diagonal patterns for the newly discovered teen market.[6] 'Ninety-eight per cent of what we made went to the ladies' tweed trade', Arthur Walsh noted. 'Most of the cloth was used to sew skirts.' Netherfield Mill spent about seven months per year making tweeds for spring styles and five months per year producing tweeds for winter styles. Profits were limited by the rules of the Utility authorities.[7] In 1950, British woollen mills delivered 185 million square yards of Utility cloth. During 1951, when the Utility programme was winding down, production fell to 143 million square yards, which was still significant.[8] Intended to check inflation as well as to use fabrics wisely, the Utility Scheme strove to ensure that consumers could buy products of a certain quality at an affordable price.

As the British government worked to fine-tune the civilian economy and consumers strove to carry on, Abraham Moon and Sons grappled with a sudden internal upheaval. On 5 June 1953, Frank Walsh, the chairman and managing director, passed away after tea one afternoon, no doubt due in part to the recent death of his wife, with whom he had been close. Three days later, his brother, the chemist Cyril Walsh, became chairman and his nephew, Arthur, became managing director and deputy chairman. The board was rounded out by the addition of a new secretary and two new directors, both production men who had been with the firm since the days of the Moon family's ownership: Alfred Dudbridge, the dyer who had joined the company in 1907, and Harry Turner Spence, the wool buyer and wool blender who had started in 1913.[9] The young Arthur suddenly found himself with a good deal of responsibility. At the age of twenty-nine, he had oversight of a Yorkshire manufacturing enterprise that had been in business for more than a hundred years. The old-timers understood the situation and took him under wing.

In those days, the managing director of a Yorkshire woollen mill wore two hats. As the boss, he was responsible for daily operations and, in the absence of a dedicated sales force, he was the ad hoc sales manager. Like other woollen mills, Abraham Moon and Sons made plain cloth for various types of uniforms: military, police, transport and so forth. The company also produced fabrics for the so-called donkey jacket worn by people in countless working-class occupations, from coal miners to road repairmen. These and other 'uniform cloths' were staples for Netherfield Mill, the bread-and-butter. But the mill also had a commitment to flexible production and design innovation. Arthur had to grapple with the disjuncture between the mill's capabilities and the realities of the postwar economy. 'After the war and after the scarcity, people were made to look after things', he remembered. 'You bought a coat and it had to last a few years, so quality came in.'[10] Arthur faced the challenge of drumming up business for fancy tweeds in a market dominated by necessity rather than fashion. It was a formidable task for a mill manager who hadn't yet seen his thirtieth birthday.

Multiples and makers-up

The supply chain in the fashion system had also evolved since the teenaged Arthur Walsh had his first exposure to the mill in the 1930s. The Second World War signalled the death knell for the wholesale merchants that had dominated the textile trade before the First World War. The new powerhouses in the textile world were the high-street multiples, whose standardised stores sold moderately priced and inexpensive ready-to-wear to the middle classes. In 1900, the multiple shops sold less than 1 per cent of ready-made garments for women and girls. By 1950, they sold up to 22 per cent of this merchandise and enjoyed a growing market share.[11]

The multiples came to dominate fashion retailing by watching their costs. They procured ready-to-wear directly from the makers-up in manufacturing centres such as Glasgow, Leeds, London and Manchester, as well as from those located in smaller cities and towns around Britain. As we have seen, those makers-up curbed their expenses by sidestepping the wholesale merchants to buy textiles and trimmings straight from the mills. Among the leading multiples in 1950 were Dorothy Perkins Ltd and Etam Ltd, each of which had between fifty and one hundred branch stores that sold hosiery, underclothing, knitwear and woollen garments. Multiples such as Morrisons Associated Companies Ltd, Willsons (London and Provinces) Ltd and Richard Shops Ltd, which specialised in outerwear, also had between fifty and one hundred stores each.[12] Starting in 1951, the variety store chain Marks and Spencer Ltd (M&S) undertook a massive building and expansion programme, bringing the total number of stores to 241 in 1968. M&S sold readymade clothing alongside general merchandise and some groceries.[13] Its major competitor in affordable ready-to-wear, C&A Modes Ltd, also expanded in this period, growing from twenty stores in 1951 to forty stores in 1966.[14]

Years later, Arthur (always referred to as 'Mr Walsh') reminisced about the changes to the distribution system. 'About ten years before I started at the mill, a good deal of Moon's trade was done through merchants. Merchants then sold the cloth on by length. So you'd supply two or three pieces to a merchant. He would then sell on to small tailors, three yards of this, six yards of that. But the trade was different after the war. It changed dramatically. Our customers were the people who made the garments.'[15] Important Leeds merchants, such as James Hare, continued to buy fabrics from Netherfield Mill, as did Leeds makers-up such as James Corson,

John Barran & Sons and Heatons. But now more often customers came from among the makers-up in other cities, including Glasgow, London and Manchester.[16]

Eliminating the middleman from the supply chain reduced prices in the stores, and put ready-to-wear within reach of a broader swathe of the population. In the postwar culture of necessity, two types of woollen clothing found a ready market: ladies' spring coats and children's coats. In the cool damp British climate, women wore lightweight woollen coats in the spring and summer, while children needed warm coats all year round and replacements in larger sizes as they grew. Although basic needs played a strong hand in consumer choice, fashion was inching its way onto the high street, influenced by Hollywood films and Paris fashions like Christian Dior's New Look of 1947. The New Look was a boon to textile mills because the new skirt—long, gathered at the waist and swirling widely at the hem—used at least twice as much fabric as the straight skirts worn during the war. British consumers saved up to buy inexpensive versions of such stylish clothing at fashion multiples like C&A Modes. Barbara Walsh fondly remembered taking her £5 bonus to C&A Modes in Leeds, where she splurged on a brown tweed outfit in the New Look mode, which she wore as Sunday best.[17]

C&A Modes was a major force in the democratisation of fashion in postwar Britain (figure 5.2). This London-based multiple, which debuted in 1922 with a large store on Oxford Street, was part of the Dutch family-run retail empire, C&A.[18] The house of C&A was founded in 1841 by the brothers Clemens and August Brenninkmeijer as a linen and cotton fabric business in Sneek, an old city in the Netherlands, southwest of Leeuwarden. In 1860, the Brenninkmeijer brothers opened their first retail store and thereafter started producing ready-to-wear at moderate prices. C&A retail stores were opened in Leeuwarden in 1881; Amsterdam in 1893 and 1896; and Berlin, Germany, in 1911. By this time, a new generation was in charge and C&A had a reputation for affordable clothing for the burgeoning middle classes.[19] The British arm, C&A Modes, ran the Oxford Street store and gradually opened high-street stores in Birmingham, Liverpool and other cities around the UK. Eventually, C&A Modes had three large stores on Oxford Street. From the start, C&A Modes had defined itself neither as a 'drapery house' nor as a 'departmental' store, but as a 'house specialising in the sale of women's and girls' outer garments' as well as millinery. It catered 'not only for the well-to-do' but also for 'a medium class trade', and interpreted 'the latest styles from London, Paris, and other centres of fashion'. British shoppers fondly referred to C&A Modes by the nickname 'Coats and 'Ats'.[20]

Abraham Moon and Sons first supplied the C&A Modes business in around 1953, just as major military orders wound up. During the Korean War (June 1950–July 1953), British troops served alongside soldiers from other countries of the UN

5.2 C&A Modes was famous for bringing 'distinctive fabric and fashion-wise styling' to the high street, often using Yorkshire tweeds in children's wear and ladies' wear as shown in this advertisement from 1960. Courtesy of The Draiflessen Collection, C&A and History of Advertising Trust.

Command involved in the anti-Communist effort. Early in 1953, Netherfield Mill made final delivery on a substantial government contract for khaki shirting and was processing a large order for serge service dress cloth.[21] Following the completion of these jobs, there was a slump in orders. Arthur Walsh had to find new business and C&A Modes looked as if it would fit the bill. By that time, C&A Modes had nineteen 'provincial branches' that sold women's and children's wear, including suits, frocks, coats and hats at competitive prices. C&A Modes never hesitated to reduce those prices to attract shoppers and move the merchandise.[22]

The mill did not directly deal with C&A Modes, but sold fabric to the makers-up that sewed apparel on the retailer's behalf. Over time, Arthur built up a business with around eight makers-up in London, Glasgow and Manchester whose major customer was C&A Modes. These manufacturers purchased two types of woollen fabrics: tweeds for ladies' coats and double cloths for ladies' and children's coats.[23] Arthur dealt personally with the manufacturers, who selected the patterns from the range and drove hard bargains on delivery and price.[24] Netherfield Mill had no input into the finished garments that were sold by C&A Modes. But this business continued the pattern established in the interwar years, when the mill first sold fabrics to manufacturer-retailers like Jaeger. Increasingly, the mill was part of a supply chain that began with the woolgrowers in Australia, New Zealand and South Africa, and ended with the multiples on the British high street.

In the early 1950s, the mill's relationship with the makers-up for C&A Modes was just getting started and more customers were needed. The company depended on agents in London, Manchester and Glasgow to sell its fabrics to garment factories, tailors and retail drapers around Britain. Arthur Walsh saw the largest customers and had overall responsibility for the direction of sales. In autumn 1953, he headed up to the City of London, concerned about the 'uncertain state of the market for the Company's woollen piece goods'. Something had to be done to find business in a market that was still driven by price and necessity. Since design innovation was in the mill's blood, cloth made from fibre blends seemed a promising avenue. Following a meeting with the London agents Fowler & Orr, at their offices at Empire House in St Martin's-le-Grand off Cheapside, Arthur proposed to introduce 'wool and cotton mixture cloths', a fabric that harked back to the union cloth made by his firm's founder, Abraham Moon.[25] By October, the 'new wool and cotton mixture cloths had been made' and were soon to be in the hands of the various agents.[26] But in November, Arthur conveyed his disappointment to the board; the wool-cotton blends hadn't met favour with the trade. This failed experiment in design innovation suggested that the mill needed to get closer to the market, where it could anticipate changing tastes.[27]

Ultimately, Fowler & Orr helped the mill strengthen its connections with smaller customers in greater London. After some deliberation, it was 'agreed that the London agent, Mr. [Alfred] Chambers, or his assistant, be asked to visit the Mill one day during next week for a discussion' with chairman Cyril Walsh.[28] Following this meeting with Victor Smith of Fowler & Orr, Cyril recommended that the 'London Agents should visit the Mill at frequent intervals'.[29] These exchanges launched a decades-long business relationship that served Abraham Moon and Sons well. Smith had joined Fowler & Orr in 1946, following a stint as a squadron leader in the Royal Air Force during the Second World War. He learned to sell cloth as the special assistant to Chambers, who relied on the younger man to carry his sample cases on visits to the customers. The seasoned agent and the strapping veteran went around metropolitan London, knocking on doors and taking orders from countless makers-up and merchants.[30] In 1957, Smith took over the Fowler & Orr business and, at the same time, the minutes of Abraham Moon and Sons recorded that he became the 'Company's agent for London and the Home Counties'.[31] He worked exclusively for Netherfield Mill, selling mostly to the ladies' trade until his retirement some twenty-five years later.[32]

The advantage of being a mill dedicated to flexible production meant that Abraham Moon and Sons could readily adapt to changing styles. Once large contracts for uniform cloths were in hand, the company could respond to requests for small orders of more complex patterns from merchants and the growing army of makers-up. In January 1954, for example, Netherfield Mill secured a substantial contract from the Ministry of Supply for 36,500 yards of 'Serge Service Dress', a durable woollen cloth for uniforms.[33] An order like this was the ideal complement to the mill's ongoing production of fabrics for the tartan skirts that were the latest high-street fashion. Tartan-loving customers demanded a great variety of patterns, sometime in short yardages. 'Tartans, kilts—women and girls were all wearing variations of them', Arthur Walsh recalled. 'We made 40 or 50 different patterns, including the very popular MacBeth, Royal Stewart and Mackenzie, among others.'[34] The mill always had to find a delicate balance between large orders for plain cloths that were relatively easy to make and smaller orders for fancy tweeds that required a greater investment in design and production.

The great demand for woollens for children's wear was tied to the need to dress the first cohort of baby boomers, born just after the war. With these clothes, convenience mattered more than appearance, which made this market vulnerable to the encroachment of man-made and synthetic fibres. The ladies' trade also had its own set of peculiarities. 'Tweed can be much in fashion', Arthur explained, 'and the women's trade is particularly fickle.'[35] High-street styles took their cues from the Paris couture houses, which for the sake of creativity or marketing might embrace tweed one season and declare nylon *de rigueur* the next. As before, it was impossible to predict if and when fashion would favour tweeds. Abraham Moon and Sons grappled with the challenges that faced all manufacturers whose products had a style element. The cyclical and unpredictable demand for fancy cloths forced the mill to assume a defensive position.

By the late 1950s, approximately 60 per cent of the mill's output went to makers-up that produced clothing for C&A Modes. 'The late 1950s was one of the most profitable eras of the mill', Arthur said. 'The per cent of profit was bigger than today. This was built on two cloths: the cloths for ladies' spring coats and the double cloths, which went to makers-up for C&A Modes.'[36] The mill's reliance on C&A Modes was consistent with broader developments in the Yorkshire woollen industry. In 1959, the *Financial Times* reported that four-fifths of British woollens ultimately ended up in ready-to-wear sold by the multiple clothing stores. The multiples carried a big stick, often squeezing their suppliers as they looked for ways to offer better prices to the consumer. Some mills tried to beat the multiples at their own game, merging with other firms to gain control of the supply chain and reduce the costs of feedstock. Such was the case when the famous worsted weaver Salts (Saltaire) Ltd merged first with a spinner and then with a wool comber.[37] But for most mills dependent on high-street multiples, large orders had to make up for the low prices.

The growing dependence on the makers-up to C&A Modes was cosy, but potentially volatile. Other mills in the Aireborough district had close relationships with powerful players on the high street. James Ives & Company; the Peate subsidiary of the West Riding Worsted and Woollen Mills; and the Springhead Mill Company (Guiseley) Ltd relied on M&S for a large proportion of their orders.[38] This was a potentially dangerous position. Arthur put it succinctly: 'You don't want a market of one if you're selling manufactured goods, do you?'[39] One way to avoid this type of vulnerability was to balance the big customers with the little customers and to explore the export trade.

Looking abroad

British woollen and worsted manufacturers had long depended on export markets. Back in 1924—the year when Charles Walsh died and Frank Walsh became managing director—the industry produced 476 million square yards of woollens and worsteds. Nearly half of this material was sold abroad. The industry's output declined during the Great Depression and the Second World War, despite the demand for military cloth. By 1947, however, production was on the upswing. British mills made 359 million square yards of wool fabrics and exported 77.5 million square yards of it. By 1953, production increased to 411 million square yards but some 25 per cent, or 105 million square yards, was exported. That year, British mills produced 98.5 per cent of the woollen and worsted fabrics used in the UK.[40] When viewed another way, in 1952, global exports of wool fabrics totalled 117 million lb. British mills produced 60 million lb. of this cloth, or just over half of the woollens and worsteds exported around the world.[41] In other words, the postwar trend was towards British manufacturers mainly supplying the British market, while seeking to rebuild their export trade in an increasingly competitive global environment.

By the early 1950s, the writing was on the wall. Major challenges were in store for exports of Yorkshire wool fabrics as textile manufacturing revived on the Continent. The years just after the Second World War had been a seller's market for British mills, as most countries were busy reconstructing their civilian economies rather than engaging in international trade. But within a few short years, the Italian textile industry had recovered from wartime devastation—and posed a major challenge to the British woollen and worsted industries. Italian competition came from three major industrial clusters: the worsted industry in Biella, a town located northwest of Milan in the Piedmont region; two giant woollen concerns near Venice; and the woollen industry in Prato, a town north of Florence in Tuscany. Prato specialised in low-priced woollens made from a blend of new wool, artificial fibres, shoddy and rags imported from Britain and America.[42]

Prato was a special menace to Yorkshire. Although Tuscan entrepreneurs had invested heavily in new machinery—the number of looms rose from 3,500 in 1938 to 6,000 in 1951—the region had few factories.[43] The Prato woollen industry was highly fragmented. The entrepreneurs functioned as converters who secured orders, purchased raw materials, coordinated the work and sent the cloth to market. The converter subcontracted specific jobs to individuals or households. Whether they did spinning, weaving, dyeing or finishing, the subcontractors rented their equipment from the converter. The lack of overheads, the low wages and the use of recycled materials kept costs down.[44] By the mid-1950s, inexpensive Italian woollens were already in great demand in Britain, France, Germany, South Africa, Switzerland and the United States.[45] The lower end of the British woollen industry felt the effects of Prato early on. By 1957, the mills in the heavy woollen district in Dewsbury, Batley and Morley—factories that made inexpensive cloth from virgin wool and shoddy— were hard hit by competition from Italy.[46]

The British wool textile industry was an important player in British overseas trade and the balance of payments. On 11 March 1941, President Franklin Delano Roosevelt had signed the Lend-Lease Act, which allowed the United States to lend or lease supplies to any sympathetic country in defence of the national security. As the bill wound its way around Capitol Hill, in Britain the Board of Trade created the National Wool Textile Export Corporation (NWTEC), a Bradford-based organisation with the remit 'to promote the exports of the Wool Textile Industry' as a means for securing dollar exchange. The NWTEC was funded by a wool levy collected by the Wool Control. Besides helping makers-up find export markets, the NWTEC joined forces with the International Wool Secretariat (IWS)—the organisation created by wool growers in the 1930s to promote wool fibres—to advertise British clothing and to help London establish 'a "British fashion" for women's suits and sports clothes'.[47] As the Second World War drew to a close, the NWTEC opened an office at 743 Fifth Avenue in New York with the aim to reignite the relationships among British mills and their pre-war American customers (figure 5.3).[48] Postwar Britain needed dollars to repay its wartime debt and to purchase food and raw materials. When the Wool Control ceased, the government in July 1950 decided to fund the NWTEC with a levy on the wool textile industry.[49] By 1951, wool textiles were Britain's 'paramount dollar-earning industry', with exports totalling a record value of nearly £177 million.[50]

North America was the largest export destination for British wool fabrics. The fate of UK woollens and worsteds was inevitably linked to US customs regulations. In 1950, the American textile industry vigorously lobbied Congress for import quotas on woollens, so as to prevent the ruin of domestic mills.[51] The next year, a worldwide recession hit the textile industry. In 1951–52, markets around the

5.3 This 1951 National Wool Textile Export Corporation advertisement featured garments designed by Davidow, an American company known for their tailored suits. Author's collection: *Harper's Bazaar* (July 1951), 10–11.

world were saturated with wool, cotton and rayon goods. In the towns and villages of Lancashire and Yorkshire, unemployment levels recalled the worst years of the Great Depression.[52] Graham Carmichael, promotion director of the NWTEC, toured the United States and Canada to assess the export market. After visiting Chicago, Montreal, New York and Toronto, he returned to Bradford nervous about prospects. 'Stores in New York were loaded up to the ceiling, particularly in men's clothes; manufacturers were clogged up with stocks of piece goods, and people were not buying.'[53] American consumers were cautious in reaction to the inflation and uncertainty created by the Korean War. But he spotted some promising signs for woollens. In 'men's wear there was a distinct swing over to what Americans call "leisure clothes", that is sports jackets and odd trousers, which normally are not used as much in the States as they are here. Some Americans were even wearing such clothes for business. This trend towards casual clothes also helped favour woollens against worsteds.'[54]

In the postwar years, the ranks of the American middle class had expanded to include more blue-collar families, some ethnic minorities, bachelors, career women and teenagers. Consumer society in the United States had become more inclusive, heterogeneous and price-conscious.[55] With one eye on tastes and the other on costs, retailers knew the tweed look appealed to some of these market segments, but tariffs stood in the way of getting the goods to the consumers. The fashion director at William Filene's Sons Company, the leading fashion retailer in Boston, explained the situation to one Irish maker-up:

> Certainly, our store—and many others, I am sure—feel that there *is* a market for casual coats, well styled in attractive hand loomed Irish tweeds. However, price will be an important factor, also, because of course they must be competitive with other casual coats we sell—in both American and imported fabrics. Unfortunately, by the time we add handling and duty to your cost in Dublin we will have to retail the coats at well over $100. This represents a very limited consumer market and would necessarily mean an extremely limited volume of business.[56]

The British woollen industry was increasingly concerned about foreign protectionism. The General Agreement on Tariffs and Trade (GATT) was the first step towards the liberalisation of global commerce, but nations had to negotiate terms among themselves. In 1947, America and Britain had agreed to a 25 per cent duty on wool fabrics imported to the United States; in the next decade, the textile lobby in the United States claimed this was too low.[57] After relentless complaints, the American mills scored a major victory on Capitol Hill. In December 1957, the US government imposed a quota on fabric imports, permitting 14.2 million lb. annually at an *ad valorem* rate of 25 per cent. Beyond that quota, fabrics were subject to duties ranging from 30 per cent to 40 per cent. The new regulations had an immediate impact. The United States began to import more cloth from low-wage economies such as Italy and Japan and less cloth from the older industrial economies of Britain and France.[58]

The Canadian woollen industry also complained of stiff foreign competition. Textiles and garments from Czechoslovakia, Britain, Japan and the United States had 'invaded the market'.[59] In 1949, 39 per cent of all British exports to Canada were textiles.[60] Two years later, British wool fabrics accounted for nearly one-third of the entire Canadian textile market and 85 per cent of those that were foreign-made: wool textile imports totalled 13.3 million linear yards, of which 11.3 million came the UK.[61] One Canadian textile executive explained: 'The shrinking demand for textiles throughout the world, the necessity for liquidation of inventories, and the shortage of dollars have turned the attention of British and European manufacturers to the last unrestricted, low-tariff, hard currency market in the world. This market is Canada.'[62]

Canada had become Britain's largest overseas customer for wool fabrics, trailed by the United States. In Montreal, all the major retailers on Saint Catherine Street—Simpsons, Eatons and Ogilvy—were keen on all types of British goods, avidly promoting them with special British Weeks.[63] In 1953, *Women's Wear Daily* reported that thirty-six of Britain's largest exporters of wool fabrics, working under the NWTEC's auspices, participated in the Canadian National Exhibition in Toronto, a major fair expected to attract 2.75 million visitors. The list of British participants was a virtual who's who of mills in Scotland and Yorkshire; the Peate subsidiary of the West Riding Worsted and Woollen Mills had a display.[64] Abraham Moon and Sons did not put up a booth, but Arthur Walsh remembered how the new realities of the export trade affected the firm. Merchants still handled most exports, but mills could sell their cloth overseas through foreign commission agents. Netherfield Mill used a Montreal agency run by the brothers Alfred and John Capper, whose family business had represented Abraham Moon and Sons since the early twentieth century. Arthur eventually developed his own Canadian links through Rae Anderson, a friend from the University of Leeds, who had moved to Montreal in the 1950s.[65]

British woollen mills also looked for new business in Continental Europe, where the various nations were taking steps to encourage international trade. In the late 1950s, they formed two major trading blocs that were committed to the gradual elimination of tariffs between member countries and the establishment of a common import policy.[66] In March 1957, the first of these trading blocs was created when six European nations—Belgium, France, Italy, Luxembourg, the Netherlands and West Germany—signed the Treaty of Rome to form the European Economic Community (EEC). The Common Market or the 'Six', as the EEC was also called, came into being in January 1958. Trade barriers between the six member states were removed on 1 January 1959 and tariffs were reduced on imports from other countries, including the UK.[67] In 1961, the *Financial Times* predicted that British wool textiles would benefit from the trade policies of the Common Market because member states such as Germany would look to the UK for high-quality woollens.[68] However, in the early days, the Common Market did little to improve the export position of the Yorkshire woollen industry because of the favourable status given to Italy as a member state. The Italian woollen mills flooded Western Europe and central Europe with inexpensive fabrics.

The second trading bloc, the European Free Trade Association (EFTA), came into being on 1 January 1960. Nicknamed the 'Outer Seven', this trading group was comprised of Austria, Denmark, Norway, Portugal, Sweden, Switzerland and the UK. Starting on 1 July 1960, tariffs between the EFTA member nations were cut by 20 per cent, with subsequent reductions planned leading up to the elimination of duties. The UK was the dominant trading partner among the Outer Seven and the only member with a large-scale wool textile industry, accounting for 77 per cent of the wool fabrics produced among the EFTA states.[69] However, the EEC constituted a much larger market for wool textiles than the EFTA. When the UK government pursued membership in the Common Market, the British woollen and worsted industry rejoiced.[70]

Canada continued to grow as the largest export market for British woollens and for tweeds by Abraham Moon and Sons. Mid-market mills desperately wanted access to the United States, but the protectionist wall kept growing taller. In 1961, the United States dropped its quota system, but increased the *ad valorem* duty on woollens and worsteds (figure 5.4). With a few exclusions, the duty went up to 38 per cent. The West Riding Worsted and Woollen Mills put it simply: 'This is a highly penal and protective rate, and it remains to be seen whether we can sell in the face of it.'[71] One Huddersfield mill, Jonas Kenyon & Sons Ltd, which exported nearly a quarter of its output to eight or ten foreign markets, did well in the United States 'in spite of the 38 percent duty'. Everyone 'has learnt to live with it', the Kenyon sales manager said.[72] In contrast, Abraham Moon and Sons was priced out of the American market. The mill continued to export to Canada, which by 1963 depended on the UK for about 70 per cent of its imported wool fabrics.[73] 'There was something like 35 per cent tariff in the states. They protected themselves to some tune', Arthur explained. 'It carried on for ages. It was lethal, really. We couldn't sell there, so we focused on Canada, which was our major export market until the late 1960s or 1970s.'[74]

Sales meets design

By 1954, the dual responsibilities of the managing directorship—looking after the mill and seeing to the customers—were becoming a chore for the busy Arthur Walsh. Once daily operations had settled into a routine after the death of Frank Walsh and the protracted settlement of his estate, the engagement between Arthur and Barbara Sutcliffe could progress to the next stage. The couple began planning for a June 1954 wedding.[75] Arthur knew that, as a family man, it would be a challenge to spend a lot of time on the road, wooing the makers-up for C&A Modes and looking for new customers. In March 1954, he noted a 'deterioration in the order position' and lamented that 'few orders were now in hand'.[76] Something had to be done to close the gap. Some of the larger Yorkshire mills had professional sales staff and Abraham Moon and Sons now took the first steps down this path.

By this time, the company was vying with foreign manufacturers for a thin slice of the global woollen market. The Italian mills in Prato were proving to be fierce rivals. Abraham Moon and Sons also competed for shares of the home trade and the export market with other vertically integrated woollen mills, such as the Peate division of the West Riding Worsted and Woollen Mills in Guiseley and

1 Ladies' tweed costume by J. R. Dale & Company, tailors and habit makers, London, c. 1900–10. Courtesy of Museum of London: Costume Collection, 85.238A–B.

2 The earliest known fabrics by Abraham Moon and Sons are these two striped dress fabrics deposited in the Design Registry in 1875; they may represent the firm's early use of synthetic dyes. Courtesy of The National Archives: registered designs 297231 and 297232.

3 The Isaac Moon memorial window, 1909, in St Oswald's Church, Guiseley. Photography by author.

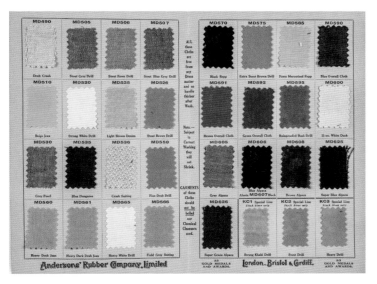

4 *Andersons' 'Rainthorne Weatherproofs' for Ladies, Gentlemen, Girls & Boys, Manufactured by Andersons' Rubber Co. Ltd., Pattern Book No. 966, Season 1927–8.* Courtesy of Museum of London: Costume Collection, 71.117/53.

5 Heatons (Leeds) Ltd advertisement for Alwetha coats in waterproof tweeds, which could have been made by Abraham Moon and Sons. © The British Library Board: *Drapers' Organiser* (February 1927), 54.

"DEEMARCO" INEXPENSIVE RANGE

(Regd.)

4563 — price 63/-
All wool Bedford
Cord Royala Vel-
our, lined art.
Satin, Skunk col-
lar, in all latest
colours, Women's
and Maids'.

2613 — price 39/11
All wool Novelty
Velour, lined art.
Silk twill, in
fauns, browns,
black and white.
Women's and
Maids'.

2611 — price 47/11
All wool Diagon-
al Velour lined
best art. Silk
twill. Collar and
cuffs in Nutria
Lamb. In all la-
test colours. Wo-
men's and Maids'.

| 4563 | 2613 | 2611 |

Novel weaves and colour effects enhance smart designs in our
range of Coats for Autumn and Winter. We invite you to visit
our Showrooms during September. Inspect the entire range and

"LOOK AT THE QUALITY OF THE CLOTH"

DICKSON MILLAR & CO.

Cardiff Address:—
7 Pembroke Terrace
(Mr. P. W. Brooks)

35/38 ALDERSGATE STREET, LONDON, E.C.1
Telephone: National 7736-7335

Glasgow Address:—
20 Springfield Court,
Queen Street
(Mr. E. J. Henry)

6 As indicated in this advertisement for Dickson Millar & Company, a Moon customer, the
stylishness of inexpensive tweeds was a boon to cost-conscious consumers during the Great
Depression. © The British Library Board: *Drapers' Organiser* (September 1931), 55.

7 Close-up of a herringbone uniform for the Women's Voluntary Service, 1942, made in Leeds by John Barran & Sons, using the type of cloth produced by Abraham Moon and Sons. Courtesy of Museum of London: Costume Collection, 80.416/2.

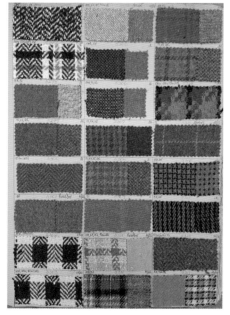

8 A pattern book from the mill's extensive design archive shows the variety of patterns during the postwar era. Courtesy of Abraham Moon and Sons.

9 Ladies' woollen suit with fur trim, purchased at C&A Modes, 1960s. Courtesy of Museum of London: Costume Collection, 70.131.1–2.

10 This woollen suit was bought at Matthias Robinson—a small chain of department stores owned by Debenhams—by a young Yorkshire woman who needed something nice to wear at a friend's wedding in 1966 or 1967; costing around £20 (a week's wages), it was a special purchase for the owner, aged 22 or 23, who normally made her own clothes. Courtesy of Yorkshire Fashion Archive: gift of Marion Ackroyd of Keighley, West Yorkshire.

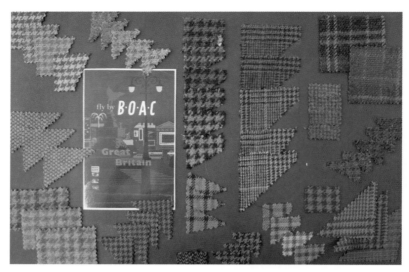

11 Mood board by Martin Aveyard, c. 1980. Courtesy of Abraham Moon and Sons.

12 The mill's Sales and Design Showroom Suite, showing the arrangement of throws in a rainbow effect, 2016. Courtesy of Abraham Moon and Sons.

5.4 The fashion houses on Seventh Avenue in New York gave tweeds a modern American look as shown by this lightweight coat for spring 1960. Author's collection.

C. & J. Hirst & Sons Ltd, in Huddersfield. The advantage of vertical integration was that Netherfield Mill controlled all aspects of production, ensuring consistency from one order to the next.[77] But a firm like Peate had further advantages because it was part of the West Riding group. By this time, the West Riding Worsted and Woollen Mills had thirteen subsidiaries, including Priestleys Ltd, a Bradford manufacturer of 'high-class worsted cloth' with a New York branch that had been in operation since 1900. Peate had more resources at its disposal, including a direct lifeline to the America market.[78]

In the main, the person responsible for the look of tweeds at Netherfield Mill was Albert Holmes, who had worked in the designers' office since the mid-1930s. Around 1950, Frank Walsh had reorganised the senior staff in response to the retirement of Hugh Busfield from the position of 'Mill Manager'. The designer Tom Walsh was put in charge of costing, a job that suited his penchant for details, and Albert was given oversight for design, weaving and finishing. This was the first step in a revision of the design process, which had not changed since the wartime focus on military needs and the Utility scheme.[79]

The mill needed a way of collecting up-to-date knowledge of consumer tastes and channelling this information into the designers' office, where it could inform the patterns for next season. Albert worked in a traditional way, designing on point paper and then trying out the patterns on an old handloom to see how they looked. He would add a blue yarn here and a red yarn there to study the contrast, to see if the pattern looked nice and to determine if all the checks were in balance. But the world had changed dramatically since the days when he had studied at the University of Leeds and designed cloth for Springhead Mills. It never occurred to Albert to read fashion magazines like British *Vogue* or to browse the high-street shops for inspiration. His approach was somewhat of a mismatch for the increasingly competitive and fashion-conscious business environment.

Netherfield Mill needed a better connection to the marketplace. In May 1954, the directors appointed Dennis R. Moulson 'to the position of Salesman'.[80] The new recruit came to Abraham Moon and Sons from the sales department at James Ives & Company, which made woollens for M&S. Dennis was familiar with the expectations of the high-street multiples.[81] He was also aware of the value of informal market research. In his first two or three years at Abraham Moon and Sons, he worked as a 'mill traveller' watching over the small customers while Arthur looked after the makers-up for C&A Modes. Although Dennis was clever at sales, his talent for matching a pattern to a market niche soon became apparent. Eventually, Albert concentrated on production and Dennis was given joint responsibility for design and sales.[82]

Thus began the slow transition towards an integrated approach to design practice. Although this shift occurred under his watch, Arthur was the first to admit that there was nothing planned or strategic about the marriage of design and sales. The two functions gradually began to interact from the 1950s onward. With his training in textiles at the University of Leeds, Arthur appreciated the complementarity of design and sales, and he encouraged synergies. 'It was very important for designers to be mixed up with sales', he explained. 'There's nothing a customer likes better than having someone who is both on the design side and the sales side, someone who knows what he or she is talking about and can say, Yes, we can do this, that, and the other, we can vary that pattern if you like, or we can do this other thing.'[83]

The link between design and sales was crucial to Abraham Moon and Sons, given the focus on fancy tweeds, the market conditions and the moment. 'It was variety that sold. We couldn't compete with people who just made one thing', Arthur explained.[84] 'We tended to have a small niche of the trade that dealt with something on a small scale. Our lines were different from the plain simple designs that our competitors could make cheaper because they didn't do all the fancy fabrics.'[85] 'If you make one thing, you can do it cheaply', he said. 'If you make a hundred things, you can't do it cheaply.'[86] The trick to the balancing act was to match the customer with the pattern and vice versa (Colour Plate 8). Every fabric buyer liked to believe that he was getting something special. 'If we sold one design to A, he wasn't happy if we sold the same design to B, C and D', Arthur elaborated. 'We had a general range of about fifty different designs, and we showed them mainly to smaller people. In addition, we had our bigger trade, mainly C&A, who were given exclusivity.'[87]

By 1960, the mill was equipped with a management team that had complementary skills in wool blending, design, weaving, finishing and sales. The dyer Alfred Dudbridge, who had worked at the mill since the time of Isaac Moon, had passed away in 1954.[88] Tom Walsh retired sometime after the war and died in 1961.[89] There were the inevitable personality conflicts, particularly between generations, but the company had the expertise and the financial standing to keep up with the times. In the long run, it was the commitment to design-driven sales, flexible production and technical innovation that allowed Abraham Moon and Sons to adapt to the changes of the third quarter of the twentieth century.

Swinging into synthetics

The profits from uniform cloths and high-street tweeds provided Abraham Moon and Sons with the cash for incremental renovations to the mill and the machinery. During the 1950s and 1960s, the company invested in a series of capital improvements that helped the mill to maintain a competitive edge. Technical upgrades to mill equipment were in part driven by necessity, as obsolete or worn machinery had to be replaced. But another important technical innovation—man-made fibres—began to reshape design and production. The multiples were swept up in the synthetics revolution, which promised to democratise clothing consumption with lower prices. As part of the high-street supply chain, Netherfield Mill turned to synthetics.

Abraham Moon and Sons had a tradition of reinvesting part of its profits in capital equipment, dating from the time of Charles Walsh and Frank Walsh. The practice continued during Arthur Walsh's term as managing director. In 1953, the company built a new willey house, which in a vertically integrated woollen mill is a space equipped with machinery for blending and oiling the wool prior to the carding process.[90] Updated dyeing equipment was purchased in 1955. The weaving shed was enlarged twice, first in 1955 and again in 1960. An extension was added above the mending room and yarn store in 1958 and a 'new designing office' for the 'designing and progress staff' was built in 1959.[91]

Despite these improvements to the physical plant, Netherfield Mill could run into trouble meeting the demand for fancy tweeds. Given the footprint of the mill property, it was difficult to expand certain departments and add more machinery. In the early 1960s, for example, space constraints made it nearly impossible to make enough weft yarn to keep the looms busy, particularly since a large variety of colours, weights and textures were needed to achieve the look that customers wanted. In 1962, Arthur reported the 'control of yarn requirements had always been a difficult problem', and Albert took measures to make the winding department more efficient.[92] A new piece-rate system provided workers with an incentive to achieve better results.[93] Besides the human element, issues with the quality of the yarn stemmed from 'the limitation imposed by the number of Carding Machines in operation, the increased range of colours which we were producing and the economic necessity of making each batch of yarn as large as possible having regard to our requirements'.[94] Variety was both a blessing and a curse.

The ability to produce woollens in a wide choice of colours and patterns favoured Abraham Moon and Sons in the buoyant consumer culture of the 1960s (figure 5.5). The necessity-driven high street of the immediate postwar era was transformed into a vibrant modern high street that tempted shoppers with affordable everyday fashion. Although many cities were still partially in ruins from the Blitz, there was a steady rise in the standard of living for the average Briton. Inexpensive ready-made clothing provided a modicum of luxury to consumers who had suffered through years of hardship. As the economy improved, the average British woman could save a few shillings here and there to treat herself and her family to new clothes, and the London dandy could indulge his taste for the latest styles.

The British ready-to-wear industry, which had steadily matured since the end of clothes rationing, was the largest garment industry in Europe and it served 'the most highly integrated retail market outside the United States'. Around 1960, Britons on average spent £25 to £30 per head annually on clothing.[95] Although it had long played second fiddle to Paris as a women's wear capital, London had come into its own as a couture centre through the activities of the Incorporated Society of London Fashion Designers, established in 1942 to help make the city into a 'centre of fashion'. In 1958, the ready-to-wear industry established the Fashion House Group

5.5 Illustrating the maxim that clothes make the man, a London dandy enjoys the early spring weather at Embankment Gardens wearing a flashy check tweed suit; his down-at-heel companion also wears wool, albeit less fashionably. Author's collection: press photo for Sullivan Williams and Company, maker of the suit, March 1959.

of London, which launched the first biannual London Fashion Week.[96] On the high street, fashion multiples exerted even greater sway over the consumer's choices. Up-market stores such as Aquascutum, Burberry and Jaeger promoted a tailored British aesthetic that revolved around country pursuits or sophisticated urban living. C&A Modes and M&S offered practical easy-care fashions to consumers who needed to watch their budgets (figure 5.6 and Colour Plate 9). This middle market was the

5.6 Marks and Spencer Ltd kept middle-class consumers supplied with stylish tweeds, such as the two check patterns shown in this fashion shot from the store's in-house newsletter. Courtesy of The M&S Company Archive: *St Michael News*, 6:9 (September 1959), 1.

largest growth area for everyday fashion. The British high street and the British consumer were in a warm embrace. British style was the new order of the day and British tweeds were very much a part of the look.

Back in 1952, Graham Carmichael of the NWTEC had returned from a trip to the United States optimistic that British wool textiles would find a place in the American market—with one caveat. The 'one cloud on the horizon' was 'the remarkable strides made by synthetic fabrics in men's wear as well as women's wear styles'. He brought fabric samples back to Britain, including '100 per cent and mixture constructions, among them Dacron (Terylene) cloths as well as nylon and rayon structures'.[97] The French textile industry had created the first man-made fibres from the cellulose in plants in the years around 1900, after which cellulose fibres such as viscose rayon and acetate were further developed in Europe and the United States. In the 1930s, two chemical giants—IG Farben in Germany and E. I. du Pont de Nemours and Company in the United States—raced to synthetise the world's first test-tube fibre made from petroleum. Just before the war, each firm invented a variation of the miracle substance that the DuPont Company called nylon. In wartime Britain, two Manchester chemists built on DuPont's nylon research to create the first polyester fibre. Imperial Chemical Industries (ICI) commercialised this invention as Terylene polyester, to which DuPont purchased the American rights. DuPont's extensive investments in laboratory research and chemical engineering generated more miracle materials. In the 1960s, the United States led the world in the production of synthetic fibres and DuPont held the reins on seven different fibres: rayon, acetate, nylon, polyester, acrylic, spandex and fluorocarbon.[98] In the UK by 1964, Courtaulds had captured the rayon market, ICI had a monopoly on polyester with the Terylene brand and British Nylon Spinners (a jointly owned subsidiary of Courtaulds and ICI) dominated nylon production. Courtaulds competed with Chemstrand in the UK market for acrylic, a type of synthetic wool. A joint venture between the Monsanto Chemical Company and the American Viscose Corporation (two American fibre manufacturers), Chemstrand had built an acrylic fibre plant in Northern Ireland expressly to serve the British market. Rayon aside, 70 per cent of the artificial fibres produced in the UK went into clothing.[99] The synthetics revolution was poised to deliver easy-care everyday fashion onto the high street.

Abraham Moon and Sons and other British tweed mills did not agree with the NWTEC position that synthetics were a 'cloud on the horizon'. In terms of price, the new fibres were highly competitive with virgin wool. The Guiseley tweed makers, along with the Dewsbury heavy woollen makers, had always looked for ways to reduce the cost of materials. In the old days, rags recycled at the Eller Ghyll facility had done the trick for Netherfield Mill. But after the Second World War, the mill saw great promise in man-made fibres from the rayon giant, Courtaulds. In November 1953, the directors had a 'discussion on the possible use of synthetic fibres' and asked wool blender Harry Spence to obtain 'a supply of rayon fibre'.[100] The demand was high and Courtaulds struggled to keep up. In December, Harry reported that 'Courtaulds were unable to generate a supply of "fibre" at the present time, and that we had ordered a bale of rayon waste'.[101] Rayon became an important cost-cutter for Netherfield Mill. In early 1960, Harry proposed to procure from Courtaulds 40,000 lb. of rayon fibre in excess of the mill's expected needs to 'ensure an adequate supply next Winter'.[102]

By the 1960s, Netherfield Mill was fully invested in rayon-wool blends, as were many weavers who wanted to be on the cutting edge. These fibre mixtures achieved the tweedy look at a reduced price. The new man-made materials freed the mills from agricultural uncertainties, such as the Australian droughts that led to wool shortages and skyrocketing prices, and made them less beholden to the Bradford wool merchants. On both sides of the Atlantic Ocean, textile manufacturers acknowledged the advantages of artificial fibres. 'The best thing about synthetics', one American mill operator told *Business Week*, 'is that they take the speculation out of inventory buying. They greatly reduce the amount of capital necessary to run this business and, for the first time, they permit us to compete on the basis of manufacturing efficiency and sales promotion—not on how well we can read the crystal ball of the wool market.'[103]

From the consumer's perspective, synthetics met the need for clothing that was affordable, easy to clean and stylish. For decades, British women had reserved colour and frivolity for special occasions. The typical consumer, much like Samantha Stewart in *Foyle's War* and the real-life Barbara Sutcliffe, thought of everyday clothes as a practical uniform, tailored and smart. Warm and serviceable, tweeds were the embodiment of traditional British styling. The executive's wife or the urban career woman shopped for her tweed outfits at up-market multiples, while the school mistress or housewife bought them from a local shop or at one of the multiples in the larger towns. The shift to casual styling was given a boost around 1956, when the Paris couture houses abandoned the New Look in favour of short, slim skirts. Gabrielle 'Coco' Chanel had re-opened her couture house and her advocacy of soft, knitted clothing that fitted the natural female form paved the way for the triumph of practicality and comfort. In novels and films, sexualised teenaged characters such as Juliette, played by the French ingénue Brigitte Bardot in Roger Vadim's controversial 1957 film, *Et Dieu … créa la femme* [*And God Created Woman*], and Lolita, from the eponymous 1955 novel by Vladimir Nabokov and the 1962 film by Stanley Kubrick, helped to popularise a fresh youthful look. But the new synthetics—which allowed garment makers to produce easy-going garments—also played a pivotal role.

Artificial fibres were in vogue at the two great high-street clothing and fashion multiples, M&S and C&A Modes. The most powerful player on the high street,

M&S first introduced consumers to synthetics through pyjamas and lingerie, but was soon using the new materials in a wide range of clothing.[104] In 1959, Mary Welbeck, the fashion writer for *St Michael News*, the M&S in-house newsletter, predicted that the new 'completely reversible Acrilan skirts'—washable and with 'pleats-that-last-forever'—would 'be politely but firmly fought over' among shoppers in the stores. Acrilan synthetic wool, she implied, was better than the real thing.[105] M&S saw the new fibres as bringing 'progress' to the consumer, providing easy-care clothes at affordable prices.[106] The dominant store on the high street had signalled that rayon, acetate, nylon, acrylic, polyester and spandex were here to stay. C&A Modes also embraced lower-priced synthetics, advancing the concept that fashion should be accessible to everyone.

The design staff at Netherfield Mill scurried to keep up with the synthetics revolution. In 1962, a new designer named John Richmond joined Abraham Moon and Sons as the assistant to Dennis Moulson. A native of Huddersfield, John had taken night classes in weaving, designing, finishing and testing at the Huddersfield Technical College and had worked for woollen and worsted manufacturers in his home town. When he started at Netherfield Mill, the bulk of the business was done in the home market with a small percentage of exports to Canada. Half of the output was woollens for children's wear (figure 5.7).[107] The mill created a favourite fabric for

5.7 In cold climates such as Canada and northern parts of the United States, children often wore woollen coats made from British tweed. Author's collection.

C&A Modes by adding a waste-yarn backing to wool tweed; this double cloth was ideal for children's wear because of its warmth and durability.[108] John soon learned that synthetic blends were suited to children's clothing because of their lightness and practicality. Mothers loved the new fabrics because they could be washed. One American woollen manufacturer summed the advantages of fabrics made from a blend of virgin wool, nylon and Orlon acrylic by DuPont: 'We have used orlon [sic] in our woolen fabric because with it the fabric becomes *hand washable* (not machine washable), crease resistant and considerably stronger without added weight. The nylon has been added mostly for strength.'[109] Synthetics were an invisible technology that was helping to modernise consumer society on both sides of the Atlantic Ocean. After years of scarcity, everyone wanted everyday life to be easier, more convenient and modern. Designers had to respond.

As British style came into its own, the fickleness of fashion compounded the uncertainties that were a matter of routine for woollen manufacturers. One detailed board minute from March 1963 gets to the heart of the matter. Arthur Walsh happily reported that Abraham Moon and Sons had approximately ten to twelve weeks of work on hand, but the backlog of orders had a downside. The mill

> now required more orders to keep our looms going than previously, as our weaving output in terms of pieces had expanded considerably in recent weeks due to the preponderance of light weight clothes being produced. More bought yarn was being used in these pieces, and the total weight of the output was down, leading to a reduced demand on our Spinning Department … The increase in the number of pieces produced had made it difficult to get the output through the finishing sections of the Mill, particularly the Mending Department, and had led to late deliveries.[110]

In April, the situation worsened when some customers, struggling with the 'difficult Spring season', cancelled their orders. Netherfield Mill was left 'with a large quantity of Stock Pieces of doubtful value which would have to be written down, and as a result our profit for the year … would be lower than expected'.[111] To recoup part of the loss, the mill re-dyed some of the unsold cloth in 'Winter Shades', but could do nothing with the 'foam-backed stock' other than store it until 'the next Spring Season' when it would have to be sold at a reduced price.[112] Meanwhile, the march of synthetics continued unabated. During 1963, for the first time, man-made fibres became the single largest type of raw material used by the British textile industry. UK textile producers were using more man-made fibres than any of the natural fibres, including cotton.[113]

Poor retail sales in spring 1963 were followed by a backlash against tweeds a year later. Abraham Moon and Sons started the year with optimism, having eleven weeks of orders on the books. To keep up with demand, the mill experimented with adding some of the new fibres to the yarns without any problems. 'Our chief difficulties at the moment arose from the increased variety of our range, leading to small lots', the directors noted in February 1964.[114] But in April, the order position deteriorated as tweeds fell out of favour. 'The Spring season had finished a month earlier than usual due to the unpopularity of woollen tweeds and although big initial orders for Winter had been received we had started making these earlier to fill in the gap and were now faced with a lull until repeat orders could be expected.'[115]

As tweed makers scrambled, the *Financial Times* paid tribute to the synthetics revolution. Among producers and consumers alike, man-made fibres had prompted an attitude change by lending 'themselves to madly impractical designs on account of their basic practicality'. British women all looked 'like schoolgirls', dressed 'almost entirely' in 'pleated skirts, white blouses, chunky knitteds, pastel colours and soft flyaway materials'—all made from materials that washed and dried in a few hours and never needed to be ironed. The synthetics revolution was helping to modernise the supply chain in the fashion system. The British ready-to-wear trade had been transformed from a fragmented collection of family businesses into 'an industry which worked with fabric producers on technical problems'. A new generation of clothing designers, who had grown up with rayon, nylon and polyester, understood the potential. By the 1960s, there was widespread enthusiasm for all things synthetic.[116]

The triumph of fashion knitwear was one of the most important outcomes of the synthetics revolution, reshaping demand in ways that would reverberate among the woollen weavers for decades. As early as 1964, about 60 per cent of the synthetic wool, or acrylic, used in Britain and Western Europe went into knitted apparel. The properties of synthetic materials—strength, shape retention, easy washing and softness of handle—were ideal for knitwear.[117] Using a new generation of advanced knitting machines, yarns could be converted into fabrics within two or three days, as opposed to the six to nine months needed to take a woven cloth from the drawing board to the delivery dock.[118] The speed of knitwear production was perfect for the emerging buy-it-now culture. The new fashion knitwear styles for sweaters, dresses, skirts and slacks embodied the youthful look of Brigitte Bardot and the equally famous London supermodels Jean Shrimpton and, later, Twiggy.

As fashion knitwear grew in popularity, the entire wool industry found itself falling behind. Abraham Moon and Sons looked to update the tweed look by creating wool-rayon blends with bright colours, bold patterns, lighter weights and better performance. Competitors such as James Ives & Company and Gibson & Lumgair Ltd, in Selkirk, Scotland, wove novelty woollens in 'the knitted look', but the effort only went so far due to the inherent lack of stretchability.[119] The woes of

5.8 Woolmark advertisement, Paris, 1966. Author's collection; courtesy The Woolmark Company.

wool extended far beyond the weaving sheds of the UK. With their livelihoods on the line, worried woolgrowers in the IWS spent £13 million to promote a positive image for wool fabrics.[120]

In early 1964, the IWS announced plans for a major public-relations campaign to put virgin wool in the public eye (figure 5.8). The Woolmark logo, inspired by a skein of wool, was officially introduced by the IWS in September. Woolmark was a Certification Trade Mark issued with approval from the Board of Trade and differed from an ordinary trademark in that the government had to be satisfied that goods bearing it met certain standards. The goal was to place the Woolmark logo on garments, knitting wools and product advertisements where it served as a guarantee of quality and authenticity.[121] 'Young people think of wool as being "square" and synthetics as being young and gay', said the UK director of the IWS.[122] The Woolmark campaign aimed to change their minds. Wool was ready for a head-on fight against man-made fibres.[123]

The 'young people' who thought woollens were old-fashioned and synthetics were modern took their cues from films, teen magazines like *Jackie*, the *Daily Mail*, the BBC music show *Top of the Pops*, Mod boutiques and high-street stores such as Dorothy Perkins and C&A Modes. By 1966, the population cohorts born during the 1940s and early 1950s were coming of age during a period of affluence built on Britain's industrial economy. These 15 to 25-year-olds had money to spend and rather than buying 'a *good* new outfit for every season', according to the *Daily Mail*, they splurged on 'new dresses or suits or separates every week'. As one of the major purveyors of mass-produced fashion, C&A Modes happily reported that skimpy trends like the mini skirt did not translate into reduced orders with textile mills 'because of the boom in sales'.[124]

In essence, C&A Modes was offering an early form of 'fast fashion' to teenagers who were hungry for 'the London look' pioneered by designers such as Mary Quant and popularised by trendy retailing districts such as the King's Road and Carnaby Street (figure 6.1). 'C&A was the first mass-market retailer to get the idea', noted the *Daily Mail*. 'It would buy new merchandise every week on a cash-and-carry basis from rag trade firms in the East End of London.' And every week, C&A sold every bit of it to teenaged girls who loved the lightweight A-line shifts and stretchy knitted tube dresses by Mary Quant and Yves Saint Laurent, but could never have worn these styles if not for high-street knock-offs.[125]

Whereas M&S offered good-value clothing for the entire family, C&A Modes focused on affordable fashion and developed niches within that speciality. It catered to mothers who needed inexpensive clothes for their children and also delivered 'low-budget garments' in edgy styles that teenagers loved.[126] It is difficult to evaluate the impact of this strategy on the financial health of C&A Modes due to the secretive culture of the parent firm, C&A. Snippets from the newspapers provide some insight. Between 1953 and 1962, earnings went from £711,087 to £1.15 million per annum and, by 1964, the chain had thirty-seven stores, 'from London's Oxford-street to Aberdeen'.[127] Following the Companies Act 1967 (which required greater financial transparency of limited companies, effective from 27 January 1968), C&A Modes moved from being registered as a limited company to being re-registered as a partnership, which permitted a higher degree of secrecy about internal operations.[128] Soon after, in 1968, C&A Modes was the 'biggest-advertised' consumer brand in the UK.[129] That year, the multiple invested £1.5 million in advertising, which accounted for more than half of the £2.8 million spent by all UK retailers.[130]

The accelerated pace of everyday fashion—much of it made from synthetics— was not without consequences for the West Yorkshire textile mills. The young styles on offer by high-street retailers such as C&A Modes, Dorothy Perkins and Richard Shops; more up-market retailers such as Matthias Robinson and Wallis shops; and by the new boutiques that catered to baby boomers, were a clarion call to woollen manufacturers (Colour Plate 10). Ralph Masters, secretary of the NWTEC, acknowledged the importance of youth culture. 'If we don't go ahead with catching the modern feeling about life, projecting the modern image, we shall all stagnate', he told the *Ambassador*, a trade journal that promoted British fabrics around the world. 'What we have to do is to latch on to the needs, the way of life, of the younger generation. We have to take note of how they are living and expressing themselves, in work and leisure, and in their home lives, and bring ourselves into line with their demands.'[131] Individual mills looked to embrace synthetics, improve design and accelerate production. 'One of the most spectacular changes has been in the way things have speeded up', one Bradford weaver said in the *Ambassador*. 'Modern living demands an unceasing quest for new ideas, and at the same time modern science has put many more fibres at our disposal … So the speed at which you can convert new ideas into cloth is really important.'[132]

Sulzer weaving machines

The synthetics revolution and the new Mod styles, coupled with unrelenting competition from Italian and Japanese woollen manufacturers, forced the Yorkshire mills to modernise or face closure. Italy was a fierce rival in the ladies' trade. The Italians offered 'women's cloths for export having attractive colours and designs, and being sold at prices that make them popular with customers and especially with big ready-made garment manufacturers abroad'.[133] The British woollen industry was roughly divided into two segments: the 'mass producers of competitively priced medium quality cloth whose main markets are in the U.K.' and the 'specialised producers of high quality, more expensive cloth, many of whose main markets are overseas'. Some 800 Yorkshire woollen manufacturers carried on a regular export trade, many selling more than half their output abroad and some small firms up to 90 per cent. The mills that made cloth for 'the multiple tailors and similar bulk buyers' sought to become more efficient by updating their equipment. The smaller mills that produced short runs for prestige customers like the Paris couture houses focused on improving their capabilities in 'cloth design and marketing'.[134]

Abraham Moon and Sons sat somewhere between these extremes. In 1965, Brian Beckett went to work at Netherfield Mill after moving from Staffordshire to Yorkshire. 'In those days, there were loads of mills', he recalled. 'You could get a job anywhere.' At age eighteen, Brian started in the weaving shed, which was under the general oversight of Albert Holmes, now production manager, and the direct supervision of weaving manager Arthur Leach. The shed was outfitted with 124 power looms, including pre-war machines made by George Hodgson in Bradford and postwar equipment by George Hattersley & Sons in Keighley. There was no formal apprenticeship system, so Brian had a seven-week crash course on how to operate the shuttle looms with senior weaver Jack Thompson. 'When Jack said you were okay', Brian explained, 'you were put to work.' Jack divided up the orders among the sixty weavers, each of whom operated two looms. Brian remembered the great variety of fabrics.[135] The fancy cloths included blended tweeds that went into coats for C&A Modes, double cloths for ladies' and children's coats, and tartans for skirts. Plainer staple fabrics included khaki for the army and steel grey flannel for men's trousers, school uniforms and the like (figure 5.9). In a typical 39-hour week, each weaver would make five pieces of cloth that were seventy-two yards in length.[136]

The mill towns of the West Riding were mindful of a new loom that could dramatically increase the productivity of the weaving sheds. Sulzer Brothers, an engineering firm in Winterthur, Switzerland, with a British division, had perfected a shuttleless weft insertion method, termed 'projectile'. Large American weaving mills such as J. P. Stevens were early adopters, followed by British weavers in cotton and man-made fibres, including Courtaulds.[137] The worsted mills of Yorkshire used the new weaving machines to make large runs of fine fabrics.[138] The woollen mills, which produced cloth with a coarser appearance, were slower to adopt. The rapidly changing commercial environment of the 1960s convinced them it was time to invest in sales and design—and the new technology. The *Ambassador* wrote of the Sulzers: 'The Yorkshire wool textile industry is in the throes of a revolution comparable to that which, nearly two hundred years ago, established Britain as the leading manufacturer and exporter of woollen and worsted cloth.'[139]

In 1965, Abraham Moon and Sons ordered twelve Sulzer weaving machines at £7,000 each for a total expenditure of £84,000.[140] They were delivered two years later and four additional machines were purchased in 1972.[141] In the Aireborough district, James Ives & Company had ordered Sulzer weaving machines in 1956 after mill owner E. Kenneth Ives saw them in a Philadelphia textile mill.[142] The Peate division of the West Riding Worsted and Woollen Mills as well as L. J. Booth and Company in Rawdon also invested in Sulzers. The Springhead Mill Company (Guidseley) Ltd, William Murgatroyd & Company and Edward Denison (Yeadon) Ltd did not.[143] 'Three of our competitors already had these Swiss looms', Arthur Walsh recalled. 'One competitor had them for ten or twelve years, so they were churning things out. We were late, but we weren't the last by any means. Of course, most of the mills with the fast looms were the mills that did plainer work. In plainer work, you get longer runs. If you're doing fancy things, the customer might just buy two pieces.'[144] Fancy work required that the looms be reset for every new pattern. It was thought this was best done on the older power looms, which had greater flexibility.

Exactly what was so innovative about Sulzer weaving machines? Weaving is a technique for making cloth on a loom by interlacing horizontal threads called the weft through tensioned vertical threads called the warp. During the Industrial Revolution, the mechanisation process included powering the flying shuttle—a long bobbin, or pirn, wound with weft yarn and moving back and forth across the shed of warp yarns. Further improvements led to the automatic loom, which, among other things, wound the bobbin and loaded the shuttle. The self-shuttling

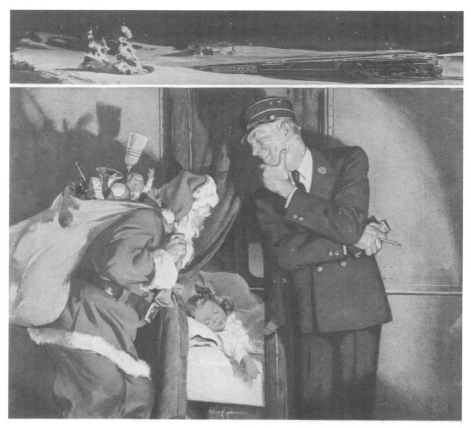

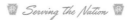

'twas the night before Christmas...

... And this little miss asleep in a cozy roomette, her stocking hung high in great expectation, symbolizes the spirit you find aboard Pennsylvania Railroad's great East-West Fleet at this season of the year. Step into cars aglow with good cheer and good fellowship . . . glance at the array of beribboned gifts heaped high in racks and rooms.

Stroll into the Dining Car and enjoy the festive foods of the day . . . get a good night's sleep in a comfortable bed—arrive refreshed. And above all, enjoy the peace of mind that comes from knowing your train will get you there—conveniently, and at low cost. All aboard . . . to a Merry Christmas and Happy New Year!

PENNSYLVANIA RAILROAD
Serving the Nation

5.9 Railway conductors around the world wore woollen uniforms tailored from blue serge, often made by British mills. Author's collection: Pennsylvania Railroad advertisement from *LIFE*, 1947.

automatic loom was widely adopted by Yorkshire woollen mills, but Netherfield Mill preferred the older power loom, which was better suited to fancy patterns and flexible production. Shortly after the Second World War, Sulzer Brothers announced the first viable shuttleless loom.[145] The engineers who designed this new weaving machine dispensed with the conventional shuttle in favour of a small one-directional projectile called a weft carrier, which gripped the weft yarn and pulled it across the open shed of warp yarns to the far side. There, the yarn ends were tucked into the selvedge and the weft carrier was sent back, via the underside of the shed, to collect another yarn. The replacement of the two-way shuttle with the one-way weft carrier permitted weaving that was faster, quieter and more economical.[146]

The Sulzer weaving machine had several advantages for a mill that made long runs of fabrics for the fashion multiples and shorter runs for a great number of small customers. First, a Sulzer weaving machine was easier and faster to programme, facilitating more delicate and intricate patterns than a conventional British power loom.[147] In addition, on the shop floor productivity dramatically increased because each weaver could tend to six looms, rather than two. Finally, the quality of the fabric was better. Fifty years later, these improvements were crystal clear to Norman Renton, who supervised the mending department at Netherfield Mill from 1966. With the old Hattersley shuttle looms, Norman needed twenty menders to repair irregularities in the cloth. Once the Sulzer weaving machines were installed, the number of menders dropped to seven.[148]

As the science writer Edward Tenner had noted, many technological improvements often create greater problems than the ones they were created to solve.[149] The Sulzer weaving machines installed in Netherfield Mill were no exception. The equipment was so efficient that the mill had to find new products to make. 'These were very fast looms', Arthur Walsh explained. 'You couldn't alter the things to run at a slow speed. So we needed to improve the quality of the yarn. We had to make certain that the blend of raw materials that we used produced yarn that was better.'[150] The Sulzer, which was ideal for the rapid production of plain weaves, required strong yarns. To maximise the capabilities of these machines, Abraham Moon and Sons started to make curtain fabrics out of Courtelle, an acrylic fibre from Courtaulds.[151] Ironically, the Sulzers, which had been purchased to bolster woollens against the onslaught of synthetics, pushed Netherfield Mill deeper into the arena of man-made fibres.

Fashion handwriting

The unbridled enthusiasm for the Sulzer weaving machine made some cautious mill owners uncomfortable. Abraham Moon and Sons had hundreds of customers in dozens of markets that wanted a wide choice of new designs every year. There was value in design experimentation and the development costs grew in direct proportion to the customer's appetite for variety. Subtle differences in colour, texture and handle owed much to the yarns. The firm that hoped to snare orders from French couture houses had to bear the cost of carrying a wide selection of unusual yarns, so it could produce small runs of highly varied fabrics at short notice. Mills specialising in variety had to stick with flexible production, the mainstay of the tweed tradition.

Some Yorkshiremen thought the woollen industry simply needed a better public image. The Woolmark campaign sought to educate the consumer, but it was the cloth buyer who decided whether woollens were 'in' or 'out'. The NWTEC publicised British cloth to foreign buyers by emphasising its British origins, but there was no consensus among woollen men on the best iconography for the industry. The symbols of British heritage that would prove to have marketing value in the twenty-first century seemed out of sync with the Mod zeitgeist of the 1960s. 'Typical British images, such as London buses and Bobbies, Beefeaters and Big Ben', reported the *Ambassador*, 'are not much in favour among cloth manufacturers.'[152] In the era of synthetics and Sulzers, many Yorkshire woollen manufacturers were keen to put aside tradition and project an image of modernity.

One discussion centred on the crucial relationship between design and sales. As Edward Symonds, the managing director of Reville, had argued decades earlier, some mill owners believed that the product was the only thing that mattered. A good product—a fabric that was distinctive and suited to its purpose—would stand out and catch the eye of the cloth buyer. 'British woollens should sell themselves through their quality and their fashion handwriting', argued one manufacturer from Dewsbury. The challenge for the Yorkshire mills was to create woollen and worsteds suited to the London-driven culture of the swinging 1960s. How could a tweed mill pique the interests of Mod fashion brands such as Mary Quant and Biba by Barbara Hulanicki? How could a provincial industry impress a Continental fabric buyer who had been bedazzled by invitation-only fashion shows in Paris, Milan and Rome? The Dewsbury manufacturer put it simply:

> A good designer has the flair to think up fantastic ideas and then bring them down to a workable basis. Price is secondary to good design. A good buyer will look at a cloth and only if he likes it will he ask the price. On the whole, though, buyers tend to play safe unless one can give them an idea in what cloths to style. If clothiers, fashion houses and merchants could collaborate more closely with cloth manufacturers this would be to the woollen industry's advantage.[153]

The sales manager from one Huddersfield woollen mill was of a similar mind. No one in the Yorkshire woollen industry hired consultants to conduct market research, but everyone understood the power of the handshake and the value of face-to-face interactions. 'Someone from the mill must visit each market regularly, someone who has good taste, and can interpret a trend—not necessarily a designer', ventured this Yorkshireman. 'The ideal situation is where a designer and a salesman can work closely together.'[154] Another Huddersfield mill reported that it was 'working much closer with customers than ever before. They come to us now because they know we're flexible and will experiment for them.'[155]

Arthur Walsh steered away from opinion forums on the state of affairs in Yorkshire. Speaking out in public about business practices had little appeal to the managers at Abraham Moon and Sons. As in earlier days, they kept to themselves and did not put all of their eggs in one basket. Netherfield Mill met the challenges of synthetics, knitwear, youth culture and cheap imports in its own time. The mill found its way by sticking to variety and flexibility. Arthur purchased Sulzer weaving machines, but he also expanded the export trade and invested in design-led sales. Technology was just one expedient. As Frank Walsh, the first technological impresario of the firm had known, new equipment was a tool, a means to end. It was the 'fashion handwriting' that really mattered.

6 Adjustments

Over 1000 pattern lengths had been ordered for next Winter's season. The number of pattern orders caused problems, but although our aim was to produce a smaller range this was difficult when forecasting and selling in the men's, ladies and export trades. (Arthur Walsh, 1978)[1]

The 1970s were a time for reflection at Abraham Moon and Sons. The UK seemed to be unravelling at the seams. The decade witnessed labour unrest, state interventions into the economy, government mandates such as the Three-Day Work Order, and the infamous Winter of Discontent. The textile industry entered a period of steep decline. Consumers no longer saw clothing as an investment, as had the young Barbara Sutcliffe during the great scarcity after the Second World War. Few teenagers and young women had a taste for classic tailoring and outfits that could be kept for years. Some consumers invested in mix-and-match classics from Jaeger or the new Country Casuals multiple, but many went for the slouchy look: easy-care knitted garments in inexpensive synthetic fibres (figure 6.1). The 1970s were an exuberant celebration of polyester, moving from bell-bottoms and safari jackets to glittery glam-rock styles, to the body-clinging disco look and to sports clothing as everyday attire. For the most part, the traditional British textile and clothing industries did not adapt well. At the end of the decade, few Yorkshire woollen mills were left in operation.

Abraham Moon and Sons was one of the survivors. In the postwar era, managing director Arthur Walsh had faced a world barricaded by tariffs and invaded by man-made fibres. The challenges of the late 1960s and early 1970s—synthetics, knitwear and Italian imports—foreshadowed greater troubles to come in the 1980s, especially in the domestic market. Arthur carved out a place for Netherfield Mill in the new world order with the help of forward-looking agents and an expanded staff in design and sales. He and finance director Kenneth Rawson took a defensive position in a declining industry.[2] It was the firm's longstanding commitment to family control, low profits, technological innovation, flexible production and design innovation that helped Netherfield Mill get through.

THE CARNABY STREET LOOK IN COURTELLE

IT'S London's Carnaby Street look — this time in washable Courtelle — part of the Group 1 collection by John J. Hilton.

The colours are wild — whoever thought of teaming publicity pink and Chelsea blue — and wistaria with Windsor green was Carnaby Street inspired — but of course!

Describe them anyway you like but if you're the 'in' group the word is 'unreal.'

Prices of the Group 1 collection are, from left to right: $18, $20, $23, $20.

Fashions are available at retail stores all over Australia.

24

WOMAN'S DAY with WOMAN, July 11, 1966

6.1 The synthetics revolution ushered in an era of easy-care clothing that was an excellent fit with the youthful styles of Carnaby Street in London; here this style together with Courtaulds' Courtelle are promoted via a Group 1 collection by John J. Hilton of Australia. Author's collection: *Woman's Day with Woman* (11 July 1966), 24.

Time for reassessment

In 1969, the British government published a special report on *The Strategic Future of the Wool Textile Industry*. Completed by W. S. Atkins & Partners, the report was commissioned by the wool subcommittee of the National Economic Development Office, a government body created in 1962 to monitor British economic performance and known by the nickname 'Neddy'. (The industry subcommittees created by the National Economic Development Office were called 'Little Neddys'.) The study, which took more than a year to complete, was based on questionnaires sent to companies; site visits to 200 firms in Scotland, the West of England and Yorkshire; and fieldwork in major markets such as Austria, Canada, Denmark, Sweden, the United States and West Germany. The Atkins Report became the document against which all developments in the British wool industry of the 1970s were measured.[3]

The Atkins Report made fourteen major recommendations for wool, woollens and worsteds. The recommendations covered production, manpower, technology, management, organisation, capital, output, sales and marketing. The last three areas are most salient to our discussion of Abraham Moon and Sons. Manufacturers were urged to standardise their ranges, but not 'to such an extent that variety of designs and quality of finished fabrics is perceptibly impaired'. They could 'combat their weak selling position by specialising more in the products and services they offer, thus increasing run lengths and efficiency, and decreasing the number of competitors in any given product'. Marketing was singled out as an important area for development; there 'should be more direct selling to customers particularly overseas'.[4] As Netherfield Mill adapted to the troubled times in the industry, Arthur made a deliberate decision to maintain the company's commitment to variety. A new focus on marketing evolved to meet changing demand, both at home and abroad. These adaptations were made in the face of several major threats, the first of which was the triumph of man-made fibres.

In 1970, the journalist on the Yorkshire beat for the *Financial Times* referenced the Atkins Report on wool and a parallel study on cotton in his discussion of major transitions underway in British textiles. Man-made fibres had elbowed their way into Lancashire and Yorkshire, challenging the dominance of traditional materials. More than half of the fibres used by the British textile industry were man-made and the amount was expected to grow to three-quarters by 1980. The Lancashire cotton mills were the hardest hit because vertically integrated textile companies such as Viyella set up fibre plants, spinning mills, weaving mills and garment factories in their backyards. The cotton industry suffered an additional blow with the rise of inexpensive clothing imports from low-wage economies that had built up their textile and garment industries after the Second World War.[5]

British fibre makers like Courtaulds were large public companies that embraced modern business practices. These giant firms were a stark contrast to the small private firms that dominated woollens and worsted manufacture. Family firms like Abraham Moon and Sons had been producing cloth in the same Yorkshire communities for generations. They did one thing and did it well, whether spinning yarn or making wool fabrics. The fibre companies, which were run by professional managers rather than family owners, sought to generate profits through advanced engineering, vertical integration and consolidation. Firms such as Viyella and Courtaulds looked to control a large part of the supply chain, from fibre production to packaged product. In emulation of American fibre giants such as E. I. du Pont de Nemours and Company and the Celanese Fibers Marketing Company, British fibre makers invested heavily in direct consumer marketing. In an early form of ingredient branding, the names of proprietary fibres such as Courtelle (Courtaulds' acrylic) and Terylene (ICI's polyester) were put before the public on clothing tags, on bolts of fabric, in window displays, in print advertisements and through television commercials. Everywhere that British consumers went, they were promised a convenient, stylish new world made possible by test-tube fabrics.

Initially, the new man-made fibres looked to be a good fit for the Yorkshire mills, whether they made worsteds or woollens. As we saw in Chapter 5, Arthur Walsh and the production team at Abraham Moon and Sons had learned to combine man-made and natural materials, creating blended fabrics that were highly competitive in price and performance. Wool-rayon blends were ideal for C&A Modes, the principal end-user of cloth from Netherfield Mill, during its relentless drive to undersell Marks and Spencer (M&S) in everyday fashion. The rivalry between these two high-street giants was a boon to Netherfield Mill, which at times sold more than half of its output to the makers-up producing garments for C&A Modes.

Another challenge for Yorkshire weavers was the growing popularity of knitwear made from synthetic yarns.[6] Knitwear had an easy-going look and feel that was a good match for casual attire and it could be produced at great speed. Weaving mills normally needed six to nine months to take a fabric from order to delivery and three to seven months to fill a repeat order. As the fashion cycle picked up, high-street multiples looked for lower-cost apparel and expected deliveries within six weeks. The knitters, who were equipped with high-speed machines, had an advantage. 'The buyers are screaming for knitteds', cried the wholesale merchants in Golden Square and the City.[7] The Bradford worsted trade, which made fabrics for the multiple tailors, responded to changing tastes by introducing knitted fabrics for men's suits. They also tried to put on a modern face by venturing into celebrity endorsements. One worsted manufacturer beefed up its image with Sulzer machines, snazzy patterns and promotions that featured the debonair actor Roger Moore, who from 1962 to 1969 had starred as the secret agent Simon Templar in the television series, *The Saint*, and who would be cast as James Bond in 1973.[8] Double-knit fabrics entered menswear and became one of the signature looks of the 1970s.

Easy-going fashions were discussed in *Your Future in Clothing*, a forecast for UK apparel consumption by the Little Neddy for the garment industry. The report predicted a rise in apparel purchases particularly at the lower end of the market. Total UK expenditure on clothing was expected to grow from £2.1 million in 1968 to £2.7 million by 1978. The most notable development was the buying power of baby boomers. Teenaged girls and young women aged fifteen to twenty-nine constituted just over one-quarter of the total adult female population, but they accounted for more than 50 per cent of ladies' apparel purchases. This demographic reality shaped clothing forecasts for the decade. Experts predicted a 5 per cent growth in sales of ladies' knitwear and separates and a 10 per cent decline in ensembles and suits. The latter were made from Yorkshire woollens.[9]

The new trends in apparel consumption went hand-in-hand with the continued transformation of the British high street. Multiples and variety chains such as Burtons, C&A Modes, F. W. Woolworth, M&S and Richard Shops were snatching more and more trade away from small apparel shops. Between 1950 and 1966, their share of the UK clothing market had increased from 27 per cent to 48 per cent, from around one-quarter to nearly half. Although growth was predicted to slow down, it was expected that these types of retailers would come to dominate clothing sales with a 55 per cent market share by 1978. The upshot was that textile mills and garment manufacturers who wanted business from the multiples had to 'accept the disciplines which such relationships demand'. Suppliers had to make products to the customer's specifications, rather than designing the ranges and putting stock patterns on offer. This was a new way of working for woollen mills. Early on, the innovative M&S chain had pioneered this new approach to merchandising—known as 'specification buying'—and other major high-street retailers followed suit to one degree or another.[10]

Everyone in the textile industry agreed that 1970 was an annus horribilis.[11] The rapid growth of the man-made fibre industry had resulted in overcapacity, which in turn encouraged consolidation. Animosity grew between the fiercely independent woollen and worsted mills and the fibre giants that had developed textile empires in the Yorkshire countryside. Since 1960, Yorkshire wool men had warily watched the Glasgow-based J. & P. Coats, the dominant global player in thread manufacturing, diversify from sewing supplies into textiles, clothing and retailing. Back in 1965, the expanded firm, known by the cumbersome name J. & P. Coats, Patons & Baldwins Ltd, had acquired Pasolds Ltd, manufacturers of Ladybird children's wear (figure 6.2), Dombros Knitwear and Chilpruf underwear and, two years later in May 1967, it swallowed Jaeger Ltd, the manufacturer-retailer of up-market outerwear and

6.2 The Ladybird brand produced woollen skirts for girls and woollen trousers for boys. Author's collection: advertisement from a British magazine, mid-1960s. Courtesy Shop Direct Ltd.

knitwear that used fabrics from Netherfield Mill. By January 1968, Coats Patons, operating under a streamlined name, controlled the West Riding Worsted and Woollen Mills, which included Nunroyd Mills, the old Peate facility in Guiseley. With the acquisition of Peates, one of the fibre giants had established a presence in the

Aireborough district.[12] Throughout the Yorkshire woollen industry, mills focused on their strength—'flexibility and variety in design'—and on new efforts to shorten the 'production pipeline' in response to the 'rapid cycles' demanded by the fashion trade. Those who ignored the 'fashion handwriting' were pushed out of business.[13]

Mill and customer

At Abraham Moon and Sons, Arthur Walsh eyed the mill's order book with some concern. The changing dimensions of the market for wool fabrics meant that Netherfield Mill operated on a hand-to-mouth basis. In June 1970, Arthur told the board of directors that the mill had a mere six weeks of work on hand.[14] Important customers included two London-based makers-up for C&A Modes: Cecil Silver Ltd— 'juvenile clothing mkrs.' with offices in Classic House at 174–180 Old Street in the City of London and a factory in Romford, Essex—and Reggie & Company Ltd, a subsidiary of the conglomerate, Cope Allman International (CAI). Run by the feisty Benny Schmidt-Bodner, the Reggie company were 'mantle mfrs.' with offices on Margaret Street near Oxford Circus and production facilities in Shoreditch in London's East End.[15] There were also substantial customers in Glasgow and Manchester, notably the children's wear manufacturer Poole Bell, which made clothing for C&A Modes.[16] In total, the business for C&A Modes accounted for about 50 per cent of the mill's output.[17] Orders for 'contract cloth'—flannel shirting for the British army and heavy coatings for uniforms worn by employees of the General Post Office and British Rail—were consistent and kept the looms running.[18] Arthur travelled around the country to drum up business, compiling orders from here and there. But no one could stop the synthetics knitwear boom that was eating away at the market for woven fabrics.

This period saw the Victorian industrial heritage of the Aireborough district slip away. By 1971, a large percentage of people in Aireborough—40 per cent— travelled to work outside the area. A major reorganisation of local government throughout England led to the establishment of the Leeds Metropolitan District Council, commonly known as the Leeds City Council, in 1974. The Aireborough Urban District Council and comparable entities were amalgamated into the new organisation and the Aireborough towns, including Guiseley, Rawdon, and Yeadon, became part of greater Leeds. These changes paralleled significant transformations in Aireborough's woollen industry.[19]

The 1969 closure of Moorfield Mills, established in Yeadon in 1877 by William Murgatroyd, was especially disturbing to people at Abraham Moon and Sons. In the early 1920s, the management at Moorfield Mills had included Charles Moon, the grandson of Abraham Moon. There were blood relations between the Walsh and

Murgatroyd families; Moorfield's founder was the great uncle of Barbara Walsh née Sutcliffe. Like Netherfield Mill, Moorfield Mills made moderately priced woollens, but the firm was unable to compete against imports, synthetics and changing fashions.[20] Then in June 1972 the premises of Springhead Mills, the modern successor to the company mill where Abraham and William Moon had processed cloth in Victorian times, was sold. The plan was to break up the property into small industrial units for let.[21]

Changes were also afoot at Nunroyd Mills, the old Peate facility in Guiseley. In May 1972, the parent company, Coats Patons, shut down poor performers in the West Riding Worsted and Woollen Group and reorganised the Woollen Division around two profitable subsidiaries: Kelsall & Kemp Ltd and J., J. L., and C. Peate (Guiseley) Ltd.[22] The new unit was called Peate, Kelsall and Kemp Ltd.[23] In January 1975, this unit was merged with the jersey knitter W. C. Forrest to form yet another subsidiary, West Riding Fabrics.[24] Working under this umbrella, Nunroyd Mills continued to make moderately priced tweeds for customers like M&S.[25]

In 1972 and early 1973, there had been an exceptionally strong global demand for wool fabrics. The Japanese were particularly keen on wool, importing vast quantities of the material for their own textile mills and coveting British tweeds.[26] But in late 1973, the global woollen boom became the global woollen slump.[27] The downturn dovetailed with the 1973 Oil Crisis caused when Arab petroleum producers embargoed Canada, Japan, the UK and the United States in protest against American support of Israel in the Yom Kippur War. In Britain, the start of the international crisis was followed by a strike on the part of the National Union of Mineworkers, and the Three-Day Work Order was initiated by Prime Minister Edward Heath as a measure to save electricity and preserve the nation's coal stocks. When the strike ended and the normal working week was restored in March 1974, the Yorkshire mills returned to full-time operation but firms at the lower and middle segments of the market struggled. Indicative of larger trends, Joseph Beaumont Junr Ltd, a small woollen manufacturer in Huddersfield, closed down one of its mills due to a slump in orders, cash-flow shortages and skyrocketing prices for raw materials.[28] In the UK generally, unemployment and inflation rose. By the summer of 1975, Britain was in the midst of a major recession, as the annual increase in the cost of living reached 26 per cent.[29]

Even in these tough times, Abraham Moon and Sons maintained its commitment to low dividends and the reinvestment of profits in new technology. The Edward Heath government introduced a Scheme of Assistance for textile manufacturers under the Industry Act 1972, providing financial aid to mills that wanted to upgrade their equipment. Modernisation funds were made available to the wool, woollen and worsted industry, with the idea that both individual firms and manufacturers' associations would contribute a larger portion of the redevelopment costs. In the first stage of the scheme from July 1973 to December 1977, the government invested £15.9 million in the industry, with more than £10 million going to Yorkshire and Humberside. With phase one projects still underway, a second assistance programme was initiated. In the second phase from November 1976 to December 1979, the government invested an additional £6.5 million in the region.[30]

Abraham Moon and Sons did not seek financial assistance from this scheme, but remained fiercely independent. During the mill's early days, Abraham Moon, Isaac Moon and Charles Walsh had supported the Chamber of Commerce and the Guiseley Conservative Club, but trade associations, government committees and group promotions were not to their liking. Independent thinking ruled the roost at Netherfield Mill. Arthur Walsh could not fathom how government intervention could repair the foundering economy or do much for woollen mills that had not been updated for decades. Yorkshire had more than its share of obsolete mills that were more like technology museums than modern factories. After years of neglecting the physical plant, these manufacturers could not keep up with changes in the market. Arthur believed that it was up to the individual firm to adapt. To meet the distinctive challenges of the 1970s, Abraham Moon and Sons looked to design, sales and exports.

In Golden Square

Netherfield Mill had a small staff and everyone wore more than one hat. Sales and design fell under the purview of designer Dennis Moulson and assistant designer John Richmond, who looked after 'mill customers' such as the remaining merchants and the smaller makers-up. Arthur attended to the major accounts such as Cecil Silver, Reggie & Company and Poole Bell, which ordered large quantities of fabrics to sew clothing for C&A Modes.[31] With an eye on popular fashion, he realised that the London market, which was headquarters for the major multiples and home to countless makers-up, required special attention. Initial efforts focused on urging the London agent, Victor Smith of Fowler & Orr in the City, to do more.[32] But it became apparent new ideas were needed. This realisation ultimately brought Trevor Brann to Abraham Moon and Sons.

In 1973, Trevor Brann joined Abraham Moon and Sons as an agent based in London. After being discharged from the army in 1959, this native son of Newcastle was about to follow his father, a surveyor, into a career with British Petroleum when a cousin who worked in a Bradford dye house made some off-the-cuff remarks that piqued his interest: 'the woollen merchants run the country' and 'it's all down to the City'. Trevor headed up to London to seek his fortune among the wholesale

6.3 The House of Dormeuil, built in 1926, dominated Golden Square in London, which was also known as 'Woollen Square'. Courtesy of Dormeuil.

merchants. As was the custom in those days, he went door to door in search of work. He got lucky at 14 Warwick Street, the Golden Square headquarters of Dormeuil Ltd (figure 6.3), which in earlier days had stocked ladies' woollens by Netherfield Mill. While awaiting his interview, Trevor sat in the impressive wood-panelled showroom, flipped through the *Wool Record* and the *Ambassador*, and educated himself about wool fabrics. Ultimately, he charmed his way into an entry-level position. The ambitious young man fancied a job in Hong Kong selling cloth to the Chinese, but instead found himself in the basement of the House of Dormeuil. The personnel manager told him, 'You have to start work at the bottom.'[33]

That basement was occupied by the Dormeuil department responsible for assembling bunches and swatch books for the house. Besides exporting cloth, the merchants in Golden Square supplied fabrics to high-class tailors in London and the provinces. Each merchant was known for the 'handwriting' of its collection, which was carefully assembled for the customers with a certain style and colour theme in mind. In the language of our own time, each merchant 'curated' a range of fabric choices for its particular customers. The bunches and swatch books were the embodiment of those curatorial efforts and were an important sales tool for the tailors. Cutting up worsted patterns allowed the young Trevor to handle a wide range of materials and to learn about the look and feel of the fabrics.[34]

By around 1960, the ladies' ready-to-wear industry was taking off, with more women having the financial wherewithal to dress in style. London stores such as Selfridges Ltd on Oxford Street, Debenham & Freebody (Debenhams Ltd) on Wigmore Street and John Barker & Company Ltd on Kensington High Street led the way with fashionable designs, and the multiples offered spin-offs at lower prices. In the wake of the devastating wartime bombing of the City, the West End had become the major London market for fabrics and fashion. By the time Trevor arrived, the West End was brimming with showrooms for all of the major British clothing labels, each looking to capture a share of the growing market for ready-made clothing. Dormeuil mainly sold worsteds for men's suits, but the house wanted to engage with the promising ladies' wear business. Identified as a young man with potential, Trevor was bumped upstairs to the women's department, which handled fabrics for haute couture and high-end ladies' tailors. He worked as a sales trainee, helping an eccentric salesman who carried large bolts of fabrics to the customers so they could see the whole cloth. The ambitious young man longed for a job in Paris, but one of the senior buyers, Frank Defeu, took him aside and explained the realities. The Paris assignments were reserved for members of the Dormeuil family and other Frenchmen. But there were other options. Defeu was keen on woollens and he had convinced Dormeuil that it was a fortuitous time to expand the woollen ranges by looking to Yorkshire and Scotland. Couture customers such as Lachasse, the up-market ladies' tailors in Mayfair, and Cristóbal Balenciaga's couture house in Paris wanted British tweeds. In planning his Yorkshire reconnaissance mission, Defeu asked Trevor, 'How would you like to go to the mills? Would you like to be a trainee buyer?'[35]

The next six months cemented Trevor's enthusiasm for all things woollen. On trips north, he and Defeu settled into the comfortable George Hotel on St George's Square in Huddersfield. In hunting down the best woollens in and around the Colne Valley, they found a number of mills that could produce fabrics to Dormeuil's demanding expectations, including but not limited to Smith & Calverley Ltd, in Lindley; John Crowther & Sons (Milnsbridge) Ltd; John Knox & Sons Ltd, in Silsden; Pearson Brothers Ltd, in Golcar; Dobroyd Ltd, in New Mill; C. & J. Hirst & Sons Ltd, in Longwood; Hirst & Mallinson Ltd, in Longwood; and John Lockwood & Sons Ltd, in Milnesbridge. Trevor soaked up the atmosphere in Huddersfield, which had been making fine woollens and worsteds since the days of the Victorian design impresario John Beaumont. One evening, he and Kenneth Lockwood of John Lockwood & Sons stood on a hill looking down on the Colne Valley. Admiring the factories, the billowing smoke and the twinkling lights, the textile manufacturer waxed on about the 'Valley of Velour'. Trevor came to understand the Yorkshire pride in the region and the product. Dealings with John Crowther and C. & J. Hirst taught him important lessons about velours and tweeds comparable to those made by a highly competitive little mill in Guiseley—Abraham Moon and Sons.[36]

But the great wholesale merchants that had long reigned over the fabric supply in the fashion system were losing ground. Retailers such as M&S and C&A Modes ruled the high street, and the makers-up that supplied them with clothing kept their costs down by purchasing fabrics straight from the mills. The traditional supply chain, with powerful merchant-tastemakers connecting textile mills to the market, was on its last legs. There would always be room for a few up-market merchants like Dormeuil to serve high-end tailors, but this was the exception that proved the rule. Defeu was near retirement and he worried about Trevor's future. He encouraged his protégé to leave Dormeuil and get started as a mill agent who sold cloth directly to the remaining merchants and mainly to the growing numbers of makers-up.[37]

In 1962, Trevor secured a place with Robert Taylor & Sons, woollen agents at 1 Golden Square who represented Yorkshire mills such as John Lockwood & Sons. During the early part of the war, the agency had offices at 16–17 Watling Street near St Paul's Cathedral, but following the Blitz attacks on London, from 1942 onward the firm operated in the West End.[38] Trevor's routine at Robert Taylor & Sons was to call on thirty or so customers per day with mill samples. Over time, a longstanding customer of Taylors, a West End velour merchant named Joseph Mortner, of J. Mortner Ltd, put two and two together: John Lockwood & Sons made fabrics with the same yarn counts as Abraham Moon and Sons. Trevor knew this type of cloth inside out and could talk about it in his sleep; he also had a personable manner that might sit well with Arthur Walsh. Acting on a hunch, Joe Mortner introduced the two men. The timing was perfect. Trevor was looking to enlarge his business and Arthur wanted to expand his firm's London presence. Arthur asked, 'Would you work for Moons?'[39]

In 1973, Trevor took over the Robert Taylor business and also began selling cloth on commission for Abraham Moon and Sons. His assignment was to complement the work of the main London agent, Victor Smith of Fowler & Orr. His immediate charge was to build up business with the makers-up and the multiples in the ladies' wear trade.[40] There was a wide field in which he could pitch woollens. Hundreds of garment factories were scattered all around England, many of which had some type of London presence. The list of well-known ladies' wear manufacturers included L. Harris (Harella) Ltd, founded by tailor's apprentice Lew Harris in London in 1919. With factories in England and Scotland, this large clothing exporter sold ladies' costumes and coats branded with labels that read, 'It's a Dream … its Harella.'[41] Another venerable London fashion house was Windsmoor (London) Ltd, established in 1933 as a wholesale clothier specialising in ladies' coats. By 1938, the Windsmoor trademark was found on tailor-made jackets and coats sold by department stores. In the late 1950s, the firm helped to advance the 'shop-in-shop' concept whereby concession boutiques sold Windsmoor lines in department stores. Recognising the purchasing power of baby boomers, the company launched the Planet collection for younger shoppers in 1979.[42]

Trevor tempted these firms with tweeds from Netherfield Mill and courted other labels or brands that made classic clothing: Alexon, Country Casuals, Deréta, Eastex, Jaeger, Mansfield Originals and Mona. All of them needed moderately priced woollens with a style element. From Golden Square, Trevor could easily and frequently call on their fabric buyers. For example, the Windsmoor buyer had an office just a few short blocks away, near Liberty's. The founder-owner of Mansfield Originals Ltd, Frank Russell, appreciated Netherfield Mill's inexpensive nylon-wool blends. Three patterns by Abraham Moon and Sons—Dallas, Houston and Texas—were used by the company's East End manufacturing facilities to make apparel with the French-sounding label, Cache d'Or.[43] Introduced in 1975 as a line of 'co-ordinate designer casualwear', Cache d'Or was a favourite among busy female executives, who wanted to 'look as sleek, secure and successful as men without looking *like* them'. They shopped at Oxford Street stores like Selfridges for Cache d'Or office attire, which looked stylish, feminine and professional.[44]

It is worth looking at a few important customers for what their stories tell us about everyday fashion, the high street and Yorkshire tweeds in this period. Deréta and Eastex were two well-established mid-market labels owned by Ellis & Goldstein Ltd, an old-guard ladies' coat manufacturer with factories on Brick Lane in London's East End that found itself adapting to the new retail environment.[45] Country Casuals was a spanking new brand and retail concept that was launched by the textile giant Coats Patons to capture an under-served market: the provincial shopper. All three brands were major users of British woollens, including fabrics made by Abraham Moon and Sons and handled by its young London agent, Trevor Brann.

The story of Ellis & Goldstein shows how Britain's largest manufacturer of ladies' outerwear adjusted to the major changes in consumer taste and high-street retailing over the course of the twentieth century. Ellis & Goldstein was formed as a public company in 1936 to continue the garment business of an older firm of the same name. The East End manufacturer made Elgora ready-to-wear until the Second World War, when, like most makers-up, it began to produce army uniforms.[46] Just after the war in 1946, Ellis & Goldstein acquired the Eastex Manufacturing Company and related ladies' wear firms.[47] By 1951, the company was selling coats and suits under the trade names Elgora and Eastex and dresses under other labels.[48] New showrooms were opened in Manchester, Leeds and Glasgow to accommodate the hungry postwar market.[49] In 1956, there were further acquisitions and the Deréta label was added to the product portfolio.[50] As Trevor remembers, this label was the creation of one Mr D. Horne and one Mr Ritter, who cobbled together 'D' and 'Ritter' to create the trade name Deréta. The original firm, D. Ritter & Company, was an apparel manufacturer-wholesaler with showrooms in Kent House, just north of Oxford Circus. By the time it became part of Ellis & Goldstein, Deréta was a recognised label among consumers who liked traditional tailored apparel and its showroom was a major destination for retail buyers who were shopping the London market. [51]

During the 1960s, Ellis & Goldstein looked to capitalise on the advent of casual styling. The firm understood that American ready-to-wear led the way with informal styles and turned to the United States for a tutorial. In late 1966, Ellis & Goldstein signed a licensing agreement with Bobbie Brooks Inc., a large American casualwear manufacturer, to make a colour-coordinated line for teenagers and sell these in boutiques at British department stores.[52] The high hopes for the Bobbie Brooks subsidiary were deflated when the American-designed casualwear failed to win favour with British shoppers, but Ellis & Goldstein liked the shop-in-shop concept.[53] By 1973, the firm had 226 boutiques that sold the Deréta, Eastex, Dumarsal and Laura Lee labels in department stores and independent shops, and a total of 1,100 sales outlets. The company began exporting the in-store boutique model to Austria, Canada, Sweden and West Germany.[54] The switch from manufacturing alone to the integration of manufacturing and marketing enabled Ellis & Goldstein to downplay its wholesaling business, lower costs and increase profits. The integrated approach led to better coordination between the factory warehouse and the retail store, allowing for rapid-fire restocking and the 'instant reaction to the customer's likes and dislikes'. Store displays filled with the latest styles were suited to the burgeoning middle market, where shoppers increasingly believed that fashion should be at their fingertips.[55]

In 1973, Ellis & Goldstein noted the strong consumer preference for casualwear and the growing tendency among younger shoppers to buy new clothes every season.[56] The idea of clothing as a 'pick-me-up' had gestated in the previous decade with Mod styling, synthetic materials, knitwear and the rising standard of living. The new attitude was the polar opposite of clothing as an investment, the philosophy of consumers who wore tweeds. By 1977, Ellis & Goldstein reported that sales of heavier outerwear—the coats and suits worn by middle-aged tweed lovers—had fallen, while sales of 'lighter, less tailored articles' were on the upswing.[57] The popularity of comfortable, casual styles was also reflected in the growth of Ellis & Goldstein's knitwear division.[58]

Shortly after he started working as a commission agent for Netherfield Mill, Trevor paid a visit to the Brick Lane facility of Ellis & Goldstein near the tube stop in Aldgate East. The regular London agent, Victor Smith, had had little success with them. Trevor hit the ground running with Ellis & Goldstein, talking up tweeds as just the thing for the classic look. Through his efforts, Abraham Moon and Sons began to make tweeds and other fabrics for the Deréta (figure 6.4) and Eastex labels.[59]

The somewhat different story of Country Casuals linked Abraham Moon and Sons to a new marketing concept: the brand-as-store aimed at a particular demographic segment. In the early 1970s, a few astute retailers acknowledged the absence of mid-range clothing in the ladies' market. As living standards improved, a certain type of consumer outside London came to want traditional woollen clothing that was neither high-end nor low. There was a demand for apparel that fell somewhere between the put-together looks of pricey labels such as Jaeger and the sensible, practical clothing in the ladies' department at M&S or the trendy, inexpensive attire at C&A Modes. As we saw in Chapter 4, Jaeger had pioneered the merchandising of stylish high-street clothing suited to the damp, chilly British weather, showcasing an up-to-date woolly look in ultra-modern shops. By the 1970s, Jaeger was the favourite shopping destination for an up-market crowd based in London. Margaret Thatcher, who needed well-tailored, colour-coordinated clothes for her high-profile job as a rising star in the Conservative Party, often shopped at the Jaeger store at the corner of the King's Road and Flood Street close to her home in Chelsea.[60] Outside London, some affluent younger women, aged twenty-five to forty, aspired to the Jaeger look but could not afford the price.

Country Casuals was created to fill this gap. Coats Patons, which owned Jaeger Holdings, launched the new multiple to offer the Jaeger look for less. Established in 1973, Country Casuals modified the tailored style favoured by Margaret Thatcher to suit the provincial woman who by habit made biannual shopping trips to London to refresh her wardrobe. Her favourite store was Aquascutum, which stocked tweeds in classic styles. Like Jaeger and Aquascutum, Country Casuals offered mix-and-match separates that could be coordinated to create an outfit 'all of a piece' but did not seem fussy. The line was created by Torun Marks, a Swedish designer who knew how to create classless clothes suited to a wide range of customers. Country Casuals started with fifty stores on the high streets of provincial towns, from Perth in the north to Truro in the south. There was a conscious decision to have no Country Casual stores in London, as the metropolitan market was already well served with shops.[61]

Country Casuals was a step forward in lifestyle merchandising, bringing the expensive, well-coordinated look to the middle market. One early publicity photo for Country Casuals showed a genteel blonde beauty posed against an English country house with an elegant golden-haired hound by her side.[62] In many respects, Country

6.4 Deréta advertisement for a tweed coat in pure new wool, from the *Sunday Telegraph*, 14 October 1979. Author's collection.

Casuals anticipated the popularity of the country weekend look sported by the young Princess Diana as she found her place in the public eye. The line was directed to the aspirational shopper who admired the royal family and fantasized about country life on the great Scottish estates. In August 1981, the media immortalised the style in the famous photographs of the honeymooning royal couple, Charles and Diana Windsor, at Balmoral Castle in the Scottish Highlands, showing the Princess in a sporty hunting suit designed by Bill Pashley in brown check tweed.[63] Country Casuals offered apparel that captured this look: respectable, durable and comfortable. The brand promoted a soft, pretty ladylike image that included Paisley dresses, silk bow ties, felt bowler hats, imitation Chanel suits and Donegal tweed jackets. This tweedy look used woollens from the Yorkshire mills, including Abraham Moon and Sons.

Fortuitously, Country Casuals was founded in the same year that Trevor Brann started working as an agent for Abraham Moon and Sons. He was quick on the uptake and served as the matchmaker for Country Casuals and Netherfield Mill. The older London agent, Victor Smith, worked in a very conventional way; he mainly called on the merchants and a select group of makers-up. Trevor went knocking on everyone's doors: the merchants, the makers-up *and* the multiples. His entrée to Country Casuals was velour, the soft 100 per cent wool fabric used for ladies' winter coats. The mill had a strong velour business with a number of makers-up, which gave him talking points with James Laden, the fabric buyer for Country Casuals.[64]

In the years between 1973 and 1983, when Trevor was getting started with the mill, the high street was in the midst of another makeover. The small clothing store, run by the independent shopkeeper who stocked goods suited to the local taste, was pushed out of the picture as the multiples, department stores and variety chains gained control of the apparel market. 'In the 1970s, there was giantism on the high street', Arthur Walsh recalled. 'You're talking about these huge conglomerates, and big companies like M&S and C&A who were buying huge quantities.'[65] Collectively by 1977, the large retailers—multiples, department stores and variety chains— accounted for 70 per cent of clothing sales. Of this figure, the multiples took a 53 per cent market share, while department stores and variety stores had 17 per cent. Major retailers such as M&S decided what to stock based on their perceptions of consumer needs in terms of price, quality and style. Serviceable style mattered far more than cutting-edge fashion.[66] C&A Modes was still known for affordable fashion geared to teenagers and families on a budget. By the early 1970s, the chain had ventured into menswear and competed heavily with M&S and the Great Universal Stores (GUS), a major mail-order retailer. C&A Modes became *the* place where suburban boys, who eschewed the multiple tailors as stuffy and old-fashioned, bought their first suit for their first job interview.[67]

In their relentless drive to undercut each other's prices, the giants of the high street increasingly looked to low-wage economies for textiles and garments. 'They were in a garment price war', Arthur observed. 'The cheap imports were driven by lower-priced currencies.'[68] Many retailers, aware of the need to reduce costs, introduced styles that were easier and cheaper to manufacture than tailored styles. Although Aquascutum, Burberry, C&A Modes, Jaeger, M&S and Windsmoor all stocked the traditional tailored coat, by 1976 this garment, which had long been the mainstay of the British woman's wardrobe, was only one of several outerwear options. Most high-street stores were filled with 'unstructured' coats in colourful synthetic blends and crocheted capes that were essentially glamorous cardigans. Consumers found that the cloth poncho, like knitwear, was forgiving in terms of fit, style and price. Women were turning away from classic tweed and velour coats—to the detriment of the British woollen industry.[69]

Moving into design-led sales

Market conditions in the 1970s led Abraham Moon and Sons to develop a new approach to design management. Dennis Moulson, the technically oriented design chief who had steered Netherfield Mill through the early years of synthetics, recognised the need for fresh talent. His thinking aligned with customers' needs. Whether they were selecting material for the home trade or for foreign markets, fabric buyers now had to be more careful in their choices. They could not 'afford to buy wrong' and were vocal about wanting face-to-face meetings with the people who designed the cloth.[70] William Neill Johnstone (known as 'Bill' Johnstone in the trade), a designer at R. G. Neill & Son Ltd in Langholm, in the Scottish Borders, lambasted the woollen industry for telling design trainees to 'look at what we sold last time, study it carefully and then vary it slightly'. The growing export market and the heightened domestic competition warranted something better than 'last season's ideas'.[71]

By this time at Netherfield Mill, John Richmond, who had come on board as assistant designer in 1962, sought out a change of routine. He felt that his 'eyes were getting old' and that he 'wanted to do something different'. He gradually moved into sales, where his design experience proved to be an asset in dealing with the customers. John knew exactly what could be produced vis-à-vis the pattern, the construction, the colour and the cost. His technical skill as a designer made conversations with the customers go smoothly and helped to build confidence in Netherfield Mill.[72] John's interactions with the customers stood in stark contrast to those of the agents, who had no technical training. Most of the agents came to the mill twice a year, gathered samples and spent four to six weeks on the road chasing

6.5 The University of Leeds continues to train designers for jobs in the textile industry; here, students plan fabric patterns, 1969. Reproduced with the permission of Special Collections, Leeds University Library: LUA/PHC/002/100.

after customers. They sold cloth by making the fabric buyer feel special, rather than helping him or her find the material that was best suited to the line. They did not have the technical background to see how the design might be adapted to the customer's needs.[73]

In 1975, Dennis Moulson recruited a bright young talent for Netherfield Mill, hiring his neighbour, Martin Aveyard—the son of an electronics engineer—as the new assistant designer. As a student in the textiles department at the University of Leeds (figure 6.5) from 1971 to 1974, Martin focused on design management with a technical bent, but found his coursework to be detached from reality. Philosophical differences among tutors generated debates over whether the University of Leeds should emphasise practice or an academic approach. These disagreements had little impact on areas like medicine or purely academic subjects such as history, but were disruptive to interdisciplinary fields such as textile design, which involved accounting, colour studies, drawing, fabric construction, history, mechanics and theory.[74]

Martin found that the Leeds textile curriculum provided students with little or no exposure to trade shows or to the fashion collections in London, Paris, Milan and Rome. Trade shows had become important sites for information exchange and customer development. They were the modern equivalents of the ancient cloth halls; exhibitors displayed their samples and liaised with fabric buyers and clothing designers who had travelled from far and wide to conduct research for next season's lines. The Spring Prêt-á-Porter show in Paris was a case in point. Members of the British Fashion Export Group, a subset of the Apparel and Fashion Industry Association, first set up displays at this fair in 1963. It was expensive to buy space and put up a booth, but major gains were to be had. 'Whereas other firms sit back and wonder what to do', one ladies' wear manufacturer told the *Wool Record*, 'we benefit by going to the Continent to pick up news, ideas, rumours. It all leads to business.'[75] In the long run, the Paris display by the British Fashion Export Group generated orders worth £800,000.[76]

Textile trade fairs provided similar opportunities. In the second half of the twentieth century, these fairs supplanted the urban wholesale districts as the major commercial spaces for fabric promotion and sales. Frankfurt's medieval textile fairs aside, most fairs showcasing a wide range of goods developed from the early twentieth century onwards. The Milan International Samples Fair opened its gates in April 1920. It started out as a modest-sized trade show with 1,233 exhibitors and grew by 1957 to include 13,000 exhibitors and more than 93,000 buyers from around the world.[77] Individual countries had national trade fairs to promote their home industries, including textiles and fashion. For example, Austria had the Dornbirn Export and Industries Fair; established in 1949, this summer event exhibited Austrian fibres, textiles and ready-to-wear to buyers from central Europe and elsewhere in the West. As discussed in Chapter 5, the launch of the European Economic Community in January 1958 and the reduction of tariffs between the member states in January 1959 had created the Common Market comprised of Belgium, France, Italy, Luxembourg, the Netherlands and West Germany. The move towards the liberalisation of trade (furthered by the establishment of the European Free Trade Association by Austria, Denmark, Norway, Portugal, Sweden, Switzerland and the UK in 1960) fostered a new approach to trade fairs, whereby local and regional shows were supplanted by international events.[78] Messe Frankfurt, a state-supported entity that organised trade exhibitions in Frankfurt am Main, West Germany, seized the moment and created Interstoff, a unique international trade fair for European textiles.[79]

Launched in July 1959, Interstoff would for a time be the most important textile trade fair in Europe. (The name combines 'Inter' for international and 'Stoff', the German word for textile.)[80] The 1963 edition of Interstoff had 311 exhibitors who attracted 7,000 visitors from thirty-six countries over the first three days.[81] Fabric buyers and clothing designers no longer had to go from mill to mill or from merchant to merchant. Located in the heart of Europe, Interstoff provided one-stop shopping. In November 1974, the *Guardian* described the fair as a 'show case for every type of cloth' and a 'melting-pot for a variety of different people: manufacturers, marketing directors, fabric research scientists, fabric designers and of course the fashion designers who come here to see what colours and textures are going to be the trend a year ahead and to gain inspiration for a new line and look'. Visitors could see 'a mass of tweeds', spy on the Italian knitters, learn about new DuPont fibres like Qiana and study the trend forecast by the International Wool Secretariat (IWS).[82] These types of reconnaissance missions were of growing importance for Yorkshire mills that looked to expand their horizons. Martin Aveyard was happy to leave behind the ivory tower and put down roots at a mill that valued this type of work.[83]

Some British woollen mills had participated in Interstoff since the early 1960s through an export drive coordinated by the National Wool Textile Export Corporation (NWTEC), in which the Board of Trade encouraged manufacturers to display their products at international trade fairs by paying for the space and the 'cost of the small cubicle'.[84] Working to help the woollen and worsted industries see the advantage of the government's Joint Venture Scheme, the NWTEC facilitated the participation of forty British mills at Interstoff in May 1963. 'Interstoff is described as an "appointments fair" at which United Kingdom principals sell to overseas buyers in closed cubicles', the NWTEC told member mills.[85] At Interstoff, 'the buyers really wade in and buy—which is very different from some other exhibitions where the exhibitor gets a shower of inquiries from would-be agents and a few requests for samples or half pieces'.[86] By the end of the decade, British participation at the biannual Interstoff fair included nearly fifty mills that made various types of fabrics, mainly for women's wear. Twenty-one woollen mills had booths at the autumn 1969 edition of the fair.[87]

By the time Martin Aveyard was settling in at Netherfield Mill, the British woollen industry acknowledged that Interstoff was 'the premier textile fair' and 'a fashion forum for the world' (figure 6.6).[88] The May 1975 show, which featured fabrics for Spring/Summer 1976, welcomed 23,000 visitors from sixty-five countries to see 800 exhibitors.[89] Special displays linked the fabrics to fashion trends. For example, the IWS had a special Woolmark pavilion filled with thousands of woollen and worsted samples from around the world, coordinated to illustrate the increasingly popular 'natural' look.[90] The NWTEC's involvement in the fair, which by this time was supported by the British Overseas Trade Board, followed an established pattern. In November 1977, more than a hundred British textile companies, including sixty-nine wool fabric manufacturers, displayed their products in a space arranged by the NWTEC. Buyers from North America, the Middle East and the Far East browsed through the British section, taking in 'sports jacketing

6.6 Cover of the official Interstoff catalogue, 1980. Courtesy of Messe Frankfurt.

fabrics, particularly tweeds, and … tartans for ladies' wear'. By this time, Interstoff was just one among several trade fairs on the NWTEC calendar. Among these were another one organised by Messe Frankfurt: the Heimtex show featuring textiles for the interiors market, a new area for many British woollen mills.[91] Abraham Moon and Sons participated in Interstoff for almost four full years, from the 38th edition in November 1977 to the 44th edition in November 1980.[92] Martin remembered minding the booth with Arthur Walsh and the agent from West Germany. Business was slow and those representing the mill wondered if going to this massive show for ladies' fabrics was a good investment.[93]

Martin Aveyard had started as an assistant designer in much the same way that Trevor Brann entered the woollen trade: cutting up fabrics into swatches. One of Martin's first jobs at Netherfield Mill was to make swatches and paste them in the large reference books that still constitute the basis of the mill's design archive. When a customer ordered samples, he processed the request by costing the order, calculating how much yarn was used in each pattern, preparing the lengths for shipment and going around the mill to check on the progress of the order. He got to know everybody on the shop floor, developed a good understanding of the types of cloth made by the mill and learned which customers preferred what type of cloth.[94]

Martin's arrival at Netherfield Mill coincided with new threats and opportunities to the woollen industry. On the downside, he witnessed the death throes of the merchants, the relentless march of knitwear and the 1978–79 Winter of Discontent. On the upside, he saw the potential of the multiples to reach the expanding middle market, the craving for stylish clothes in everyday life and the foreign passion for British high-street fashion. Journalists reported sightings of chic Parisians, mad about the classic tweed look, streaming across the English Channel on cheap excursion tickets to stock up on 'terribly, terribly traditional British' clothes from Burberry, Jaeger and M&S.[95] It seemed as if everybody except the British wanted British tweeds. This reality coincided with Arthur Walsh's heightened attention to foreign markets. The export cocktail was not to everyone's palate but Martin was young and open-minded, and he developed a taste for it.

Italian invasion

All over Yorkshire, there was a wringing of hands in the woollen and worsted industries over foreign competition, mostly from Italy. The home market, which had been at Yorkshire's fingertips since the Second World War, had been captured by foreign mills. In 1975, imported woollen cloth accounted for 34 per cent of the UK home trade; by 1978, the figure had climbed to 55 per cent.[96] The trend towards casual attire favoured woollens over worsteds, but unfortunately for the Yorkshire mills, most of this demand was met by Italian imports. The enemy were the woollen men of Prato, Italy.

The Prato woollen manufacturers dominated the three largest European markets—Italy, France and West Germany—and were hungry for more. In the early to mid-1960s, they went after trade in the Common Market and virtually put the wool textile industry of the Netherlands out of business.[97] After the UK joined the Common Market in 1973, the Italians fixed their eyes on the little island nation that had the most highly developed clothing industry and retailing system in Europe. Almost immediately, Italians stepped up their exports to Britain. By 1974, more than 64 per cent of the 'wool-predominant cloths' imported to the UK came from Italy.[98]

The Prato textile manufacturers had gathered steam during the 1960s, the years of the 'Italian economic miracle', during which their industry was recovering from the Second World War. As the rest of the world was swept up in the synthetics revolution, Prato benefited from Italian snobbery about man-made fibres. Italian mills, makers-up and consumers preferred cotton and wool to artificial materials.

Many British mill owners believed that Prato's extensive 'black economy'—the widespread reliance on outworkers who laboured in their homes or in small workshops—was the secret to its success. By 1982, Prato had 10,000 textile firms, mainly small family-run operations, and 65,000 textile employees, being an average of only 6.5 employees per firm. Because of the outwork system, the Prato woollen manufacturers had low overheads and avoided the social welfare costs associated with employing a large workforce in a mill.[99]

Concerned about the long-term effects of imports, British textile manufacturers looked to public authorities for some protection as goods passed through customs.[100] Textiles were a major topic among policymakers concerned with the balance of trade between the advanced industrial economies and the developing economies. In 1974, the General Agreement on Tariffs and Trade set up the Multi-Fibre Arrangement (MFA) to rationalise global trade in textiles and garments. The MFA permitted bilateral agreements that allowed a developed country to set quotas on imports of textiles and garments from an emerging economy.[101] In 1977, as talks were underway to renew the MFA, the British textile and clothing industries cried foul. Manufacturers were angry about the large volume of imports to the UK from emerging economies, but their protests were in vain. Between 1978 and 1979, the volume continued to grow; textile imports expanded by more than 20 per cent and clothing imports by 33 per cent. The man-made fibre industry was greatly affected. Courtaulds, the UK's largest textile conglomerate, announced 5,000 lay-offs spread across fibre making, spinning, knitting and apparel manufacturing. In the same period, some 7,000 jobs were lost in the British wool textile industries.[102] In wool fabrics, the major threat came not from the developing economies, but from European competitors such as Italy.

As the British textile industry struggled to cope with the flood of imports, some observers laid the blame on the high street. Britain's well-developed retail network, with so many department stores, variety chains and multiples, made the UK an easy mark for clothing importers. 'In other words a few calls in the London head offices of the major chains are enough to secure nationwide distribution of imported products', wrote the *Financial Times*. 'In France, by contrast, the fragmentation of the retail sector means that much more legwork is required to achieve a similar penetration.' The barrage of foreign-made textiles and clothing associated with the MFA was exacerbated by the Common Market's decision to permit additional textile imports, first from low-wage Mediterranean countries such as Greece, Portugal, Spain and Turkey, and then from China.[103]

Arthur Walsh took matters into his own hands. One day, he walked into an unassuming office building in Golden Square with grave determination. He wanted to track down George Portland, a commission agent who sold British woollens to the large ready-to-wear industry in West Germany.[104] By the time Arthur landed on Portland's doorstep, British woollen manufacturing was in crisis. The formidable triumvirate—the synthetics revolution, casual knitwear and Italian woollens— was marching across Yorkshire and mills were falling like dominoes. The Prato competition appeared unstoppable—except for one fact. In West Germany, a clash of cultures boded ill for Prato. The Germans were disillusioned by the Italian habit of missing delivery deadlines and they looked to British mills as a reliable alternative.[105]

Arthur recognised that the survival of Abraham Moon and Sons depended on his ability to capitalise on the Italians' shaky record with the Germans. He needed an entrée into the large market for heavyweight menswear fabrics in West Germany, and Portland had the right connections. He had a long history that tied him to central Europe. Born in Bratislava in 1920 with the Jewish surname Pollack, he had escaped Hitler's invasion of Czechoslovakia in 1938 by way of Italy and France, finding his way to England where the Free Czechoslovak Army was encamped. In 1944, he participated in the Normandy landing with the 11th Armoured Division of the British army, known as the Black Bull, and after the war he became a competitive swimmer in the British Army Championships. Once demobilised, Portland landed a job with a Golden Square export merchant in 1947 and in the following year went to work for a City merchant who exported to South America. From a well-to-do background, Portland was fluent in the native tongues of his father, a Slovak, and his mother, a Hungarian, and he also spoke English, French, German and Italian. There was no better fit for the international woollen trade than this multilingual Jewish émigré with a clipped German accent. Portland was a 'larger than life' character with a colourful past—all of this made for a good salesman. With a loan from a Piccadilly banker, he eventually set up his own export agency in Golden Square.[106]

Portland was honest and blunt, and Arthur was smart and genteel. Their talents and personalities were in balance and they struck a deal. Portland took on Abraham Moon and Sons, while continuing to represent a few other British mills. Initially, the effort to introduce tweeds from Netherfield Mill to the West German menswear market did not go smoothly. After three disastrous seasons with very few orders, Portland and Arthur had a heart-to-heart talk. The mill's prices were right, Portland said, but all of the 'shetlands and tweeds contained Nylon'. The customers in West Germany were not only pernickety about delivery, but they were also sticklers about product quality. Put simply, the German man who dressed like a peacock was a wool snob and it was imperative that Netherfield Mill make cloth to the standard of the International Wool Secretariat, that is, from 'pure wool IWS, otherwise we shall not succeed'. Arthur agreed to give all-wool menswear fabrics a try. Within two years,

'Moon was known in Germany and business increased fast', due the quality of the all-wool cloth and Portland's 'knowledge of the market'. Thus began a decades-long relationship between Netherfield Mill and one of its most important agents in foreign markets.[107]

Export drive

The late 1970s were by no means easy for Abraham Moon and Sons. The recollections of Gary Martin Smith, who started at the mill straight out of school at the age of fifteen in 1976, are particularly apposite. He followed in the footsteps of his father, a mill employee who had gone from the yarn store to production management. After a starter job collecting wool waste from the mull spinners, Gary went into a permanent position in the warehouse, which shipped orders out of the mill. He got to know the customers' names and preferences, much as did Martin Aveyard through his work on the range books. When Gary started, some 10 per cent of the mill's output was plain cloth created for uniforms and 75 per cent of the output was double cloth intended for children's outerwear, mostly for C&A Modes. Many of the double cloths had a brightly coloured pattern on the front and a purple backing made from waste material on the reverse. These fabrics went into children's coats sewn up by customers such as Cecil Silver, Reggie & Company and Tinyfolk Wear Ltd, another London maker-up.[108] Many of the little coats eventually found their way onto the racks at C&A Modes.

The mill's export drive stands out in Gary's memory. The desperate situation from 1973 onward prompted Arthur Walsh to grab his winter coat and go worldwide to cold climates looking for orders. The hunt took Arthur and Portland on travels through Eastern Europe. In 1976, they ventured behind the Iron Curtain to Budapest, Hungary, in search of business. While trying to strike a deal with the state-owned Hungaretex company, the two men found themselves in the presence of state buyers, all women, who plied them with vodka to negotiate a better deal on the price on winter coatings.[109] The quest for exports also took Arthur across the Atlantic Ocean to more genteel surroundings in Canada, where the cold weather guaranteed the popularity of tweeds. Canada had long been an important export market and it would continue to be a major destination for the mill's fabrics in the decades ahead. Clothiers such as Golden Brand Clothing Inc., Peerless Clothing Inc. and Coppley Noyes & Randall Ltd, as well as the Canadian retail conglomerate Dylex (an acronym for 'damn your lousy excuses') used cloth from Netherfield Mill to make men's jackets. Arthur found a growing interest in heavier cloth for coats with S. Cohen & Company Ltd, a menswear manufacturer based in Montreal.[110]

Arthur also made inroads in the United States, which had always been a tough nut to crack because of the prohibitive tariffs. Through the mill's New York agent (see Chapter 7), he established connections with Norman Lichtenstein, who ran the Norlic Import Company at 1290 Avenue of the Americas, not far from Rockefeller Center. The Norlic Import Company imported and sold British woollens, including women's wear fabrics, making this firm an ideal customer for Netherfield Mill.[111] In other instances, the route to the American market was circuitous. Arthur discovered a treasure in Eisenberg International, based in San Fernando, California. This company ordered large quantities of woollen fabric—500 to 600 pieces in one go—to be shipped directly to the Commonwealth of the Northern Mariana Islands in the north-western Pacific Ocean. When these islands became a territory of the United States in 1975, they were exempted from federal immigration and minimum wage laws in order to encourage manufacturing. In the early 1980s, a large garment industry developed on the island of Saipan, using Asian immigrant labourers to sew garments bearing the label 'Made in the U.S.A.'[112] By 1986, the Northern Mariana Islands were given special duty-free trade status, meaning that products made there entered the United States without any customs fees.[113]

In the late 1970s, Arthur, together with the designers Dennis and Martin, and production manager Danny Spence, all travelled abroad to evaluate the market. Martin accompanied Arthur to the United States and West Germany, visited France with Dennis and then went to France on his own. It was an exciting time for the budding designer, who was finally getting into the woollen business and meeting customers.[114] He looked around Yorkshire and thought that most of the mills were not very creative. They approached design in a formulaic way and asked, 'Why should we change?'[115] Besides contributing to the general education of the young designer, the overseas research trips brought insights about the global marketplace into the company.

Martin recalled how his interactions with Ferry Grad, the mill's French agent, were especially influential on his development as a creative thinker. Abraham Moon and Sons did a prosperous trade exporting woollens to the fashionable French menswear market through Grad's Paris-based commission agency, Copaex. An Egyptian Jew by birth, Grad spoke fluent English and dressed like an elegant Frenchman.[116] European customers had preconceived notions about what constituted British style and Grad had developed a distinctive 'mix and match' approach, selecting from Italian, French and British fabrics to create the British look as imagined on the Continent.[117] He took Martin under his wing and became the young man's mentor. The Copaex offices were located in a stylish Art Deco building just off rue Montmartre in the heart of the commercial second arrondissement, on the Right Bank not far from the Louvre. The showroom was filled with fabric samples from numerous mills, carefully arranged by pattern and colour. Copaex sold fabrics to French clothing manufacturers at the middle to upper end of the market. Important customers included the YSL Diffusion line made by the Bidermann Group; Daniel Hechter (figure 6.7 and figure 6.8); and Vestra. Grad employed three stylists who liaised with the special customers on a routine basis. Mario Beconi

6.7 Daniel Hechter advertisement, 1976. Author's collection.

Daniel Hechter le sait, on ne peut utiliser
que ce qu'il y a de mieux : des tissus en pure
laine vierge contrôlés Woolmark.
        C'est la pure laine vierge qui leur donne
leur tombant, leur allure, leur souplesse.
(La veste 640 F environ, la jupe 370 F environ).

**WOOLMARK
LE MEILLEUR DE
LA LAINE.**

Pour tous renseignements : Secrétariat International de la Laine, 23 avenue de Neuilly, 75116 Paris. Tél. 758.11.31.

6.8 One of a two-page Daniel Hechter advertisement for the new look in unstructured menswear made from pure new wool. Author's collection: *Paris Match*, 1538 (17 November 1978), 76–7, courtesy The Woolmark Company.

handled YSL Diffusion, Gianni Caporale dealt with Daniel Hechter and Geles Prezpowlowski took care of Bidermann.[118]

Copaex served as an 'idea crucible' for French clothing designers, who often visited the showroom for brainstorming sessions on their new collections. Grad and his stylists would help each designer coordinate a new ensemble, perhaps pairing a jacket of Italian cloth with British trousers in fabric by Abraham Moon and Sons.

The emphasis was always on bright, bold hues. Grad had a taste for flamboyant colour and he dared to create unusual juxtapositions. He was always looking and learning, and encouraged those around him to follow suit. Martin remembered how Grad urged him to keep an open mind. The British designer found himself trailing the French agent around the Paris flea markets, where they would pick up vintage clothing to use as inspiration pieces. Walking down rue Montmartre, Grad told his British friend, 'Open your eyes, look at everything.'[119]

Grad's integrated approach to design and sales left a mark on the young Martin, who had a natural flair for colour. As a schoolboy, his favourite art lessons had dealt with colour and, as a teenager, he honed his chromatic eye by painting with oils. Few Yorkshire woollen designers of the older generation had an interest in colour and colour theory. A solid mathematician, Dennis Moulson created technically competent woollen patterns, but he never looked at the yarn colours to study how they related to each other. For Martin, the entire design process began with colour. As his confidence grew, the new designer began to discuss his ideas on colour in woollen ranges with the Copaex stylist, Caporale, who appreciated the exchange. Other British mills would go to Paris and show their patterns to Copaex without asking for feedback, but Martin found that a give-and-take approach helped him back in Yorkshire. He started to do things differently as he found his footing at Netherfield Mill.[120]

Martin developed a sales tool that laid the foundation for a whole new way of interacting with the customers. Back in the designers' office at Netherfield Mill, he created mood boards, or forecasts (Colour Plate 11), that embodied his ideas for next season's fashion trends. The mood boards were comprised of swatches from the previous seasons that were glued on to craft paper, along with suggestive imagery from colourful postcards. The manufacturer of the fabric was irrelevant. The cuttings might have come from Netherfield Mill, from its competitors, or from vintage clothing. The goal was to create a thematic prediction of fashion trends around which to have a conversation. Martin hit the road with the new sales tool in hand. In Canada and the United States, he and the agents showed the mood boards to customers who were used to seeing a pre-set group of ranges and pointing to the cloth they wanted. Martin gave the customers the opportunity to play off his ideas about emerging trends and, going from there, to specify which colours and patterns might work with their plans for the new season. He put new questions on the table, 'What do you want? What can we make for you?' These open-ended queries replaced the show-and-point method that was the norm in fabric buying. Here was an innovative approach to interactions between the mill and the customer. This was the beginning of design-led sales, a boutique or bespoke way of designing that empowered the customer and put them at the centre of the decision-making.[121]

Under Grad's influence, Martin took Abraham Moon and Sons down another new path that would serve the mill well in the future. Few Yorkshire mills sold their cloth under a label or a brand and Grad saw this as a missed opportunity to build an identity for the business. He encouraged Martin to develop a unique trade symbol that could go on woven labels to be sewn into French garments alongside the manufacturer's label. Co-branding and heritage resonated with the status-conscious French fashion consumer. The new label consisted of two crossed Union Jack flags and the words 'Yorkshire Tweed by Abraham Moon'. Thus in the years around 1980, the mill had ventured into co-branding, using a theme from British heritage.[122] It was a sign of things to come.

The trips abroad fortified the mill's commitment to variety in design and flexibility in production. Following one tour of foreign textile mills, Arthur Walsh and Danny Spence reported to the board that the weaving department at Netherfield Mill was in top form, but suggested adjustments to the ranges. The foreign mills 'were producing very fancy cloths' but because they offered less variety, their development and production costs were low. The directors debated whether to reduce the scope and breadth of the line. The designer Dennis Moulson was adamant about variety, which had been the lifeblood of the mill since the days of Charles Walsh. In Dennis's view, variety was the key to customer satisfaction. A wide selection of patterns was needed to satisfy brands like Jaeger and Windsmoor (figure 6.9), which were always looking for something distinctive: 'in the higher end of the ladies trade customers wanted cloths confined and therefore a larger range was required'. Arthur reiterated the need for a wide selection of patterns and for 'the design of the range' to meet 'market requirements'.[123] This was the polar opposite of what the Atkins Report had recommended, but the decision to stick to its commitment to diversity would serve the mill well.

The overseas missions also paid off in terms of sales. By the late 1970s, exports accounted for a major portion of the turnover at Abraham Moon and Sons. For the financial year ending March 1977, these were 19 per cent of sales. By March 1978, the figure had grown to 27.5 per cent. An even more dramatic increase occurred in the nine months between April and December 1978, when exports totalled 40 per cent of sales. Finance director Kenneth Rawson analysed the numbers and predicted that, in the 1978–79 financial year, exports would exceed £1 million.[124] The largest export markets were France, Canada and the United States.[125]

The sales upturn at Abraham Moon and Sons preceded the British economic crises of the late 1970s. In 1978–79, the Winter of Discontent saw crippling strikes that ultimately, in the spring of 1979, led to the ascent of Margaret Thatcher as Prime Minister. She was known for her classic sense of style, but it was generally not a good time for high-street fashion. The economic downturn of September

HARRODS
A GREAT BRITISH
TRADITION

Boldly elegant three-piece
and scarf (not shown). Checks
of Brown/Camel or Beige/
Cream, with plain bolero.
10 to 16. **£137.95**
Windsmoor Room. First Floor.
Personal shoppers only.

Windsmoor

6.9 By gentlemen's agreement, brands such as Windsmoor expected textile mills to provide them with 'confined' patterns that differentiated their lines from those of the competition. Courtesy of Yorkshire Fashion Archive: British *Vogue* (May 1977), 160.

1978 to February 1979 dealt hammer blows to high-street retailers and the weather made thing worse. The early months of 1979 were the coldest winter since 1962–63, bringing in blizzards and keeping people away from the shops. The freezing cold start to 1979 was followed by unusually warm weather at the end of the year. When the weather was balmy, nobody wanted to think about buying a winter coat, even a floppy poncho.[126]

If weather woes were not trouble enough, by 1980 the British fashion industry seemed out of touch with what women actually wanted to wear. As consumers rejected garments with 'uncomfortably tight' waists and 'space-age' shoulders, retailers were burdened with large inventories of unsold stock. Even the small shops that traditionally catered to the wives of businessmen, barristers and the like, saw their trade reduced by half. Stagnation on the high street stretched back along the supply chain, affecting the apparel factories, the button and zip-fastener makers, and the textile mills.[127] If the early years of the decade had been troublesome, the closing years were a nightmare.

While Britain suffered through the Winter of Discontent, the weaving machines at Netherfield Mill hummed away. In April 1979, the mill was overbooked with orders. The production team looked for ways to boost the output of the Sulzer weaving machines and contemplated three shifts to keep the mill running around the clock.[128] By November, the boom had levelled off. Canadian orders had slowed down, but the mill expected a steady income from 'contract work' on uniform cloth.[129] Abraham Moon and Sons had weathered the Winter of Discontent better than most, but its luck was soon to run out.

The question of woollen imports was still a political 'hot potato'. In London, leaders from the Labour Party locked horns with Conservatives from Margaret Thatcher's government. Labour politician John Silkin, the Shadow Secretary of State for Industry, held that the crisis in the woollen industry could turn into a catastrophe. Cecil Parkinson, a Conservative junior minister in the Department of Trade, accused Opposition leaders of exaggeration. 'Whether we like it or not,' Parkinson argued, 'we live in a harsh competitive world and we will not reverse our industrial decline if we permanently shelter the textile or any other industry from these realities.'[130] Later, in a 1980 speech related to the renewal of the MFA, Parkinson got down to brass tacks with the Manchester Chamber of Commerce. 'What the Government cannot do is to regulate fashion changes, protect firms that do not update their designs, protect workers who will not operate modern machines effectively, or generally stop or control imports of textiles from other developed countries, many of which have wage costs far in excess of our own.'[131] Only a textile mill with a history of innovation could clamber out of this morass.

Presentation and marketing

At the end of the 1970s, Abraham Moon and Sons began to think less like a
Yorkshire woollen mill and more like a modern marketer. One prescient discussion
about the future was captured in the board minutes for November 1978. Exports
were growing, contracts for uniform cloths rolled in and the domestic menswear
trade held steady. Business was improving—except for the fact that the 'ladies trade
was poor'. The slouchy knitwear look was taking its toll on weavers and the directors
discussed a strategy. Should Netherfield Mill look down-market for customers?
Design chief Dennis Moulson warned that 'it was a mistake to produce cheaper
cloths for the ladies range as these were not competitive with firms specialising in
cheap cloths', including foreign mills. Netherfield Mill could only lower its prices so
far before the profits would disappear. The board compiled a list of concerns: 'the
excessive size of the Company's ranges, inadequacies in our set-up for showing, lack
of feed-back from the home trade, the question of motivating our London Agents
and greater involvement of the sales force in product planning'.[132]

The practice of making continuous technological improvements to the physical
plant, a policy set by Frank Walsh, meant that Netherfield Mill was a more efficient
operation than many of its Yorkshire counterparts. The machinery was up to date and
there was a noticeable absence of old looms and other museum pieces. But the focus
on technology and the big export drive had diverted some of the firm's attention away
from product design and development. The absence of marketing know-how was
not unique to Netherfield Mill. Historically, the woollen trade had been subject to its
own internal rhythms and practices, being mainly a face-to-face business wherein
deals were struck over a sample case filled with bunches. The NWTEC and the IWS
promoted wool and wool fabrics, but individual firms did little on their own.

Over the course of the 1970s, the rules of the game changed and the commercial
sphere began to take on its modern contours. Milestones included international
trade fairs, catwalk shows, competing multiples, casual dressing, transatlantic jet
travel and inklings of the next wave of globalisation. Like many British woollen
manufacturers, Netherfield Mill needed to find its way through this unfamiliar
terrain. In November 1978, board member David C. Walsh, the younger brother of
Arthur and CEO of Ellis & Everard, a Bradford-based chemical company, hit the
nail on the head when he 'suggested that the Company should have a Market Plan'.
Indeed, one of the great challenges before Abraham Moon and Sons in the ensuing
decades would be 'presentation and marketing'.[133]

7 What's next?

It was becoming more necessary to work with customers. (Abraham Moon and Sons, 1982)[1]

In 1979, the British textile industry acknowledged the importance of fashion by participating in Fashion Fabrex, the new biannual London trade show for fashion and fabrics. The first Spring edition took place in April 1979 at Earl's Court, where 140 textile manufacturers displayed their collections for Spring/Summer 1980. More than 5,000 buyers attended the show.[2] The first Autumn edition, Fashion Fabrex '79, took place in the National Hall at Olympia from 30 October to 2 November 1979 (figure 7.1). The brochure for the latter explained how the show continued the 'ancient tradition of the British Cloth Fair… which was held annually in London for 700 years' and presented 'a wealth of British textile expertise and fashion, alongside friendly competition from the Continent of Europe'.[3]

That autumn, Abraham Moon and Sons was one of forty British woollen and worsted mills that exhibited at Fashion Fabrex '79 in a space created by the International Wool Secretariat (IWS). The goal was to promote the new range for Autumn/Winter 1980–81 under the Woolmark banner of the IWS.[4] Trevor Brann, the mill's young London agent, manned the company's display (figure 7.2).[5] Like the other textile trade fairs, Fashion Fabrex was a place where managers, designers and fabric buyers could look over the range for the next season, and place orders for samples.[6] It was also a mechanism for the mill to get acquainted with the customers and learn more about their needs.

As the textile trade show calendar solidified, Fabrex was advertised as 'Britain's International Apparel Fabrics Exhibition' or 'Britain's International Fashion Fabric Exhibition'. Some of the advertisements implied that Fabrex was the meat in the sandwich between the cutting-edge Première Vision show in Paris, discussed below, and the nuts-and-bolts Interstoff show for ladies' wear fabrics in Frankfurt am Main.[7] Within a few years, the reputation of Fabrex grew, with some 8,000 visitors attending the three-day event. Most visitors were from the UK, but foreign buyers came from Canada, Europe, the Middle East, Scandinavia and the United States.[8] The presence of Abraham Moon and Sons at Fabrex and other trade shows signalled

7.1 Cover of Fashion Fabrex '79 brochure. Courtesy of Abraham Moon and Sons.

a new outlook at Netherfield Mill. Marketing had never been a strong point among British woollen manufacturers, but those mills aiming to capitalise on the changing fashion-industrial complex had to increase their visibility by participating in trade fairs.

Abraham Moon and Sons had spent the 1970s adjusting to the deindustrialisation of Britain and adapting to the first stirrings of modern globalisation. At that time, Netherfield Mill had cast a wide net in search of customers at home and abroad. The quest for new markets continued in the 1980s, accompanied by ongoing reflection. Back in Edwardian times, the designers Charles, Frank and Tom Walsh helped the Moon family to create patterns that resonated in the export trade, particularly in Canada. The mid-twentieth century designers, Albert Holmes and Dennis Moulson, had a strong technical focus that suited the seller's market. In the 1970s and 1980s, major changes to the woollen industry, the British high street and the global fashion system required a special type of design thinking. Martin Aveyard built on his experience with Ferry Grad

7.2 The young Abraham Moon and Sons' London agent, Trevor Brann, on the company stand at Fabrex '79. Courtesy of Trevor Brann.

and helped the mill understand that designers could have profitable conversations with their customers. An expanded creative staff pioneered an active role for designers in sales and laid the groundwork for design-led sales, which was to become a hallmark of the company. Textile trade shows were one important avenue for meeting new customers and for sitting down with old customers to discuss their needs.

Farewell, Cecil Silver

1980 was another bleak year for Yorkshire textiles. In March, the Wool Textile Economic Development Committee—the wool industry's 'Little Neddy'—published a progress report on the state of affairs in wool, woollens and worsteds. The good news was that the steep decline in woollen production that occurred from 1968 to 1975 had levelled off and output had stabilised. However, imports of wool fabrics from Italy had increased dramatically, with no sign of a let up. In previous eras, classic British woollens were world-renowned for quality and design, but in the 1970s, the global reputation of the Yorkshire mills had spiralled downward. The report of the wool industry's Little Neddy faulted uninspired colour and design, non-existent marketing and the failure to follow fashion.[9]

To add insult to injury, the Confederation of British Wool Textiles urged the Yorkshire woollen industry to 'think Italian'. More appropriately, this trade association, formed around 1980 to tackle the industry's problems and convey its concerns to the government, criticised the lack of imaginative British woollen designs and proposed to coordinate an identity makeover. In emulation of the Italians, the idea was to create a new British image for British woollens. Each season, the leading mills were to decide on a common British theme for their displays at the trade shows. Each mill was to interpret this theme in its own unique way, demonstrating its own particular flair for British styling. The hope was to wrestle part of the European trade away from the Italians, starting with imports into West Germany.[10]

Abraham Moon and Sons was already on the export bandwagon under the management of Arthur Walsh. Sales to Canada, France and the United States continued to grow, with 'favourable comments on the new ranges from Germany and France and also from home customers such as Burtons'.[11] The company's German agent, George Portland, was making headway among makers-up and retail brands in West Germany. Japan began to show an interest in woollens from Netherfield Mill. The American Ivy League style, complete with flannel, tweeds and tartans, gained currency among young Japanese men in the postwar era and had been immortalised in a popular style handbook, *Take Ivy*, published in Japan in 1965. During the late 1970s, Ivy League style spilled over to women's wear with the introduction of the 'North American schoolgirl look' for young Japanese fashionistas.[12] The early Japanese orders to Netherfield Mill were for menswear fabrics in subtle colours and designs to use in jackets.[13] Gary Smith, who now works as one of the mill's sales managers, remembered orders from Takisada, an importer-wholesaler that specialised in textiles, that came in through Mike Ueda & Company around 1980. Ueda was an important Japanese agent for British textile mills and Takisada was one of his largest customers.[14]

In contrast, Yorkshire mills that mainly focused on the UK trade did not envision a robust future for their products. In 1979, one of the major woollen manufacturers in the Aireborough district shut its doors. James Ives & Company in Yeadon had been in the hands of the same family since its establishment in 1848. After E. Kenneth Ives died suddenly on his way to dinner at a trade fair in Basle, Switzerland, in September 1967, the firm passed to his widow Elsie Mary Ives, who served as chairman and joint managing director. She was a figure head and some of the men who had worked for her husband ran the operation. For a time, the two Ives plants—Manor Mill and Leafield Mills—continued production, weaving medium-priced woollens for apparel by Marks and Spencer (M&S) and other high-street retailers. But in 1979, the firm ceased operations and closed both mills. Thirty of the company's fifty Sulzer weaving machines were purchased at auction by Italian bidders and found their way to Prato, while a selection of other machinery went to the industrial museum at Armley Mills in Leeds.[15] Manor Mill was demolished in 1980, Leafield Mills in 1983.[16] The signs of ruin were evident all around Yorkshire. In April 1982, David Gaunt, chairman of Reuben Gaunt & Sons Ltd, a worsted and woollen manufacture with facilities in Farsley and Pudsey, shared some startling statistics with his shareholders. Over the past year, 'no fewer than 1280 textile companies failed; an average of about 5 for every working day… These are truly frightening figures and underline the extent to which the textile industry is being laid waste by the artillery of world recession and cheap imports.'[17]

Late in the autumn of 1980, disconcerting news from London rattled Netherfield Mill. At the December board meeting, Arthur Walsh gave his monthly report on orders and made the announcement. 'Our major home customer was closing down and there was no prospect of a replacement during the next six months', stated a board minute. 'We must assume that the next six months will be difficult and reduce costs accordingly.'[18] He was referring to the fact that, after October 1980, there would be no further orders from Cecil Silver, the reliable London customer that made children's wear for C&A Modes.[19] The Jewish garment manufacturer was getting on in years and, given the uncertainties within the trade, he had decided to retire. For decades, the hard-driving businessman had kept his customers on their toes with demands for better quality and lower prices. He was a colourful character with a residence just off the Kensington High Street. He always put on a good show, driving up to a meeting in a battered Ford Cortina instead of his beautiful Bentley. Silver knew how to make a deal.[20] The effect of his firm's closure was devastating for Abraham Moon and Sons. During the previous decade, the makers-up for C&A Modes had at times purchased half of the cloth made by Abraham Moon and Sons. But the signs of a possible shake-up had been evident for quite some time. Back in the 1950s and 1960s, C&A had started to source clothing from low-wage economies around the world for sale in Europe. By the early 1980s, sales of woollens for children's apparel were generally in a slump, largely because mothers preferred to dress their youngsters in washable synthetics. 'The big hole', John Richmond remembered, 'came when Cecil Silver gave up.'[21]

The race ensued at Abraham Moon and Sons to find new business at home and abroad. In December 1981, mill salesman Roy A. Hammond provided an update to the directors. A year had passed since Silver had shut down. 'There is now the return of demand from C&A for the former C. Silver business, spread over three or four companies, Truly–Fair, Glenmore Fashions, Peacock and possibly

L. C. Tailorwear… Perhaps the *total* business may yield 50/60 per cent of the former quantities ordered when C. Silver was their supplier.'[22] Some of this demand was for woollens for kids' clothing, as Truly-Fair (International) Ltd was a London-based children's wear manufacturer with offices at Grafton House in Golden Square.[23] Roy also commented on some the major trends affecting the woollen trade. 'C&A have experienced losses on running a cheaper Italian version of our style of cloth.' 'The tweed ladies coat has generally been out of vogue for the last 3 or 4 years. Velours are over supplied and much less demanded, as the casual look has been dominant in latter years.' In terms of jackets, the market for tweeds made from pure new wool 'has suffered badly, due to the leap in demand for casual wear'.[24]

Expanding exports

Ultimately, exports filled the gap caused by the closure of Cecil Silver and the flagging demand for wool fabric for children's clothing. Abraham Moon and Sons was already expanding its international business and Arthur Walsh ramped up the effort to secure export orders. Back in December 1978, exports had accounted for 40 per cent of sales and the overseas business was on the upswing. In 1982–83, total sales were £3.26 million, of which exports were 53 per cent.[25] In 1980, the major overseas markets were Canada, France, Germany and Ireland (in descending order by volume). There were the inevitable shifts as the mill found its way with overseas accounts. In 1983, the major markets were France, Germany, Canada and the United States.[26]

To expand exports, Abraham Moon and Sons had to increase its international visibility. Commission agents such as George Portland, who by this time was billed in the London city directories as handling 'silk scarves and accessories' from 12a Golden Square, knew the ins and outs of particular foreign markets and helped the mill find its legs abroad.[27] When Netherfield Mill first ventured into the West German trade, the market had a preference for heavyweight menswear fabrics in sombre shades of grey, brown and blue. But as German men developed more confidence with fashion, there emerged a greater demand for colour. By the 1980s, they looked like handsome peacocks dressed in purple suits and bright red jackets.[28] Portland introduced the mill's fabrics to dozens of garment manufacturers and brands in Austria and West Germany.[29] With his eye for colour, Martin Aveyard thrived in this fashion-conscious environment. He relished the opportunity to create new colourways and to design new tweeds with unusual treatments. Martin was soon in regular contact with chief designer Werner Baldessarani and his staff at Hugo Boss, AG, which became a major customer through Portland.[30]

But the mill needed greater exposure in more overseas markets. The void created by the demise of the wholesale merchants and their international connections was filled by textile trade shows such as Interstoff in Frankfurt. For better or worse, Messe Frankfurt, the trade-show company that ran Interstoff, had no professional expertise in fabrics or fashion. The show gathered all types of fabric at every price point under one roof in an industrial exhibition hall on the Frankfurt fair grounds. In the 1960s and 1970s, nearly everyone in the fashion business flocked to Frankfurt, explained the New York-based journalist Mary Lisa Gavenas, not because Interstoff was glamorous or particularly helpful but because there was little else. Messe Frankfurt always seemed to schedule Interstoff at the wrong time of the year for the fashion cycle, too late for brands and retailers to make fabric selections for the upcoming season and far too early for the next cycle.[31]

As explained in Chapter 6, the National Wool Textile Export Corporation (NWTEC) guided British woollen mills through the mysteries of the trade-show world, commencing with Interstoff and expanding to others. In earlier years, the NWTEC had created its own public-relations activities to put British woollens and worsteds before the public eye. During the late 1960s, for example, the organisation's branch offices in New York and Düsseldorf orchestrated a series of store promotions with major retailers to stimulate consumer interest in British wool fabrics.[32] Elsewhere, the NWTEC championed British woollens and worsteds at British Week promotions held in European cities such as Bruges, Brussels, Dornbirn, Esbjerg, Lille, Salzburg, Stockholm and Vienna.[33] But over the course of the 1970s and 1980s, the NWTEC increasingly turned its attention to trade shows, which were becoming essential spaces for sales and marketing in textiles and fashion. Besides Interstoff, by the 1980s there were Première Vision and Salon International de l'Habillement Masculin (SEHM) in Paris, Fabrex in London, Wol en Handwerken in Amsterdam, Heimtextil in Frankfurt, new shows such as the Men's Wool Club and the Material 9 Convention in Japan, and more. By 1983, four executives at the NWTEC devoted a major part of their time to trade-show promotions. That year alone, they attended twenty-four trade shows—seven in the UK and seventeen overseas—for an average of one every fortnight. This level of activity testified to the growing importance of trade fairs to a business that once relied on wholesale merchants.[34]

The NWTEC introduced British woollen mills to the trade show that became one of the most influential marketing forces in fashion: Première Vision Tissus Création in Paris (figure 7.3). Back in October 1973, fifteen French silk weavers launched a tiny trade show called Première Vision Tissus de Lyon. The idea was to pre-empt other trade events, notably Interstoff, and give silk customers a 'first look' at the collections for the following autumn. The emphasis was on high-quality silk fabrics with a distinctive fashion element, rather than the homogenised designs that dominated Interstoff. The show moved to Paris in 1974 and its scope gradually expanded beyond French silks to other fabrics and other nations. The

7.3 Première Vision became Europe's most important textile trade fair by assembling the best fabric mills under one roof and playing an active role in trend forecasting, here looking forward to Autumn/Winter 1989–90. By kind permission of Leeds Library and Information Services: *International Textiles* 695 (1988), 20–1.

timing was carefully arranged to dovetail with Prêt-à-Porter (a trade show for women's wear that evolved into Paris Fashion Week) so that business visitors to Paris could look at both fabrics and fashion. In 1980, other high-end European textile manufacturers that passed jury selection were allowed to exhibit, with the exception of the Italian mills because they were direct competitors to the French. In 1983, the show finally admitted the Italians; that October, the name was shortened to Première Vision.[35]

In 1980, the Lyon silk weavers met with officials at the British Embassy in Paris to discuss the possibility of establishing a British wool presence at Première Vision.[36] Soon afterwards, Première Vision's founder and general director Bernard Dupasquier and fashion director Micheline Alland visited Yorkshire to liaise with the wool textile industry. Peter Ackroyd, the senior promotion executive at the NWTEC, recognised an unprecedented opportunity to connect British woollens and worsteds to a textile trade fair that focused on the upper end of the market. The emphasis on quality, the admission by jury and the location in Paris (the fashion capital of Europe) were just what the doctor ordered for the British wool fabrics industry. The NWTEC responded to Dupasquier's invitation by agreeing to facilitate the participation of fourteen British woollen and worsted mills at Première Vision commencing with the Spring

1980 edition.[37] The results were promising and the NWTEC decided to repeat the experience. In April 1981, Ackroyd was 'in Paris supervising the new Joint Venture at the Premiere Vision exhibition'.[38] With funding from the British Overseas Trade Board and the sponsorship of the NWTEC, twenty-three British mills participated in the Spring 1981 edition of Première Vision, which coincided with the Prêt-à-Porter salon at Porte de Versailles, just outside Paris.[39]

Abraham Moon and Sons was pleased with the outcome of its display at Première Vision. The Paris agent Ferry Grad, who continued to serve as an informal adviser on matters of style, had urged the mill to participate in the show. Première Vision showcased fabrics by the most 'creative' companies and Grad thought that participation in this elite juried exhibition would attract important fashion customers to the mill. A display there would tell the fashion world that Abraham Moon and Sons was on the cutting edge.[40] The designers Dennis Moulson and Martin Aveyard created the Spring/Summer 1982 lines with exports in mind and the *Wool Record* reported that Netherfield Mill had received 'many sample orders'.[41]

Première Vision proved to be a boon for British textile mills. The NWTEC expanded its remit to include the coordination of the British presence at this biannual fair. The NWTEC secured additional space for British exhibitors as more mills decided to participate.[42] 'The Show was becoming as important as Interstoff', the NWTEC noted in March 1982, 'and could take over as the leading fabric show, within the next 18 months.' That spring, the British section at Première Vision had thirty-five exhibitors, including twenty woollen and worsted manufacturers.[43] The show provided woollen manufacturers with much-needed international exposure among 'all the right people'. Influential French attendees included Pierre Cardin, the Paris designer who built a global fasion empire through licensing agreements, and Ted Lapidus, who pioneered the unisex look; representatives from fashion houses such as Cacharel and Bidermann International; and Guy Dormeuil of the venerable house of luxury fabrics, Dormeuil Frères.[44] With the location in Paris and the emphasis on fashion, Première Vision would challenge the dominance of Interstoff and eventually put it out of business.

Across the Atlantic Ocean, the NWTEC worked to raise the profile of British woollens and worsteds in the United States. New York manufacturers in the famous Seventh Avenue garment industry had started to reinvent themselves around the concept of designer brands. Despite high tariffs, the burgeoning consumer society of the United States had great potential as a market for British fabrics. As in earlier decades, all things British had snob appeal in America, particularly at the upper end of the market. In August 1980, the New York office of the NWTEC organised the first British Woollens Show at the luxurious Waldorf-Astoria Hotel at 901

Park Avenue just north of Grand Central Terminal (also known as Grand Central Station). Twenty firms participated in the exhibition over three days. Abraham Moon and Sons was there, along with competitors such as C. & J. Hirst & Sons Ltd, from the Colne Valley.[45] The second edition of the British Woollens Show, held in 1981, attracted 'nearly all major American and Canadian buyers'.[46] In 1982, the show had twenty-three exhibitors who were excited to meet representatives from New York brands such as Perry Ellis and Halston. 'The British have such a lively sense of textiles', the Halston fashion scout told *Women's Wear Daily*, 'and the quality is marvelous.'[47] The British Woollens Show ran until 1985, when unfavourable exchange rates for sterling forced a hiatus that lasted until 1993, upon which time the show enjoyed a very brief revival.[48]

Closer to home, the NWTEC sponsored the biannual Dorchester Exhibition in London.[49] In October 1981, Abraham Moon and Sons joined thirty other up-market British woollen and worsted manufacturers at the first of these shows, which was named after the venue: the prestigious Dorchester Hotel overlooking Hyde Park. Working a year in advance, the Autumn/Winter menswear range for 1982–83 was put out on view. John Richmond handled the display of fabrics by Abraham Moon and Sons. The Dorchester Exhibition filled a gap in the trade-fair calendar. It came after Première Vision in Paris and before Fashion Fabrex in London. The two larger shows were open to many types of textiles, while the Dorchester Exhibition focused on high-end British woollens and worsteds. The exclusivity of the show, combined with the posh surroundings, was designed to give the impression that British menswear fabrics were something really special. The main display was in the ballroom, while individual mills rented suites for private consultations with the customers. In these early days, the Dorchester Exhibition attracted buyers from around the UK and a smaller number from overseas, including Americans who loved to soak up the affluent atmosphere of Mayfair. The show was also popular with Japanese buyers.[50]

The NWTEC, as a facilitator of trade exhibitions in Frankfurt, Paris, New York and London, helped to create spaces where British woollen and worsted mills and their international customers could meet on a regular basis. The intention was to enable NWTEC member firms 'to make closer acquaintance with actual buyers in the market, outside the normal agent/importer channel'.[51] Under the old modus operandi, mill salesmen went door-to-door with their sample cases, as did many foreign agents. But customers in the new fashion-industrial complex wanted closer contact with the mills themselves. This is not the place to discuss the origins of sales engineering, but suffice it to say that large fibre makers such as the DuPont Company and ICI helped to change the terms of engagement by introducing fabric development specialists to customers further along the supply chain, from the New York 'garmentos' to the Paris couturiers. As a result, customers expected to receive technical support from their suppliers. The British woollen and worsted mills were just catching up with this new way of doing business. By leading the way with trade fairs, the NWTEC acted as a broker between the mills and their customers, helping British manufacturers to develop a feel for marketing.

Hello, high street

Abraham Moon and Sons also shopped the high street for new customers. The closure of James Ives & Company in Yeadon meant that its accounts were up for grabs. At the time of its 125th anniversary in 1973, Elsie Ives stated that her firm was the 'largest *private* woollen mill in England, if not in Europe'—*and* the 'largest supplier of textiles' to 'a little firm in London' called M&S.[52] Like the Springhead Mill Company (Guiseley) Ltd and the Nunroyd Mills of the West Riding Worsted and Woollen Mills, James Ives & Company had supplied moderately priced woollens to the high-street giant.[53] It was big business. Looking to pick up some of the pieces, in 1981 the board at Abraham Moon and Sons asked designer Dennis Moulson to 'take charge of promoting sales to Marks and Spencer'.[54] After six months, he reported some happy news. The people from M&S had been impressed by the mill's patterns at the Dorchester Exhibition and Dennis followed up with a visit to the M&S head office on Baker Street in central London. Sample orders had been submitted to the M&S departments in charge of clothing for men, women and children. Arthur Walsh was set to meet with one of the executive directors early in 1982.[55]

The interaction with M&S was a learning experience for Abraham Moon and Sons. The management and design staff at Netherfield Mill discovered they were dealing with a labyrinthine corporate culture that was dramatically different from the entrepreneurial culture of the woollen trade. The woollen business was largely a handshake business, wherein deals were struck by sitting down with the samples. It was difficult for a manufacturer accustomed to this way of doing business to get its bearing with M&S. The strict system of quality control—the bedrock of the M&S reputation for fail-safe merchandise—meant that all fabrics had to meet fastidious specifications set by the testing laboratory and that the patterns had to fit into a larger seasonal merchandising plan. The internal M&S policy to move personnel from job to job made hopeful suppliers feel as if they were standing on quicksand. By January 1982, the M&S executive director for menswear had moved on and the menswear buyer was 'reluctant to act' until his new boss 'could be consulted'. On the 'ladies side the tester did not consider our cloths good enough, but according to the buyer there are possibilities for next Autumn.' However, things looked more positive on 'the children's side'. Netherfield Mill was supplying '2000 metres of duffle-coating in a pilot scheme' set up by the high-street leader.[56]

Netherfield Mill continued to do business as usual, trying to find an entrée into M&S by using the personal touch. By February 1982, the great hope for menswear orders dampened when Arthur was 'unable to arrange our appointment with the new director in charge of Marks & Spencer's menswear.' The fact that the menswear 'buyer still holds out hope for future transactions' was a small comfort. On the ladies' wear side, Dennis had plans to 'to try and show the Spring range in order to keep in touch'.[57] By May 1982, the effort to secure orders from M&S had stalled. 'The Chairman reported that he had not yet contacted the menswear director', and the 'ladieswear buyer was not interested in looking at our Spring range'. The tenacious Dennis planned to 'approach them early for winter'.[58] In June 1982, he reported that 'M&S Menswear had expressed an interest in British Wools. We had sent them a pattern but they had not yet commented.'[59] M&S was a tough nut to crack. Besides the cultural differences, another roadblock was the Yorkshire competition. Arthur pointed to the success of local rivals at M&S: 'two of our competitors are well entrenched'. In the trying times of the early 1980s, any mill fortunate enough to have large orders from M&S was not about to let go.[60]

Elsewhere in London and Yorkshire, the troubles of longstanding customers and their textile suppliers proved to be a blessing in disguise—at least for Abraham Moon and Sons. Ellis & Goldstein remained a steady customer and continued to order woollens for the Deréta (figure 7.4) and Eastex labels. By 1981, Ellis & Goldstein was opening more shop-in-shop concessions and diversifying beyond traditional coats and suits into casual clothing. The great hope was to reach the 'middle-class, middle-aged retailing clientele' whose favourite shopping destination—the small independent store—was an endangered species.[61] By 1982, those shop-in-shop enterprises that carried the Eastex and Deréta labels absorbed more than 60 per cent of Ellis & Goldstein's output, compared with 40 to 45 per cent a few years earlier when independent retailers were more vibrant.[62] In February 1982, Deréta sent extra orders to Abraham Moon and Sons, following the closure of competitor C. & J. Hirst & Sons, which had operated Sunny Bank Mills in Longwood and a sales office in Golden Square.[63] The Hirst orders were warmly received at Netherfield Mill, which was under strain. 'Apart from Deréta the home market was difficult and sales were now in fewer hands', noted the board minutes. 'The men's trade was producing few sales, there was some improvement in the children's trade and, in the ladies trade the larger orders were from accounts on which we spent a lot of time.'[64] It was a godsend to have loyal customers like Ellis & Goldstein, which saw Netherfield Mill as the pinnacle of dependability. But Arthur Walsh knew that the

Deréta
speaks louder than words.

Boucle cardigan jacket £49.50
pleated skirt £27.50
blouse with jabot £19.50
other boucle jackets include,
with braid detail £52
Chanel style £47.50.
Dereta coats, suits, casuals,
at all good fashion shops
and stores.

Dereta (Dept TMD) Box 5 Northolt Middx UB5 5QT

7.4 Deréta updated the classic British woollen look with this bouclé cardigan jacket and pleated skirt, using the types of fabrics made by Netherfield Mill. Author's collection: *Sunday Telegraph*, 5 October 1980.

firm would not survive by catering to old-type customers when the high street was undergoing such dramatic change.

Next: a bit of magic

By the early 1980s, British apparel retailing was becoming the famous British high-street fashion industry. Women's fashion was 'one of the most exciting growth areas' in the UK economy. From 1980 to 1986, sales in the multiples and department stores increased by more than 78 per cent. The rise of consumers' disposable incomes, greater access to credit and better-designed merchandise contributed to these figures.[65] Growth encompassed the high-end designers and boutique brands at one end of the market, and the mass-market multiples and variety chains at the other end. A larger portion of the British consumer's budget was spent on high-street fashion, which only whetted her appetite for more.

Practicality and price, which had served the British woman well since Utility days, were no longer the principal selling points. The old values were replaced by a heightened consumer awareness of new styles and trends. 'We're finding that because of the way prices have risen, women want the best available within their chosen price category—and then they want a bit of magic as well', explained Clare Stubbs, the merchandise manager at Harvey Nichols, a high-end fashion retailer with its flagship store in Knightsbridge, London. 'They think about clothes more now in the way that the Europeans have been used to doing; they plan them and colour co-ordinate and what they want, above all, is mileage clothes.'[66] In the Utility days, mileage meant durability; in the 1980s, mileage meant glamour and versatility. The consumer now wanted to mix and match different articles of clothing to create an endless stream of unique outfits that expressed her many different moods. Design was an important factor in the new 'express-yourself' fashion environment.

Despite the rising importance of everyday fashion, some brands and retailers lamented the lack of appealing fabrics being made in Britain. It was difficult to attract design talent to the mass-market fashion industry, which in the words of the *Financial Times*, seemed to be 'starved of the creative energy it needs'. There was a disjuncture between design education and the design marketplace. The London art schools had little contact with the Northern textile mills and students were encouraged to seek their fortunes at the glamorous upper end of the fashion business, where very few would succeed.[67] In the industrial regions, the textile programmes struggled to gain scientific legitimacy, which created an entirely different set of problems. In the previous chapter, we saw how Martin Aveyard while a student at the University of Leeds was unsure of where his studies were leading him. He had wondered what designers actually did in a textile mill.

All the signs suggested that a greater attentiveness to design had market value. The experience of the Scottish woollen industry demonstrated how the marriage of quality and marketing could generate sales. Serving the higher end of the woollen market, the Scots had fared better than their Yorkshire counterparts during the 1970s. Some 73 per cent of Scottish woven cloth was exported and, when garments were counted, the proportion exceeded 80 per cent. The Common Market was the main destination, accounting for 57 per cent of all Scottish cloth sales in 1980. The United States was the second largest market, taking 19 per cent of Scottish cloth by value.[68] Other evidence buttressed the case for good design. Some business analysts of the Italian textile miracle argued that high-quality, reasonably priced products were a major factor in Prato's success. The majority of UK textile buyers believed that Yorkshire mills made good-quality woollens and met delivery deadlines. However, few of them thought Yorkshire prices were competitive or found Yorkshire designs to be fashionable.[69]

Abraham Moon and Sons took measures to combat these stereotypes by strengthening the reputation of its cloth at home and abroad. Following the ideas of board member David Walsh on 'presentation and marketing', the firm undertook a protracted analysis of its approach to design and sales. This analysis was not conducted in any scientific way or according to any management textbook. It was largely a hit-or-miss discovery process. Over the course of the 1980s, Netherfield Mill made adjustments to personnel and practice that allowed it to respond with greater agility to customer expectations. Unconsciously, the mill was evolving a design management policy that gave the firm a competitive edge and ensured its survival against the odds.

During the early 1980s, discussions of marketing repeatedly popped up in board meetings as the directors tried to find a new way forward.[70] When Arthur Walsh presented his analysis of 1981 sales, one particular weak spot in the home trade stood out. Sales by the agents were strong, but 'accounts serviced from the Mill' comprised a mere 7.5 per cent of the total turnover. The poor results stemmed from transformations on the high street and the changing needs of the mill's important Yorkshire customers. Burtons Group, which had once been the UK's leading multiple tailor, tried to cope with the collapse of the market for men's suits by increasing women's wear lines. In 1979, Burtons had acquired Dorothy Perkins and turned to Netherfield Mill for ladies' fabrics. The orders from Burtons were steady and complemented the other mill accounts. Fashion aside, wool was still used for utilitarian workwear such as the uniforms worn by soldiers, postmen and railway conductors. Orders for this 'contract cloth' were also steady, but not large. The low turnover from the mill led to a board discussion on the sales organisation and the proper role of the designers. As early as December 1981, the mill discussed whether 'more designer involvement in selling' would lead to larger orders from customers like Burtons or from the newer high-street players that wanted semi-bespoke cloth.[71]

The debate over the designer-customer interface came into tighter focus between 1982 and 1989, when a number of new retailers appeared on the British high street. The first new kid on the block was Next, the innovative women's wear multiple that raised the bar for everyday fashion. Next was created by the charismatic merchandiser George Davies, who opened the first seven Next stores on 12 February 1982 for the Hepworth Group, another down-trodden Leeds menswear multiple that was trying to reinvent itself. Next filled a gap in the ladies' wear market, offering 'designer' office ensembles to fashion-conscious young professionals.[72] The launch was accompanied by a high-profile advertising campaign in British *Vogue, Cosmopolitan, Woman, Woman's Own, She* and *Women's Journal*.[73] Davies took inspiration from Benetton, an Italian mass-market chain that offered colour-coordinated casual clothing to younger shoppers in Italy, Germany and France. The target audience for Next was a new UK demographic: the woman aged twenty-five to forty-five who had a job outside the home and shopped on the high street for clothes that were appropriate for the white-collar work environment. In her younger days, this consumer may have worn minis and maxis from C&A Modes, but she now wanted office-appropriate outfits—'quality and fashion' without 'Jaeger prices'.[74] Abraham Moon and Sons was immediately on the case. On 19 February 1982, Arthur Walsh pressed the board to consider the mill's 'future policy regarding sales and design staff'. At his request, the designer Dennis Moulson 'described his visit to "Next" Ltd, a company aiming at the age 25+ women's market'.[75]

Arthur noted that Next's product development policies were 'a good example of the types of marketing required as against a salesman's approach'.[76] From the start, Next worked closely with all of its suppliers, including the textile mills and the makers-up. George Davies described the process: 'We would control our product right the way through, from the raw materials to the finished garment in the shop. While in other organisations the majority of buyers were coming in half-way through the process, at Next we would be making the decisions about every dye batch and every button. It's attention to that sort of detail that gives you the quality of garment we had in mind.'[77] Another innovative aspect of Next was the store design. Conran Associates, the major company for Hepworth chairman Terence Conran, helped Davies to build the Next brand by creating store interiors, facades and a logo, all in grey and burgundy, that provided continuity with the clothes. Even more than with Jaeger's merchandising strategies in the interwar period, the stores and the clothes conveyed the same aesthetic and thus the unity of the Next brand. Close relationships with suppliers allowed Next to 'react to trends swiftly and repeat on the winning ranges'.[78] The lessons for Abraham Moon and Sons were clear. Arthur advocated 'more designer involvement, and marketing as distinct from selling'.[79]

The debut of Next, which was built around product development and identity branding, served as a focusing device for Netherfield Mill. Board-level discussions about design and sales intensified. In January 1983, Arthur took the initiative and pressed for a 'policy regarding sales and design'. The elephant in the room had grown larger and was pressing up against the walls. 'It was becoming more necessary for designers to work closely with customers and to market and sell their designs.'[80] Design chief Dennis Moulson was set to retire within a few years and succession planning was needed. 'The appointment of an additional designer could allow Mr. Moulson to take on more responsibility for sales', while the 'Sales Manager, Mr. Richmond, could manage mill sales on the same basis as London and Export Sales rather than being directly involved in selling'. It was agreed to advertise for a 'designer with an interest in marketing, approximate age 20 to 30'—someone who could relate to the Next demographic.[81]

Within a few months, Abraham Moon and Sons had a new ladies' wear designer and serious consideration was being given to 'combining sales with design'.[82] Rona Stean came to Netherfield Mill in March 1983 having completed her studies at the Scottish College of Textiles in Galashiels, Scotland, and having two years of work experience as a textile designer for Butterworth & Roberts in Holmfirth, near Huddersfield. She brought Scottish design sensibilities and a familiarity with ladies' wear fabrics to Netherfield Mill.[83] The hiring of a female designer was a novelty, as most professional designers in the Yorkshire textile mills and most design students at the University of Leeds were male.[84] Things were generally looking up. There was excellent news on sales from the mill, with 'good orders from Next and Burtons'. Exports were promising: 'We had hopes of orders from Germany and good early orders from U.S.A.'[85] When a major fire in the warehouse for the Ministry of Defence destroyed the military's entire stock of olive green cloth, Netherfield Mill made thousands of metres of replacement material, which was shipped to a maker-up in Northern Ireland to be sewn into shirts and sleeping bags.[86]

By the early 1980s, London was the dominant customer in the UK market. This was a major change from the days of Isaac Moon or Frank Walsh, when the makers-up, multiple tailors and wholesale merchants in the Northern industrial belt—Bradford, Huddersfield, Leeds and Manchester—gobbled up much of the cloth. During the 1970s, Victor Smith at Fowler & Orr had handled most of the routine trade with the London merchants and Arthur Walsh had dealt with established ladies' wear manufacturers such as Reggie & Company, which made the Miss Smith line (figure 7.5). The go-getter Trevor Brann dealt with the 'exceptional accounts': Deréta, Mansfield Originals and Country Casuals.[87] For the financial

7.5 Black and white check jacket from Miss Smith by Reggie & Company, an important customer for the mill. Courtesy of *Twist Magazine*, formerly *Wood Record* and by kind permission of Leeds Library and Information Services: from *Wool Record*, 147 (November 1988), 81.

year 1982–83, the London trade constituted 47 per cent of UK sales; contract cloths were 34 per cent; mill sales to local customers such as Burtons 16 per cent; and furnishings fabrics (an experimental line) 3 per cent.[88] With the pre-eminence of London, Arthur and the board re-evaluated the need to have a mill salesman, a practice left over from the days when Leeds ruled. The question of who could most effectively speak to customers about the cloth was still undecided. However, the

London situation was clear. Trevor was a dynamic salesman who understood the new dimensions of the metropolitan trade; he became the sole London agent for Abraham Moon and Sons when Smith retired in July 1983.[89]

1984: new order of the day

In 1984, the arrival of another new face—Arthur's son, John P. T. Walsh—ultimately led to the reorganisation of sales, design and marketing. Dennis Moulson, John Richmond and Martin Aveyard were textile polymaths who switched between design and sales. They interacted with the customers and brought in orders. The mill was building a new customer base at home and abroad, but formal expertise in marketing was missing. John Walsh had studied business at the University of Manchester and, through a graduate training programme offered by Courtaulds, he spent three years working on technical textiles at the Marglass division of Courtaulds in Dorset. There, he met Julie Hallam, a recent physics graduate from Newcastle University and his future wife. When Courtaulds sold the Marglass weaving and finishing company to United Merchants & Manufacturers, John turned away from big business and returned to Yorkshire to join the family business.[90]

John's arrival at Netherfield Mill in August 1984 filled everyone with optimism, as it was clear that he would one day take the reins at Abraham Moon and Sons. Shortly after his arrival, the newcomer was alerted to the realities in the woollen industry when he attended a mill auction and saw spinning equipment that appeared to date from the nineteenth century. He was shocked to see how some firms had failed to reinvest in new equipment that would have given them a competitive edge. The experience engendered in John an appreciation for cutting-edge technology that would shape his decision-making in the years ahead.[91]

The major concern at Abraham Moon and Sons was the relationship between the product and the market. In the boardroom that summer, David Walsh continued to emphasise 'the importance of planning for the future on sales policy'. Once John was on staff, the board buckled down for a serious discussion of 'the overall co-ordination of sales and design staff'.[92] In September 1985, Dennis was appointed marketing director with responsibility for design and sales and Martin became the head designer.[93] John Walsh put his business training to good use as the mill's new sales director. In this capacity, he started visiting the United States and Canada two or three times per year and went to Japan, South Korea, Germany and other European markets at least once a year.[94]

By this time, a new pattern of demand had started to emerge. Next had proved to be a boon to Netherfield Mill. The new multiple expected quick delivery, but the size of its repeat orders was impressive.[95] In 1984, Next was the mill's largest domestic customer. Other important UK customers included the Burton Group, which owned ladies' wear multiples such as Dorothy Perkins, Evans, Principles and Top Shop; Ladybird, the children's wear manufacturer that was part of Coats Patons; Briggs Jones and Gibson, a maker-up that produced uniforms for the Post Office and British Rail; and the Continental Quilt Company, which used khaki shirting to make sleeping bag covers for the army.[96]

The revolution in casual styling was in full swing. Although women could still find traditional tailored styles in stores like the Wallis shops (figure 7.6), unstructured clothing was growing in popularity. As in ladies' wear, menswear was swept away by the new vogue. Everywhere in the West, fashion magazines, celebrity endorsements by sports figures, Hollywood movies and syndicated American television series helped to reorient men's tastes around the casual aesthetic. In 1980, the Hollywood crime drama *American Gigolo* starred Richard Gere as the male escort Julian Kaye, a fashion lover with a penchant for unstructured suits by Giorgio Armani, a rising star in Italian menswear. The Milan-based Armani created his signature easy-going jacket by knocking out the stuffing, dispensing with the lining and replacing tweed and flannel with softer fabrics such as wool crepe, which gave the garment the fluid look of a knitted cardigan. *American Gigolo* helped launch Armani's international reputation, which in turn portended the decline of the formal tailored suit from Savile Row and didn't do much for tweeds either.[97]

The rise of casual menswear styling was given a boost on American television. From 1984 to 1989, the National Broadcasting Company (NBC), one of the three commercial TV networks in the United States, ran the popular crime drama *Miami Vice*. The handsome Don Johnson and his suave sidekick Philip Michael Thomas played two plainclothes detectives, James 'Sonny' Crockett and Ricardo 'Rico' Tubbs, from the Metro-Dade Police Department. In the hot humid Miami weather, the macho heroes gunned down villains while wearing big hair, three-day stubble and cool pastel outfits in colours that matched the Art Deco architecture of South Beach. The show put European menswear before the average television viewer, popularising German designs by Hugo Boss and Italian designs by Gianni Versace and Giorgio Armani. Don Johnson did much to promote the 'Armani look' from Milan, typically wearing an unstructured sports jacket over an expensive T-shirt, linen trousers and loafers minus socks. He rolled up the sleeves and turned up the collar on his Italian jacket to make his character look like a dishevelled party animal.[98] Here was the new relaxed silhouette for men, a step beyond double-knit leisurewear and several steps away from dyed-in-the-wool tailored tweeds. Armani-driven metrosexual style had a major impact on menswear and the tweed jacket was relegated to the back of the closet.

It would be impossible to explore how all of the mill's UK customers were affected by the triumph of casual apparel, but one example is telling. Ellis & Goldstein

7.6 This suit, a Wallis Exclusive in brown wool check from the late 1970s or early 1980s, was worn by Mary Bodman Rae (1925–2015), a fashion-conscious seamstress and retailing professional who had worked as a trainee buyer at Jaeger in Regent Street, London. Courtesy of Yorkshire Fashion Archive: gift of the Rae family of Ilkley, West Yorkshire.

struggled when sales of its Eastex and Deréta labels plateaued. In 1983, the firm introduced the Dash line of up-market sports leisurewear for women aged twenty-five to fifty; the clothing was made in Southeast Asia and sold in stand-alone stores and at shop-in-shop concessions. In 1986, Dash had 170 locations, had broadened to include men and teens, and helped profits grow from £2.34 million to £3.55 million.[99] The same year, Ellis & Goldstein further targeted women in the Dash demographic with a new range of office wear marketed under the name 'Jenni Barnes'. Two years after its launch, the Jenni Barnes range was foundering and was set for a makeover. Meanwhile, observers criticised Ellis & Goldstein for allowing the Eastex and Deréta labels to 'languish'. In 1988, a rival women's wear group, Berkertex, launched a takeover bid for Ellis & Goldstein, claiming the firm had failed 'to respond to the changing retail environment'.[100] The bid was unsuccessful but Ellis & Goldstein's time was limited. The *Financial Times* dryly noted the firm's 'all-too-evident vulnerability to the vagaries of fashion'.[101] By 1989, Ellis & Goldstein would be part of the Alexon Group, which manufactured the Alexon and Eastex brands.[102]

Growing sales at home and abroad

Between 1984 and 1988, sales at Abraham Moon and Sons grew from £4.12 million to £5.24 million. This 27 per cent growth in sales came not from selling more fabric, but from selling better-quality fabric. The results could be attributed to the new focus on customer service. In 1984, the mill sold 1.16 million metres of cloth and, in 1988, just over 1 million metres. The number of full-time employees grew from 152 to 163. Efficiency gains were reflected in the number of metres finished per employee (7,600 in 1984 as against 6,600 in 1988) and sales per employee (£27,000 in 1984 against £32,000 in 1988).[103]

By 1987, exports accounted for 44 per cent of sales at Abraham Moon and Sons; a year later in 1988, they amounted to 58 per cent of sales.[104] At mid-decade, there was a major shift in the composition of the mill's export markets, which in turn pushed the mill deeper into fabrics for menswear. George Portland consistently secured strong jacketing orders from Germany; Copaex was active with brands in France; the St. Andrews Textile Company in New York worked to penetrate the US menswear market; and Anderson Crowe Textiles of Montreal linked the mill to Canada, where cold winters demanded heavy woollens. Trained as a tweed designer in the Galashiels tradition, Rae Anderson had emigrated from Huddersfield to Montreal a few years after the war and, starting around 1980, he and his business partner, Les Crowe, became the Canadian agent.[105] While Europe and North America were strong markets, Asia started to play an important role. At the start of the 1980s, the mill's major markets, as noted earlier, were in Europe and North

America, but as the decade unfolded, the company developed its export trade with Hong Kong and especially Japan.[106] By 1988, the leading export markets for the mill were Germany (23 per cent); the United States and France (20 per cent each); Canada (13 per cent); and Japan (12 per cent).[107]

This pattern was consistent with larger trends in the woollen industry. Japan grew as a market for British tweeds after UK retailers such as Aquascutum, Burberry, Daks and Dunhill established a presence there. In 1981, Paul Stuart, a New York private-label menswear retailer headed by Clifford Grodd, opened two stores in Tokyo's exclusive retailing districts, Aoyama and Ginza. The stores offered Japanese men an expensive American interpretation of British style.[108] The younger generation of Japanese consumers accessed the British look via Paul Smith. Working with Japanese partners, the quirky London-based designer adapted his vintage-inspired menswear to the market and established stand-alone shops and shop-in-shop sales points in department stores.[109] The strong British presence in Japan invigorated the Ivy League style and stimulated the demand for Yorkshire woollens. In the words of NWTEC executive Ackroyd, 'The Japanese love British style. They do it very smart. They dress like the British better than the British do.'[110] The NWTEC reported that, for 1988 by value, the five major export destinations for British woollens were Japan, West Germany, the United States, Belgium and Luxembourg, and Italy.[111]

As the sales director, John saw the importance of exports—and recognised that a focus on established markets was not good enough. Entrepreneurial intuition led him to see the global future and he worked to develop connections to untapped markets in Europe and Asia. Convinced that Italian men would appreciate Yorkshire tweeds, he headed off to Italy against the advice of colleagues who said he was 'trying to sell sand in Egypt or coals to Newcastle'. In 1985, he established a relationship with an Italian agency run by Osvaldo Franco, who represented a Huddersfield mill and wanted to expand his British offerings. John recalled the experience:

> We didn't start out too well. Osvaldo hired a car, an Alfa Romeo, to drive from Milan to Turin to visit customers. He was feeling ill so asked me to drive. On the return journey the brakes failed in the fast lane at 120 k.p.h. We just about managed to avoid hitting several cars before coming to a hand-brake stop. It didn't bode well for future business dealings and after a year we parted company. Osvaldo sold mainly to tailors and we needed to sell to the up-and-coming super brands: Armani, Prada, Gucci and Dolce & Gabbana.[112]

At one edition of Première Vision, a London textile agent introduced John to Riccardo Negrini, a Milan-based agent who began working with the mill in March 1987. Around this time, John also established relationships for the mill with agents in Austria, Australia, Belgium, Hong Kong, the Netherlands, Norway, Portugal, South Korea and Spain, laying the foundation for global expansion.

From dolls' clothes to Yorkshire tweeds

Abraham Moon and Sons was coming to grips with the proper relationship between design and sales. In January 1987, John Walsh was elected to the board of directors and, six months later, Dennis Moulson retired after thirty-three years.[113] The new management team assessed the design and sales departments. The mill traveller Roy Hammond was due to retire within a few years and the board needed to make some tactical decisions. The firm was successfully venturing deeper into menswear, but something was amiss in ladies' wear. The selection of patterns did not seem to resonate with customers. As sales director, John argued for new blood 'on the ladies' side', and production director Danny Spence proposed to hire a new designer.[114]

Netherfield Mill was unusual in the level of authority that it invested in the design staff. Some of the other Yorkshire mills used consultant designers to create their ranges and outsourced the production of sample patterns to commission mills. Reuben Gaunt & Sons followed this practice until 1981 and only then hired a full-time designer and installed a pattern production department. Chairman David Gaunt believed that the 'greater emphasis on… fancy production' would allow the company to become 'more competitive in the fashion textile market both at home and abroad'.[115] Abraham Moon and Sons was ahead of the curve by having recruited Martin Aveyard in the mid-1970s and two additional designers, Rona Stean and Kathryn Robbins, in the mid-1980s.[116]

The directors started to acknowledge that Martin had benefited from his contact with Ferry Grad and that designer-customer interactions had value. After Martin started visiting the Japanese agents and customers in their home territory around 1983, he came to understand the cultural similarities and differences between East and West. The Japanese loved to borrow and adapt styles from other cultures and they never hesitated to create a pastiche of British, Italian and American motifs. Japan seemed 'so alien in every way', but 'everyone was so friendly' and wanted to show him the way. Martin learned to appreciate Japanese aesthetics as embodied in everything from the raw fish in the sushi to the simple hotel décor, and learned to 'change the check size for Japanese bodies and tone down the colours'. Only someone who was attuned to the nuances of material culture would have fathomed the need for this level of attention. Grad had encouraged Martin to look and learn, and so he did. His focus on little details led to big changes in the look of the fabric and resulted in a steady increase of Japanese orders.[117] Despite this success, it took some time for Netherfield Mill to work out the balance between design and sales.

The quest for new talent in design-led sales focused on ladies' wear, which was a growth area in the home market and the United States. In June 1988, the young Judith Webb (later Judith Coates) responded to the mill's newspaper advertisement for a designer. Born in Broughton, a village in Cambridgeshire, she learned to sew from her mother, a professional dressmaker, and at age five, she began to make clothes for her dolls. With a passion for fabrics, Judith studied art, history, and dress and textiles for her A-levels and enrolled in the three-year bachelor's degree programme in textile design at the University of Leeds in 1984. After graduation in 1987, she worked as a textile designer for Double Two, a shirt factory in Wakefield, West Yorkshire. The job at Double Two focused on creating new shirt patterns in stripes and checks. The young designer found little satisfaction in the work from either a technical or a creative perspective. The situation was different at Abraham Moon and Sons, where she found herself having to swim 'at the deep end'. The February before her arrival, assistant designer Rona Stean had left the mill for a position at Whiteley & Green in Holmfirth and, shortly after she started, Kathryn Robbins accepted a job in the United States. Another designer, Joanna Fox, would be hired in due course, but Judith found herself 'very involved from the get go'.[118]

Judith joined Abraham Moon and Sons at a crucial moment in its design history and her experience was indicative of a sea change in woollen marketing. After a decade of deliberation, the board of directors officially acknowledged that designers had something unique to contribute to sales. By this time, customers in the United States were extremely important for the mill, which was assisted in the development of the American market by the St. Andrews Textile Company, an importer and agent in mid-town Manhattan. Almost immediately, Judith was on the road, attending to customers at major international trade shows such as Première Vision—the Autumn 1988 edition had more than seventy British exhibitors, including fifty-six woollen and worsted mills—and flying to New York to promote the new ranges through St. Andrews.[119]

The St. Andrews Textile Company dated to the interwar years and, in those early days, it was run by Frank L. Swayze, a veteran of the dry-goods trade who had been in the business since 1900. American garment manufacturers were keen to buy European fabrics, but they did not want to deal with foreign currencies, strange languages and unfamiliar customs. Importers stepped in to fill the gap. Swayze built the reputation of St. Andrews as an importer of up-market European fabrics, serving as the American agent for mills such as Picardie of France; Holmes & Allan of Glasgow, Scotland; and William Yates & Sons Ltd, of Manchester, England.[120] The stock included colourful Scottish tweeds with bouclé effects for ladies' autumn ensembles and fine cottons for better shirts, pyjamas, robes and neckwear.[121] By the late 1930s, St. Andrews had a design staff that worked with women's wear manufacturers and retailers to create fabrics in bespoke colours, textures and patterns. 'Designing is all done here, often with customers in on the plans, and forwarded to the mills', wrote *Women's Wear Daily* of the company. 'Almost everything is "confined" at least as far as color is concerned.'[122] By 1950, St. Andrews was focused on importing Scottish textiles for men's and women's apparel. Passionate about woollens, the ageing Swayze continued to visit the office, but he sold the business to William E. Dreschel, formerly a buyer and merchandise manager for two major Chicago retailers: Carson Pirie Scott & Company and Wilson Brothers. Dreschel moved the showroom from East Forty First Street to 240 Madison Avenue and homed in on high-fashion fabrics from England, Scotland, Ireland and the Netherlands.[123]

By the 1980s, the St. Andrews Textile Company was in the hands of the son, John Andrew Dreschel, who had been at the firm since 1960. 'Andy' Dreschel had worked with Arthur Moon for some time and he introduced Abraham Moon and Sons to one of its most important American customers, Polo Ralph Lauren. Although not trained as a designer, he was an accomplished stylist in his own right, based on decades of experience. He took Judith under his wing and helped her understand how North American fabric buyers and fashion designers did business. There was a well-defined division of labour between the mill and the importer. Judith visited St. Andrews twice a year, once to promote the Autumn/Winter range and again to promote the Spring/Summer range. The importer purchased the fabrics from the mill and handled the pricing, deliveries and payments among the customers.[124]

By the late 1980s, St. Andrews had a luxurious suite of six showrooms at 135 West Fiftieth Street, close to Rockefeller Center and not far from the heart of the fashion district. Judith was free to use the space as needed to meet with customers. Everything about the luxurious interior was meant to evoke Old World heritage and to make the customer feel special. The wood-panelled walls were embellished with oil paintings and with photographs of golfers and rugby players. The wooden floor was covered with plush Indian carpets and the antique furniture was upholstered with Scottish tartans. The atmosphere was meant to transport the customer from the hustle-and-bustle of mid-town Manhattan to the picturesque town of St Andrews, Scotland, a golf resort on the North Sea, or some imaginary version of it.[125]

The American market had distinctive requirements, much as it had in the interwar years when Swayze set up St. Andrews and when Frank Walsh tried to make inroads through Charles David. By the mid to late 1980s, the European market had taken a turn towards bright bold colour. Designer menswear collections and brands from France, Germany and Italy were known for their dramatic style shifts from season to season.[126] Many American men found European cuts and shades to be effeminate, preferring conservative designs. Among the New York fashion houses, Polo Ralph Lauren had achieved a mediation between Euro-chic and American 'preppy' styles by offering consumers a romanticised version of the British country look. Like Swayze before him, Andy Dreschel recognised the gap between European and American tastes and he employed a fifteen-person staff of designers and salespeople to help the British textile mills connect to the US market. When she got to New York, Judith would show the new collection to Andy and his staff, who would then arrange appointments with the merchandising offices at Polo Ralph Lauren, Brooks Brothers, J. Crew and other New York-based brands. Judith would take it from there, going over to the customer's offices to meet with the fabric merchandisers, fabric buyers and clothing designers. The discussions revolved around colour, texture, pattern, weight and price, and modifications that might be required to fit into the customer's line for the upcoming season.[127]

Another feature of the North American market was the 'gentleman's agreement' that each pattern would be exclusive or 'confined' to a particular customer. One such customer was the high-end fashion retailer Saks Fifth Avenue. Saks needed distinctive fabrics for its private label fashions, which were sold by the flagship store in mid-town Manhattan and by branch stores in smart locations across the United States. The buyers from major menswear manufacturers such as Hart Schaffner & Marx (HSM) of Chicago and Peerless Clothing Inc. of Canada, would visit the St. Andrews showrooms when they were in New York. They sat down with Judith to examine swatches, discuss their needs and make arrangements to receive sample lengths of patterns that had been tweaked to meet the requirement for exclusivity.[128]

Shortly after Judith started at the mill, a major trade agreement went into effect that proved to be a game changer for Abraham Moon and Sons. Taking cues from the EFTA and similar free-trade policies negotiated under the GATT, Canada and the United States signed the Canada-United States Free Trade Agreement (CUSFTA), which opened commerce between the two countries, starting in January 1989.[129] CUSFTA was a life-saver for British mills that wanted more of their fabrics to reach the United States. New York was the major textile market for North America, offering one-stop shopping to fabric buyers who could visit the sales offices of a dozen mills or importers on a single trip. Once the borders opened up, Canadian companies like Peerless relentlessly pursued the large US market for tailored menswear. Peerless purchased British fabrics in New York, made the garments in Canada and exported them back to the United States. With a new young designer on board, Abraham Moon and Sons could cater to customers like Peerless by offering bespoke patterns that suited the distinctive tastes of the American consumer. It was a win-win situation for mill and customer.[130]

New demand cycle

By the late 1980s, the textile and clothing market in the UK was being squeezed by problems on all sides: increasing imports, sluggish exports and erratic demand from customers. Inexpensive imported fabrics and apparel were making inroads on the high street. In 1986, most clothing sold under the Windsmoor label was made in the UK, but up to 40 per cent by value was produced overseas, mainly in Europe and Hong Kong.[131] The bottom soon fell out of the British textile industry. Among those hardest hit were the man-made fibre producers, which had over-expanded their manufacturing facilities. Europe's largest textile group, Coats Viyella (formed from a merger of Vantona Viyella and Coats Patons in early 1986), saw profits fall by 36 per cent in 1988. The strength of sterling against both the American dollar and Asian currencies weakened the export market for British textiles. These realities led Coats Viyella to sell the Country Casuals chain, which had 172 stores, to a buy-out group in 1989.[132] The turmoil at Coats Viyella was indicative of broader troubles on the high street and at various nodes in the supply chain for the fashion system. Close to home in the Aireborough district, those difficulties were reflected in Coats's closure of the old Peate facility, Nunroyd Mills, and the factory's demolition in 1987.[133]

Abraham Moon and Sons survived the tumultuous 1980s because it had developed a winning formula. Family control, low dividends, quality and investment in new technology were constant (figure 7.7). Two important new elements had evolved over the course of the 1980s: the relentless pursuit of overseas customers and the focus on designer-led service and sales. But the company was not unaffected by the shift to casual dressing. No sooner was Netherfield Mill on its feet again after the closure of Cecil Silver than fashion dealt it another blow. An unfortunate new demand cycle for woollens was becoming evident. The mill had plenty of orders in the first half of 1985, but things turned sluggish after the summer holidays. In October, Arthur Walsh reported on 'the order position which was generally poor but would have been abysmal without the pieces of khaki on order'.[134] The stagnation continued into December. With the exception of army shirting, the company had few new orders. Arthur hoped to find 'possible orders for piece dyed cloths' to keep the mill running.[135]

Until the late 1960s, there had been a year-round demand for woollen fabrics. Traditionally, British consumers had worn wool clothes twelve months of the year. Woollen skirts, jackets, trousers and coats were the perfect cover-ups for the

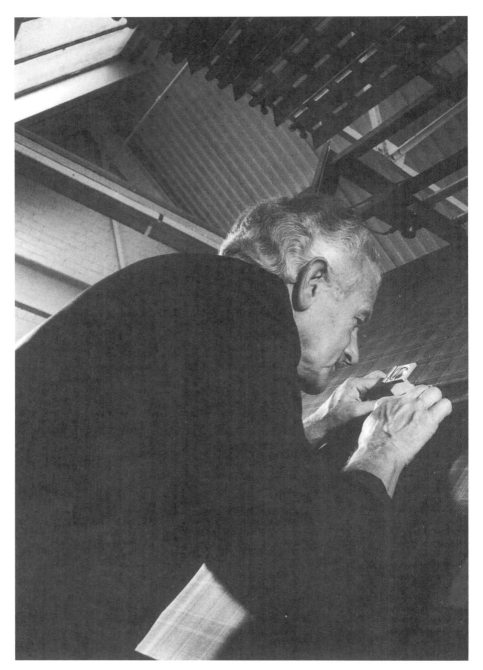

7.7 Good quality control has long been a distinguishing feature of Netherfield Mill; here, the finishing manager Malcolm Wood examines cloth on a 'perch'. Courtesy of Abraham Moon and Sons: *Creating the Cloth* brochure, early 1990s.

relatively mild, but damp, British weather. But over the course of the 1970s and especially the 1980s, woollens fell out of favour for spring and summer garments. As buildings were modernised and central heating was installed, there was less of a need to wrap up indoors. Whereas the woman of Barbara Sutcliffe's generation wore a light woollen coat in spring, the 1980s' woman kept warm with a knitted sweater, poncho or jacket made from polyester, acrylic or nylon. The modern consumer who drove his or her own car, rather than taking the train or the bus, had no need for both a winter and spring coat. Modern children played sports in washable coats and went to school in jackets sewn from fabrics composed of man-made fibres. For summer, men had switched from classic tweed jackets to loose-fitting linen jackets, Armani style. With the exception of the man's power suit made from worsteds, the demand for lightweight year-round wool fabrics had disappeared.

By the late 1980s, Netherfield Mill received steady orders from January to June, but almost no orders rolled in during the second half of the year. Some production statistics get to the heart of the matter. In the winter of 1989, the mill sold 15,029 pieces of cloth to customers in the UK, Germany and Austria, France, the United States, Canada and smaller markets around the world. The contrast with the following year was striking. In spring 1990, the mill sold a mere 1,930 pieces of cloth.[136]

In March 1989, there was a generational shift at Abraham Moon and Sons. Early in the month, board member David Walsh—the great advocate of marketing—died. At the end of the month, Arthur Walsh retired as managing director and handed the baton to his son, John.[137] The older man continued as chairman until 2010, watching from the sidelines and trying to be helpful and not intrusive. Like his father before him, John became the managing director at Abraham Moon and Sons as a young man aged only twenty-nine. He had read a few management textbooks, served as marketing trainee at Courtaulds and watched internal disagreements between the old-timers and younger generation at Netherfield Mill. Now John had to grapple with the perplexing problem of running a family business in a declining industry.[138] That story takes us to our conclusion.

8 Reinvention

> The luxury brands want authenticity and a story. Now we are a brand. We are selling that identity. (John P. T. Walsh, 2013)[1]

Over the past twenty-five years, Abraham Moon and Sons has been swept up in the massive changes wrought by the new era of globalisation. Netherfield Mill entered the closing decades of the twentieth century with significant experience as an exporter that was finding its way with design-driven sales. But the rapidly changing marketplace placed relentless demands on the company. In this postmodern context, stories and storytelling—and the conversion of history into heritage—became important marketing tools.

The Victorian clothier Abraham Moon had displayed his fabrics in the Coloured Cloth Hall in Leeds and the Edwardian designer-manager Charles Walsh had depended on merchants in Bradford, Glasgow, Leeds, London and Manchester to sell his woollens. By the late twentieth century, new ways of selling cloth had come to dominate the scene. Mainly, textile trade shows and fashion trade shows became much more important for connecting fabric manufacturers to customers from around the world. The designers, salesman and agents who worked for Netherfield Mill were constantly on the go, either visiting customers in their home offices and design studios or taking sample orders from them at international shows. After the New Millennium, the calendar proved more demanding as trade shows proliferated, particularly in East Asia. In 2004, for example, Première Vision China was launched in Shanghai to provide fabric mills with greater access to Asian customers.[2]

As globalisation advanced, stories about origins—the local, the regional and the national—gained a good deal of currency. Retailers and brands had to fight tooth and nail to differentiate themselves from their competitors. Some of the mill's up-market customers in Germany, Japan, the United Kingdom and the United States started to view 'Britishness' as a means for enhancing the prestige of their brands. In the new global order, there was a certain irony to the fact that nationhood and place-specific identities came to be important tropes in international branding. In a way, traditional motifs and stories emerged as cultural anchors to help customers and consumers find their moorings in an uncertain global world.

Although the National Wool Textile Export Corporation (NWTEC) had been touting British style for some time, branding was relatively new for Yorkshire woollen and worsted mills. Abraham Moon and Sons was one of the first to adopt the concept of mill branding and to help customers establish unique identities through co-branding. Netherfield Mill looked deep into the past and its archives to create a new image rooted in authenticity. Stories about the past—from the humble origins of tweeds as a twill weave to the fabric's popularity among film stars like Cary Grant—became part of the firm's marketing strategy. History was recast as heritage as the Yorkshire mill reinvented itself as a global brand.

Entrepreneurial thinking

John Walsh had spent the 1980s learning the ins-and-outs of the woollen business. When he first joined the company in 1984, the 24-year-old sales director worked with agents in Canada, France, Japan, the United States and West Germany. There was no better way to learn the woollen trade than riding on the coat-tails of a master salesman like George Portland. During a typical tour around West Germany, the men called on the customers during the day and John browsed through the stores in the evening to 'see the market from the consumer's point of view'. 'I was thrown into the deep end', he reminisced, echoing Judith Coates, 'and had to swim.'[3]

The young entrepreneur soon learned how much the Yorkshire woollen industry was wedded to old ways. All around him, John sized up the signs of neglect, including shuttered mills filled with machinery that was five decades old. Working in various jobs at the mill to learn the business, he observed the 'old thinking' and ingrained work habits that inadvertently led to slippages in quality. The Italian woollen and worsted industries continued to be highly competitive, so he studied their fabrics at trade shows and visited Italy to look at the production facilities. Slowly but surely, John began to understand that, despite Netherfield Mill's continued reinvestment in new technology, the external environment had changed more dramatically. He 'tried to bring new thinking to the mill' and posed tough questions: 'What are the faults, and where do they come from? What do we need to do to achieve zero defects?'[4]

The areas of sales, quality control and information processing were targeted for evaluation and improvement. For starters, Netherfield Mill had no computers. Every iota of information was tracked on paper, starting with the agents' orders and ending with the packing slips in the shipping department. The large number of customers and the wide variety of patterns was especially troublesome for the designers, who had to spend a lot of time on the shop floor helping set up new production runs. John spent eighteen months collaborating with a software developer in Glasgow to create a bespoke computer package suited to a vertically integrated textile mill. The system was up and running by 1986. 'Computers enabled the mill to grow', John explained. 'Process control allowed for more systemisation.'[5]

The new manufacturing efficiencies only served to heighten John's concerns about the decline of the British woollen industry. In November 1988, the Confederation of British Wool Textiles (CBWT) documented the dismal state of affairs. Between 1986 and 1988, there had been a dramatic increase of woollen and worsted imports from China and Turkey and no respite was in sight. In this brief two-year period, woollen imports from China alone grew from 36,000 to 433,000 square metres.[6] The CBWT chairman highlighted the difficulties for 'woollen manufacturers, with several companies having to resort to short-time working and, in some cases, redundancies'. Looking to explain the spiral, he pointed to fashion changes, high wool prices, unfair competition, skyrocketing interest rates, the instability of sterling and the laissez-faire policies of Prime Minister Margaret Thatcher.[7] The UK was not alone in its troubles; even the normally buoyant American clothing market was in turmoil. 'The situation in the USA was not a happy one, with a very poor demand for clothing', the CBWT noted. 'There was no strong fashion trend to induce consumers to buy—this was the only time since the last war that clothing sales had gone contrary to the trend of consumer spending.'[8]

In 1989, the British textile industry accounted for almost £4 billion in exports and was the UK's most successful trading partner with Japan.[9] But textile and clothing manufacturers, including those in the wool fabric sector, were reeling from the effects of international policies created to encourage global trade. Under the Multi-Fibre Arrangement (MFA), developed economies had some control over imports, but the emerging economies proved 'adept at using tariff and non-tariff barriers to deny … access to their markets'.[10] The British mills battled for a share of the global market, while combating imports on their home turf. One problem was the rising competition from state-supported textile mills in the Eastern Bloc.[11] In 1988, for example, *International Textiles* reported on 'fashion conscious' fabrics from mills in the Centrotex organisation in Czechoslovakia, advising the European ready-to-wear industry to 'Czech the winter scene'. Centrotex offered 'country tweeds', 'career girl' plaids and 'sporty brights' that rivalled the colours and textures of the Yorkshire mills—and at much lower prices.[12]

In January 1990, the House of Commons held a session on the MFA and learned about the avalanche of cheap East European imports directly from Yorkshiremen. 'We manufacture wool crepe which we sell to the makers up at about £6.50 to £6.70', explained John Knox, the managing director of Aire Valley Mills in Silsden. 'A very similar fabric is bought by a merchant from Poland at £4.65 and sold to the same makers up at £6.25.'[13] The collapse of the Soviet Union was likely to exacerbate things. 'Imports over the last few years have grown at a greater rate than our domestic market. It would seem that already we must brace ourselves for a fresh avalanche of imports from Eastern Europe as they sell us one of their new tradeable commodities (fabric and clothing) for hard currency. We would doubt if their prices would represent the actual cost of manufacture.'[14] Who was to blame? The MP from Keighley, a mill town within greater Bradford, pointed to the high-street multiples, to 'the relatively small number of distributors and retailers who account for over half the clothing sales in the United Kingdom' and 'make us peculiarly vulnerable' to imports 'from countries whose own markets remain relatively restricted'.[15]

The adverse effects of trade policies were compounded by the continued casualisation of everyday life, which had an impact on people's fashion choices. Most consumers continued to move away from highly structured clothing made from woven fabrics in favour of easy-going knitwear. In North America and Western Europe, retailers filled their stores with ever-cheaper, increasingly casual apparel imported from the low-wage economies of East Asia, Eastern Europe and North Africa. Whereas British consumers had once worn lightweight woollen jackets in the summer, this style preference had virtually disappeared. In the United States, the 'cool cat' of the 1950s, who had smoked his briar pipe and listened to jazz records in a jacket of velvet or tweed, was now middle aged.[16] The *Christian Science Monitor*, published in Boston—where the tweed jacket with elbow patches was the standard uniform of the male college professor—referred to this style as the 'Old Fogey Look'.[17] The fashion-conscious consumer had soured on tweed, which was the antithesis of the cosmopolitan aesthetic inspired by Italian brands such as Armani and Gucci.[18]

The British woollen and worsted industries were a shadow of their former selves. In 1988, there were just over 200 mills and 30,000 workers, compared to the immediate postwar era's 3,000 mills and 180,000 workers. The signs of industrial decline were evident all around Yorkshire, as old mills were demolished to make way for shopping centres. An especially poignant symbol of change could be seen in Bradford, once famous as the wool capital of the world. The Bradford Wool Exchange—the Gothic Revival building from whence the global wool supply had been managed—was no longer used as a trading space. Some dedicated woollen men kept a stiff upper lip. 'No Yorkshireman, no Scot, will go down the tubes if he doesn't want to', asserted Geoffrey Richardson, a larger-than-life character who directed the NWTEC.[19] But observers in the City of London, the financial heart of the UK, were circumspect. 'Twenty years ago there were seven textile mills in and around the tiny town of Guiseley', the *Financial Times* wrote in 1989. 'Today, Abraham Moon, a family-owned spinner and weaver, is the sole survivor. The last of the other mills closed four years ago, to re-open as a drive-in McDonald's.'[20]

Heritage marketing

One mark of an entrepreneur is the ability to anticipate trends before they become mainstream. John Walsh not only recognised the rising tide of globalisation, but also understood the commercial potential of British heritage. In the United States, the blockbuster exhibition, *The Treasure Houses of Britain*, attracted nearly one million visitors during its five-month run at the National Gallery of Art in Washington DC, in 1985–86. The show stimulated the American appetite for British style and luxury.[21] In the American capital to promote all things British, Prince Charles and Princess Diana attended a gala dinner at the White House as the guests of President Ronald Reagan and First Lady Nancy Reagan. Wearing an ink blue velvet evening gown, Princess Diana famously danced with the American movie star John Travolta to the music of his 1977 film *Saturday Night Fever*. Diana's pale complexion, swept-back blonde hair and Edwardian-influenced style complemented the old-fashioned Hollywood elegance of the Reagan White House and the glamour of TV soap operas such as *Dallas* (1978–91) and *Dynasty* (1981–89).[22] Old World elegance, with a British twist, was thrust into the public eye.

In the United States, structured clothing with a vintage touch came to be redefined as classic. Aspirational consumers at the upper end of the middle market had developed a taste for understated tailored attire. The 'preppy' mode, which might be best described as a low-key style rather than a fashion statement, was inspired by an imagined version of British heritage. In the New York fashion industry, retailers and brands such as Banana Republic, Brooks Brothers, Ralph Lauren and Tommy Hilfiger turned back the pages of history and adopted nostalgic motifs from the past. Starting in the 1970s, the entrepreneur Ralph Lauren had reimagined dapper British country clothing from the interwar years as an 'old money look' for middle-class consumers who longed to rub shoulders with 'the establishment' in the Hamptons. Ralph Lauren understood the need for status, the desire to belong and the way in which 'clothes that could last for years' suited the 'traditional man' and the 'unfashionable fashion girl … with enough authority to carry off very tailored clothes in a feminine way'. His designs for apparel and home furnishings were informed by this understanding. Natural materials such as suede, leather, camel hair, cashmere and tweed were suited to the new understated style, with its strong heritage accents.[23]

On its home turf, British heritage was going strong. In greater Bradford, the gigantic worsted mill built in Victorian times by Titus Salt ceased production in 1987 and shortly thereafter, Jonathan Silver—a local developer with an eye for vintage architecture—began converting the property into a mixed-use facility for business, residential and cultural activities.[24] On the high street, the up-market retailer Laura Ashley offered merchandise inspired by 'traditional English country values'. Inch by inch, the Laura Ashley brand had extended its signature romantic look, made famous by 'farm girl' dresses, to a home-furnishings range. *The Laura Ashley Book of Home Decorating*, which sold more than 475,000 copies between 1981 and 1985, was a go-to manual for amateur decorators keen on British country style.[25]

The retro phenomenon held great promise for Abraham Moon and Sons, whose history could be traced back to the 1837 partnership between the half-brothers Abraham and William Moon. The challenge to John Walsh was how to turn the mill's venerable history into heritage so as to sell more tweeds.

Netherfield Mill had experimented with heritage marketing some time before when Martin Aveyard and Ferry Grad created the 'Yorkshire Tweed by Abraham Moon' label for co-branding with French menswear manufacturers. As more brands embraced the heritage concept, the mill attracted new customers who engaged with the past in product design and development. One such account was the GB Clothing Company, a maker-up in Castleford, near Leeds, which produced trousers for Next but also made its own quirky line of menswear (figure 8.1 and figure 8.2). GB Clothing welcomed the chance to collaborate with Martin on the creation of bespoke fabrics that were colourful and unique. The designer at GB Clothing sketched out some ideas, gave them to Martin and said, 'go from here'—which suited the latter just fine. GB Clothing embodied the vintage fashion zeitgeist of the moment, creating distinctive menswear that combined slouchy informality with unconventional textured tweediness. The edginess was achieved by using bouclé and other ladies' wear fabrics, bold colours, unusual silhouettes and contrasts between the rough and the smooth. 'Many of the fabrics have been created by GB's design team', one press release announced, 'and actually produced in the company's Yorkshire heartland.'[26]

Another customer, Gant (figure 8.3), used the mill's tweeds to develop a rugged heritage-inspired look for the European market. This brand, which originated in America, was established internationally through licensing agreements. Founded in 1920s' New York by the shirt-maker Bernard Gantmacher, in the postwar years, Gant Inc. had relocated to New Haven, Connecticut, and developed its signature look: boldly coloured Oxford shirts for Ivy League college students and Madison Avenue advertising executives. Gant borrowed the design of the button-down shirt from Brooks Brothers, one of its customers, which in turn had been inspired by British polo players.[27] After 1968, Gant changed hands and, in 1980, Pyramid Sportswear of Stockholm acquired the licence to design and market products under the Gant trademark in Sweden and elsewhere (except the United States until

8.1 GB Clothing Company, Leeds, menswear line, Winter 1985, using tweeds by Abraham Moon and Sons. Courtesy of Abraham Moon and Sons.

1999, when the global rights were acquired). Around 1988, some Pyramid staff walked on to the stand of Abraham Moon and Sons at Première Vision (which had moved to the Parc des Expositions near the Charles de Gaulle Airport in 1984) and ordered samples. The aim was to adapt the American preppy look, popularised by L. L. Bean and Polo Ralph Lauren, to practical clothes for the changeable European

8.2 GB Clothing Company, Leeds, menswear line, Winter 1985, using tweeds by Abraham Moon and Sons. Courtesy of Abraham Moon and Sons.

weather. Gant used the mill's fabrics in menswear jackets commencing with their 'Martha's Vineyard' range for Autumn 1989. Shetland tweeds in check patterns brought brilliant colour and imaginary heritage styling to the line, which Pyramid called 'Gant American Sportswear'.[28]

The British look and beyond

Back in the 1960s, the Yorkshire mills distanced themselves from British symbols such as the Union Jack, Bobbies, red telephone boxes and double-decker buses as

8.3 Pyramid Sportswear, the European licensee for the Gant brand, used the mill's cloth to make this check jacket that harked back to an imaginary Anglo-American preppy utopia where real men wore colourful British tweeds. Courtesy of Abraham Moon and Sons: *Gant Martha's Vineyard Fall Collection 1989*, 10.

they looked to project a modern image to the world. The heritage boom of the 1980s led to an about-face. The NWTEC redoubled its effort to promote the British look in woollens and worsteds at local, national and international trade shows.[29] With their eyes on global customers, John Walsh and Martin Aveyard began to understand the need to redefine the business as a brand and to engage in heritage marketing (figure 8.4 and figure 8.5). The legal name of the company, Abraham Moon and Sons Ltd, was cumbersome, old-fashioned and difficult to remember. The creation of a new logo with a shortened name, 'Moon', was the first step in the reinvention of the firm as a heritage brand.[30]

British business, following the American example, had begun to embrace corporate-identity branding. Names such as Rolls Royce and St Michael—the in-house clothing label for Marks & Spencer (M&S)—were well established, but other companies looked for ways to enhance their visibility in the global business environment. In 1982, the glassmaker Pilkington launched a new identity and, two years later, British Airways flaunted a livery designed by Landor Associates in San Francisco. In textiles, Courtaulds collaborated with the design consultancy Lloyd Northover on a new visual identity that would win the inaugural Grand Prix Design Effectiveness Award, sponsored by the Design Business Association, in 1989.[31] Aside from Courtaulds, John and Martin knew that the Alexon Group, a ladies' wear customer, had a cameo logo and that a rival tweed mill, R. G. Neill & Son Ltd of Langholm, Scotland, used a thistle trademark. The Department of Trade and Industry (DTI) provided advice and financial support to firms that wanted to improve their marketing programmes. In December 1988, a representative from the Leeds office of the DTI visited Guiseley to assess the mill's branding efforts. The DTI agent summed it up: 'Mr Aveyard is quite clear that the company needs a logo that would immediately link the company with their product in their customers mind.'[32]

The mill capitalised on its long history to launch a branding effort around the heritage theme. A small grant was used to hire Elmwood Design, a creative agency with headquarters in Guiseley.[33] Today, Elmwood is a £13 million Leeds-based design and brand identity consultancy with a global presence, but three decades ago, it was an inexperienced start-up with a modest turnover of £1 million.[34] When Elmwood's graphic designers proposed ultra-cute logos with sheep, Martin turned to his old Paris collaborator Gianni Caporale for help. The Italian stylist advised the mill to build on its success with 'Yorkshire Tweed by Abraham Moon', the label created for French co-branding. The design simply needed a facelift, and a short snappy name like 'Moon' in a classic typeface would do the trick. After all, Caporale said, 'That's what all the big brands do.'[35] With the new logo in hand, the mill asked the Haluk Gurer graphic design agency in Derby to apply the finishing touches; they designed promotional materials around the logo and added the tagline, 'Creating the cloth'.[36] The new

8.4 The management team, left to right: Arthur Walsh, Danny Spence, Martin Aveyard and John Walsh. Courtesy of Abraham Moon and Sons: *Creating the Cloth brochure*, early 1990s.

presentation embodied the themes of creativity and heritage that were coming to define the mill and set a classy tone that would resonate among up-market customers.

But the uneven seasonal demand for apparel fabrics was persistent and troublesome. At one 1993 board meeting, the directors pondered the 'losses arising during the autumn period' caused by the lack of demand for winter tweeds. Production director Danny Spence reported that the 'general trading conditions' were the worst he had ever seen. The mill 'seemed to be in a cycle of 5 good, 3 lean and 3 bad months

8.5 Finance director Graham Lockwood was another member of the management team. Courtesy of Abraham Moon and Sons.

every year', explained Arthur Walsh, and the 'costs of supplying the wide variety and high number of patterns' were high. John Walsh addressed the paradox: 'when times were hard … it was necessary to try and obtain business wherever it could be found and therefore a wide variety of ranges were necessary'. The slow period in the autumn allowed the mill to 'produce the numbers and variety of patterns' needed to supply the large number of customers. Design director Martin Aveyard believed 'it was up to the design department to make the best range possible and inevitably this would mean producing the widest possible range of cloths'. He urged the board 'to identify the markets that we intended to serve and to target the range at only those markets'.[37] One Yorkshire mill dealt with the seasonality problem in another way. In 1996, the chairman of R. Gaunt & Sons (Holdings) Ltd, of Pudsey, explained the situation to his stockholders: 'Wool textiles in Yorkshire suffers from a lack of orders and consequently a lack of activity in the autumn and winter of each year. Reuben Gaunts has been afflicted in the same way as the rest of the industry and what profit that has been made in the summer has been lost in the winter. We … are changing the emphasis of our ranges of cloth to have greater activity in winter.'[38] Eventually, the company landed on a simpler solution and sold off its cloth manufacturing division.[39]

Abraham Moon and Sons was more tenacious and more venturesome. At the Autumn 1996 edition of Première Vision, the mill introduced two collections—'Moon' and 'Phase 2'—that stressed the colourful aspects of tweed. Promotional materials for Phase 2 poked fun at double-decker buses (figure 8.6), the Queen's Guard and other British icons, while suggesting that tweed makers had a sense of humour.[40] More importantly, in the same year, John Walsh took a major step towards overcoming the uneven demand cycle by diversifying into accessories with a line of scarves in traditional tweed and tartan patterns. The mill had created

8.6 A bit of British humour from 'Moon Phase 2' advertising leaflet, 1996. Courtesy of Abraham Moon and Sons.

scarves for Polo Ralph Lauren in a small way, but they became more important with Gant's request for them.[41] In 1997, George Portland was appointed the mill's 'agent for our range of scarves for selected accounts in and around the London area'. The scarves were sold to UK customers such as the House of Fraser, the John Lewis Partnership and the Scotch House (the famous heritage woollen and cashmere retailer with stores in Regent Street and Knightsbridge); to the London buying offices for Isetan Japan and Mitsukoshi Japan; to C&A in Europe; and to importers in the United States.[42]

By this time, the company had around fifty British competitors in Yorkshire and Scotland. They all produced fabrics for menswear and ladies' wear, but there was a substantial difference in the scope of their markets. While other mills sold fabrics mainly to North America and Japan, Abraham Moon and Sons not only had a presence there, selling through their own agents, but also operated in Europe. Under John Walsh as sales director, the mill had started to expand its geographical reach, growing the customer base in Benelux, Denmark, Finland, Italy, Norway, Portugal, South Korea, Spain and Sweden. By the 1990s, the largest customers included Alexon and Daks Simpson in the UK; the ladies' brands Raven and Huche, and the menswear brands Konen and Baumler in Germany; Hart Schaffner & Marx (HSM) in the United States; Takisada in Japan; and Dylex in Canada. In 1994, the mill's exports totalled £5 million; the largest market by far was Germany (£1.4 million) with healthy sales (in descending order) to France, the United States, Italy, Japan, Portugal, Canada and Spain.[43]

The conquest of Italy was especially significant given the rivalry between Yorkshire and Prato. The Italian woollen and worsted industries were at the height of their power and British mills faced fierce competition from fifty or so producers in Biella and mainly in Prato.[44] John Walsh decided to fight back. At the Autumn 1986 edition of Première Vision, he had met Riccardo Negrini, an Italian textile agent who had operated out of Turin from 1974 to 1977, when he relocated to the great fashion city, Milan. The mill was selling '2,000 pieces per (winter season) in Germany and France' and John wanted to 'emulate this achievement in Italy'. In 1987, Negrini's agency—Ennetex s.a.s di R. Negrini & c. (which from 1990 was known as Essevi s.a.s di R. Negrini & c., or Studio Negrini/Essevi)—came to represent the mill in the Italian market.[45] The early experience in Italy was etched John's memory. He explained:

> Riccardo was rotund, young and ambitious with a sense of humour and popular with customers. I'm sure his jokes were funny in Italian but translated into his version of English they were hilarious. Design ideas flowed between Martin Aveyard, Riccardo's father (an outstanding stylist as well as an agent) Sergio Negrini and the customers' own stylists and designers. In those early years we sold to a long list of customers including

> Gruppo GFT, Lubiam, Canali, Corneliani, Etro and later with the super brands. Our
> Euro-British look was a winner. No other UK woollen mill was offering this look; they
> were still largely serving the British high street.[46]

Other Yorkshire mill owners were sceptical about John's decision to go after
accounts in Italy, where Prato reigned supreme.[47] Still organised around small
production units, the Prato woollen industry had largely abandoned the use of
recovered wool and recycled rags, and was known internationally for fine, well-
designed fabrics made from pure new wool, alpaca, camel hair, cashmere, and
mohair.[48] As the mill's exports to Italy were just getting started in the early 1990s,
the sales staff warily watched customers like Planet and Mansfield, two important
UK ladies' wear brands, buy 'expensive Italian velour'.[49] In 1996, however, John had
his satisfaction when the *Yorkshire Post* reported favourably on the mill's triumph in
Italy.[50] Global thinking was emerging as a hallmark of the company.

The new global order

In 1995, the World Trade Organization (WTO) was established in Geneva,
Switzerland, as an outcome of the Uruguay round of negotiations under the General
Agreement on Tariffs and Trade. The aim of the WTO is to open markets around the
world and to support trade barriers only when they are needed to protect consumers
or to prevent the spread of disease. In the organisation's own words, 'The system's
overriding purpose is to help trade flow as freely as possible—so long as there are no
undesirable side effects—because this is important for economic development and
well-being.'[51] In terms of textiles and clothing, the WTO would eliminate the vast
majority of tariffs, quotas and other trade barriers by 2005. The woollen industry
would have to adapt.

The venerable French merchant, Dormeuil, saw the writing on the wall. During
its 150th anniversary in 1992, the firm described itself as 'French by pedigree,
English in image and international in operation'. The birthday celebration took
place, not at the House of Dormeuil in Golden Square but at a relatively new French
headquarters, in Palaiseau, just outside Paris. By that time, Dormeuil had fourteen
offices around the world, but its presence no longer dominated Golden Square.
The House of Dormeuil had closed and the British branch of the company had
relocated to a refurbished office-showroom to the west of Regent Street, close to the
elite tailors on Savile Row. By 1994, the House of Dormeuil itself, once the Grande
Dame of Woollen Square, was divided up into rental office units.[52] Dormeuil's exit
from Golden Square was a symbol of change; by that time, trade shows, rather than
merchants, were the major intermediaries between manufacturers and brands and

promising markets were emerging on the other side of the world. Within a few short years, Dormeuil opened a Singapore office to service prestige accounts in Thailand, Malaysia and Vietnam and was looking to high-end customers in India and Mainland China.[53]

The British Wool Textile Export Corporation (BWTEC), as the National Wool Textile Export Corporation was renamed in 1993, prepared for the new order of the day with a global marketing strategy.[54] Over the next few years, the scope of the BWTEC's trade show programme became more international, building on the effort that had been underway for decades. Peter Ackroyd, who succeeded Geoffrey Richardson as director in 1992, was an enthusiastic globetrotter and, like John Walsh, he understood that the world was getting smaller. The BWTEC continued to liaise between British mills and various trade-fair authorities, arranging for space and coordinating group themes at the shows. The roster of events for 1996–97 included the usual textile, yarn and fashion trade shows in Europe and North America, new ones further afield—the British Textile Show in Seoul, South Korea; Intertextile in Shanghai; and Woolmeet in New Delhi, India—and special promotional missions to New York, Japan and Hong Kong.[55]

In 1996, Abraham Moon and Sons received the coveted Queen's Award for Export Achievement for selling woollen fabrics to Asia, Europe and North America.[56] Arthur Walsh and an entourage from the mill, including Norman Renton, the veteran mending-room supervisor, went to Buckingham Palace to accept the award from HM Queen Elizabeth, and a private celebration was held at the Royal Armouries Museum in Leeds.[57] Whether in Italy or Japan, the mill had learned to fathom the overseas customer's perception of British style and tweaked the pattern, colour and texture to deliver on those expectations. 'The whole range has our handwriting', John Walsh said in a *Financial Times* interview on the coveted export award, 'but our success lies in adapting our colours to the nuances of each market … We cannot sell to Japan, without getting on a plane to Osaka, and talking to people.'[58]

Around this time, the *New York Times* journalist Thomas L. Friedman identified the need for companies to adopt a 'multi-local' approach as they ventured into markets around the world. To succeed globally, they had to learn the local customs in the host country and become 'glocal'.[59] Abraham Moon and Sons was evolving into a glocal company. 'Our design and sales teams are travelling, designing and modifying all the time', John commented. 'We have agents in more than 20 countries, and are in constant touch with them, and with our customers.'[60] The mill's designers—Martin Aveyard, Sarah Dietz, Amanda Dougill and Judith Webb (by then Judith Coates)—all worked closely with international accounts in their home offices or at trade shows (figure 8.7). They knew how to modify the tweedy British look to suit polar opposites: the Japanese desire for subtlety as opposed to the

8.7 The Moon design team, left to right: Judith Webb (now Judith Coates), Amanda Oakes (now Amanda Dougill) and Martin Aveyard. Courtesy of Abraham Moon and Sons: *Creating the Cloth* brochure, early 1990s.

Continental taste for precision and flash. 'In Japan we can't use bright yellows', John explained, 'so we go for lots of greys and blues. The Italians love the British look.'[61] 'But their idea of British is more classical and exact than ever the British look was', he told the *Financial Times*. 'In France the British look can be positively oddball: an acrid yellow, or wacky green ... We have to modify everything and we have to keep coming up with new ideas. If we stood still, we would die.'[62]

By 1997, exports accounted for 70 per cent of sales at Abraham Moon and Sons, with the major foreign markets being France, Germany, Italy, Japan and the United States. British customers like M&S ordered substantial amounts of cloth to be shipped to their German makers-up—80,000 metres went to Dressmaster Bekleidungswerke that year. These orders evinced the growing internationalism of the fashion supply chain; fabrics made in the UK were sewn into apparel in Germany and shipped back to the UK to be sold on the high street.[63] The mill's direct sales to foreign markets ebbed and flowed. With the exception of Hugo Boss, German brands struggled in the face of Italian competition, as did Konen Herrenkleiderfabrik and BAWI Bekleidungswerke. At the mill, increased orders from Italy served as a counterpoint to the diminishing business from Germany. Eventually, the big Italian luxury brands, such as Dolce & Gabbana and Prada, replaced the lost German customers.[64]

Towards bespoke exclusivity

In 2000, *A National Strategy for the UK Textile and Clothing Industry* was published by the Textile and Clothing Strategy Group, a committee comprised of trade associations, manufacturers, retailers, unions, academics and the DTI. By that time, 70 per cent of the clothing sold on the British high street was made overseas. M&S was the UK's largest clothing retailer with a 16 per cent market share; half of the apparel it sold was sourced abroad—and even more would come from abroad in years to come.[65] In June 2000, C&A Modes announced the decision to close all of its 109 stores, which were losing £1 million per week. Back in 1995, the Dutch parent company, C&A, looked to reduce costs by consolidating its buying operations at two Continental locations, Düsseldorf and Brussels. As a result, it was difficult for C&A to cater to the taste variations in the twelve different countries where it had stores. In the UK, C&A Modes struggled to compete against discount retailers such as Matalan and Primark and speciality chains such as the Gap, which sold inexpensive sporty apparel imported from low-wage economies. 'The UK middle market is going', C&A's managing director of British operations told the *Financial Times*. 'To survive you have to be a discounter or a brand.'[66]

Back when Arthur Walsh ran the mill, nobody talked about discount retailers or brands. The great rivals on the high street, M&S and C&A Modes, had provided the average British consumer with quality apparel at moderate prices. Consumers of the postwar era had defined themselves as middle class in part through their material goods, choosing apparel, appliances, cars and furnishings to project their identity. By the New Millennium, the society that once valued possessions had transformed into the throwaway society, in part encouraged by ever-cheaper imports from low-wage economies. As fewer people purchased investment clothing, the demand for wool fabrics continued to shrink. A niche market remained for mid-range and high-quality woollens and worsteds, but the mills in Britain, France and Italy had to compete for that business against low-cost producers in Eastern Europe and China.

China weighed heavily in the minds of mill managers all around Yorkshire. To capitalise on the growing East Asian market, Messe Frankfurt launched the Interstoff Asia trade show in Hong Kong, which was on its fifth edition by the autumn of 1991.[67] Building on this effort, it put on the first Intertextile trade show at the China International Exhibition Center in Beijing from 30 October to 1 November 1995. The next year, Intertextile was moved to the Shanghai Exhibitions Center in Shanghai; the BWTEC helped British mills present their fabrics commencing with this edition, which ran from 30 October to 1 November 1996.[68] At the 1998 edition, the BWTEC put up a large 'Britain in China' display, funded by the DTI, with exhibits of yarns, fabrics and fashions, and trend forecasts and photomontages on London as a style capital. It was hoped that the Chinese would buy British fabrics, but some unsettling cultural differences interfered. In one mill just outside Shanghai, John Walsh was flabbergasted to see cloth marked with the words 'Woven in Huddersfield'. The Chinese had little regard for the Western concept of intellectual property rights and freely copied patterns. In the years ahead, the BRICs—the emerging economies of Brazil, Russia, India and China—earned a global reputation as copycats. The copying of Western designs was so prevalent among mills in China that Peter Ackroyd called it 'the nation's national sport after table tennis'.[69] Design piracy, which had plagued British woollen manufacturers in the Victorian and Edwardian eras, had returned in a new guise.

The terrorist attacks on the United States on 11 September 2001 threw the textile and garment industries into recession. European textile exports to the United States 'almost totally collapsed' and attendance at major trade fairs such as Expofil and Première Vision in Paris declined.[70] A year after the attacks, James Sugden, managing director at Johnstons of Elgin in Scotland explained how high-end apparel sales had been affected: 'Even before September 11 world markets were ailing and exports were down … The luxury market suffers if people are not travelling, … our cashmere business is down by at least 20 per cent.'[71] At Première Vision in September 2002, a group of high-level industrialists attributed the recession to the post-9/11 loss of consumer confidence, the high cost of labour and raw materials, customers' uncertainty about the euro (adopted in January 1999) and the rise of China and India as global players.[72] In 2003, the War in Iraq deepened the unease.[73] In September, Sugden put it bluntly: 'I can say that the last 12 months have been the most demanding of my 35 years in the business.'[74]

In the midst of the recession, John Walsh kicked off the New Year 2002 by becoming, at the age of forty-two, the youngest-ever chairman of the BWTEC. The world was shrinking and everybody—including Première Vision—was adjusting to the new global order. That autumn, Europe's most prestigious juried show for apparel fabrics welcomed the first non-European exhibitors, including mills from Uruguay and Japan.[75] Under the BWTEC's auspices, Prince Andrew, the Duke of York, toured the British exhibits at the Spring 2003 edition. Among the 800 booths showing fabrics for Spring 2004, the exhibition of woollens and worsteds included 420 mills from Italy, 158 from France and 70 from the UK. All together, the British woollen industry employed 12,500 people, about 10 per cent of the number in the early 1950s. The 200 or so remaining companies in Yorkshire and Scotland collectively generated £700 million in sales, exporting 70 per cent of their output, mainly to Germany, Italy, Japan, Korea and the United States and catering to niche markets.[76]

Netherfield Mill had been moving towards niche products and bespoke exclusivity for some time with its Japanese accounts, the GB Clothing Company and Gant. However, in 2003, the mill's bets on heritage styling received a major blow. For several years, the largest export account had been the American brand, Lauren by Ralph Lauren. In October 1995, the Polo Ralph Lauren Corporation licensed the Jones Apparel Group to produce, launch and distribute a new lifestyle brand, Lauren by Ralph Lauren, in North America commencing in August 1996.[77] Sold in concept shops within department stores, the 'Lauren Ralph Lauren Collection' brought 'the classic ideals, worldliness and elegance of Ralph Lauren to a new group of customers' who wanted 'the premium designer label at affordable prices'.[78]

The new label offered better career casualwear and outerwear, using woollens from Netherfield Mill. Initially, the design team for Lauren by Ralph Lauren selected the fabrics, but designers from the mill gradually came to play a larger role.[79] Lauren by Ralph Lauren was one of Jones's most successful brands, generating more than $400 million in wholesale volume in North America by 1999.[80] In 2000, Jones secured the licence to distribute the brand to 'all international locations', with a special eye to Europe.[81] The honeymoon soon ended. In 2002, Jones informed shareholders of a dispute over royalties and at the end of 2003, Polo Ralph Lauren severed the licensing agreement, three years prematurely.[82] The effect on Abraham Moon and Sons was devastating. With Jones out of the picture, the Lauren by Ralph Lauren business was lost—and the mill had to scramble to redevelop ties to this important brand.[83]

Around the same time, the St. Andrews Textile Company, the mill's importer and agent in New York, ceased operations.[84] Andy Dreschel had started working at St. Andrews in 1960, during the glory days of the city as a garment centre and witnessed the transition to brands over the next few decades. By the New Millennium, the New York fashion business was alien territory. The rise of offshore production, of discount retailers and fast-fashion chains, and of leisurewear as everyday attire started to kill off the fabric importers. On April Fool's Day in 2003, Dreschel gathered his staff and sadly announced the closure of the firm. Although St. Andrews was gone, American brands still needed woollens for skirts, jackets and coats, and Abraham Moon and Sons was left to find its own way. International trade shows like Première Vision became even more important as venues for meeting with the customers.[85]

Learning about furnishings

The uneven demand for apparel fabrics was like a sore that would not heal.[86] It was a real psychological drain to cope with the situation. In April 1999, for example, the mill had '3,438 pieces on order to weave', but there were 'very few orders' for July and 'very little hope of Spring business apart from some development work that was being carried out for M&S "Ladies"'.[87] After the New Millennium, the loss of the Lauren by Ralph Lauren business and of American contacts through St. Andrews served to focus John Walsh's strategic thinking. What if the slow time in the mill could be used to the company's advantage, producing fabric to stock? The puzzle was what to make. Could the mill weave some type of material for the UK trade that would complement the apparel fabrics made for export?

During the 1980s, Abraham Moon and Sons had exported a blanket line to the United States through St. Andrews without much success. Since the mid-1990s, John had contemplated a venture into the UK upholstery market, where there was 'a gap … for any product constructed in wool or wool blends'.[88] One day in London, he wandered through the Design Centre at Chelsea Harbour, an up-market venue with more than one hundred showrooms filled with decorator fabrics by prestigious brands such as G. P. & J. Baker, Colefax and Fowler, and Sanderson. Whether they were embellishing a hotel or a private residence, interior designers and decorators shopped at Chelsea Harbour for fabrics, furnishings and accessories. In one showroom after another, John's proposals for woollen upholstery were rebuffed: 'We don't use wool in furnishings.'[89]

Minimalism was the preferred style in fahionable glossy magazines such as *Elle Decoration*, whose pages were filled with pared-down furniture, a subdued grey-and-beige palette and unembellished fabrics in synthetic blends.[90] But

Country Homes & Interiors, a magazine for the suburban do-it-yourself decorator, featured carpets, sofas, cushions, chairs and even a doggie bed upholstered in checks and stripes that looked to be made of wool.[91] British manufacturers such as the Isle Mill in Perth, Scotland—part of the Macnaughton group, a major producer of paisley shawls and Highland and Celtic wear—were already supplying the furnishings market in the UK and abroad. The Isle Mill offered a line of stock-supported worsted furnishings fabrics that were sold to professional interior decorators and hobbyists inspired by home 'make-over' programmes on television.[92] Netherfield Mill needed to find a toehold in this unfamiliar territory. John believed that 'just as customers loved to wear tweeds by Abraham Moon and Sons in their garments, surely they would equally love the same kinds of fabrics in their homes'.[93]

In 2003, John hired a design and marketing consultant to help launch a range of furnishings fabrics. The key was to develop style options that would appeal to the urban sophisticates who read *Elle Decoration* and the cosy suburbanites who preferred *Country Homes & Interiors*. Based on the consultant's input, Martin Aveyard created two ranges, both for the mid to high-end furnishings markets. The plan was to bypass the wholesalers, using the mill's own agents to establish a direct line to the customers: furniture manufacturers, cushion makers, interior designers and fabric retailers. The fabric was to be shipped worldwide from stock in the warehouse, offering 'just in time' delivery that could bring in a premium price.[94]

In 2004, the mill launched the Moon Furnishing Collection at Heimtextil, the annual Messe Frankfurt trade fair for home and contract textiles in Frankfurt am Main, Germany. The collection consisted of coordinated furnishings fabrics in contemporary and classic designs called Urban and Heritage, respectively. The Urban line (figure 8.8) included Retro Squares, Zig Zags and Spots in black and white, turquoise, red, denim and berry, showing 'how Wool can be used in a modern environment in an exciting new way!' The Heritage range featured 'Tartans, Meltons, Boucles and Ethnic stripes' in berry, old gold, denim blue, moss green, champagne and eau de Nil, a 'twist on the traditional!'[95] When the UK's 2004 Design and Decoration Awards were announced, Abraham Moon and Sons was pleased to find the Urban line among the finalists.[96] Within a short time, other Yorkshire mills saw the potential and diversified into furnishings, while the International Wool Textile Organisation—an authority established in 1930 to oversee standards for the global wool industry, from farm to retail—commissioned a study on the image of wool in interiors.[97]

By the mid-2000s, the British textile industry had lost most of its mid-market weavers. Peter Ackroyd of the BWTEC explained the realties to the *Daily New Record*, the New York-based newspaper for the menswear trade. The remaining British mills survived by catering to high-end markets in Italy, Japan and the United States. Many of them also sold cloth to China but no one knew if the product was being used there

8.8 Urban furnishing fabrics were introduced at Heimtextil, 2004, and this line became a finalist the UK's Design and Decoration Awards in the same year. Courtesy of Abraham Moon and Sons.

or was being resold to other markets.[98] British woollens and worsteds were appealing because of their distinctiveness. 'People want things made in England because of the quality and the reputation of the product', he said, predicting that, as living standards improved, the appetite for British goods would spread to Russia and China.[99]

Everyone had an eye on China, but Abraham Moon and Sons concentrated on developing new ranges for three product areas: accessories, apparel and furnishings. Accessories were a great help with the problem of cyclical demand; the mill wove scarves (figure 8.9) when the demand for apparel fabrics was low, from July to September. But the dominance of knitwear made it difficult to sell woven scarves in some markets, including the United States. 'The style of the Moon's scarf collection is not something they have seen before and some intend to use it as a move on from the knits that have been used in the past', stated one report on a visit to American retailers. 'The Mens departments have been more interested, whilst womenswear like the look, they still prefer the knitted products.'[100] The mill tried to innovate by introducing some scented scarves—'Moonscents' for adults and 'Snifty' for children— but the idea never really took off.[101] In the early 2000s, John Pickles was hired to sell scarves to customers such as Gant, John Lewis and M&S. He disliked the scented scarves and made it known to the management committee, arguing that the mill

8.9 *Moon Accessories* brochure showing a throw that could double as a shawl or scarf, 1990s. Courtesy of Abraham Moon and Sons.

should be frying bigger fish. In 2005, John promoted Pickles to sales director, freeing up his own time to focus more intently on management and strategic thinking.[102]

Turning point: bespoke exclusivity

The years 2005 to 2008 were the toughest in John Walsh's memory. When China joined the WTO in 2001, its garment industry had 45,000 manufacturers, 3.7 million employees, produced 22 billion garments and did an export business worth $36 billion to Europe, Japan, south Asia and the United States.[103] By 2004, Chinese clothing exports accounted for one-quarter of the global total.[104] In terms of wool textiles, China's share of world production grew from 10 per cent in 1993 to 23 per cent in 2003. By one estimate, China made sixteen million cashmere sweaters in 2002 and exported seven million of them. As the *Wool Record* noted, traditional wool textile centres in the UK and Europe feared they would be 'completely eclipsed in the longer term because of China's growing might'.[105]

After the WTO initiated quota-free global trading on 1 January 2005, the West was flooded with poor quality, inexpensive garments from China, Bangladesh and elsewhere in East Asia. In the first three months of 2005, the European clothing and textile industry saw fifty firms shut down and an average of 1,000 jobs lost per day.[106] UK retailing was coming to resemble the value-driven sales environment of the United States, with everyday low prices and endless markdowns. Between 1997 and 2005, women's wear prices fell by some 34 per cent, while menswear prices dropped by around 21 per cent.[107]

The great middle market—with its major tweed users of years past such as Austin Reed, Country Casuals, M&S and C&A Modes—was disappearing. Well-known companies exited the field as their market shares plummeted. For example, Coats PLC divested itself of two classic ladies' wear lines—Jaeger and Viyella—as part of a strategy to dispose of its fashion-retail division in order to privatise and sell thread globally.[108] The growth of internet retailing added to the distress of traditional brick-and-mortar stores that served an older demographic.

A new group of clothing retailers, some of them associated with the 'fast fashion' concept, benefited from cheap clothing imports. The multiples that sold their own brands—Next, the Arcadia Group (Top Shop, Top Man, Evans, Dorothy Perkins, Burton, Wallis, Miss Selfridge), the Mosaic Fashion Group (Oasis, Coast, Karen Millen, Whistles), River Island, New Look and Zara—emphasised price, fashion and speed. New entrants like Zara delivered the latest catwalk looks, quickly made up in its own factories, at mainstream prices. At the lower end of the high street, 'value retailers' and supermarkets such as Primark, the Peacock Group (Peacocks, Bonmarché), George at Asda and Tesco (Florence & Fred) tempted prudent shoppers with fast-fashion fads that were in-and-out in one season.[109] The merchandise was more stylish than that found at the world's largest discount retailer, Wal-Mart (which had owned Asda since 1999), but as in that case, the everyday low prices were made possible by offshore production.

John Walsh discovered that some customers were taking patterns by Abraham Moon and Sons to China to have them copied cheaply. In response, the mill experimented with sourcing some cloth from China, giving its customers the option to buy fabrics made there or in the UK.[110] But after a while, the firm realised that what was gained in price was lost in quality and the practice was discontinued. With China looming large, some Yorkshiremen thought the best option was to admit defeat. Entrepreneurial thinkers like James Sugden saw another way forward. 'The biggest change we now face is learning to become a niche player, a high-added-value producer of textiles', he told the Huddersfield Textile Society. When he first started at Johnstons in 1987, he 'could never understand why a yard of tartan cloth woven in and sold out of Scotland always commanded a premium over Yorkshire cloth with the same yarns, same overheads and similar wages'. The reason, he learned, was the 'marketing of Scotland'—the creation of a romantic aura around the entire country.[111] Peter Ackroyd simply called it British style and urged the industry to 'reclaim its heritage'.[112]

In Guiseley, John pondered these options as he monitored the progress of the new furnishings venture. Although the diversification into interiors garnered media attention, the publicity did not immediately translate into sales. The high-end interiors market was still shackled to modernism and it would take a while for the reversal described in 2005 by style guru Ilse Crawford (the launch editor of *Elle Decoration*) to take hold. 'Today, some of the strongest trends are towards the comfortable—things that speak of intimacy, privacy, sensuosity and beauty, that balance the more clinical design of recent years.'[113] That was the company's first full year of furnishings production, and Abraham Moon and Sons had £500,000 of these fabrics in the warehouse and few orders on the books. It was a pensive moment for John. Turnover totalled £8 million, but profits were small. The downward spiral of the Yorkshire woollen industry, combined with the rise of China as the workshop of the world, did not bode well. Measures were taken to safeguard the firm against catastrophic financial loss. The business was divided into two companies: Abraham Moon and Sons for manufacturing and Tempest Bailey to manage the firm's cash and property and to seek new investment opportunities.[114]

In 2006, the company experienced a small loss, but strategic thinking started to pay off. British tweeds began inching back into favour due to the trend for 'smart casual' office attire for 'dress-down Friday'.[115] A new approach to work attire emerged and the standard office uniform for men—the classic worsted suit—was replaced by chinos and a woollen jacket. 'Dress styles are evolutionary', explained the chairman of Dormeuil. 'The internet has brought about a change of mentality', offering 'a real choice' that fostered a 'move to individualism'.[116]

As the concept of smart casual Fridays gained ground, brands at the upper end of the apparel market looked to British woollen mills for something different. 'A tweed herringbone jacket, topcoat or vest can be worn casual with denim', John told the *Daily News Record*.[117] Mix-and-match was the new fashion and it was a good fit with bespoke exclusivity. Retailers such as Jack Wills, L. K. Bennett and Hobbs looked to distinguish themselves by offering better-quality fashion to the brand-conscious consumer.[118] Hobbs described itself as 'quintessentially English' and pushed for a revival of the smart tailored look.[119] Tweeds by Abraham Moon and Sons found favour with these British brands as well as with Armani, Burberry, Canali, Chanel, Coach, Dolce & Gabbana, Fat Face, Gucci, J. Crew, Polo Ralph Lauren, Prada, The White Company and White Stuff.[120] For the financial year ending March 2006, exports totalled £4.64 million, with major sales (in descending order) going to Italy, Germany, Hong Kong, Spain, the United States, Portugal and Japan.[121] Many mill owners adhered to their old ways, but John went against the grain. 'We let everyone else have China and decided to do something else', he later explained. 'We decided to stay in the UK and to focus on bespoke exclusivity.'[122]

Growth through acquisition

For almost two centuries, the mill's success had been based on sales to merchants and makers-up. All of the mill's customers were in apparel and when John Walsh started in 1984, 'the only way we knew to grow our business was to chase sales'.[123] Between 2003 and 2009, he came to understand that the business could follow other paths, not only diversifying the product portfolio but also growing through acquisition. This realisation went hand-in-hand with the idea that the mill's heritage could be tapped to develop 'Moon' as a brand.

Around 2005, John explored the possibility of acquiring Neill Johnstone Ltd, in Langholm, Dumfriesshire, in the Scottish Borders. This small textile manufacturer was the brainchild of William Neill Johnstone, the visionary designer at R. G. Neill & Son Ltd, whom we met briefly in Chapter 6. Bill Johnstone had worked for R. G. Neill & Son, his family's company, since 1961, and after that firm became part of the Illingworth Morris Group in 1965, he became its managing director in 1970. In this capacity, he transformed R. G. Neill & Son into a design-led business that produced innovative textiles for men's and women's fashions. In 1985, he left to establish two of his own companies, including Neill Johnstone Ltd, a year later. With a strong design focus, the new mill sold luxury fabrics and some furnishings fabrics to up-market customers in Europe and the United States, winning the Queen's Award for Export Achievement in 1992.[124] By the mid-2000s, the fad for textured, glittery, highly coloured tweeds was at its peak and Neill Johnstone had important European accounts such as Chanel and the German brand Escada.[125] After protracted discussions, John and finance director Graham Lockwood decided against the deal. As the latter put it, 'We went to the altar but never married.'[126]

The experience helped the management team at Abraham Moon and Sons understand the need to consolidate their brand-building efforts around the heritage concept. By 2006, Netherfield Mill made products for three now clearly defined sectors—apparel, furnishings and accessories. As John happily told his colleagues in the BWTEC, the 'manufacturing of accessories' was 'helping to redress the imbalance of seasonality' that had long plagued the mill.[127] But variety had a price; there were too many customers and too many price points. The mill needed to channel its energies more efficiently and provide the core customers with superior products and service. In one sales planning meeting, it was decided to 'focus on the top 20/30 customers more, in both terms of design and sales'. In apparel, this included brands and retailers such as Brook Taverner, Brooks Brothers, Hobbs, J. Crew, Jones New York, Massimo Dutti, M&S, Paul Smith and Polo Ralph Lauren. For the first time, Abraham Moon and Sons articulated a strategy for heritage branding. The goal was to emphasise 'key values, giving customers "reason to buy"' and to 'Push the Moon brand', which had a 'story to tell in terms of Heritage/history and modern manufacturing/flexibility'.[128]

On 27 April 2007, Abraham Moon and Sons purchased a small Yorkshire worsted manufacturer that was in financial trouble: Wallass & Company Ltd in Baildon, near Bradford. Founded in 1999 by Jon Wall, the firm made worsteds for suits, uniforms and blazers that were used by universities and rugby clubs and it already produced worsteds on behalf of Abraham Moon and Sons. A critic of the throwaway lifestyle, Jon advocated a return to 'quality and design' in UK manufacturing as a salvo against 'the Chinese onslaught'.[129] After the acquisition, the Baildon plant was closed and all fourteen workers were transferred to Netherfield Mill to make worsteds under Jon's watch. The worsted business was not as seasonal as the woollen business, with decent orders during the autumn slump. Customers could now order woollen and worsted cloths created by the designers at Netherfield Mill and produced to exacting standards under one roof.[130]

That year, John also pressed ahead with an idea that had been tossed around among the mill's managers for decades. Isaac Moon had been a fan of lawn bowling and cricket and, at some point, the bowling green across from Netherfield Mill had been converted into a cricket ground. In October 2007, Abraham Moon and Sons, working through Tempest Bailey, announced a plan to raise capital by selling the property.[131] The funds would be used to expand Netherfield Mill in the years ahead.

In March 2009, Abraham Moon and Sons strengthened its standing in the accessories business with another acquisition: J. D. Matthewman (Textiles) Ltd (JDM). This family business was owned by a father-and-son team—John D. Matthewman and J. Richard Matthewman—and operated a small twelve-loom mill in Morley, a town within the City of Leeds metropolitan borough, which ran round the clock to make scarves, throws and rugs. JDM started off with tartans and diversified into 'trendy' throws, designing everything on the loom. The strategy worked brilliantly for a while, with throws under the brands Bronte Tweeds and Highland Tweeds sold in up-market stores such as Harrods and Selfridges. The industrious little mill had also 'mopped up' the Scottish and North American trade in heritage merchandise, serving customers such as the National Trust, English Heritage, tourist shops on the Royal Mile in Edinburgh, outlet stores in the Scottish countryside and Scots-Irish shops in North America. Besides Bronte Tweeds and Highland Tweeds, the mill made woollen waffle blankets for the National Health Service. But by the mid-2000s, sales had slowed down and the mill was having difficulties.[132]

The timing was fortuitous for John Walsh, who was looking for ways to grow the accessories business. He was less interested in waffle blankets than in how the demand cycle for Bronte Tweeds might complement that of apparel fabrics. Besides scarves, Netherfield Mill had a small line of throws, about a dozen altogether, but there was no good customer list and no understanding of the retail accessories trade. Scottish manufacturers such as the Isle Mill and Johnstons of Elgin were successful with worsted and cashmere throws, respectively.[133] JDM had a veteran salesman, Richard Edward Wilkinson, who knew the retail side of the throws business inside out. This native Yorkshireman—known to everyone as Edward Wilkinson—had spent fifteen years at Tweedmill Ltd, formerly the Afonwen Woollen Mill, a Welsh firm that sold scarves and throws. Edward moved to JDM in the 1990s and helped the mill transition from wholesale to retail in the UK, using the major gift shows to build a reputation for Bronte Tweeds. He also tackled the Japanese market, developing an understanding of the culture by going to Japan on trade missions sponsored by the DTI. Back in Britain, Edward secured orders for throws from the London buying offices of Japanese department stores and, when those accounts dried up, he built up the business with major trading companies such as the Marubeni Corporation, the Itochu Corporation and the Kanematsu Corporation.[134]

Between people and products, JDM had assets that complemented those of Abraham Moon and Sons. The manufacture of Bronte Tweeds was moved to Netherfield Mill, where the throws could be made to stock during the autumn slump.

The acquisition brought in a customer list of seaside shops, gift shops, interior design stores and independent retailers. JDM was well established among up-market home décor retailers, including John Lewis, Selfridges and Liberty, and among shops run by Historic Scotland and the Edinburgh Woollen Mill.[135] The brand Bronte Tweeds was also a good fit with the country look that was popular among middle-class consumers. By 2009, *Country Homes & Interiors* was advising the home decorator to soften the look of rough interiors with 'comfortable furniture and natural fabrics' and touted the woven blanket or throw as a must-have accessory for 'country living rooms with beams and stone walls'.[136]

The JDM acquisition brought additional know-how to Abraham Moon and Sons. Richard Matthewman was asked to run the accessories division and Edward Wilkinson became part of the sales team. The latter was instrumental in helping the mill to understand the retail environment for home accessories. JDM was the first woollen throw manufacturer to 'colour-blend' its product displays and to help retailers tell a 'colour story' around the merchandise. At a Harrogate home and giftware show in the summer of 2009, Edward experienced a 'eureka moment' that had a lasting impact on merchandising at Abraham Moon and Sons. Faced with a pile of mismatched samples from the two manufacturers, he arranged the throws into a pleasing rainbow display. 'You can't sell twenty-three great throws without stories', he later said. 'The stories are about *colour*. It's about the look and how you sell the look.'[137]

Design director Martin Aveyard saw the booth and began to think about colour in new ways. Bright bold patterns had given the mill a competitive edge during the synthetics revolution of the 1960s and during the European menswear fashion revolution of the 1980s. Moving forward, colour coordination became a vital part of how the mill displayed Bronte Tweeds at trade shows, in its own showroom, in promotional booklets and on the internet. The mill began to suggest how customers might display the throws in a store or how consumers might use them in the home.[138] In 2011, 'Bronte by Moon' was introduced to connect the 'Bronte' and 'Moon' brands. Abraham Moon and Sons was soon a regular presence at major giftware trade shows from the UK to China.[139]

The right time for luxury

The Great Recession, which started in the United States in December 2007 and ended in June 2009, affected most countries around the world and was the longest economic downturn since the Second World War. The economic crisis gave pause to the Western fashion industry. Before the recession started, the Paris-based American journalist Dana Thomas published *Deluxe: How Luxury Lost Its Luster*, an exposé that blew the whistle on high-end fashion houses that sourced products in China but labelled them as European.[140] In December 2007 on public television in Italy, the 'Report' programme on channel Rai-3 exposed the 'good, the bad and the ugly' of the Italian fashion system, contrasting the extreme glamour of Milan Fashion Week with the harsh conditions in the 'dubious factories off the autostrada between Florence and Prada'. The fashion victims were the 'poor souls toiling away in the Valdarno for €3 an hour' and the shoppers 'spending €700.00 on a Fendi bag that cost less than €30 to produce'.[141] A small group of consumers, mainly at the upper end of the market, started turning their backs on cheap fast fashion and demanded to know the origins of the product. This great awakening was in part fed by the sustainability movement and in part by the growing knowledge that most fashion worn in the West was made in third-world sweatshops.[142]

The top end of the apparel industry was suddenly preoccupied with integrity and looked for ways to validate added value. Abraham Moon and Sons capitalised on the moment. The year 2007 marked the 170th anniversary of the original 1837 partnership between Abraham and William Moon and the mill celebrated by introducing a Heritage Collection of tartan, Shetland and Donegal fabrics based on historic pattern books in the design archive (figure 8.10). Design director Martin Aveyard researched romantic

8.10 'British Wool Tweed' swatches from the Heritage Collection, 2007. Courtesy of Abraham Moon and Sons.

stories and vintage images to go with the swatches. A thick stack of sample cards, printed on parchment-like paper, associated Moon tweeds with historic figures such as King Edward VII, who as the Prince of Wales wore a variation of the Glen Urquhart check while shooting in Scotland.[143] Bearing the Woolmark label, the Heritage Collection was made from pure virgin wool that had been carefully selected and blended under the auspices of production director Kevin Cockerham, who succeeded Danny Spence in that position upon the latter's retirement.[144]

Although the mill was ahead of the game in terms of heritage marketing, it was operating in the red. It was difficult to establish a toehold for furnishings in the United States. Brands such as Polo Ralph Lauren liked the mill's throws, especially the 'simple stuff, overchecks, … and herringbone', but major furniture retailers like Ethan Allen were not 'interested in wool fabrics' because they were 'too expensive'. But in 2008, even as the world was in the midst of the Great Recession, the mill's sales of furnishings fabrics started to pick up. The line caught on the UK, as the nesting impulse took hold and consumers channelled discretionary income into the home. That year, the mill made a profit on substantially increased turnover.[145] From 2008 onwards, there was a psychological shift within the company—a boost of confidence. The management team began to articulate a new ambition: to be 'the best tweed mill in the world'.[146]

By 2009, the UK had forty worsted and woollen mills that focused on apparel; menswear textiles accounted for about 85 per cent of their output, which was mainly exported to Japan, Italy and the United States.[147] Although the future was promising for this elite group of mills (who had found their niches in the shrunken market), things were bleak for trade organisations in the British woollen and worsted industries. In March, the BWTEC ended its long run as the major advocate for British woollens and worsteds internationally. Based on input from manufacturers, the Department for Business Enterprise and Regulatory Reform, the successor agency to the DTI, discontinued the statutory levy on the wool industry that had supported the organisation since 1940.[148] In September, the CBWT merged with the Textile Centre of Excellence, a non-profit business with whom it had been sharing premises in Huddersfield for some months previously. The goal was to create 'a "one-stop shop" for a wide range of services for companies in the textile industry' supported by public funding. It was not clear that a trade body focused on overseas marketing and an industry organisation dedicated to management issues were needed by niche mills that focused on 'origins, provenance, heritage, and quality'.[149]

Heritage and quality were 'in'. High-end apparel brands like Boden (figure 8.11), a major customer for the mill, did not want to pay a premium for goods made in anonymous Asian sweatshops. Labour costs in China were rising, which made it

8.11 Boden uses traditional fabrics with a new twist, to create the 'Boden New British' look; offered in 2016, their Tweed Dress employs woollen cloth by Abraham Moon and Sons. Courtesy of Boden; model Cato van Ee at Viva London; photo by Heather Favell, LGA Management.

more expensive for Western brands to outsource production there. Further, there was a stylistic backlash against the gaudy over-embellishment that had dominated global fashion since 2005, when the WTO had liberalised trade and unleashed cheap Asian production. The 2011 royal wedding of Prince William, Duke of Cambridge, and Catherine Middleton focused consumer attention on understatement. The bride and her sister Pippa Middleton, the maid-of-honour, wore dresses designed by Sarah Burton at Alexander McQueen in London. The wedding inspired an interest in subtle styling, high-quality fashion and British design.[150] 'There is a trend for all things British', explained Martin Aveyard. 'That means authentic fabrics with awareness of heritage, traceability and sustainability.'[151]

Heritage marketing

By 2011, Abraham Moon and Sons was the only family-owned vertically integrated tweed mill in England.[152] The firm had taken risks and had weathered the storm. As always in business, not every decision generated successes and, by trial and error, it was discovered that worsteds were not a good fit for the mill. Production was discontinued, with Jon Wall leaving the company to pursue other textile interests.[153] However, over the course of 2011, sales grew by 18.4 per cent to £14.7 million, with healthy profits.[154] The mill's strength in exports combined with the new tripartite product portfolio—apparel, furnishings and accessories—had saved the day.

The actual stories associated with cloth manufacturing—the romance of woollen production—were increasingly important to brands at the upper end of the high street and in the global luxury business. By 2012, 'Made in Britain' was the new moniker among global luxury brands such as Chanel, Hermès, Louis Vuitton, Prada and Ralph Lauren, which were turning to 'Britain's heritage factories' for supplies of cashmere, tweeds and leather footwear. The 'new luxury' was about 'small production runs, provenance, purity and attention to detail'. The high-end fashion designer Victoria Beckham had one of her dress collections made up in East London and even the mass-market retailer Top Shop, part of the Arcadia Group, turned to British factories to sew its classic Boutique range. Among manufacturers, success stories included Burberry, whose factory in Castleford, near Leeds, employed a hundred tailors to sew trench coats, and Johnstons of Elgin, whose latest innovation was making crocheted biker jackets for the Scottish-born London-based fashion designer Christopher Kane. 'Buying British', wrote the *Sunday Times*, 'is now seen as synonymous with buying investment pieces that last.'[155]

Abraham Moon and Sons, which had inched into heritage marketing over the course of three decades, was nicely positioned to provide fashion brands with tweeds that were imbued with Britishness. One successful example was the collaboration with the Italian brand Dolce & Gabbana in 2011. 'They had a military theme for their catwalk', John Walsh explained, and wanted a 'product that was actually used and not some kind of modern variant'. At the mill, the design staff perused the historic swatch collection and created a new fabric modelled after cloth that Netherfield Mill had made for British military trench coats during the Second World War.[156] That level of authenticity, and the history attached to it, had tremendous value in the luxury market. Closer to home, British style enjoyed a revival on the high street. In 2013, M&S launched a three-year collaboration with the British Fashion Council that resulted in the Best of British, a capsule collection of menswear and women's wear made in the UK from British materials.[157] The Best of British collection hit the shops in October with suits, outerwear, knitwear, shirts and shoes from domestic manufacturers, including menswear tweeds from Abraham Moon and Sons.[158]

The quest for authenticity and the interest in British heritage extended to the home. In Autumn/Winter 2014–15, the House of Fraser launched Dickins & Jones Home, an eclectic country-inspired collection that blended 'heritage prints, modern design and a fresh vibrant colour palette' into this 'Quintessentially British' line. Colourful cushions by Abraham Moon and Sons were included in the collection: 'You can't beat classic tweed for a chic country house feel.' *Country Homes & Interiors* put a purple cushion and matching throw in 'Home Notes' in the front of the magazine with the tagline, 'Love all things wool.'[159] Bronte Tweeds were found at Highgrove House in Gloucestershire, the private residence of Charles, Prince of Wales, and Camilla, Duchess of Cornwall, and at Chatsworth House, the stately country home of the Duke and Duchess of Devonshire in Derbyshire. Further afield, First Lady Michelle Obama and her interior decorator chose the mill's furnishings fabrics for seating in the White House.[160]

Back in the 1920s, Frank Walsh had set the tone for a century of management practice when he established the policy to keep dividends low and invest in modern machinery. This precedent shaped management policy under Arthur and John Walsh. For example, when John won a Business Thinking award in Yorkshire, the money was ploughed back into the business. A major capital improvement project was already underway, in part drawing on funds from the sale of the cricket ground and in part on loans. In early 2013, a large extension of 45,000 square feet was built next to the weaving shed, bringing the total space in the mill to 200,000 square feet.[161]

In 2015, a bright new Sales and Design Showroom Suite (figure 8.12) was opened on the first floor of a mid-twentieth century building that had once housed the mending department.[162] The spacious interior exuded the company's newfound confidence. The judicious use of vintage architectural elements and the arrangement of Bronte Tweeds to resemble a colour card (Colour Plate 12) celebrated the mill's commitment to its Yorkshire heritage and design innovation. On any one weekday

8.12 The mill's Sales and Design Showroom Suite, opened in 2015. Courtesy of Abraham Moon and Sons.

at Guiseley station, one might see an entourage of Japanese or Italian customers disembark from the Leeds train and walk the short distance to Netherfield Mill for meetings with the sales, design and management staff in the new Sales and Design Showroom.

John Walsh's commitment to Yorkshire had paid off. The revenue for 2015 was double that of 2008.[163] By 2015, many brands that had been sourcing fabric in China were turning to British manufacturers because the price differential between Chinese goods and British goods had dropped considerably. The gap had narrowed to around

25 per cent and there was a major difference between Chinese and British products in terms of quality and design.[164] The decision to stay in Yorkshire rather than move to China, made against the advice of others in the woollen business, had been right on the money.[165] The reinvention of Abraham Moon and Sons around branding and British identity proved a fitting strategy for the twenty-first century.

9 Fashionability: the way forward

From 17 to 19 January 2016, Abraham Moon and Sons had an accessories display at the Top Drawer trade show at the Olympia London exhibition centre. Established in 1984, Top Drawer has evolved into a major international trade show for design-led brands in four key sectors: home, gift, fashion and craft. The mill's stand, located in the home section, showed the full range of Bronte Tweeds and Highland Tweeds: throws, cushions, baby blankets and knee rugs for the home, and scarves, stoles and, for fashionistas, poncho-style ruanas. There was a steady stream of customers from among the interior design consultancies and home goods retailers.[1]

The participation of Abraham Moon and Sons in Top Drawer spoke to the major changes that took place at the firm in the New Millennium. By 2016, the mill had a diversified product range: 50 per cent of sales were in apparel fabrics, 25 per cent in furnishings fabrics, and 25 per cent in accessories. The exhibit at Top Drawer showcased the company's heritage-inspired, design-driven philosophy in a way that was decidedly different from Première Vision, where the mill's designers helped customers with apparel fabrics. The Top Drawer stand demonstrated to retailers and interior designers how to display Bronte Tweeds and Highland Tweeds to best advantage. The merchandise was tastefully arranged according to colour families, inspired by Edward Wilkinson's eureka moment at the Harrogate gift show. He and other staff from sales and marketing, including Martin Ellis, John Pickles and Julian Smith, minded the booth and attended to the customers (figure 9.1).[2]

Fashionability by design

The fashionable home goods exhibited at Top Drawer testified to the company's evolution as a heritage-informed, design-led business and its ability to adapt traditional patterns to suit the contemporary home. The selection included reversible throws, often woven as double cloths to present a different colour and pattern on each side. Double cloths have long been a part of the mill's history, whether khaki double cloths produced for military greatcoats during the Second World War or

9.1 The sales and marketing staff from the mill interact with a guest viewing the display of Bronte Tweeds and Highland Tweeds at the Top Drawer trade show, London, January 2016. Author's collection.

patterned double cloths woven from wool-rayon blends for the C&A Modes business in the postwar era. In response to the twenty-first century penchant for natural fibres, Abraham Moon and Sons made its double cloth throws entirely from virgin wool.[3]

The most important feature of the double cloth throws is invisible, indiscernible to all but expert eyes. As Kirsty Anderson, one of the mill's designers, explained, double cloths are complex fabrics that require a high level of technical skill in both design and production. Trained at the School of Textiles and Design at Heriot-Watt University in Galashiels on the Scottish Borders, Kirsty had worked at the Isle Mill before joining Abraham Moon and Sons in August 2008. At Netherfield Mill, she is one of four staff designers who create apparel fabrics, furnishings fabrics and accessories under the auspices of Martin Aveyard, now the creative director, and Judith Coates, the new head of design. Double cloths, she explains, actually take longer to design than other fabrics. The designer first works out the intricate relationships between the different coloured yarns using pen and paper (figure 9.2), and then consults with the production team about the loom set-up to get the weaving right.[4] In the end, then, the Top Drawer stand was a fashion statement that benefited not only from a heritage-informed approach to marketing but also from advanced technical capabilities in woollen design.

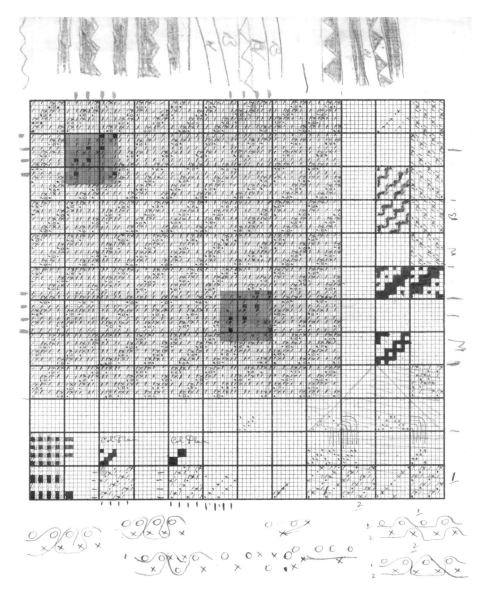

9.2 A hand-drawn point paper showing a design for a complex double cloth with a square motif.
Courtesy of and copyright Abraham Moon and Sons.

Heritage: made in Britain

The adjacent stand of Welsh rival Tweedmill featured woollen accessories in bright colours, advertised by a prominent sign announcing that the products are developed in Britain.[5] 'What's distinctive about Moon is that it is a vertical mill', said Pam Birchenall, a designer who joined the firm in 2015. Another graduate of the Scottish college of textiles in Galashiels, she has worked for several Yorkshire mills, including Joshua Ellis & Company, a high-end cashmere manufacturer in Batley. 'Many mills only exist as an "office"', she explained.[6] Fabrics and accessories by Abraham Moon and Sons are designed, developed and made in Britain.

At the start of the New Millennium, managing director John Walsh had chosen to keep Netherfield Mill going when many others looked to China's mills. The commitment to manufacturing in the UK went against the grain, but ultimately, this counterintuitive measure proved to be on trend. British production was an asset in British branding. The industrious little Guiseley mill had been ahead of the game when it partnered with vintage-inspired customers like the GB Clothing Company, Polo Ralph Lauren and Gant in the mid- to late 1980s. By 2016, heritage branding had become a favourite marketing strategy among retailers and brands from the middle market upwards. Motifs and stories from the past were seen as tools for distinguishing pedigreed or aspirational brands from the upstarts. British retailers like Boden, Hobbs and M&S, and global luxury brands such as Chanel and Dolce & Gabbana, sought to capitalise on heritage, which gave their products considerable cultural cachet. John had bet on British manufacturing and British heritage—and won.

Tariffs and technology

The international political economy has long been an important influence on the design history of Abraham Moon and Sons. For better or worse, tariffs and trade policies were always on the minds of woollen manufacturers and determined what types of cloth they made. The free trade policies of the Victorian era created a favourable climate for woollen manufacturers who were exporters. For a short period, it seemed as if everyone wanted British tweeds, and the Yorkshire mills had the world at their fingertips. But the tariff wars that commenced in the 1880s transformed into the isolationist policies of the Great Depression and the complex protectionist regime under the General Agreement on Tariffs and Trade. Tweed mills fought for slim slices of the market at home and abroad: price, quality and novelty were the ammunition. Mill owners bemoaned the pattern wars that swept across West Yorkshire as manufacturers clamoured for shares of the export market. They groaned the loudest when discussing the rampant pirating of British patterns by importers and textile mills in Continental Europe, North America and, eventually, Asia.

Few histories of design and fashion consider the relationships among trade policies, technology and product innovation. Over two centuries, Abraham Moon and Sons reeled from the effects of foreign protectionism, but found a way through the quagmire. In the 1920s, Frank Walsh invested in the latest mill equipment as a way to increase productivity, improve the quality of the cloth, reduce prices and stay ahead. His efforts to compete with Scottish tweeds in New York never got off the ground, but his investment in technology paid off during the Great Depression. Canny consumers looked for inexpensive woollen clothing with some fashion flair, and tweeds from Netherfield Mill proved to be just the thing. A quarter-century later, Arthur Walsh engaged another type of technology—man-made fibres—as a winning weapon when he ventured into rayon-wool blends for the mass market served by C&A Modes. The end result was a marvellous range of moderately priced tartans and tweeds that delighted countless British consumers who lived on a budget.

The decision to compete in a protectionist world by producing a wide variety of patterns for many different customers was not unique to Netherfield Mill. Other tweed makers in Scotland and Yorkshire followed a similar path. What differentiated Abraham Moon and Sons from most of these mills was the continued willingness of the Walsh family to reinvest the profits into the business, mainly on new equipment and the general improvement of the physical plant. Early on, John Walsh learned about the follies of neglect when he went to equipment auctions for shut-down companies and found factories filled with antiquated machinery. These sorry sights impressed on him the importance of continued improvement—not only of the product, but also of the mill itself.

In the Victorian woollen industry, nobody uttered the words 'corporate strategy', but everyone talked about tariffs and trade. Guiseley, like countless other manufacturing towns, was linked to the global economy by a network of merchants, warehouses, railroads, canals and ships that delivered Yorkshire woollens to port and then to markets around the world. Like John Walsh, the pioneer factory owners of what became the Aireborough district—James Ives, Abraham Moon, William Murgatroyd and Jonathan Peate—found their way as entrepreneurs by experimenting with different strategies until they landed on something that worked. They combined design and technology to develop Guiseley Waterproof Tweeds—the ideal wet weather gear for the British Isles, Central and Northern Europe and North America—and had a good run for a while. Ultimately, these early mill owners found themselves adrift when the major industrial powers engaged in a ferocious tariff war that continued well beyond their lifetimes. When the World Trade Organization liberalised markets in the years either side of 2000, this presented a new problem for UK woollen mills: Chinese competition. Then, after 24 June 2016, John Walsh and other mill owners faced an uncertain future in the light of Brexit, the UK's vote to leave the European Union and its zero-tariff trading conditions. 'Britain had a good deal in Europe', said Andrew Seal of SIL Holdings, a textile conglomerate in Bradford, but the 'warmth has gone to some extent.'[7] There is nothing surprising about the parallels to the tariff worries of Victorian times. To paraphrase the American writer Mark Twain, no occurrence is a one-off event, but it repeats something that has happened before.

'Terribly Tasty Tweed': keeping up with the customers

Over the past four decades, Abraham Moon and Sons learned the value of close collaboration with their customers. The clothiers of early modern times depended on woollen merchants to help them understand the vagaries of fashion. The 1870s' swatches in the Design Registry at the National Archives in Kew show that Netherfield Mill used the new aniline dyes to make eye-catching patterns, but no one knows exactly how Abraham Moon and his sons, Abraham Moon the younger and Isaac Moon, decided which designs and colours to make. There is greater certainty about the relationship between the mill and its twentieth-century customers. This period was first dominated by the woollen merchants, then the makers-up and finally by powerful high-street multiples. During the interwar years, tastemakers from London looked north and offered free advice. They believed that if Yorkshire mills put more thought into aesthetics, the cloth would sell itself.

The Yorkshire mill owners knew better. Mass-market tweeds—with their delightful patterns, unusual colours and affordable prices—actually did well during periods of scarcity. In the postwar sellers' market, Arthur Walsh grew the business by selling ranges created by skilled technical designers. In response to the cultural upheavals of the 1960s, some Yorkshire woollen and worsted mills began to ask the customers what they wanted. The late twentieth century was a turning point for fashionability and design practice at Netherfield Mill. The infusion of young creative talent; the interactions with agents in Paris, Milan, Montreal, New York and Tokyo; and innovative new customers like Next, Gant and Daks brought design, sales and marketing together. One-on-one meetings between the designer and the fabric buyer became part of the customised service offered by Abraham Moon and Sons.

Designers such as Amanda Dougill and Claire Pearson have spent a good deal of their careers minding the customers. 'You can't design in a bubble', said Amanda, who started at the mill in 1992 after finishing her studies in textile design at the University of Leeds. 'You can't sit in Yorkshire and design. You have to travel and bring in ideas.' As the mill developed its trade with European fashion houses, the design staff were constantly on the road, attending textile trade fairs and visiting customers in France, Germany and Italy.[8] The pace had accelerated by the time Claire, a designer trained at Nottingham Trent University, landed at Abraham Moon and Sons after their 2007 acquisition of Wallass & Company Ltd, where she had worked on striped worsteds for blazers. Today, she specialises in women's wear fabrics, working with other members of the creative team to plan the next season's ranges, patterns and colours. She attends all the major trade shows for apparel fabrics, including Première Vision Paris and the London Textile Fair, and works closely with London agent Trevor Brann on British women's wear brands such as Boden, Crew Clothing, Hobbs, Jaeger, L. K. Bennett and Laura Ashley. After the customers have studied their sample lengths, they may ask, 'Can you change this pink?'[9] Bespoke exclusivity and fashionability are built on incremental changes.

Today, the close interaction between mill and customer is a trend among boutique fabric manufacturers. Other high-end woollen mills, including the cashmere manufacturer Joshua Ellis & Company, offer similar consultations. Abraham Moon and Sons has the largest creative staff—six designers altogether— and makes the yarn and the fabric on site.[10] The fact that the yarn is spun and the cloth is woven at the mill provides the designers with a high level of quality control that translates into satisfaction on the part of the customer and the ultimate consumer. One discerning North American consumer, who bought a J. Crew blazer made of cloth from the mill, wrote: 'The quality of the fabric is fantastic … There are no visible flaws anywhere. The herringbone pattern on the grey version looks terrific.' Back in 1905, the journalist for *Textile World Record* who saw 'Guiseley tweed' in the woollen warehouses of Manchester and Bradford admired it as a 'very tasty thing'. This consumer, writing in 2015, loved his new jacket made from 'Terribly Tasty Tweed.' [11] A century of tradition translated into happy tweed fans.

Provenance, sustainability and the future of wool

Abraham Moon and Sons has combined design, technology, heritage and customer service into a successful strategy for the twenty-first century. The focus on provenance and design-led sales, along with the Walsh family's commitment to the company, has enabled the mill to overcome some tough challenges: the avalanche of synthetics and knitwear, the backlash against classic styling and the rise of fast fashion, and the triumph of East Asia as a manufacturing centre. The mill ventured into heritage-informed design in the 1980s, when middle-class consumers still used clothing as a demarcation of social class, but in more recent years has adapted vintage styling to the higher end of the market, where better-off consumers look for historical anchors to moor them in an uncertain global world. The mill's recent successes with heritage branding and co-branding owe much to the West's growing nostalgia for the motifs of its own past, which is a response to globalisation, albeit a relatively benign one compared to Brexit and the swell of nationalism in the United States and Europe. Consumers at the upper end of the apparel market want something other than faceless mass-produced goods, and fashion houses have responded with co-branded heritage merchandise. One example is the American retailer J. Crew, which tags its herringbone menswear blazers with the co-branding label 'MOON Quality British Cloth Since 1837'.[12] Abraham Moon and Sons has emerged as one of the fashionable faces of Britain's woollen heritage.

The affluent consumer's interest in woollen fabrics has an environmental dimension that has been articulated by a number of wool advocacy initiatives, including The Campaign for Wool. In January 2010, John Walsh was among a select group of specialists from the British fashion, textile and retail industries who attended an invitational event organised by Charles, Prince of Wales, at Wimpole Home Farm near Cambridge, England, to discuss the future of wool. Prince Charles unveiled The Wool Project—an effort to raise awareness of the advantages of this natural fibre—funded by two organisations: the British Wool Marketing Board in Bradford and Australian Wool Innovation, a successor several times removed from the International Wool Secretariat.[13] The initiative eventually became The Campaign for Wool, with Prince Charles as the royal patron (figure 9.3). This campaign sponsors an annual Wool Week and other programmes to stimulate interest in wool as a sustainable material for fashion and home decoration.[14] Ultimately, the campaign was launched in Australia, France, Germany, Japan, Korea, the Netherlands, Scandinavia, Spain and elsewhere. In 2012, its reach was extended to China to capitalise on the buoyant fashion industry and the growing consumer market, and to the United States to target the interiors trade, which is dominated by synthetics. Although the original plan was for the initiative to last five years, in 2013 it was decided to make The Campaign for Wool permanent.[15] In 2016, the campaign issued The Dumfries House Wool Declaration, which outlined ten key points about the versatility and renewability of wool as a natural resource.[16]

One goal is to educate the younger generation—consumers who are already attuned to green issues—on the benefits of wool as a sustainable resource. Wool today accounts for a mere 1 per cent of the world's fibres, but advocates like James Sugden, the former chairman and managing director at Johnstons of Elgin, believes that the niche for wool fabrics has tremendous growth potential.[17] Peter Ackroyd, the former director of the British Wool Textile Export Corporation who migrated to executive positions at the International Wool Textile Organisation and The

9.3 In 2015 Prince Charles visited the mill as part of his ongoing work with The Campaign for Wool. Courtesy of Abraham Moon and Sons.

Campaign for Wool, echoes those sentiments. Woollens and worsteds, as natural fibres, press all the right environmental buttons.[18]

Besides ecological matters, concerns over labour conditions in Asian factories have furthered the wool renaissance. Consumer awareness of third-world sweatshops increased after the widespread press coverage of two tragedies in the Bangladeshi garment industry—the fire at the Tazreen Fashions factory in November 2012 and the collapse of the Rana Plaza building, the eight-story home to several clothing factories, in April 2013.[19] Discount stores and fashion retailers such as Bonmarché, C&A, H&M, KiK, Mango, Primark and Wal-Mart came under fire from trade unions and human-rights groups around the world. Critics of the have-it-now culture noted how the millennial generation's experience-driven lifestyle—based on fast food, fast tech and fast fashion—had replaced the investment consumer culture of earlier times.[20] Some socially-conscious consumers with discretionary incomes looked to revive the slower way of life, turning to upscale retailers for ecologically-sound brands with British roots. The sustainability message—wool is biodegradable—resonated in premium markets, where companies like J. Crew, the co-branding customer mentioned earlier, has policies for socially responsible supply-chain management.[21]

Fashionability: yesterday, today and tomorrow

This book has examined the history of a single firm in a single industry in a single country over the course of 180 years. The story started with a small clothier in rural Yorkshire and ended on the global stage of international commerce. The intention has been to use microhistory to tell the tale of one firm and its competitors, and to link those examples to macrohistorical developments within the fashion-industrial complex. Another goal has been to demonstrate the importance of design thinking to one of Britain's oldest industries, and thus open the door onto a new history of fabrics and fashion.

The British woollen industry has always been a global industry, but its links to the wider world have changed over the past two centuries. Merchants, telegraphs, sailing ships and steamers have been replaced by international trade shows, the internet, jet aeroplanes and container ships. The profoundly local character of Abraham Moon and Sons—it is a small mill (figure 9.4) in a town that is now a suburban community within greater Leeds—is paralleled by its thoroughly global disposition. A global outlook has shaped the company since the days of Abraham Moon the elder, who strategically built his factory next to a railway line that provided ready access to Leeds, Bradford and foreign markets. Today, international textile and fashion fairs connect the firm to its global customers, but foreign trade has never been out of the mill's sight.

The British wool textile industry modernised in the nineteenth century by consolidating production into factories, but it was the strong focus on design and design management that provided certain mills with a competitive edge. Now forgotten figures such as John Beaumont—the most famous woollen and worsted designer in Victorian Yorkshire—laid the foundation for a strong design ethos. Each generation seeks to improve upon the work of its parents and is often oblivious to the achievements of its grandparents. Hence, the commitment to product innovation ebbed and flowed, but ultimately, it was rediscovered and foregrounded by companies such as Abraham Moon and Sons, Joshua Ellis & Company, Neill Johnstone Ltd, and Johnstons of Elgin. These mills recognised that bright creative people could help to reinvent British wool fabrics, putting them back in fashion and securing the custom of up-market retailers and global luxury brands.

9.4 The office and one of the two gates at Netherfield Mill, Guiseley. Courtesy of Abraham Moon and Sons.

Place and heritage have been crucial to the recent reinvention of the industry. British woollens, with their deep historical roots, have benefited from the contemporary consumer's yearning to feel grounded in an uncertain global world. As Beryl Gibson, a trend consultant to the UK Fashion and Textile Association, explained, 'Traceability and manufacturing with superb heritage and expert time-honoured skills is seen as a quality as important as the actual fabric ... Today, discerning consumers want to know exactly what they are buying with perceived value both real and emotional.'[22] Tradition and heritage have indeed become fashionable as people evaluate the pros and cons of the often stormy effects of globalisation. Metaphorically, traditional motifs and heritage styling provide safe harbours.

Finally, the history of Abraham Moon and Sons tells us much about the resilience and the importance of family capitalism. This mill and others like it have survived not simply because of private ownership but because of the families' willingness to endure financial losses during hard times with hopes for a brighter future. The owners were patient and tenacious, not merely lucky. Such was the case during the tariff wars of the Victorian and Edwardian eras, in the Great Depression and during the industry's downward spiral in the late twentieth century. Several generations of Moons and Walshes embraced change, encouraged creativity and maintained their optimism in the face of adversity. The commitment to local production kept people employed at a time when many UK factories closed their doors. Their modus operandi offers food for thought in a world dominated by multinational corporations that are mainly focused on increasing shareholder value.

What does the future hold for firms like Abraham Moon and Sons? Historians are not fortune tellers who look into crystal balls to make predictions, but we do analyse the path travelled and can shine a light on the crossroads. Two centuries ago, nearly everyone in the West wore wool clothing to stay warm, but in our time, few people in the developed economies have to worry about bundling up against the cold. Once ubiquitous for everyday apparel, wool has been reinvented as a luxury fibre, and heritage has been added to enhance its fashion appeal. Abraham Moon and Sons has adapted to the new fashion system within which a discriminating group of consumers demand clothing, accessories and home décor that are ecologically sound and heritage-inspired. The era of mass customisation for luxury markets has arrived and appears to be here to stay.[23] The mill's commitment to design, technology, heritage and customer service has proven to be a valuable asset in this new business environment—with its distinctive demands for fashionability.

Acknowledgements

Every author is indebted to administrators, archivists, editors, librarians and funders who enable their research. For this book, I was blessed with unrestricted access to the historical archive at Abraham Moon and Sons Ltd and had the opportunity to speak with people affiliated with the firm, both today and yesterday. I am grateful to John P. T. Walsh, the chairman and managing director, for approaching the University of Leeds with the idea for a history of his company, and for his receptiveness to the idea of my writing an expansive history that situated the mill within the context of the British woollen industry and the global fashion system. Special thanks go to Barbara and Arthur Walsh for welcoming me into their home and to the ever-charming Trevor Brann for my London education on the wholesalers and makers-up of the City, Golden Square and the East End. Peter Ackroyd graciously provided me with access to the archive of the National Wool Textile Export Corporation and helped me to understand its important role in linking the British woollen and worsted industries to the wider world.

This project benefited from extensive research in repositories around the UK, which are listed in the Select Bibliography. I am grateful to the many administrators, archivists, curators and librarians who facilitated my research at those institutions, including Fiona Blair, Emily Abbey, Nick Brewster, Katherine Carter, Katherine Chorley, Elaine Evans, Timothy Long, Paul McShane, Eve Read, Michelle Ridge, Claire Watson and Jill Winder. For assistance with local history, I extend my gratitude to Carlo Harrison, Gerald Long and Alex Willoughby at the Aireborough Historical Society for imparting their knowledge of the Yorkshire woollen industry, and to Jane Blake and Deborah Myers, the current residents of Crooklands, for giving me a tour and sharing documents related to Isaac Moon's former home. I appreciate David Tebb and Rick Lamb having shown me the sights in Guiseley. Kudos goes to Keith Williams at the Leeds City Council for opening my eyes to the cityscape and its many woollen warehouses.

For editorial guidance, I am grateful to Mary Schoeser and Diane Mackay, who served as the book's subeditor and permissions researcher, respectively, and who have contributed to making this a better book in many ways. At Manchester University Press, Emma Brennan showed her faith in the project from the start and ushered the project through the system. Special thanks go to other people working for the press, including Paul M. Clarke, Bethan Hirst, Alun Richards, Lianne Slavin and Susan Womersley. Every reasonable effort has been made to contact or trace copyright holders. No harmful or malicious intent was intended in the reproduction of images, and if any errors have been inadvertently made, please contact either the publisher or the author so any corrections might be made for subsequent editions.

At the University of Leeds, I am much indebted to Professor Graham Loud who during his tenure as head of the School of History put me touch with John Walsh and encouraged me to develop projects with industry; to his successor, Professor Simon Hall; and to the School's research directors, Professor William Gould and Professor Simon Ball, for continued support. I am further indebted to Professor Abraham Lenhoff in the Department of Chemical and Biomolecular Engineering at the University of Delaware for a visiting scholar appointment that has given me continued access to Morris Library and its many resources in the history of industry, technology and society.

Funding for this project came from a number of sources: Abraham Moon and Sons, the School of History at the University of Leeds and the European Commission. An EU initiative called Humanities in the European Research Area II (HERA II) funded my three-year collaborative research project, The Enterprise of Culture: International Structures and Connections in the Fashion Industry since 1945 [12-HERA-JRP-CE-OP-050] under the 'Cultural Encounters' programme from August 2013 to October 2016. This book was my major research output for that project. HERA II provided funds for research leave and for archival research, for which I am very appreciative.

Notes

Introduction

1 Première Vision Paris, *Map Guide 15–17 Sept 2015*; Première Vision Paris, www. premierevision.com/ (accessed 1 May 2016).

2 Ivan Green, conversation with author, Première Vision Paris, 15 September 2015.

3 Author's observations, Première Vision Paris, 15–17 September 2015.

4 Notable exceptions include works such as M. Schoeser and C. Boydell (eds), *Disentangling Textiles: Techniques for the Study of Designed Objects* (London: Middlesex University Press, 2002); B. M. King, *Silk and Empire* (Manchester: Manchester University Press, 2005); P. A. Sykas, *The Secret Life of Textiles: Six Pattern Book Archives in North West England* (Bolton: Bolton Museums, Art Gallery and Aquarium, 2005); P. M. Hitchon, *Chanel and the Tweedmaker: Weavers of Dreams* (Carlisle: P3 Publications, 2012); F. Anderson, *Tweed* (London: Bloomsbury Academic, 2016).

5 J. Smail, 'The sources of innovation in the woollen and worsted industry of eighteenth-century Yorkshire', *Business History*, 41:1 (January 1999).

6 A. J. Willoughby and G. Long, interview by author, Yeadon, West Yorkshire, 29 September 2016.

7 J. Sugden, telephone interview by author, 21 October 2016; J. Sugden, email to author, 21 October 2016; M. Keighley, 'Johnstons take fashion on a Highlands tour', *Wool Record*, 151 (September 1992), 37; 'Scottish trade reaches a decisive turning point', *Wool Record*, 154 (September 1995), 17–19; 'Famous Scottish company are celebrating 200th anniversary', *Wool Record*, 156 (April 1997), 16–19.

8 Sugden interview.

9 J. P. T. Walsh, interview by author, Weeton, North Yorkshire, 23 May 2015.

10 R. L. Blaszczyk, 'Rethinking fashion', in R. L. Blaszczyk (ed.), *Producing Fashion: Commerce, Culture and Consumers* (Philadelphia: University of Pennsylvania Press, 2008), pp. 1–5.

11 J. Banks and D. de la Chapelle, *Tartan: Romancing the Plaid* (New York: Rizzoli, 2007), pp. 10–11, 24–5, 32–3, 49, 53, 134–47, 162–6.

12 E. P. Harrison, *Scottish Estate Tweeds* (Elgin, Scotland: Johnstons of Elgin, 1995), pp. 186–7; Abraham Moon and Sons Ltd, Guiseley, West Yorkshire, Design department files, promotional materials for Heritage Collection, 2007.

13 *Brief Encounter*, 1945, directed by D. Lean.

14 Blaszczyk, 'Rethinking fashion'; R. L. Blaszczyk, *Imagining Consumers: Design and Innovation from Wedgwood to Corning* (Baltimore: Johns Hopkins University Press, 2001); R. L. Blaszczyk, *The Color Revolution* (Cambridge, MA: The MIT Press, 2012); R. L. Blaszczyk and V. Pouillard (eds), *European Fashion: The Creation of a Global Industry* (Manchester: Manchester University Press, 2018).

15 J. H. Clapham, *The Woollen and Worsted Industries* (London: Methuen & Company, 1907); H. Heaton, *The Letter Books of Joseph Holroyd (cloth-factor) and Sam Hill (clothier): Documents Illustrating the Organisation of the Yorkshire Textile Industry in the Early 18th Century* (Halifax: F. King, [1914]); H. Heaton, *The Yorkshire Woollen and Worsted Industries, from the Earliest Times Up to the Industrial Revolution* (Oxford: Clarendon Press, 1920); W. B. Crump (ed.), *The Leeds Woollen Industry, 1780–1820* (Leeds: Thoresby Society, 1931); N. B. Harte and K. G. Ponting (eds), *Textile History and Economic History: Essays in Honour of Miss Julia de Lacy Mann* (Manchester: Manchester University Press, 1973); D. T. Jenkins, *The West Riding Wool Textile Industry, 1770–1835* (Edington, Wiltshire: Pasold Research Fund, 1975); D. T. Jenkins and K. G. Ponting, *The British Wool Textile Industry, 1770–1914* (London: Heinemann Educational Books, 1982); and P. Hudson, *The Genesis of Industrial Capital: A Study of the West Riding Wool Textile Industry, c. 1750–1850* (Cambridge: Cambridge University Press, 1986).

16 One of the best discussions of pattern books is Sykas, *The Secret Life of Textiles*.

17 Blaszczyk, *The Color Revolution*.

18 West Yorkshire Archive Service, Leeds, WYL2139: Records of A. W. Hainsworth and Sons Ltd, box 51, Letterbook, 1934–48, R. G. Hainsworth, Milan, to A. W. Hainsworth & Sons Ltd, West Yorkshire, 25 April 1934.

19 P. Ackroyd, telephone interview by author, 21 October 2016.

1 The case of the grey tweed

1 P. Slater, *History of the Ancient Parish of Guiseley* (London: Hamilton, Adams & Company, 1880), p. 150.

2 'Charge of fraud against a Pudsey cloth manufacturer', *Leeds Mercury* (27 January 1866); 'Charge of fraud against a Pudsey cloth manufacturer', *Leeds Mercury* (3 February 1866); 'The robbery from the Coloured Cloth Hall, Leeds', *Leeds Mercury* (30 January 1866); 'Theft from the Coloured Cloth Hall by a manufacturer's son', *Leeds Times* (3 February 1866); *Charlton and Anderson's Directory of the Woollen Districts of*

Leeds, Huddersfield, Dewsbury, and the Surrounding Villages (Leeds: Samuel Moxon, 1864), pp. 69, 134; and W. White, *Directory of Leeds* (Sheffield: William White, 1866), pp. 33, 108.

3 'Charge of fraud' (27 January 1866). Abraham Moon's stock book has not survived, but it may have been comparable to the pocket notebook used by Abimelech William ('young Bim') Hainsworth; West Yorkshire Archive Service, Leeds (hereafter cited as WYAS–L), WYL2139: Records of A. W. Hainsworth and Sons Ltd (hereafter cited as WYL2139), box 23, A. Wm. Hainsworth, 'Manufacturing Book', 10 April 1865.

4 *Report of the Tariff Commission*, vol. 2: *The Textile Trades, Part 2—Evidence on the Woollen Industry* (London: P. S. King, 1905), item 1635.

5 S. Burt and K. Grady, *The Illustrated History of Leeds*, 2nd edn (Derby: Breedon Books, 2002), pp. 58–62; J. R. McCulloch, *A Statistical Account of the British Empire*, vol. 2 (London: Charles Knight, 1837), p. 51; 'A day at a Leeds woollen-factory', *Penny Magazine*, 12 (November 1843), 464.

6 'A cloth manufacturer charged with felonious receiving', *Manchester Guardian* (4 January 1870).

7 'Charge of fraud' (27 January 1866).

8 *Report from the Select Committee on the Laws Relating to the Stamping of Woollen Cloth. Ordered, by The House of Commons, to be Printed, 19 April 1821*; and WYAS–L, WYL2139, box 23, *Regulations of the Woollen Cloth Trade within the West-Riding of Yorkshire*, 1821, pp. 1–2.

9 'Charge of fraud' (27 January 1866); 'Henry Foggitt' and 'Hannah Moon', in Ancestry. com, *West Yorkshire, England, Marriages and Banns, 1813–1935* [database on-line] (Provo, UT: Ancestry.com Operations, 2011); 'Henry Foggitt', in Ancestry.com, *1861 England Census* [database on-line] (Provo, UT: Ancestry.com Operations, 2005).

10 E. R. Kelly (ed.), *The Post Office Directory of the West Riding of Yorkshire* (London: Kelly and Company, 1867), p. 347.

11 *Ibid.*, pp. 348, 1,550; 'Charge of fraud' (3 February 1866).

12 'Charge of fraud' (3 February 1866).

13 'The robberies from the Leeds Coloured Cloth Hall', *Sheffield and Rotherham Independent* (30 January 1866); 'The robberies from the Leeds Coloured Cloth Hall', *Supplement to the Manchester Courier and Lancashire General Advertiser* (3 February 1866); 'The robberies from the Leeds Coloured Cloth Hall', *Dundee Courier and Argus* (31 January 1866); 'Robberies from the Leeds Coloured Cloth Hall', *Manchester Guardian* (29 January 1866).

14 D. T. Jenkins and K. G. Ponting, *The British Wool Textile Industry, 1770–1914* (London: Heinemann Educational Books, 1982), pp. 77–91, 125–65; R. G. Wilson, *Gentleman Merchants: The Merchant Community in Leeds, 1700–1830* (Manchester: Manchester University Press, 1971), pp. 6–7.

15   M. W. Beresford and R. Unsworth, 'Locating the early service sector of Leeds: The
     origins of an office district', *Northern History*, 44:1 (March 2007), 75–109.

16   M. R. Mitchell, *A History of Leeds* (Bath: Phillimore & Co., 2000), pp. 23–9.

17   Burt and Grady, *Illustrated History of Leeds*, pp. 19, 24–6, 33, 55, 65.

18   W. White, *Directory and Topography of the Borough of Leeds, and the Whole of the
     Clothing District of the West Riding of Yorkshire* (Sheffield: Robert Leader, 1843), n.p.

19   Burt and Grady, *Illustrated History of Leeds*, p. 135.

20   *Ibid.*, p. 134.

21   S. Wrathmell, *Leeds* (New Haven: Yale University Press, 2005), pp. 60–73, 83–8; J.
     Mayhall, *The Annals of Yorkshire from the Earliest Period to the Present Time*, vol. 3:
     1866–1874 (Leeds: C. H. Johnson, [1875]), pp. 55, 208.

22   P. Leach and N. Pevsner, *Yorkshire West Riding: Leeds, Bradford and the North* (New
     Haven: Yale University Press, 2009), pp. 405–6, 409, 428; Wrathmell, *Leeds*, pp. 103–4.

23   *Handbook for Travellers in Yorkshire*, rev. edn (London: John Murray, 1874), p. 393.

24   *Ibid.*, pp. 405, 411; M. D. T. Rigg, *Round and About Aireborough*, vol. 3 (Guiseley: M. D.
     T. Rigg, 1990), p. 71; M. Rigg, *Round and About Aireborough*, vol. 4 (Guiseley: M. D. T.
     Rigg, 1992), p. 37.

25   Aireborough Civic Society, 'A Brief History of Guiseley', at www.
     aireboroughcivicsociety.org.uk (accessed 15 September 2016).

26   P. Hudson, *The Genesis of Industrial Capital: A Study of the West Riding Wool Textile
     Industry, c. 1750–1850* (Cambridge: Cambridge University Press, 1986), pp. 26–9.

27   For Abraham Moon's date of birth, see 'Guiseley Baptisms, 1800–1809', at Genuki: UK &
     Ireland Genealogy, available at www.genuki.org.uk (accessed 14 February 2015). He was
     baptised on 4 April 1806; see 'Abraham Moon', in Ancestry.com, *England, Select Births
     and Christenings, 1538–1975* [database on-line] (Provo, UT: Ancestry.com Operations,
     2014). John Moon married Ann Oddy on 31 July 1805; see WYAS–L, Microfiche:
     Records of Guiseley Parish, Marriage Register for the Year 1805, No. 127.

28   S. A. Caunce, 'Complexity, community structure and competitive advantage within the
     Yorkshire woollen industry, c. 1700–1850', *Business History*, 39:4 (October 1997), 26–8.

29   WYAS–L, BDP29: Records of Guiseley Parish (hereafter cited as BDP29), item 122,
     'Answers to the Questions proposed by the Committee of Magistrates at Wakefield
     appointed to correspond with the Board of Agriculture', Guiseley, 10 October 1795.

30   E. Baines, *Directory and Gazetteer of the County of York, vol. I—West Riding* (Leeds:
     Edward Baines, 1822), unnumbered page; p. 512.

31   The apprenticeship records for Guiseley Parish deal with paupers and do not shed light
     on Abraham Moon's training; WYAS–L, BDP29, item 113, Apprenticeship indentures,
     1796–1829.

32   WYAS–L, BDP29, item 121, S. Robinson, 'An Assessment for the necessary Relief of the
     Poor', 12 June 1829.

33   *General and Commercial Directory of the Borough of Leeds* (Leeds: Baines and Newsome,
     1834), pp. 326, 329.

34   'Abraham Moon', record of marriage to Susannah Waite, 2 September 1832, in Ancestry.
     com, *West Yorkshire, England, Marriages and Banns, 1813–1935* [database on-line]
     (Provo, UT: Ancestry.com Operations, 2011), and 'Hannah Moon', baptism record, 7
     July 1833, in Ancestry.com, *West Yorkshire, England, Births and Baptisms, 1813–1910*
     [database on-line] (Provo, UT: Ancestry.com Operations, 2011).

35   For a view of the village, see 'Tracks in Time: The Leeds Tithe Map Project', tithe map
     for Guiseley Parish, 1838, Map Reference DBP29_39, at http://tithemaps.leeds.gov.uk
     (accessed 16 September 2016).

36   Marriage of Abraham Moon and Elizabeth Clapham, 25 November 1835, in Ancestry.
     com, *West Yorkshire, England, Marriages and Banns, 1813–1935* [database on-line]
     (Provo, UT: Ancestry.com Operations, 2011). It has been difficult to establish the blood
     relationship of Abraham Moon and the older William Moon, but both men had a father
     called John Moon. They may have been half-brothers.

37   William Moon and Hannah Clapham married on 15 May 1836, with Abraham Moon
     as one of the witnesses; Ancestry.com, *England, Select Marriages, 1538–1973* [database
     on-line] (Provo, UT: Ancestry.com Operations, 2014).

38   Jenkins and Ponting, *British Wool Textile Industry*, pp. 125–30.

39   J. James, *History of the Worsted Manufacture in England* (London: Longman, Brown,
     Green, Longmans, and Roberts, 1857), p. 477.

40   'The court for relief of insolvent debtors', *Leeds Mercury* (3 June 1837); *London Gazette*
     (2 June 1837), pp. 1, 427–8.

41   'Partnerships dissolved', *Examiner* (London) (2 September 1838); 'Partnerships
     dissolved', *Leeds Mercury* (8 September 1938).

42   'Otley', *Leeds Mercury* (14 December 1839).

43   T. W. Leavitt, 'Fashion, commerce and technology in the nineteenth century: the shawl
     trade', *Textile History*, 3:1 (1972), 52–4; S. Daly, 'Kashmir shawls in mid-Victorian
     novels', *Victorian Literature and Culture*, 30:1 (2002), 238.

44   'Yorkshire (West Riding.), report from H. S. Chapman, Esq.', in *Sessional Papers Printed
     by Order of the House of Lords, or Presented by Royal Command, in the Session 1840*. vol.
     37: *Reports from Commissioners: Hand-Loom Weavers* (London: 1840), pp. 549–50.

45   'Abraham Moon', in Ancestry.com, *1841 England Census* [database on-line] (Provo, UT:
     Ancestry.com Operations, 2010).

46   'William Moon', in Ancestry.com, *1841 England Census* [database on-line] (Provo, UT:
     Ancestry.com Operations, 2010.

47   WYAS-L, GB–GAU: Diary of Reuben Gaunt, Pudsey, 1841–54, transcription 1975,
     entries for 13 October 1841, 12 July 1842, 22 November 1842, 17 January 1843 and
     29 April 1843; Jenkins and Ponting, *British Wool Textile Industry*, pp. 92–4.

48 J. R. McCulloch, *A Descriptive and Statistical Account of the British Empire*, 3rd edn, vol. 1 (London: Longman, Brown, Green, and Longmans, 1847), p. 660.

49 F. J. Glover, 'The rise of the heavy woollen trade of the West Riding of Yorkshire in the nineteenth century', *Business History*, 4:1 (December 1961), 1–21; F. J. Glover, 'Thomas Cook and the American blanket trade in the nineteenth century', *Business History Review*, 35:2 (summer 1961), 226–46, and F. J. Glover, 'Government contracting, competition and growth in the heavy woollen industry', *Economic History Review*, n.s., 16:3 (1964), 478–98.

50 'Report of the woollen trade', *Leeds Times* (2 August 1845).

51 Abraham Moon and Sons Ltd, Guiseley, West Yorkshire, Archival files, newspaper clipping, 'Death of Mr. Isaac Moon, Guiseley' (20 August 1909); Electoral Register for Guiseley, 1845, in Ancestry.com, *West Yorkshire, England, Electoral Registers, 1840–1962* [database on-line] (Provo, UT: Ancestry.com Operations, 2013).

52 The British Ordnance Survey map describes Spring Head Mill as a mill for 'Scribbling and Fulling'. National Library of Scotland, map of Yorkshire 187, surveyed 1847–48, published 1851, at http://maps.nls.uk/view/102344863 (accessed 16 September 2016).

53 Rivers Pollution Commission, *Third Report of the Commissioners Appointed in 1868 to Inquire into the Best Means of Preventing the Pollution of Rivers*, vol. 2: *Evidence* (London: HMSO, 1871), p. 97.

54 'Alleged forgery in Bradford', *Bradford Observer* (20 November 1869).

55 E. P. Dobson and J. B. Ives, *A Century of Achievement: The History of James Ives & Company Limited, 1848–1948* (London: William Sessions, 1948), pp. 25–6.

56 *Ibid.*, pp. 24–8.

57 'Report on the history of joint stock company woollen mills', in *First Report of the Select Committee on Joint Stock Companies; Together with the Minutes of Evidence (Taken in 1841 and 1843), Appendix and Index* (London: House of Commons, 1844), p. 349. Besides the use of expensive equipment, a clothier gained social capital and a political voice through his investment in a company mill. The shares counted as property, and each shareholder was qualified to cast a ballot in public elections. See, for example, the Electoral Register for the Otley Polling District, 1858, in Ancestry.com, *West Yorkshire, England, Electoral Registers, 1840–1962* [database on-line] (Provo, UT: Ancestry.com Operations, 2013).

58 J. Nussey to W. Aldam, 9 August 1843, in *First Report of the Select Committee on Joint Stock Companies*, p. 348.

59 *Ibid.*

60 W. Aldam to W. E. Gladstone, 12 August 1843, in *First Report of the Select Committee on Joint Stock Companies*, p. 348.

61 Electoral Register, 1845, entries for Guiseley, pp. 11–13, in Ancestry.com, *West Yorkshire, England, Electoral Registers, 1840–1962* [database on-line] (Provo, UT: Ancestry.com Operations, 2013).

62 'Abraham Moon', in Ancestry.com, *1851 England Census* [database on-line] (Provo, UT: Ancestry.com Operations, 2005).

63 'William Moon', in Ancestry.com, *1851 England Census* [database on-line] (Provo, UT: Ancestry.com Operations, 2005).

64 K. Chaffer, *Victorian Village: Guiseley, Yorkshire, An Intimate View* (Harrogate: The Author, 1988), p. 62; *Post Office Directory of Yorkshire* (London: Kelly & Company, 1857), pp. 233–4.

65 'The history and progress of British wool manufactures', *The Economist* (11 June 1910), 1,291–2.

66 *Post Office Directory of Yorkshire* (1857), p. 234; 'Guiseley Agricultural Society', *Leeds Mercury* (22 October 1863).

67 WYAS–L, BDP29, item 232, 'Rector's letter', *Guiseley Parish Messenger* [April 1907], not paginated.

68 'Leeds, Tuesday', *Manchester Guardian* (5 May 1858).

69 Nussey to Aldam, in *First Report of the Select Committee on Joint Stock Companies*, pp. 348–9.

70 *Ibid.*, p. 349.

71 *First Report of the Select Committee on Joint Stock Companies*, pp. 351–2.

72 'Alleged forgery by a Yorkshire manufacturer', *Sheffield and Rotherham Independent* (3 February 1870).

73 'Abraham Moon' and 'William Moon', in Ancestry.com, *1861 England Census* [database on-line] (Provo, UT: Ancestry.com Operations, 2005).

74 'Worsteds, serges, woollens: Designs and markets', *Textile Recorder*, 32 (15 March 1915), 355.

75 P. T. Marsh, *Bargaining on Europe: Britain and the First Common Market, 1860–1892* (New Haven: Yale University Press, 1999), pp. 8–27.

76 D. Lazer, 'The free trade epidemic of the 1860s and other outbreaks of economic discrimination', *World Politics*, 51:4 (July 1999), 447.

77 F. Trentmann, *Free Trade Nation: Commerce, Consumption, and Civil Society in Modern Britain* (Oxford: Oxford University Press, 2008), p. 6.

78 M. Lampe, 'Explaining nineteenth-century bilateralism: Economic and political determinants of the Cobden-Chevalier network', *Economic History Review*, 64:2 (2011), 644–68.

79 Kelly (ed.), *Post Office Directory of the West Riding* (1867), pp. 348, 1550.

80 'Woollen trade of Leeds, Friday', *Leeds Mercury* (2 February 1867); 'Woollen trade of Leeds, Friday', *Leeds Mercury* (12 January 1867).

81 'The woollen trade of Leeds', *Yorkshire Post and Leeds Intelligencer* (29 February 1868).

82 ['The foundation stone of a new mill'], *Bradford Daily Telegraph* (29 July 1868); 'Guiseley', *Yorkshire Post and Leeds Intelligencer* (28 July 1868).

83 West Yorkshire Archive Service, Wakefield (hereafter cited as WYAS–W), West Yorkshire Registry of Deeds (hereafter cited as WYRD), No. 1869-627-546-674, Memorial of an Indenture, William Wells and Thomas Holmes to Abraham Moon, Abraham Moon Jr. and Isaac Moon, registered 8 September 1869.

84 WYAS–W, WYRD, No. 1869-627-549-676, Memorial of an Indenture, Abraham Moon, Abraham Moon Jr., and Isaac Moon to Francis Hawkesworth Fawkes and Ayscough Fawkes.

85 M. Sharples, 'The Fawkes-Turner connection and the art collection at Farnley Hall, Otley, 1792–1937: A great estate enhanced and supported', *Northern History*, 26:1 (1990), 134–9.

86 Sharples, 'The Fawkes-Turner connection', 131–2.

87 M. Sharples, 'The Fawkes family and their estates in Wharfedale, 1819–1936', *Publications of the Thoresby Society*, 2nd ser., 6 (1995), 12, 65; National Library of Scotland, map of Yorkshire 187, surveyed 1847–48, published 1851.

88 Aireborough Historical Society, Yeadon, West Yorkshire, Messrs. James S. Taylor and Henry Foggitt to Messrs. Abraham Moon, Isaac Moon and Arthur Moon, 'Conveyance of the share and interest of the late Mr. Abraham Moon the Elder deceased in Freehold hereditaments at Guiseley in the County of York', 28 June 1879, mentions two mortgages from the Fawkes family, from the 1860s and 1870s. Another document, WYAS–W, WYRD, No. 1888-25-222-122, 'Memorial of an Indenture of Reconveyance', Emma Beatrice Shidd?, Frederick Jolliffe Bayly and Edward Osborn Williams to Abraham Moon, Abraham Moon Jr. and Isaac Moon, registered 30 August 1888, suggests that distant investors also lent money to the Moons, perhaps through the Fawkes's social network.

89 Tithe map for Guiseley Parish, 1838.

90 'Cricket', *Leeds Intelligencer* (20 August 1864).

91 'To contractors', *Leeds Mercury* (2 May 1868); 'The pollution of the becks at Bradford', *British Architect* (2 April 1875), 195.

92 *Guiseley Conservation Area Appraisal and Management Plan* (Leeds: Leeds City Council, 2012), pp. 7–8, 16.

93 Slater, *History of the Ancient Parish of Guiseley*, p. 150.

94 WYAS–L, WYL2139, box 38, notebook of C. Hainsworth, 'Chemistry Experiments, Yorkshire College, Leeds', 1897; Bradford College, Bradford, West Yorkshire, Bradford Textile Archive, TAPC No. 0517, 'Prints to show suitable & unsuitable cloths for proofing', ca. 1900.

95 The Leeds firm of Thomas Boyd provided cloth manufacturers with milling, finishing and waterproofing services. See University of Leeds, Brotherton Library, Special Collections, BUS/Boyd: Records of Thomas Boyd, finishers' books, vols 13–16, 1893–1913.

96 A. A. Whife, 'Mens dress 1890–1914', *Costume*, 1:suppl. (1967), 37–41.

97 Alexander Grant, advertisement, *Bedfordshire Times and Independent* (28 November 1868).

98 'Markets: Leeds', *Bradford Daily Telegraph* (17 October 1868).

99 'The pollution of the River Aire', *Bradford Observer* (20 March 1875).

100 Rivers Pollution Commission, *Third Report*, vol. 2, pp. 96–8.

101 WYAS–W, WYRD, No. 1869-627-549-676, Memorial of an Indenture.

102 Rivers Pollution Commission, *Third Report*, vol. 2, p. 97.

103 Jenkins and Ponting, *British Wool Textile Industry*, pp. x, 223–4. For exports figures, see E. M. Sigsworth and J. M. Blackman, 'The woollen and worsted industries', in D. H. Aldcroft (ed.), *The Development of British Industry and Foreign Competition, 1875–1914* (London: George Allen & Unwin, 1968), p. 135.

104 'Abraham Moan [sic]', 'Abraham Moon Jr', 'Isaac Moon' and 'William Moon', in Ancestry.com, *1871 England Census* [database on-line] (Provo, UT: Ancestry.com Operations, 2004).

105 *Guiseley Conservation Area Appraisal and Management Plan*, p. 7.

106 WYAS–L, BDP29, item 124, 'Sealed Order of the Poor Law Board to Wharfedale Union, 20 February 1861', p. 3; P. Higginbotham, 'The Workhouse: The Story of an Institution', at www.workhouses.org.uk (accessed 16 September 2016).

107 'Wharfedale Union', *Leeds Mercury* (18 April 1865).

108 'Wharfedale Poor-Law Union', *Bradford Observer* (15 April 1871); 'Parochial matters', *Leeds Times* (15 April 1871).

109 'New workhouse for the Wharfedale Union', *Leeds Mercury* (30 November 1871); 'The new Wharfedale Union workhouse at Otley', *Yorkshire Post* (30 November 1871); 'The new Workhouse for the Wharfedale Union', *Leeds Times* (7 June 1873).

110 'Guiseley—New church schools', *British Architect* (15 May 1874), 314; 'New national schools at Guiseley', *Bradford Observer* (14 September 1874); WYAS–L, BDP29, item 99, leaflet, 'Bazaar for the Guiseley new parochial schools', [December 1874]; 'Guiseley new parochial schools', *Bradford Observer* (16 August 1875).

111 'Woollen', *Leeds Mercury* (18 January 1873).

112 Auction notice for Green Bottom Mill, *Yorkshire Post and Leeds Intelligencer* (3 January 1874).

113 'To-morrow [Wednesday]', *Yorkshire Post* (7 December 1875).

114 WYAS–W, WYRD, No. 1888-25-222-122, Memorial of an Indenture.

115 'Fatal carriage accident at Yeadon', *Leeds Mercury* (22 August 1877); 'The fatal accident to a manufacturer at Yeadon', *Leeds Mercury* (23 August 1877); 'Fatal accident to a manufacturer at Yeadon', *Leeds Mercury* (25 August 1877).

116 'Abraham Moon', in Ancestry.com, *West Yorkshire, England, Deaths and Burials, 1813–1985* [database on-line] (Provo, UT: Ancestry.com Operations, 2011).

117 'Abraham Moon', in Ancestry.com, *England & Wales, National Probate Calendar (Index of Wills and Administrations), 1858–1966* [database on-line] (Provo, UT: Ancestry.com Operations, 2010); WYAS–W, Abraham Moon, Last Will and Testament, 9 March 1875, proved at Wakefield, 7 March 1878.

118 Mayhall, *Annals of Yorkshire*, pp. 101–3.

119 J. Thomas, 'A history of the Leeds clothing industry', *Yorkshire Bulletin of Economic and Social Research*, occasional paper no. 1 (January 1955), 50–1.

120 Hepper & Sons, advertisement, *Yorkshire Post and Leeds Intelligencer* (4 April 1885).

121 *The Illustrated and Technical Guide to the Yorkshire Exhibition of Arts and Manufactures* (Leeds: Charles Goodall, 1875), p. 34; *Yorkshire Exhibition of Arts and Manufactures, Leeds, 1875* (Leeds: Inchbold & Beck, 1875), entry 23; 'The Duke of Edinburgh in Leeds', *Yorkshire Post and Leeds Intelligencer* (14 May 1875); 'The Yorkshire Exhibition at Leeds', *Yorkshire Post and Leeds Intelligencer* (27 May 1875); 'The Yorkshire Exhibition in Leeds', *Leeds Mercury* (29 May 1875); 'The Yorkshire Exhibition in Leeds: Woollen', *Yorkshire Post and Leeds Intelligencer* (16 October 1875).

122 Jenkins and Ponting, *British Wool Textile Industry*, pp. 170–1.

123 'The Yorkshire Exhibition in Leeds: Woollen'.

2 Looking good

1 Worshipful Company of Clothworkers, London (hereafter cited as CC), microfilm reel 25, p. 191, Minutes of the Trusts and General Superintendence Committee meeting, Clothworkers' Hall (hereafter cited as Minutes), 28 May 1873.

2 *Reports from Commissioners, Inspectors, and Others: Thirty-Five Volumes*, vol. 10: *Explosives; Factories and Workshops* (London: HMSO, 1905), item 2028.

3 Abraham Moon and Sons Ltd, Guiseley, West Yorkshire, Archival files (hereafter cited as AM–AF), envelope: old shipping documents, 1896, Midland Railway, consignment notice, 18 August 1896; D. T. Jenkins, 'The response of the European wool textile manufacturers to the opening of the Japanese market', *Textile History*, 19:2 (1988), 273.

4 F. Anderson, 'Spinning the ephemeral with the sublime: Modernity and landscape in men's fashion textiles, 1860–1900', *Fashion Theory*, 9:3 (2005), 283-304; F. Anderson, 'This sporting cloth: Tweed, gender and fashion, 1860–1900', *Textile History*, 37:2 (2006), 166-86; F. Anderson, *Tweed* (London: Bloomsbury Academic, 2016).

5 L. Taylor, 'Wool cloth and gender: The use of woollen cloth in women's dress in Britain, 1865-85', in A. de la Haye and E. Wilson (eds), *Defining Dress: Dress as Object, Meaning and Identity* (Manchester: Manchester University Press, 1999), pp. 30–47.

6 G. A. Sala, *Twice Round the Clock; or the Hours of the Day and Night in London* (London: Richard Marsh, 1862), p. 83.

7   J. Smail, 'The sources of innovation in the woollen and worsted industry of eighteenth-century Yorkshire', *Business History*, 41:1 (January 1999), 1–15; J. Smail, *Merchants, Markets and Manufacture: The English Wool Textile Industry in the Eighteenth Century* (New York: St. Martin's Press, 1999).

8   J. R. McCulloch, *A Statistical Account of the British Empire*, 2nd edn, vol. 1 (London: Charles Knight & Company, 1839), p. 639.

9   My research on the advent of the woollen designer is sympathetic with the findings of W. B. Crump and G. Ghorbal, *History of the Huddersfield Woollen Industry* (Huddersfield: Alfred Jubb & Son, 1935), pp. 120–6; P. Bentley, *Colne Valley Cloth: From the Earliest Times to the Present Day* (London: Curwen Press, 1947), pp. 55–7; T. A. Stillie, 'The evolution of pattern design in the Scottish woollen textile industry in the nineteenth century', *Textile History*, 1:3 (1970), 309–31; and A. M. M. Lyons, 'The textile fabrics of India and [the] Huddersfield cloth industry', *Textile Industry*, 27:2 (1996), 184–6.

10 'Fancy trade near Huddersfield', *Leeds Mercury* (29 November 1829).

11 'Leeds, Saturday, October 3', *Leeds Mercury* (3 October 1829).

12 'Meeting of fancy woollen designers', *Huddersfield Chronicle* (15 August 1857).

13 On Bolton quilting, see 'Ashton petty sessions', *Manchester Times* (7 February 1829); 'Unclaimed corpse', *Liverpool Mercury* (27 May 1825); 'Obtaining goods under false pretences', *Huddersfield Chronicle* (19 February 1859).

14 J. Beaumont, 'The Jacquard machine, and its introduction into Huddersfield', *Textile Recorder*, 4 (15 April 1886), 279–80; J. Beaumont, 'The Jacquard machine, and its introduction to Huddersfield', *Textile Recorder*, 4 (15 May 1886), 14–15; 'The introduction of the Jacquard loom into Huddersfield', *Huddersfield Daily Chronicle* (29 March 1886).

15 'To pattern designers', *Leeds Mercury* (28 February 1835); 'Wanted, a designer and pattern weaver', *Leeds Mercury* (22 April 1837); 'To pattern designers', *Leeds Mercury* (6 March 1841).

16 Beaumont, 'The Jacquard machine', *Textile Recorder* (15 April 1886), 280; 'Textile institutes', *Textile Recorder*, 1 (15 October 1883), 131; N. Rothstein, 'The introduction of the Jacquard loom to Great Britain', in V. Gervers (ed.), *Studies in Textile History in Memory of Harold B. Burnham* (Toronto: Royal Ontario Museum, 1977), pp. 284–5.

17 'A designer wanted for Jacquard looms', *Leeds Mercury* (23 October 1841).

18 'Report of the woollen trade', *Leeds Times* (2 August 1845).

19 University of Leeds, University Archive (hereafter cited as UL–UA), Yorkshire College, Register of Students.

20 Crump and Ghorbal, *History*, p. 122; 'The late Professor John Beaumont', *Journal of the Yorkshire College Textile Society* (1891), 3–8; 'The late Professor John Beaumont', *Textile*

Recorder, 7 (14 September 1889), 112; CC, microfilm reel 25, p. 475/12, J. Beaumont to
Chairman of the Yorkshire College of Science, Leeds, 28 April 1875.

21 'The late Professor John Beaumont', *Journal of the Yorkshire College Textile Society*, 8; J.
Beaumont to Chairman of the Yorkshire College of Science; D. Bremner, *The Industries
of Scotland: Their Rise, Progress, and Present Condition* (Edinburgh: Adam and Charles
Black, 1869), pp. 200–2.

22 'The right of designers to the possession of patterns', *Huddersfield Chronicle* (9 April 1864).

23 'Manufacturers and designers', *Huddersfield Chronicle* (16 April 1864).

24 'Meeting of fancy woollen designers'.

25 'The right of designers'.

26 *Paris Universal Exhibition of 1867: Catalogue of the British Section* (London: HMSO,
1867), pp. 78–9.

27 J. Halls, 'Questions of attribution: Registered designs at the National Archives', *Journal
of Design History*, 26:4 (2013), 416–32; D. Greysmith, 'Patterns, piracy and protection in
the textile printing industry, 1787–1850', *Textile History*, 14:2 (1983), 165–94; L. Kriegel,
'Culture and the copy: Calico, capitalism, and design copyright in early Victorian
Britain', *Journal of British Studies*, 43:2 (April 2004), 233–65.

28 'Exposition of Manufactures and Industrial Art' and 'Manchester School of Design', *Art-
Union*, 88 (1 December 1845), 1; J. Timbs, *The Year-Book of Facts in the Great Exhibition
of 1851* (London: David Bogue, 1851), pp. 10–13.

29 The National Archives, Kew, Records of the Board of Trade and successors, Design
Registry (hereafter cited as TNA–BT43), search in the online catalogue for 'other fabrics'
made in 'Huddersfield', 'Leeds', and 'Guiseley', 1 September 2015.

30 TNA–BT, BT43/399/260178.

31 TNA–BT, BT43/400/297231 and BT43/400/297232.

32 'Leeds', *London Evening Standard* (23 September 1867).

33 *Executive Documents Printed by Order of the House of Representatives During the Third
Session of the Fortieth Congress, 1868–69 in Fourteen Volumes*, vol. 14: *Commercial
Relations* (Washington, DC: GPO, 1869), p. 18.

34 *Paris Universal Exhibition of 1867*, p. 79.

35 R. L. Blaszczyk, *The Color Revolution* (Cambridge, MA: The MIT Press, 2012), pp. 21–33.

36 'Isaac Moon', 'Abraham Moon' and 'Arthur Moon', in Ancestry.com and The Church
of Jesus Christ of Latter-day Saints, *1881 England Census* [database on-line] (Provo, UT:
Ancestry.com Operations, 2004).

37 C. P. Kindleberger, 'The rise of free trade in Western Europe, 1820–1875', *Journal of
Economic History*, 35:1 (March 1975), 41, 46–7; A. A. Stein, 'The Hegemon's Dilemma:
Great Britain, the United States, and the international economic order', in C. Lipson and
B. J. Cohen (eds), *Theory and Structure in International Political Economy* (Cambridge,
MA: MIT Press, 1999), p. 299.

38 'Commercial markets: Leeds, Saturday', *Manchester Guardian* (12 January 1880).

39 *Reports from Commissioners*, items 1652–3.

40 'Woollen', *Leeds Mercury* (1 January 1883).

41 'Abraham Moon', entries for 1888 and 1891–92, in Ancestry.com, *British Phone Books, 1880–1984* [database on-line] (Provo, UT: Ancestry.com Operations, 2007); 'To be let: Warehouses, offices, &c.', *Yorkshire Post* (5 July 1887); Charles E. Goad, Ltd, Insurance Plan of Leeds: sheet 6, 1886, at British Library, 'Fire insurance maps and plans: England', www.bl.uk/onlinegallery (accessed 17 September 2016).

42 For another discussion of the political views of clothiers-turned-industrialists, see S. A. Caunce, 'Houses as museums: The case of the Yorkshire wool textile industry', *Transactions of the Royal Historical Society*, 13 (2003), pp. 341–2.

43 'Opening of a Conservative Club at Guiseley', *Yorkshire Post and Leeds Intelligencer* (30 January 1882); 'Mr. W. L. Jackson, M. P., and his constituents', *Yorkshire Post and Leeds Intelligencer* (2 February 1883); 'Otley division of the West Riding', *Yorkshire Post* (26 August 1885).

44 West Yorkshire Archive Service, Wakefield (hereafter cited as WYAS–W), West Yorkshire Registry of Deeds (hereafter cited as WYRD), Copy memorandum of agreement between Abraham Moon, Isaac Moon and Arthur Moon, and Henry Foggitt, 16 March 1887; 'Henry Foggitt', in Ancestry.com, *1891 England Census* [database on-line] (Provo, UT: Ancestry.com Operations, 2005).

45 'The woollen shipping trade', *Leeds Mercury* (4 August 1888).

46 E. R. Kelly (ed.), *Kelly's Directory of the West Riding of Yorkshire, 1881* (London: Kelly & Company, 1881), p. 479.

47 'Wool and woollen', *Leeds Mercury* (27 June 1888).

48 Patent no. 679, for 'An Improved Cloth', filed by Isaac Moon and Arthur Moon on 14 January 1889 and assigned on 2 March 1889.

49 'Leeds, Friday', *Manchester Guardian* (16 August 1890).

50 'Guiseley Polling District', 1889, in Ancestry.com, *West Yorkshire, England, Electoral Registers, 1840–1962* [database on-line] (Provo, UT: Ancestry.com Operations, 2013).

51 AM–AF, clipping, 'Death of Mr. Isaac Moon, Guiseley', 20 August 1909. Crooklands was divided into two residences in the 1930s. I am grateful to Deborah Myers and Jane Blake for allowing me to see the interiors of these homes and for sharing historical documents, 24 January 2016.

52 'Yeadon District Chamber of Commerce', *Leeds Mercury* (28 January 1892).

53 United States House of Representatives, 'Historical Highlights: The McKinley Tariff of 1890', at http://history.house.gov/HistoricalHighlight (accessed 17 September 2016).

54 'Yeadon, Guiseley, and District Chamber of Commerce', *Leeds Mercury* (30 December 1890).

55 J. H. Clapham, *The Woollen and Worsted Industries* (London: Methuen & Company, 1907), pp. 285–7.

56 'Yeadon and Guiseley', *Leeds Mercury* (27 December 1892).

57 'The woollen shipping trade', *Leeds Mercury* (3 December 1892).

58 D. O. Whitten, 'The Depression of 1893', at http://eh.net/encyclopedia (accessed 17 September 2016).

59 D. T. Jenkins and K. G. Ponting, *The British Wool Textile Industry, 1770–1914* (London: Heinemann Educational Books, 1982), p. 235.

60 'Abraham Moon [Jnr]', in Ancestry.com, *UK and Ireland, Find a Grave Index, 1300s–Current* [database on–line] (Provo, UT: Ancestry.com Operations, 2012); 'The funeral of Mr. Abraham Moon', *Yorkshire Post* (23 March 1891); 'Abraham Moon [Jnr]', in Ancestry.com, *England & Wales, National Probate Calendar (Index of Wills and Administrations), 1858–1966* [database on-line] (Provo, UT: Ancestry.com Operations, 2010); WYAS–W, Will of Abraham Moon Jnr, probated 15 May 1891; Aireborough Historical Society, Yeadon, West Yorkshire (hereafter cited as AHS), Mrs Hannah Moon and others to Messrs Isaac and Arthur Moon, 'Assignment of the Share of Abraham Moon deceased in the business of 'Abm. Moon & Sons' Guiseley', 30 October 1891.

61 AHS, Messrs Isaac Moon and Arthur Moon to Mrs Hannah Moon and Others, 'Mortgage', 30 October 1891.

62 'Fashionable marriage at Yeadon', *Leeds Mercury* (12 February 1892); AHS, Messrs Abraham Moon and Sons, 'Articles of Partnership', 3 August 1894.

63 'The woollen trade', *Manchester Guardian* (6 July 1895).

64 'Leeds woollen weekly trade report', *Leeds Mercury* (6 July 1895).

65 'The woollen shipping trade', *Leeds Mercury* (6 July 1895).

66 WYAS–W, WYRD, 1895-38-327-150, 'Memorial of Certificate of Appointment of Trustee in Bankruptcy', 14 November 1895; 'Notices of dividends', *London Gazette* (21 February 1896).

67 'The Bankruptcy Acts, 1883 and 1890: Receiving orders', *Huddersfield Daily Chronicle* (30 October 1895); 'Partnerships dissolved', *The Times* (9 November 1895); 'From the "London Gazette" of Friday evening: Partnerships dissolved', *Manchester Guardian* (11 November 1895).

68 AHS, Mr James William Close and others to Mr Isaac Moon, 'Conveyance of Hereditaments & Premises situate at Guiseley in County of York', 15 December 1900.

69 AHS, John Bowling Esq. to Isaac Moon Esq., 'Conveyance of Freehold Mills Lands and hereditaments Situate at Guiseley in the County of York', 24 October 1898.

70 'Yeadon, Guiseley, and Rawdon', *Leeds Mercury* (28 December 1896).

71 Whitten, 'The Depression of 1893'.

72 Jenkins and Ponting, *British Wool Textile Industry*, p. 236.

73 AHS, Close et al. to Moon, 'Conveyance of Hereditaments & Premises situate at
    Guiseley in County of York'; 'Guiseley manufacturer's affairs', *Yorkshire Evening Post*
    (23 February 1900); 'The affairs of Messrs. Moon & Sons, of Guiseley', *Yorkshire Post and
    Leeds Intelligencer* (24 February 1900).

74 'Charles Moon' and 'Walter Smith Moon', in Ancestry.com, *1901 England Census*
    [database on-line] (Provo, UT: Ancestry.com Operations, 2005). Isaac Moon had an
    older son, Sam, who died prematurely in New Zealand; see 'Deaths', *Yorkshire Evening
    Post* (22 April 1899).

75 'Arthur Moon', in Ancestry.com, *1901 England Census* [database on-line] (Provo, UT:
    Ancestry.com Operations, 2005); 'Arthur Moon', in *1911 England Census* [database
    on-line] (Provo, UT: Ancestry.com Operations, 2011).

76 'Big blaze at Guiseley', *Leeds and Yorkshire Mercury* (13 August 1902); 'North Country',
    Manchester Courier and Lancashire General Advertiser (13 August 1902); 'Mills
    destroyed by fire', *Daily Mail* (Hull) (13 August 1902); 'Guiseley mill gutted', *Supplement
    to the Manchester Courier* (16 August 1902).

77 C. Giles and I. H. Goodall, *Yorkshire Textile Mills: The Buildings of the Yorkshire Textile
    Industry, 1770–1830* (London: HMSO, 1992), pp. 39–44.

78 Between 1888 and 1891, one Yorkshire mill produced nearly 300,000 yards of
    'Metropolitan Police Contract Cloths' for a single uniform maker. See West Yorkshire
    Archive Service, Leeds (hereafter cited as WYAS–L), WYL2139: Records of A. W.
    Hainsworth and Sons Ltd, box 23, folder: Various Correspondence, John Hammond &
    Company, Newcastle under Lyme, to Hainsworth & Sons, Farsley, 16 August 1888, and
    'Quantities in yards and dates for delivery'.

79 Jenkins and Ponting, *British Wool Textile Industry*, pp. 242–59.

80 AHS, Mrs Hannah Moon to Isaac Moon Esq., 'Reconveyance', 1 December 1906.

81 AM–AF, 'Death of Mr. Isaac Moon, Guiseley'.

82 'Henry Foggitt', in Ancestry.com, *West Yorkshire, England, Church of England Deaths
    and Burials, 1813–1985* [database on-line] (Provo, UT: Ancestry.com Operations, 2011);
    AHS, The Personal Representatives of Mr Henry Foggitt, deceased, to The Trustees of
    the Will of Mr Isaac Moon, deceased, 'Reconveyance and Release of Netherfield Mills
    and land and other hereditaments and premises situated at Guiseley in the County of
    York', 6 December 1913.

83 WYAS–W, WYRD, Will of I. Moon, probated 28 October 1909.

84 AM–AF, 'Death of Mr. Isaac Moon, Guiseley'.

85 'Mr. Isaac Moon', *Litchfield (Staffordshire) Mercury* (12 November 1909); 'Latest wills',
    Manchester Courier (8 November 1909). Henry Albert Martin, head of Martin, Sons, and
    Company (Limited), worsted manufacturers in Huddersfield, left an estate of £417,489
    in 1910; see University of Leeds, Brotherton Library, Special Collections, BUS/Clay: J. T.
    Clay and Sons Ltd, scrapbook, clipping of 'Recent wills', p. 7.

86 'Legal notices', *Leeds Mercury* (30 September 1837); 'Partnerships dissolved', *Morning Post* (London) (4 October 1837).

87 'James Walsh', in Ancestry.com, *1851 England Census* [database on-line] (Provo, UT: Ancestry.com Operations, 2005); 'James Walsh', in Ancestry.com, *1861 England Census* [database on-line] (Provo, UT: Ancestry.com Operations, 2005); 'Three boys drowned', *Leeds Mercury* (14 July 1857).

88 'Thomas Walsh', in Ancestry.com, *1861 England Census* [database on-line] (Provo, UT: Ancestry.com Operations, 2005).

89 'Marriages', *Leeds Mercury* (11 October 1860); *Post Office London Directory, 1860* (London: Kelly & Company, 1860), p. 1,375.

90 WYAS–L, BDP29: Records of Guiseley Parish (hereafter cited as BDP29), item 73, minute book on churchyard extension, 1859–60, flyer on 'Guiseley Church Yard', 1 December 1859, and notebook of churchwarden James Walsh, 1859–60.

91 WYAS–W, WYRD, No. 1867-ZO-727-836, Indenture, 1 June 1867.

92 'Charles H. Walsh', in Ancestry.com, *1861 England Census* [database on-line] (Provo, UT: Ancestry.com Operations, 2005).

93 'Deaths', *Leeds Mercury* (16 December 1865).

94 WYAS–W, WYRD, No. 1866-ZF-712-795, Indenture, 21 November 1866.

95 'Charles H. Walsh', in Ancestry.com, *1871 England Census* [database on-line] (Provo, UT: Ancestry.com Operations, 2004).

96 CC, microfilm reel 25, p. 317/1-3, Yorkshire College of Science, 'Constitution', 30 April 1874.

97 T. Nussey, 'Report on carded wool and woollen fabrics (Class 30)', in *Reports on the Paris Universal Exhibition, 1867*, vol. 3 (London: HMSO, 1868), pp. 64–5.

98 CC, microfilm reel 25, p. 191/13, *Yorkshire College of Science: Provisional Committee* [1872].

99 CC, microfilm reel 25, p. 191/2, *The Yorkshire College of Science: Report of the Committee Appointed to Investigate, Consider, and Propose the Best Means to be Adopted for the Establishment of a 'Yorkshire College of Science'* (Leeds: Edward Baines and Sons, 1872), [p. 1].

100 CC, microfilm reel 25, p. 95/1–10, G. H. Nussey and A. Nussey, *Technical Institution for Leeds and District* (Leeds: Edward Baines and Sons, 1867), pp. 8–9, 15.

101 For the standard account, see R. Reynolds, 'The beginnings of the Yorkshire College: First notice', *The Gryphon*, 2 (1898), 22–4, and R. Reynolds, 'The beginnings of the Yorkshire College: Second notice', *The Gryphon*, 2 (1898), 42–4.

102 'The Clothworkers' Company', *Textile Recorder*, 1 (15 February 1884), 220–1.

103 CC, microfilm reel 25, pp. 183–4, Minutes, 30 April 1873, and pp. 190–6, Minutes, 28 May 1873; 'The late Professor John Beaumont', *Textile Recorder*, 112.

104 CC, microfilm reel 25, p. 191, Minutes, 28 May 1873.

105 CC, microfilm reel 25, p. 192, Minutes, 28 May 1873.

106 'Textile institutes', *Textile Recorder*, 3 (15 October 1885), 137.

107 CC, microfilm reel 25, p. 194, Minutes, 28 May 1873.

108 P. Leach and N. Pevsner, *Yorkshire West Riding: Leeds, Bradford and the North* (New Haven: Yale University Press, 2009), p. 472; Kelly (ed.), *Kelly's Directory of the West Riding of Yorkshire, 1881*, p. 618.

109 'The Clothworkers' Company', 221.

110 'City and Guilds of London Institute', *Textile Recorder*, 2 (14 June 1884), 36; 'City and Guilds of London Institute', *Textile Manufacturer* (15 October 1879), 345–6; and 'City and Guilds of London Institute II', *Textile Manufacturer* (15 November 1879), 383–4.

111 'City and Guilds of London Institute', *Textile Recorder*, 36–7.

112 University of Leeds—An Archive of International Textiles (hereafter cited as ULITA), *Report of the Work of the Textile Industries and Dyeing Departments for the Session Beginning October 5th, 1880, and ending June 24th, 1881, To the Worshipful Company of Clothworkers of the City of London*.

113 UL–UA, Yorkshire College, Register of Students.

114 UL–UA, Yorkshire College, *Calendar for the Ninth Session, 1882–3*, pp. 97–100, 128.

115 UL–UA, Yorkshire College, *Calendar for the Tenth Sesion, 1883–4*, pp. 99, 102, and Yorkshire College, *Calendar for the Eleventh Session, 1884–5*, p. 145.

116 R. M. Baker, 'Nineteenth century synthetic textile dyes: Their history and identification on fabric' (PhD thesis: University of Southampton, 2011), pp. 18–20.

117 'Charles H. Walsh', in Ancestry.com, *West Yorkshire, England, Marriages and Banns, 1813–1935* [database on-line] (Provo, UT: Ancestry.com Operations, 2011).

118 'Charles H. Walsh', in Ancestry.com and The Church of Jesus Christ of Latter-day Saints, *1881 England Census* [database on-line] (Provo, UT: Ancestry.com Operations, 2004).

119 WYAS–L, BDP29, item 228, 'Burials', *Guiseley Parish Magazine* (March 1880), not paginated.

120 WYAS–L, BDP29, item 229, 'Baptisms', *Guiseley Parish Magazine* (February 1882), not paginated; 'Burials', *Guiseley Parish Magazine* (May 1882), not paginated; 'Burials', *Guiseley Parish Magazine* (August 1882), not paginated.

121 CC, microfilm reel 25, p. 475, Minutes, June 1875, and pp. 474–5, H. H. Sales, Yorkshire College of Science, to Clothworkers' Company, 5 June 1875. Beaumont was hired after William Walker, the appointee in 1874–75, was unable to fulfil his obligations; see CC, microfilm reel 25, pp. 440–7, Minutes, 28 April 1875.

122 'Textile institutes', *Textile Recorder*, 2 (15 July 1884), 56.

123 ULITA, J. Beaumont, 'Textile Industries Department', in *Report of the Work of the Textile Industries and Dyeing Departments*, Sixth Session, 1881–82, p. 1.

124 ULITA, J. Beaumont, 'Textile Industries Department', in *Report of the Work of the Textile Industries and Dyeing Departments*, Ninth Session, 1882–83, p. 2.

125 UL–UA, Yorkshire College, *Calendar for the Ninth Session, 1882–3*, pp. 71–2.

126 Beaumont, 'Textile Industries Department', in *Report*, 1882–83, p. 2.

127 'The Yorkshire College', *Yorkshire Post* (21 June 1884); 'Yorkshire College textile exhibition', *Leeds Mercury* (21 June 1884).

128 UL–UA, Yorkshire College, *Calendar for the Ninth Session, 1882–3*, p. 133.

129 UL–UA, Yorkshire College, *Calendar for the Tenth Session, 1883–4*, p. 140, and Yorkshire College, *Calendar for the Eleventh Session, 1884–5*, p. 152.

130 ULITA, J. Beaumont, 'Textile industries classes (eleventh session)', in *The Yorkshire College, Leeds, Report on the Work of the Textile Industries and Dyeing Classes for the Session 1884–5*, p. 5.

131 'Frank Tempest Walsh' and 'Arthur Cyril Walsh', in Ancestry.com, *West Yorkshire, England, Births and Baptisms, 1813–1910* [database on-line] (Provo, UT: Ancestry.com Operations, 2011).

132 'Otley Division Conservative Association', *Yorkshire Post* (18 February 1887).

133 For Charles Walsh as a 'designer', see *Slater's Royal National Commercial Directory of Yorkshire*, 10th edn (Manchester: Isaac Slater, 1887), p. 129. For him as a 'Clerk', see 'Jessie Walsh', in Ancestry.com, *West Yorkshire, England, Births and Baptisms, 1813–1910* [database on-line] (Provo, UT: Ancestry.com Operations, 2011).

134 'Charles H. Walsh', in Ancestry.com, *1891 England Census* [database on-line] (Provo, UT: Ancestry.com Operations, 2005).

135 S. Burt and K. Grady, *The Illustrated History of Leeds*, 2nd edn (Derby: Breedon Books, 2002), pp. 60, 134.

136 'Partnerships dissolved', *Huddersfield Chronicle* (24 January 1885); 'Mr. Jonathan Peate dead', *Yorkshire Evening Post* (13 December 1924); W. Cooper, *Bygone Guiseley* (Guiseley: M. T. D. Rigg, 1995), p. 136; P. Slater, *History of the Ancient Paris of Guiseley* (London: Hamilton, Adams & Company, 1880), p. 149.

137 Clapham, *Woollen and Worsted Industries*, pp. 128–9.

138 'Ordinary grade', *Yorkshire College Textile Magazine*, 2:3 (25 January 1895), 50; 'Thomas Walsh', in Ancestry.com, *1901 England Census* [database on-line] (Provo, UT: Ancestry.com Operations, 2005).

139 'Frank T. Walsh', in Ancestry.com, *1901 England Census* [database on-line] (Provo, UT: Ancestry.com Operations, 2005). After Frank died on 5 June 1953, the board noted that he 'had been associated with the company for over fifty years'; see AM–AF, Minutes of the Board of Directors, 8 June 1953.

140 UL–UA, University of Leeds, Register of evening students, pp. 103, 127, 161; P. Gosden, 'From county college to civic university, Leeds, 1904', *Northern History*, 42:2 (September 2005), 317–28.

3 The wider world

1   *Report of the Tariff Commission*, vol. 2: *The Textile Trades, Part 2—Evidence on the Woollen Industry* (London: P. S. King, 1905), item 2281.

2   'The woollen and worsted trades of the West Riding', *The Economist* (24 September 1911), 603.

3   *Ibid.*

4   'Wholesale drapery results', *Financial Times* (2 February 1910); S. Chapman, 'The decline and rise of textile merchanting, 1880–1990', *Business History*, 32:4 (November 1990), 175.

5   'The woollen trade outlook', *Financial Times* (6 December 1898).

6   *Report of the Tariff Commission*, vol. 2, items 1642–5.

7   *Ibid.*, item 1626.

8   A. S. Thompson, 'Tariff reform: An imperial strategy, 1903–1913', *Historical Journal*, 40:4 (1997), 1,033–54.

9   'The Tariff Commission: Completion of the textile evidence', *Manchester Courier and Lancashire General Advertiser* (7 November 1904).

10   *Report of the Tariff Commission*, vol. 2, items 1356–60.

11   *Ibid.*, item 1312.

12   *Ibid.*, items 1312, 1429.

13   *Ibid.*, item 2028.

14   *Ibid.*, item 2004.

15   *Ibid.*, item 1635.

16   *Ibid.*, item 1638; A. Laurence, *Murgatroyd: The Yeadon Legends* (n.p.: no publisher [after 2005]), p. 3.

17   *Report of the Tariff Commission*, vol. 2, item 2280.

18   *Ibid.*, item 1615.

19   *Ibid.*, item 1639.

20   *Ibid.*, item 1499.

21   *Ibid.*, item 1640.

22   *Ibid.*, item 1498.

23   *Ibid.*

24   *Ibid.*, item 2280.

25   *Ibid.*, item 2228.

26   *Ibid.*, items 1361–2.

27   *Ibid.*, items 1362–4, 1944.

28   *Ibid.*, item 1364; 'The Tariff Commission and the woollen industry', *The Economist* (16 December 1905), 2,016.

29   *Report of the Tariff Commission*, vol. 2, items 1637, 1940.

30 *Ibid.*, item 1355.

31 'English notes', *Textile World Record*, 30 (November 1905), 120.

32 'The manufacturing end', *American Wool and Cotton Reporter*, 21 (10 January 1907), 59.

33 K. W. Taylor, 'Tariffs', in W. S. Wallace (ed.), *The Encyclopedia of Canada*, vol. 6 (Toronto: University Associates of Canada, 1948), pp. 102–8; W. S. Wallace, 'Imperial Preference', in *Encyclopedia of Canada*, vol. 3, pp. 254–5.

34 Departmental Committee on the Textile Trades, *Report of the Departmental Committee Appointed by the Board of Trade to Consider the Position of the Textile Trades After the War* (London: HMSO, 1918), p. 71.

35 'Wool and textiles', *Supplement to the Yorkshire Post* (27 December 1911).

36 'Manufactures', *Supplement to the Yorkshire Post* (27 December 1911).

37 Abraham Moon and Sons Ltd, Guiseley, West Yorkshire (hereafter cited as AM), Archival files (hereafter cited as AM–AF), C. H. Walsh and W. S. Moon to Abraham Moon and Sons Ltd, 'Agreement for the sale and purchase of the business of A. Moon & Sons Woollen Manufacturers and Merchants', 28 May 1913.

38 University of Leeds, University Archive, box 149, folder: Textiles—General, 1915–1919, typed list of alumni in textile studies at the Yorkshire College of Science and successor institutions, 14 May 1915, lists 'C. H. Walsh' and 'Thos. Walsh' at 'A. Moon & Sons, Guiseley', as 'Partners or Heads of Firms'. 'Charles Herbert Walsh', 'Frank Walsh', and 'Thomas Walsh', Ancestry.com, *1911 England Census* [database on-line] (Provo, UT: Ancestry.com Operations, 2011).

39 'Charles Moon', in Ancestry.com, *1901 England Census* [database on-line] (Provo, UT: Ancestry.com Operations, 2005); 'Walter Moon' and 'Charles Moon', in Ancestry.com, *1911 England Census* [database on-line] (Provo, UT: Ancestry.com Operations, 2011).

40 'Dog show at Guiseley', *Yorkshire Post* (11 April 1910); 'Harrogate show: Agriculture and horticulture', *Yorkshire Post* (16 August 1911).

41 'Chas. H. Walsh', in Ancestry.com, *West Yorkshire, England, Tax Valuation, 1910* [database on-line] (Provo, UT: Ancestry.com Operations, 2014); 'Charles Herbert Walsh', in Ancestry.com, *1911 England Census* [database on-line] (Provo, UT: Ancestry.com Operations, 2011); 'C H Walsh Mr', in Ancestry.com, *1911 England Census Summary Books* [database on-line] (Provo, UT: Ancestry.com Operations, 2010).

42 West Yorkshire Archive Service, Leeds (hereafter cited as WYAS–L), BDP29: Records of Guiseley Parish, item 146: St Oswald's Parish Church, *Village Fair* (Bradford: G. F. Sewell, 1910).

43 'The woollen trade', *Manchester Guardian* (16 November 1912).

44 Departmental Committee on the Textile Trades, *Report*, p. 71. Imperial markets absorbed between 43 per cent and 50 per cent of exported British woollens; see E. M. Sigsworth and J. M. Blackman, 'The woollen and worsted industries', in D. Aldcroft

(ed.), *The Development of British Industry and Foreign Competition, 1875–1914* (London: George Allen & Unwin, 1968), pp. 156–7.

45 'For graduated tax to big incomes', *New York Times* (13 March 1913); 'Calls extra session to meet on April 7', *New York Times* (18 March 1913); 'New tariff in', *New York Times* (8 April 1913); and 'Wait Wilson's move as tariff maker', *New York Times* (1 April 1913).

46 'The woollen trade, Dewsbury, Friday', *Manchester Guardian* (2 August 1913).

47 R. L. Blaszczyk, *Imagining Consumers: Design and Innovation from Wedgwood to Corning* (Baltimore: Johns Hopkins University Press, 2000), p. 89.

48 'Women workers of Guiseley may cause lock-out of 3,000 operatives', *Yorkshire Evening Post* (10 April 1913); '2,000 workers thrown idle', *Yorkshire Evening Post* (23 May 1913); 'Unique sequel to strike', *(Dundee) Courier* (24 May 1913); 'Yeadon and Guiseley lock-out', *Yorkshire Evening Post* (31 May 1913).

49 Some 35 per cent of British woollen manufacturers had adopted limited liability by 1912 compared to 2 per cent in 1870. See Sigsworth and Blackman, 'The woollen and worsted industries', p. 152.

50 M. Chatfield, 'Companies Acts', in M. Chatfield and R. Vangermeersch (eds), *The History of Accounting: An International Encyclopedia* (New York: Garland, 1996), pp. 136–9.

51 'New Companies', *Financial Times* (17 July 1909); 'Mr. Jonathan Peate dead', *Yorkshire Evening Post* (13 December 1924).

52 Board of Trade, *Companies: Twenty-Third General Annual Report by the Board of Trade* (London: HMSO, 1914), p. 64; AM–AF, 'Agreement for the sale and purchase of the business of A. Moon & Sons', 28 May 1913; AM–AF, Minutes of the Board of Directors (hereafter cited as Minutes), 28 May 1913.

53 'The wool trade', *The Economist* (12 July 1913), 91.

54 'Yeadon's great distress', *Yorkshire Evening Post* (14 July 1913).

55 'Yeadon and Guiseley lockout', *Yorkshire Evening Post* (12 June 1913); '"Hunger march" to Leeds', *Yorkshire Evening Post* (17 June 1913).

56 'Woollen trade dispute ended', *Manchester Courier* (28 July 1913); 'The woollen trade, Dewsbury, Friday', *Manchester Guardian* (2 August 1913); 'Weavers of heavy woollens granted an increase', *Bulletin of the National Association of Wool Manufacturers*, 43 (September 1913), 340.

57 'Guiseley village cross restored', *Yorkshire Post* (11 August 1913).

58 'Fat show at Leeds', *Aberdeen Daily Journal* (3 December 1913).

59 AM–AF, Ledger, '1913–1914', covering the period July 1913–March 1919 (hereafter cited as Ledger, July 1913–March 1919).

60 Departmental Committee on the Textile Trades, *Report*, p. 63.

61 AM, Ledger, July 1913–March 1919, entries for Devas, Routledge and Company; and J. & C. Boyd & Company Ltd, and Hitchcock, Williams & Company.

62 Chapman, 'The decline and rise of textile merchanting', 171–2.

63 'The drapery companies', *Financial Times* (11 February 1890).

64 'Drapery companies' shares', *Financial Times* (30 August 1892).

65 'Destructive fire in the city', *Financial Times* (20 November 1897).

66 D. A. Farnie, 'John Rylands of Manchester', *Bulletin of the John Rylands University Library of Manchester*, 56:1 (autumn 1973), 39, 41–2, 86; 'Wholesale drapery results', *Financial Times* (2 February 1910); 'Thomas Wallis and Company', *Financial Times* (28 February 1902).

67 AM, Ledger, July 1913–March 1919, entries for Rylands & Sons Ltd (W 18 Dept); Aireborough Historical Society, Yeadon, West Yorkshire, box: James Ives & Company, 'Amounts Paid to a/c of J. H. Ives', 21 June 1901.

68 S. Chapman, *Merchant Enterprise in Britain: From the Industrial Revolution to World War I* (Cambridge: Cambridge University Press, 1992), p. 167.

69 Chapman, 'The decline and rise of textile merchanting', 174.

70 *Ibid.*, 176.

71 'The piece goods trade', *Wool Record*, 40 (3 December 1931), 17.

72 'London—The metropolitan market of the woollen trade', *Textile Recorder*, 32 (15 February 1915), 319; 'The piece goods trade' (3 December 1931).

73 T. Brann, interview by author, London (6 June 2016).

74 'London—The metropolitan market of the woollen trade', *Textile Recorder*, 32 (15 January 1915), 289.

75 C. Breward, *The Suit: Form, Function and Style* (London: Reaktion Books, 2016), pp. 33, 37, 46–9.

76 'London—The metropolitan market of the woollen trade', *Textile Recorder*, 32 (15 January 1915), 290; Breward, *The Suit*, p. 52.

77 *Farrs Centenary: The Golden Square Story* [London: F. Farr and Company, Ltd, 1963], pp. 24–6.

78 P. Lorin, *Dormeuil: The History of Fabric Is Woven into the Fabric of History* (London: Dormeuil Frères, 1992), p. 56.

79 Brann interview. My understanding of the West End is based on research for a new book tentatively called 'Selling fashion'.

80 AM–AF, Ledger, July 1913–March 1919, entries for Dormeuil; Lorin, *Dormeuil*, pp. 21–2, 58–63; *Post Office London Directory for 1914* (London: Kelly's Directories, 1914), p. 884; *Post Office London Directory for 1926* (London: Kelly's Directories, 1926), p. 1,531.

81 *Post Office London Directory for 1920* (London: Kelly's Directories, 1920), p. 1,491; *Post Office London Directory with County Suburbs for 1929* (London: Kelly's Directories, 1929), p. 1,669.

82 *The City of Leeds and Its Manufactures* (London: Ed. J. Burrow & Company, 1918), p. 12.

83 'Leeds wholesale clothing', *Wool Record*, 41 (24 March 1932), 24.

84 AM–AF, Ledger, July 1913–March 1919, entries for James Marshall, Son, & Company; *The City of Leeds and Its Manufactures*, pp. 17, 98.

85 AM–AF, Ledger, July 1913–March 1919, entries for Ashworth, Brown & Company Ltd; *The City of Leeds and Its Manufactures*, pp. 16, 96.

86 'Demand for higher grade cloth', *Wool Record*, 40 (10 September 1931), 29.

87 'The drapery companies', *Financial Times* (24 January 1891).

88 'Winter dress goods in Bradford, England', *Textile World Record*, 30 (November 1905), 122–3.

89 *Post Office London Directory for 1905* (London: Kelly's Directories, 1905), pp. 1,088, 1,235 and 1,367.

90 'Woollen trade terms', *Financial Times* (30 March 1901).

91 'Wholesale drapery results', *Financial Times* (2 February 1910).

92 'Pending issues: Sparrow, Hardwick & Company', *Financial Times* (15 March 1924); 'Sparrow, Hardwick & Company', *Financial Times* (17 March 1924).

93 AM–AF, Ledger, July 1913–March 1919, entries for Sparrow, Hardwick & Company.

94 'Winter dress goods in Bradford, England', 124.

95 'London—The metropolitan market of the woollen trade', *Textile Recorder*, 32 (15 April 1915), 387.

96 WYAS–L, WYL434: Records of John Barran & Sons Ltd, boxes 27–28: Scrapbook and newspress book, John Barran & Sons Ltd, to Arnold N. Shimmin, Guiseley, 16 June 1926 and 'Notes', pp. 2, 4–5.

97 K. Honeyman, 'Style monotony and the business of fashion: The marketing of menswear in inter-war England', *Textile History*, 34:2 (2003), 171–91; E. M. Sigsworth, *Montague Burton: The Tailor of Taste* (Manchester: Manchester University Press, 1990).

98 K. Honeyman, *Well Suited: A History of the Leeds Clothing Industry, 1850–1900* (Oxford: Oxford University Press, 2000), p. 29.

99 *Ibid.*, p. 13.

100 *Ibid.*, p. 271; AM–AF, Ledger, July 1913–March 1919, entries for James Corson & Company.

101 Honeyman, *Well Suited*, pp. 21, 78, 260–2; D. Ryott, *John Barran's of Leeds, 1851–1951* (Leeds: E. J. Arnold & Son, Ltd, 1951), 4–11; AM–AF, Ledger, July 1913–March 1919, entries for John Barran & Sons Ltd.

102 Ryott, *John Barran's of Leeds*, pp. 16–21; Leeds Central Library, Local and Family History Library (hereafter cited as LCL), *Fashion Illustrations of Half-Tone and Line Blocks* (Leeds: John Barran and Sons Ltd, 1908), pp. 11, 18–19, 31, 35.

103 *A Tailormade Career* (Leeds: Thomas Marshall (Marlbeck) Ltd, [1947]), p. 6; AM–AF, Ledger, July 1913–March 1919, entries for Thomas Marshall & Company; Honeyman, *Well Suited*, p. 288; LCL, J. Marshall, untitled article, *Marlbeck Annual*, 2 (Christmas 1933), 9–11.

104 'The waterproofing trade', *The Economist* (18 September 1909), 545; S. Mierzinski, *The Waterproofing of Fabrics* (London: Scott, Greenwood & Son, 1903); A. F. Barker, *Textiles* (New York: D. Van Nostrand Company, 1919), p. 202.

105 AM–AF, Ledger, July 1913–March 1919, entries for Hepton Bros. Ltd; Honeyman, *Well Suited*, p. 281.

106 AM–AF, Ledger, July 1913–March 1919, entries for Heatons (Leeds) Ltd; Honeyman, *Well Suited*, pp. 81, 280; WYAS–L, WYL1008: Records of Heatons of Leeds Ltd, folder 5/1–4: Publicity, 1901–1908: *Spring 1906* (London: Herbert E. Coleman, 1906), and *1908 Spring and Summer Ladies' Tailor-Made Costumes, Coats and Skirts. Latest Designs* (Leeds: E. L. H., 1908).

107 'The Scotch tweed trade', *The Economist* (23 October 1909), 805–6.

108 'The woollen trade', *Manchester Guardian* (12 July 1913).

109 S. Brierley and G. R. Carter, 'Fluctuations in the woollen and worsted industries of the West Riding', *Economic Journal*, 24 (September 1914), 379.

110 'The wool trade', *The Economist* (8 August 1914), 296.

111 'The wool trade', *The Economist* (15 August 1914), 333; 'The wool trade', *The Economist* (22 August 1914), 369.

112 'The wool trade', *The Economist* (12 September 1914), 477; 'The wool trade', *The Economist* (28 November 1914), 978.

113 'The Bradford trade annual review for 1900', in U.S. Department of State, Bureau of Foreign and Domestic Commerce, *Commercial Relations of the United States with Foreign Countries during the Year 1900*, vol. 2 (Washington, DC: GPO, 1901), p. 855.

114 'A day at the Yorkshire worsted-factories', *Penny Magazine*, 13 (27 January 1845), 35.

115 *The Penny Cyclopaedia of the Society for the Diffusion of Useful Knowledge*, vol. 27 (London: Charles Knight and Co., 1843), p. 549.

116 J. Banerjee, 'Wool Exchange, Bradford, by Lockwood & Mawson', at The Victorian Web, at www.victorianweb.org/art/architecture/lockwood/1.html (accessed 2 November 2016); W. Cudworth, *Historical Notes of the Bradford Corporation* (Bradford: Thomas Brear, 1881), pp. 155–6.

117 Cudworth, *Historical Notes of the Bradford Corporation*, pp. 191–2, 199.

118 C. G. Wanford Lock (ed.), *Spons' Encyclopedia of the Industrial Arts, Manufactures, and Raw Commercial Products*, vol. 2 (London: E. & F. N. Spon, 1882), p. 2,060; W. A. Graham Clark, *Manufacture of Woollen, Worsted, and Shoddy in France and England and Jute in Scotland* (Washington, DC: GPO, 1908), pp. 34–5, 42–3.

119 'B.A.W.R.A. sale in Bradford', *Wool Record*, 20 (1 December 1921), 15.

120 AM–AF, Minutes, 3 December 1914, and 30 December 1914; AM–AF, Agreement between C. H. Walsh and W. S. Moon and T. Musgrave, 29 December 1914.

121 'Peter William Musgrave', Ancestry.com, *England & Wales, National Probate Calendar (Index of Wills and Administrations), 1858–1966* [database on-line] (Provo, UT: Ancestry.com Operations, 2010).

122 AM–AF, Minutes, 30 December 1914; AM–AF, 'Special resolution of Abraham Moon & Sons, Limited, Passed December 30th 1914 [and] Confirmed January 18th 1915'. The salary for C. H. Walsh was £1,000 per annum; the salary for W. S. Moon was reduced to £950 per annum.

123 J. Tynan, *British Army Uniform and the First World War: Men in Khaki* (Basingstoke: Palgrave Macmillan, 2013), pp. 5, 32–3.

124 D. M. Zimmern, 'The wool trade in war time', *Economic Journal*, 28:109 (March 1918), 13–14; 'The wool trade', *The Economist* (20 January 1917), 120.

125 'Worsteds, serges, woollens: Designs and markets', *Textile Recorder*, 32 (15 March 1915), 355; 'Khaki and crossbreds', *Wool Record*, 7 (11 March 1915), 222; 'The flannel trade', *Wool Record*, 11 (8 March 1917), 18.

126 J. Tynan, 'Military dress and men's outdoor leisurewear: Burberry's trench coat in First World War Britain', *Journal of Design History*, 24:2 (2011), 140–1.

127 'The wool trade', *The Economist* (20 January 1917).

128 'Huddersfield trade', *Wool Record*, 6 (15 October 1914), 356.

129 'Worsteds, serges, woollens: Designs and markets', *Textile Recorder*, 32 (15 March 1915), 35.

130 'Boom in woollen trade', *Financial Times* (22 October 1914).

131 Zimmern, 'The wool trade in war time', 13.

132 'Profits in the wool trade', *Wool Record*, 17 (29 January 1920), 266.

133 The operations of the Wool Control were covered in depth by *Wool Record*.

134 'The wool situation', *Wool Record*, 11 (24 May 1917), 11–12.

135 AM–AF, Ledger, July 1913–March 1919, entry for the Royal Army Clothing Department. Abraham Moon and Sons was among the textile mills with government contracts listed in the *Wool Record*.

136 AM–AF, Minutes, 19 July 1915.

137 AM–AF, Minutes, 16 August 1915.

138 'Worsted, serges, woollens: Designs and markets', *Textile Recorder*, 33 (15 December 1915), 224.

139 AM–AF, Minutes, 20 December 1915.

140 'Martha Moon', in Ancestry.com, *UK and Ireland, Find a Grave Index, 1300s–Current* [database on-line] (Provo, UT: Ancestry.com Operations, 2012).

141 'Wharfedale Show', *Yorkshire Post* (27 May 1916).

142 The National Archives, Kew, Records of the War Office (hereafter cited as TNA–WO), WO 374/71545, personal file for Frank Tempest Walsh, 1916–20; TNA–WO, WO 372/20/202383, Medal card of Frank Walsh, 1914–20.

143 Zimmern, 'The wool trade in war time', 14.

144 P. Reed, 'Uniforms and equipment of the Great War, 1914–18', at http://
     battlefields1418.50megs.com/uniforms_ww1.htm (accessed 20 September 1916).

145 'Khaki and crossbreds'.

146 'The woollen trade', *Wool Record*, 7 (11 February 1915), 133.

147 'The wool trade', *The Economist* (30 December 1916), 1,246.

148 AM–AF, Minutes, 21 February 1918.

149 AM–AF, Minutes, 11 November 1918, 13 November 1918, 20 November 1918, 19
     December 1918, 19 March 1919, 24 July 1919, 24 November 1919 and 26 July 1921.

150 AM–AF, W. S. Moon to C. H. Walsh, handwritten note offering to sell his interest in
     Abraham Moon and Sons for £20,000, 8 November 1919.

151 AM, Executive files, 'Analysis of Financial Accounts, 1900–1919'.

152 AM–AF, Minutes, 12 January 1920, 5 February 1920; AM–AF, 'Messrs Abraham Moon
     & Sons Limited and its liquidators to Messrs Abraham Moon & Sons Limited, agreement
     for sale and purchase', 5 February 1920.

153 My estimate is based on the tools available at MeasuringWorth.com, 'Five Ways to
     Compute the Relative Value of a UK Pound, 1270 to Present', at www.measuringworth.
     com/ukcompare/ (accessed 13 December 2016).

154 AM–AF, Minutes, 5 February 1920.

155 AM–AF, Register of allotment of shares.

156 AM–AF, Minutes, 19 August 1921, 1 May 1956; AM–AF, Register of allotment of shares;
     AM–AF, Copy of register of directors or managers.

157 B. Walsh, interview by author, Burnsall, North Yorkshire (3 May 2014).

158 'Big spinning establishment sold', *Textile World Journal*, 58 (23 October 1920), 67.

159 'Big spinning establishment sold'; 'Transfer of mills in Bradford district', *Yorkshire
     Evening Post* (17 April 1919); 'Fact and comment', *Textile World Journal*, 53 (2 March
     1918), 39; 'A leading light in the Bradford trade', *Yorkshire Evening Post* (25 February
     1920).

160 'The Guiseley District', *Yorkshire Evening Post* (20 January 1920).

4 Moving up-market

1 'Yorkshire change to better fabrics starts: Announcement by Moon of new policy
   confirms general movement', *Women's Wear Daily* (6 September 1927).

2 'The influence of fashion', *Wool Record*, 17 (4 March 1920), 12.

3 Abraham Moon and Sons rented 'Higher Gill Mill Eller Ghyll Otley' from Jonathan
   Peate starting in 1915, and used the facility to shred and grind rags. Commonly known
   as Eller Ghyll Mill, this facility was the original manufacturing plant of the Peate
   brothers. See Abraham Moon and Sons Ltd, Guiseley, West Yorkshire (hereafter cited

as AM), Archival files (hereafter cited as AM–AF), Minutes of the Board of Directors (hereafter cited as Minutes), 11 January 1915; AM–AF, 'Messrs Abraham Moon & Sons Limited and its liquidators to Messrs Abraham Moon & Sons Limited, agreement for sale and purchase', 5 February 1920; AM–AF, 'Inventory of the freehold estates known as Netherfield Mills, Guiseley,… the property of Abraham Moon & Sons Limited, woollen manufacturers', August 1920.

4 AM–AF, 'Inventory', August 1920; George Hodgson Ltd, announcement, *Financial Times* (23 May 1898).

5 R. Beaumont, *Woollen and Worsted: The Theory and Technology of the Manufacture of Woollen, Worsted, and Union Yarns and Fabrics*, 4th edn (London: G. Bell and Sons, 1920), vi.

6 AM–AF, studio photograph of an unidentified man whom I have identified as Roberts Beaumont based on comparisons with photographs of the professor as an older man.

7 'Notes from the sections', *Journal of the Society of Dyers and Colourists*, 37:12 (December 1921), 304; AM–AF, Minutes, 18 February 1920, 21 June 1920, 25 June 1924 and 22 October 1924.

8 AMAF, Registration District of Wharfedale, County of York, certified copy of an entry of death for Charles Herbert Walsh, 24 November 1924.

9 'The late Mr. C. H. Walsh, of Guiseley', *Yorkshire Post* (24 November 1924).

10 'Recent wills', *Yorkshire Post* (1 July 1921); 'Mr. Jonathan Peate dead', *Yorkshire Evening Post* (13 December 1924); 'Walter Smith Moon', in Ancestry.com, *UK and Ireland, Find a Grave Index, 1300s–Current* [database on-line] (Provo, UT: Ancestry.com Operations, 2012); 'Deaths', *Yorkshire Post* (29 July 1927).

11 Jane Blake, Guiseley, West Yorkshire, Papers related to Crooklands, 'Trustees of Mr. Isaac Moon, deceased, to John Edward Boden Esq. and Mrs. Georgina Robinson Boden, Conveyance of a dwelling house known as "Crooklands"', 29 February 1924.

12 AM–AF, Mrs Walsh & Others to Mr T. Musgrave, 'Agreement for the sale of shares in Abraham Moon & Sons Ltd', 22 March 1926.

13 AM–AF, Register of allotment of shares.

14 'Statistics of the wool industry', *Textile Recorder*, 44 (15 March 1927), 49.

15 'Cheaper dress goods in demand', *Drapers' Organiser* (December 1924), 49.

16 'Wool textile stoppage almost complete', *Yorkshire Post* (25 July 1925).

17 'Believe London purchases by U.S. buyers curtailed due to new American prices', *Women's Wear* (21 August 1925).

18 'Continental mills making inroads on British trade', *Women's Wear* (15 September 1925).

19 'The woollen trade', *Financial Times* (12 November 1925); 'Yorkshire dress goods mills revive clamor for protection', *Women's Wear* (5 November 1925).

20 M. Keighley, 'From four pages to global influence', *Wool Record*, 167 (July 2008), 34.

21 'Need seen for confining of cloth patterns', *Women's Wear* (12 May 1926).

22 'Reduced operations of British mills still hamper deliveries', *Women's Wear* (6 August 1926).

23 'Worsted industry anxious', *Financial Times* (10 October 1927).

24 'Warm weather and changed customs in styles held to affect woolen demand', *Women's Wear* (3 August 1925).

25 'Dearer fabrics mean less material in garments, says English manufacturer', *Women's Wear* (6 March 1925).

26 'West of England type fabric favored in London at present', *Women's Wear* (12 May 1925).

27 'The woollen industry', *Financial Times* (29 June 1925).

28 The National Archives, Kew (hereafter cited as TNA), Records of the War Office (TNA–WO), WO 372/20/202383, Medal card of F. T. Walsh, 1914–20.

29 AM–AF, Minutes, 2 December 1925.

30 AM–AF, Minutes, 23 March 1927.

31 'Yorkshire change to better fabrics starts'.

32 'Guiseley trade', *Yorkshire Post* (12 January 1928).

33 AM–AF, Minutes, 5 August 1925, 1 September 1925 and 23 June 1926; *Post Office London Directory with County Suburbs for 1925* (London: Kelly's Directories, 1925), p. 1,535.

34 AM–AF, Minutes, 21 February 1926, 19 July 1927, 26 July 1927, 24 October 1928, 24 February 1930, 24 March 1930, 22 October 1930, 24 February 1931 and 24 March 1931.

35 AM–AF, Minutes, 18 December 1929.

36 AM–AF, Minutes, 23 September 1925, 9 February 1926, 19 May 1926, 23 June 1926, 20 January 1927, 25 January 1927, 19 September 1928 and 6 November 1928.

37 'Textiles in Canada: Is the British preference undermined?', *Wool Record*, 41 (7 January 1932), 24.

38 'Advertising fabrics', *Textile Recorder*, 42 (25 August 1924), 26; Scottish Woollen Trade Mark Association, 'Order your spring overcoat suit or lady's costume to-day', advertisement in *Punch* (2 February 1921), vi; Scottish Woollen Trade Mark Association, *Pure New Wool—And Scottish* (1924), short film, at National Library of Scotland. movingimage.nls.uk/film/0571 (accessed 28 October 2016). The association generated a good deal of publicity in the trade journals; see, for example, 'South of Scotland woollens', *Wool Record*, 17 (26 February 1920), 21.

39 'English newspaper sees British woolens sold U.S. by advertising', *Women's Wear* (3 August 1925).

40 'Tweed for women's styles predicted, as foremost houses make selections', *Women's Wear* (13 July 1925).

41 'Some aspects of British export trade', *Wool Record*, 40 (8 October 1931), 26–8.

42 AM–AF, Minutes, 23 October 1929; 'Netherfield Mills name David's agent', *Women's Wear* (20 February 1928).

43 'Novel designs and colors features in display of woolens for autumn', *Women's Wear* (18 February 1924).

44 'Jacquard patterns in pastel tones appear in extensive import line', *Women's Wear* (8 October 1925).

45 'Soft-surfaced coatings backed with cloth matched by dress fabric, for ensembles', *Women's Wear Daily* (9 April 1928).

46 'Charles G. David returns from abroad', *Women's Wear Daily* (10 September 1926); 'C. G. David sails tomorrow', *Women's Wear Daily* (18 May 1927).

47 AM–AF, Minutes, 23 October 1929.

48 West Yorkshire Archive Service, Leeds (hereafter cited as WYAS–L), WYL2139: Records of A. W. Hainsworth and Sons Ltd (hereafter cited as WYL2139), box 21, J? T? Garnett, G. Garnett & Sons Ltd, Apperley Bridge, to C. Hainsworth, A. W. Hainsworth & Sons, Stanningley, 4 September 1933.

49 AM–AF, Minutes, 21 October 1931.

50 'How British manufacturers are meeting the tweed boom', *Daily Mail* (4 September 1929).

51 'Six textile companies purchased', *Financial Times* (13 November 1943).

52 'Correspondence: Wool textile industry', *Yorkshire Post* (13 January 1931).

53 'Wool stoppage begins', *Manchester Guardian* (11 April 1930).

54 'Wool crisis', *Manchester Guardian* (5 April 1930).

55 'Wool textile dispute', *Manchester Guardian* (8 January 1930); 'Wool textile inquiry to be private', *Manchester Guardian* (24 January 1930).

56 'Wool stoppage begins'; 'Lord Macmillan's proposals', *Manchester Guardian* (7 March 1930); 'Wool trade in "critical state"', *Manchester Guardian* (7 March 1930).

57 'A hard choice', *Manchester Guardian* (25 March 1930); 'Wool wages crisis', *Manchester Guardian* (25 March 1930); 'Wool notices to be posted to-day?', *Manchester Guardian* (31 March 1930); 'Wool notices posted', *Manchester Guardian* (1 April 1930); 'Wool unions' proposals', *Manchester Guardian* (7 April 1930); 'Numbers working', *Yorkshire Evening Post* (17 April 1930); 'Wool stoppage drifts on', *Manchester Guardian* (17 April 1930).

58 'Demand for higher grade cloth', *Wool Record*, 40 (10 September 1931), 29.

59 'Wool and woollens: Huddersfield, Tuesday', *Manchester Guardian* (21 May 1930).

60 'Woollen mills open and close again', *Manchester Guardian* (31 May 1930).

61 'Wool and woollens: Huddersfield, Tuesday'.

62 'Wool textile dispute', *Manchester Guardian* (9 April 1930).

63 'Strikers' tribute', *Yorkshire Post* (24 May 1930).

64 'Wool textile dispute'; 'Numbers working'; 'Drifting back to textile mills', *Yorkshire Evening Post* (25 April 1930).

65 'Breakdown at Guiseley', *Manchester Guardian* (7 May 1930); J. B. Perkins, 'Yorkshire woolen workers return as strike nears end', *Women's Wear Daily* (29 May 1930); 'The wool stoppage', *Manchester Guardian* (20 June 1930); 'Wool trade wages dispute', *Manchester Guardian* (24 June 1930); 'Textile trade', *Manchester Guardian* (1 December 1930); J. B. Perkins, '1,500 Yeadon wool workers back on job', *Women's Wear Daily* (25 June 1930).

66 'Gleanings from Golden Square', *Wool Record*, 40 (10 December 1931), 24; 'The piece goods trade', *Wool Record*, 40 (31 December 1931), 17.

67 D. A. Irwin, 'Avoiding 1930s-style protectionism: Lessons for today', 6 May 2009, available at http://siteresources.worldbank.org (accessed 19 May 2016).

68 *Ibid.*; National Institute of Economic and Social Research, *Trade Regulations and Commercial Policy of the United Kingdom* (Cambridge: Cambridge University Press, 1943), pp. 21–41; D. L. Glickman, 'The British imperial preference system', *Quarterly Journal of Economics*, 61:3 (May 1947), 442.

69 'Imperial preference', *Encyclopedia Britannica*, 1 April 2004, at www.britannica.com/topic/imperial-preference#ref115604 (accessed 6 December 2016).

70 'Forward!', *Wool Record*, 43 (5 January 1933), 2.

71 'The shipping trade', *Wool Record*, 41 (28 April 1932), 83.

72 'The piece goods trade', *Wool Record*, 41 (7 January 1932), 17.

73 'Gleanings from Golden Square', *Wool Record*, 40 (31 December 1931), 26.

74 WYAS–L WYL2139, box 21, [R. G. Hainsworth], A. W. Hainsworth & Sons, Stanningley, to [Leeds & District Woollen & Worsted Manufacturers' Association], Leeds, 22 March 1933 and 5 April 1933.

75 WYAS–L, WYL2139, box 21, D. Moffat, Glasgow, to R. G. Hainsworth, Stanningley, 8 December 1933, and typewritten report 'for information of Mr R. G. Hainsworth', 1.

76 S. Stemp, 'Lachasse', in A. de la Haye and E. Ehrman (eds), *London Couture, 1923–1975: British Luxury* (London: V&A Publishing, 2015), pp. 60–5.

77 On tweeds in ladies' wear, see Williams and West Ltd, 'Will West Sportswear', advertisement in *Drapers' Organiser* (July 1931), 37; 'British light weight woollens meet fashion's latest demands', *Drapers' Organiser* (February 1932), 183; 'When autumn comes tweed coat time again', *Drapers' Organiser* (July 1932), 24–5; 'Coats', *Drapers' Record*, 175 (25 August 1934), 20; John Harold Ltd, 'In line with fashion's decree', advertisement in *Drapers' Record,* 175 (25 August 1934), 44–5.

78 'Fashion in 1927', *Drapers' Record*, 148 (31 December 1927), 848; 'Knitted wear and tweeds spring into new life', *Drapers' Organiser* (December 1931), 28; 'Tweeds de luxe', *Drapers' Organiser* (December 1931), 29.

79 'The piece goods trade', *Wool Record,* 40 (26 November 1931), 17.

80 E. M. Vigers, 'Fashion marshalls her forces', *Daily Mail Atlantic Edition* (5 September 1930).

81 'British fabrics at the Fashions Exhibition', *Daily Mail* (3 September 1930).

82 Vigers, 'Fashion marshalls her forces'.

83 'Heavy woollens', *Wool Record*, 40 (4 June 1931), 28.

84 'Gleanings from Golden Square', *Wool Record*, 40 (26 November 1931), 26.

85 'Gleanings from Golden Square', *Wool Record*, 41 (7 January 1932), 27.

86 'District which is enjoying a "boom"', *Manchester Guardian* (27 February 1931).

87 'Readjustment', *Wool Record*, 40 (11 June 1931), 2; 'Exchange gossip: Over-industrialisation and a way out', *Wool Record*, 40 (9 July 1931), 73.

88 'Artificial silk progress during the past year', *Drapers' Organiser* (February 1931), 143; 'Rayon piece goods', *Wool Record*, 40 (23 July 1931), 28.

89 WYAS–L, WYL2139, box 27, 'Trade and industry in 1934. Incorporating the chairman's remarks at the annual ordinary meeting of Reuben Gaunt & Sons, Ltd, on December 14th, 1934', 29 December 1934, p. 9.

90 'Fashion and tariffs', *Wool Record*, 40 (8 October 1931), 31.

91 AM, Executive files (hereafter cited as AM–EF), 'Analysis of Financial Accounts, 1920–1939'.

92 A. J. P. Walsh, interview by author, Burnsall, North Yorkshire (3 May 2014); University of Leeds, University Archive, Ledger for evening students, entry for A. Holmes, 1928–29.

93 Springhead Mills had sales offices on Queen Street in Glasgow and in St Paul's Churchyard in the City; see Springhead Mill Company (Guiseley) Ltd, advertisement in *Wool Record*, 40 (29 October 1931), 40.

94 AM–AF, address book, 1930s.

95 'Wholesaler and retailer', *Drapers' Record*, 147 (16 July 1927), 145.

96 'Leeds of to-day', *Financial Times* (29 June 1925).

97 'Clothing trade situation', *Financial Times* (29 June 1925).

98 AM–AF, Ledger, '1913–1914', covering the period July 1913–March 1919; AM–AF, address book, 1930s.

99 Thomas Marshall & Company, 'Marlbeck Tailor Mades', advertisement in *Drapers' Record*, 175 (25 August 1934), 79.

100 James Corson & Company, 'Corsonia Tailor Mades', advertisement in *Drapers' Record*, 175 (15 September 1934), lxx; James Corson & Company, 'Fashion's "in the air" again', advertisement in *Drapers' Organiser* (March 1938), 31.

101 Dickson, Millar & Company, '"Deemarco" inexpensive range', advertisement in *Drapers' Organiser* (September 1931), 55.

102 'Hitchcock, Williams & Company', advertisement in *Drapers' Record*, 145 (5 March 1927), 653; Hitchcock, Williams & Company, 'New coat frocks', advertisement in *Drapers' Record*, 145 (19 March 1927) lxiv–lxv.

103 E. M. Sigsworth, *Montague Burton: The Tailor of Taste* (Manchester: Manchester University Press, 1990), 34.

104 Lewis Hyland & Company, 'The Burberry', advertisement in *Bexhill-on-Sea Observer*
     (4 May 1912); 'Burberry Motor Dress', advertisement in *Illustrated London News* (8 May
     1915); 'Burberry airylight weatherproof summer dress', advertisement in *Illustrated
     London News* (31 July 1915); MacGregor & Grant, 'Burberry exhibition', advertisement
     in *Yorkshire Evening Post* (11 November 1922); Burberry, 'In every quarter of the globe',
     advertisement in *Illustrated London News* (Christmas 1935).

105 'London—the metropolitan market of the woollen trade', *Textile Recorder*, 32 (15 March
     1915), 358.

106 *A History of Burberry* ([London: Burberry], 2006).

107 AM–AF, Address book, 1930s, entry for Burberry's Ltd.

108 Westminster City Archives, London (hereafter cited as WCA), 1327: Jaeger Archives
     (hereafter cited as 1327), 1327/27, A. V. May, 'The Jaeger Legend', 7–9, 11, 17–22,
     29–30; University of Glasgow Archive Services, UG–C, folder: UGD 199/1/20/17:
     Jaeger Acquisition Papers, 1967, 'Offers by Morgan Grenfell & Co. Limited
     on behalf of J&P Coats, Patons & Baldwins Limited to acquire … Jaeger Holdings
     Limited.

109 WCA, 1327, May, 'The Jaeger Legend', 22–8; WCA, 1327/569, 'Shops in stores', *Jaeger
     Staff Review*, 53 (summer 1935), 8.

110 AM–AF, address book, 1930s.

111 'Move to stop manufacturers supplying woollens direct to retailers', *Tailor and Cutter*,
     71 (11 December 1936), 1,590.

112 AM–AF, address book, 1930s; *Post Office London Directory with County Suburbs for
     1930* (London: Kelly's Directories, 1930), pp. 1,441, 1,552.

113 'Sparrow, Hardwick & Company', *Financial Times* (17 March 1924).

114 Sparrow, Hardwick & Company, 'Autumn show', advertisement in *Drapers' Record*, 147
     (27 August 1927), xxxii.

115 Leeds Central Library, Local and Family History Library, *A Retrospect and Record of the
     House of James Hare, Ltd, Leeds and London* ([Leeds: James Hare, 1936]), n.p.

116 'Why the Mrs. Smiths prefer madame shops', *Drapers' Record*, 175 (8 September
     1934), 18.

117 'Do national brands diminish retailers' individuality?, *Drapers' Record*, 175 (14 July
     1934), 33.

118 M. Keighley, *Wool City: A History of the Bradford Textile Industry in the 20th Century*
     (Ilkley: G. Whitaker & Co., 2007), p. 80.

119 Aireborough Civic Society, 'Guiseley', at www.aireboroughcivicsociety.org.uk (accessed
     1 October 2016).

120 'Leeds wholesale clothing: Cautious buying', *Wool Record*, 40 (6 January 1938), 9.

121 Keighley, *Wool City*, p. 82.

122 AM, Minutes, 25 January 1938.

123 Encyclopaedia Britannica, 'Munich Agreement', 10 February 2015, at www.britannica. com/event/Munich-Agreement (accessed 13 November 2016).

124 A. Briggs, 'The framework of the Wool Control', *Oxford Economic Papers*, 8 (November 1947), 18–19.

125 Briggs, 'The framework of the Wool Control', 28; University of Leeds, Brotherton Library, Special Collections, LAVC/NSP/38: Leeds Tailoring Industry Papers, folder 1, C. H. Hargreaves, undated typescript on the history of Montague Burton Ltd.

126 'The human element in industry', *Manchester Guardian* (9 May 1941).

127 'Concentration in wool textiles', *Manchester Guardian* (16 July 1941); TNA, Records of the Board of Trade and successors, Wool Concentration (hereafter cited as TNA–BT64/855), folder: Board of Trade, Concentration of production, General policy—Woollen & worsted industry, 'Note on Wool Concentration', [1941], 'Wool Concentration', [1941]; TNA–BT64/855, M. Watkins, 'Concentration in the woollen and worsted industry', 8 August 1941.

128 'Wool textile regulation', *Manchester Guardian* (16 June 1941).

129 'Concentration in wool textiles', *Manchester Guardian* (16 July 1941); TNA–BT64/855, folder: Board of Trade, Concentration of production, General policy—Woollen & worsted industry, Central Concentration Association, 'Concentration Scheme for the wool-textile industry', 14 July 1941.

130 AM–AF, Minutes, 25 July 1941.

131 AM–AF, Minutes, 26 November 1940.

132 AM–AF, Abraham Moon and Sons Ltd, 'Netherfield Mills, Guiseley, nr. Leeds, schedule and valuation of buildings, plant & machinery, April 1941'.

133 TNA–BT64/855, folder: Board of Trade, Concentration of production, General policy— Woollen & worsted industry, 'Wool Control', n.d. [1941].

134 AM–AF, Minutes, 2 January 1942.

135 'Labour and output in wool textiles', *Manchester Guardian* (3 December 1941); 'Nucleus wool textile mills', *Manchester Guardian* (22 October 1941); '"Lost" cotton workers urged to return to mills', *Manchester Guardian* (31 October 1941); 'Wool and woollens', *Manchester Guardian* (18 March 1943); TNA–BT64/855, folder: Board of Trade, Concentration of production, General policy—Woollen & worsted industry, C. M. W., 'Concentration of the woollen industry', 7 August 1941.

136 'The human element in industry'; 'Concentration for wool textiles', *Manchester Guardian* (2 May 1941); 'Concentration in wool textiles', *Manchester Guardian* (15 August 1941).

137 Imperial War Museums, L. Clouting, '8 facts about clothes rationing in Britain during the Second World War', available www.iwm.org.uk (accessed 13 November 2016).

138 *Ibid.*

139 Briggs, 'The framework of the Wool Control', 34–5.

140 'Burberrys, Ltd: net profit doubled', *Manchester Guardian* (22 October 1943).

141 TNA–BT64/855, folder: Board of Trade, Concentration of production, General policy—Woollen & worsted industry, 'Memorandum of a visit to Bradford, 3rd and 4th July 1941'.

142 AM–AF, Minutes, 22 December 1944.

143 AM–AF, Minutes, 23 January 1945.

144 AM–AF, Minutes, 2 May 1946.

145 A. J. P. Walsh interview (3 May 2014).

146 *Ibid.*; A. J. P. Walsh, interview by author, Guiseley, West Yorkshire, 28 April 2015; AM–EF, G. G. Lockwood to J. P. T. Walsh, 2 May 2008.

147 A. J. P. Walsh interviews (3 May 2014 and 28 April 2015).

148 AM–EF, *Moon: The Abraham Moon Story*, booklet, 2012.

149 International Wool Secretariat, 'Do you recognize her?', advertisement in *Fashions and Fabrics*, 66 (December 1946), 7.

150 'West Riding Worsted and Woollen Mills', *Financial Times* (27 March 1948).

151 'Labour force in Yorkshire mills almost halved', *Manchester Guardian* (22 January 1947).

152 Keighley, 'From four pages to global influence', 34.

153 A. Draper, 'Fine prospects for the weaver', *Guardian* (24 March 1964).

154 'Labour force in Yorkshire mills almost halved'.

5 From necessity to fashion

1 B. Walsh, interview by author, Burnsall, North Yorkshire (3 May 2014).

2 *Foyle's War*, created by Anthony Horowitz, ITV, 2002–15.

3 B. Walsh interview (3 May 2014); B. Walsh, interview by author, Burnsall, North Yorkshire (24 May 2014).

4 B. Walsh interview (24 May 2014).

5 A J. P. Walsh, interview by author, Burnsall, North Yorkshire (3 May 2014).

6 'Loose boxy jackets with slim skirts', *Fashions and Fabrics*, 71 (January 1950), 36; *Fashion and Fabrics*, 72 (May 1950), cover; 'Teen-and-twenty adaptables', *Fashion and Fabrics*, 72 (July 1950), 41.

7 A. J. P. Walsh interview (3 May 2014).

8 'Utility wool cloths', *Wool Record*, 81 (24 January 1952), 275.

9 A. J. P. Walsh, interview by author, Guiseley, West Yorkshire (21 June 2016); Abraham Moon and Sons Ltd, Guiseley, West Yorkshire, Archival files (hereafter cited as AM–AF), Minutes of the Board of Directors (hereafter cited as Minutes), 8 June 1953.

10 A. J. P. Walsh and J. P. T. Walsh, interview by author, Guiseley, West Yorkshire (5 May 2014).

11 J. B. Jeffreys, *Retail Trading in Britain, 1850–1950* (Cambridge: Cambridge University Press, 1954), p. 349.

12 *Ibid.*, p. 340.

13 G. Rees, *St Michael: A History of Marks and Spencer* (London: Weidenfeld and Nicolson, 1969), p. 229.

14 'Dalton tells the housewives to hold off buying', *Daily Mail* (15 September 1951); P. Sergeant, 'C&A go dividend crazy', *Daily Mail* (19 March 1966).

15 A. J. P. Walsh and J. P. T. Walsh interview.

16 A. J. P. Walsh, interview by author, Guiseley, West Yorkshire (21 June 2016).

17 B. Walsh interview (3 May 2016).

18 'C&A Modes open apparel store in London', *Women's Wear Daily* (3 October 1922).

19 C&A Company, Origins, at www.c-and-a.com/uk/en/corporate/company/about-ca/story/history/ (accessed 29 October 2016); M. Spoerer, *C&A: A Family Business in Germany, the Netherlands and the United Kingdom, 1911–1961* (Munich: Verlag C. H. Beck, 2016).

20 'C&A: Birmingham's new home of fashion', *Tamworth Herald* (25 September 1926).

21 AM–AF, Minutes, 19 January 1953.

22 'Dalton tells the housewives to hold off buying', *Daily Mail* (15 September 1951).

23 A. J. P. Walsh interview (3 May 2014); A. J. P. Walsh, interview by author, Guiseley, West Yorkshire (7 May 2015).

24 A. J. P. Walsh interview (21 June 2016).

25 AM–AF, Minutes, 21 September 1953, 28 September 1953; *Post Office London Directory 1953* (London: Kelly's Directories, 1953), p. 1,408.

26 AM–AF, Minutes, 19 October 1953.

27 AM–AF, Minutes, 9 November 1953.

28 *Ibid.*

29 AM–AF, Minutes, 23 November 1953.

30 A. J. P. Walsh, interview by author, Guiseley, West Yorkshire (28 April 2015); T. Brann, interview by author, London (17 April 2015).

31 AM–AF, Minutes, 5 September 1957.

32 A. J. P. Walsh interview (28 April 2015).

33 AM–AF, Minutes, 11 January 1954, 1 February 1954, and 1 March 1954.

34 A. J. P. Walsh and J. P. T. Walsh interview.

35 A. J. P. Walsh interview (28 April 2015).

36 A. J. P. Walsh interview (3 May 2014).

37 'Revival continues in wool textile industry', *Financial Times* (22 December 1959).

38 A. J. P. Walsh interview (28 April 2015); G. Long, interview by author, Yeadon, West Yorkshire (19 April 2016); T. Brann, interview by author, London (27 June 2016); B. Beckett, interview by author, Guiseley, West Yorkshire (17 March 2015).

39 A. J. P. Walsh interview (7 May 2015).

40 Peter Ackroyd, Saltaire, West Yorkshire, Records of the National Wool Textile Export
    Corporation (hereafter cited as PA–NWTEC), *Exports of Wool Textiles, 1953–1954*
    (Bradford: Export Group, National Wool Textile Executive and National Wool Textile
    Export Corporation, [1954]), p. 34.

41 *Ibid.*, p. 36.

42 'Italian wool prospects', *Financial Times* (13 September 1955); 'Heavy wool trade hit',
    Financial Times (11 November 1957).

43 'Italian wool problems', *Financial Times* (31 March 1952).

44 E. Ritaine, 'Prato: An extreme case of diffuse industrialization', *International Studies
    of Management and Organization*, 20:4 (1990), 64–5; 'Little firms that loom large',
    Financial Times (29 June 1982).

45 'Italian wool prospects'; R. Dodi, 'Problems in textiles', *Financial Times* (23 April
    1957).

46 'Heavy wool trade hit by cheap imports from Italy', *Financial Times* (11 November
    1957); L. Holroyd, 'Woollen manufacturing: Some apprehension about the future', *Wool
    Record*, 103 (11 January 1963), 62–3.

47 'The National Wool Textile Export Corporation', *Manchester Guardian* (1 March
    1941); 'Wool textile exports', *Manchester Guardian* (3 March 1941); 'Levy for publicity',
    Manchester Guardian (28 March 1941); 'Promoting exports of textiles', *Manchester
    Guardian* (24 February 1942).

48 'British exports of woolens sought', *New York Times* (10 January 1945); 'British textile
    offices open in New York', *New York Times* (11 January 1945).

49 'Wool export levy', *Manchester Guardian* (22 July 1950); 'Wool "shop window" in New
    World', *Manchester Guardian* (26 July 1950); 'Wool textile export levy', *Manchester
    Guardian* (1 August 1950).

50 'Wool textile exports', *Manchester Guardian* (17 May 1952).

51 'Woollen imports in U.S.', *Manchester Guardian* (20 June 1950).

52 'United Kingdom: Foreign affairs', *The Round Table*, 42 (1952), 243.

53 'British wool textiles in U.S.A. and Canada', *Wool Record*, 81 (3 January 1952), 34.

54 *Ibid.*

55 R. L. Blaszczyk, *American Consumer Society, 1865–2005: From Hearth to HDTV*
    (Hoboken, NJ: Wiley, 2009), Part III.

56 Boston Public Library, Boston, MA, Filene's marketing archive (hereafter cited as BPL–
    FA), folder: Fashionations correspondence, Harriet Wilinsky, Paris, to Jack Clark, J. N.
    Clarke Ltd, Dublin, 18 July [1953].

57 PA–NWTEC, *Exports of Wool Textiles, 1956–1957* (Bradford: Export Group, National
    Wool Textile Executive and National Wool Textile Export Corporation, [1957]),
    pp. 13–15.

58 PA–NWTEC, *Exports of Wool Textiles, 1958–1959* (Bradford: Export Group, National
    Wool Textile Executive and National Wool Textile Export Corporation, [1959]), pp.
    16–18; 'Some winter misgivings in the wool trade', *Financial Times* (7 December 1961).

59 'Canada's imports of wool goods', *Wool Record*, 81 (10 January 1952), 101–2.

60 'Imported textiles in Canada', *Wool Record*, 81 (7 February 1952), 473–4.

61 'Topics of the week', *Wool Record*, 81 (7 February 1952), 433.

62 'Credit restrictions in Canada', *Wool Record*, 81 (24 January 1952), 305–6.

63 D. Iddon, 'Now it is "go west, young salesman"', *Daily Mail* (15 April 1953).

64 '36 UK woolen exporters to take part in Canada exhibit', *Women's Wear Daily* (6 August
    1953).

65 A. J. P. Walsh interview (21 June 2016); AM–AF, Minutes, 23 June 1926.

66 'West Riding Worsted and Woollen Mills Limited', *Financial Times* (24 January 1961).

67 PA–NWTEC, *Exports of Wool Textiles, 1959–1960* (Bradford: Export Group, National
    Wool Textile Executive and National Wool Textile Export Corporation, [1960]), pp. 5–7.

68 'Some misgivings in the wool trade', *Financial Times* (7 December 1961).

69 *Exports of Wool Textiles, 1959–1960*, pp. 36–7; 'Trading with Europe', *Textile Recorder*,
    77 (January 1960), 49.

70 'The Common Market', *Textile Recorder*, 78 (September 1961), 63; 'No time to relax',
    Textile Recorder, 80 (March 1963), 43.

71 'West Riding Worsted and Woollen Mills Limited'.

72 M. O'Connor, 'Yorkshire's new dynamic outlook', *Ambassador* (October 1965), 62.

73 A. Paterson, 'Canada: Cloth production down but imports up', *Wool Record*, 103 (11
    January 1963), 98.

74 A. J. P. Walsh interview (3 May 2014); 'US wool cloth duty equals 50 percent of its value',
    Wool Record, 103 (25 January 1963), 6.

75 B. Walsh interview (24 May 2014).

76 AM–AF, Minutes, 1 March 1954.

77 A. J. P. Walsh interview (21 June 2016).

78 'West Riding Worsted and Woollen Mills', *Financial Times* (30 March 1949); 'West
    Riding Worsted and Woollen Mills', *Financial Times* (11 February 1953); 'West Riding
    Worsted and Woollen Mills', *Financial Times* (10 February 1956).

79 Albert Holmes was added to the board in October 1962, resigned from the board in
    March 1970, and retired from his job as production manager in October 1971. AM–AF,
    Minutes, 3 November 1949, 3 October 1962, 13 March 1970 and 29 October 1971; A. J.
    P. Walsh interview (3 May 2014); A. J. P. Walsh and J. P. T. Walsh interview.

80 AM–AF, Minutes, 15 March 1954, 7 April 1954 and 5 May 1954.

81 J. Richmond, interview by author, Guiseley, West Yorkshire (7 May 2015).

82 A. J. P. Walsh interview (3 May 2014).

83 A. J. P. Walsh and J. P. T. Walsh interview.

84 A. J. P. Walsh interview (3 May 2014).

85 A. J. P. Walsh and J. P. T. Walsh interview.

86 A. J. P. Walsh interview (3 May 2014).

87 A. J. P. Walsh and J. P T. Walsh interview.

88 AM–AF, Minutes, 11 November 1954.

89 AM–AF, Minutes, 21 December 1961.

90 AM–AF, Minutes, 3 August 1953, 21 September 1953 and 28 September 1953.

91 AM, Minutes, 19 January 1955, 16 February 1955, 23 February 1955, 21 September 1955, 5 October 1955, 1 November 1955, 11 February 1958, 20 January 1959 and 18 February 1960.

92 AM–AF, Minutes, 13 November 1962.

93 AM–AF, Minutes, 5 March 1963.

94 AM–AF, Minutes, 18 December 1962.

95 'The fashion industry in the United Kingdom', *Textile Recorder*, 78 (February 1961), 33; S. Black, 'New dimensions for the fashion designer', *Financial Times* (16 March 1964).

96 E. Ehrman, 'Supporting couture: The Fashion Group of Great Britain and the Incorporated Society of London Fashion Designers', in A. de la Haye and E. Ehrman (eds), *London Couture, 1923–1975: British Luxury* (London: V&A Publishing, 2015), p. 33; R. O'Byrne, *Style City: How London Became a Fashion Capital* (London: Frances Lincoln, 2009), p. 12.

97 'British wool textiles in U.S.A. and Canada', 34.

98 R. L. Blaszczyk, 'Styling synthetics: DuPont's marketing of fabrics and fashions in postwar America', *Business History Review*, 80:3 (autumn 2006), 485–528.

99 M. Shanks, 'The battle of the fibres', *Financial Times* (16 March 1964); A. R. Milne, 'Polyester's share of growing market', *Financial Times* (16 March 1964); 'This is Chemstrand', *Chemical and Engineering News*, 35 (1957), 24–5.

100 AM–AF, Minutes, 23 November 1953.

101 AM–AF, Minutes, 7 December 1953.

102 AM–AF, Minutes, 19 January 1960.

103 BPL–FA, folder: Miracle Fabric Promotion, clipping, 'Blended synthetics can offer any cloth you want', *Business Week* (19 April 1952), 33.

104 University of Leeds, Marks and Spencer Company Archive (hereafter cited as UL–M&S), box B2–5, 386, 'Pyjamas—there's been a big improvement', *St Michael News*, 9 (October 1953), [4]; 'It's glamour—all the way', *St Michael News*, 10 (October 1953), [1]; UL–M&S, box B2–5, 387, 'Nylon—talking point in ranges', *St Michael News*, 11 (November 1953), [3].

105 UL–M&S, box B2–5, 396, 'Forthcoming attractions', *St Michael News*, 6 (September 1959), 2.

106 R. Worth, *Fashion for the People: A History of Clothing at Marks & Spencer* (New York: Berg, 2007), p. 110.

107 Richmond interview.

108 A. J. P. Walsh, interview by author, Guiseley, West Yorkshire (29 May 2015).

109 BPL–FA, folder: Miracle Fabric Promotion, Barbara Duke, J. P. Stevens & Company, New York, to Helen Tyler, William Filene's Sons Company, Boston, 30 April 1952.

110 AM–AF, Minutes, 5 March 1963.

111 AM–AF, Minutes, 9 April 1963.

112 AM–AF, Minutes, 28 May 1963.

113 'Man-Made fibres progress', *Textile Recorder*, 81 (March 1964), 51.

114 AM, Minutes, 25 February 1964.

115 AM, Minutes, 21 April 1964.

116 Black, 'New dimensions'.

117 N. Ireland-Smith, 'High standards in acrylics', *Financial Times* (16 March 1964).

118 H. Morris, 'British man-made fibres and world markets', *Financial Times* (4 July 1966).

119 'Novelty weaves top British woollen ranges', *International Textiles*, 302:4 (1958), 116–17.

120 'IWS to spend £13 millions on wool promotion', *Wool Record*, 103 (28 June 1963), 5.

121 'Campaign to promote wool starts this autumn', *Financial Times* (5 June 1964); 'Modifications to the "Woolmark" scheme', *Textile Recorder*, 82 (May 1964), 49–50; 'Woolmark introduced', *Textile Recorder*, 82 (October 1964), 53–4.

122 'Improving wool's image', *Wool Record*, 103 (10 May 1963), 12.

123 'Wool on the attack', *Textile Recorder*, 82 (October 1964), 61.

124 'M. Ogden, 'Mini skirts: Are cloth manufacturers feeling the draught?', *Daily Mail* (3 June 1966).

125 B. Polan and A. Chubb, 'Cheap chic and snappy suits that helped the 1960s swing', *Daily Mail* (16 June 2000).

126 P. Tisdall, 'Wait-to-see policy by shoppers', *The Times* (10 October 1970).

127 C. Lloyd, 'How are things with the private shopping empires?', *Daily Mail* (2 January 1964).

128 M. Allen, 'How to use *The Times 1000*', *The Times* (15 October 1971).

129 'Detergent giants head the list of big spenders', *The Times* (12 February 1969).

130 P. Tisdall, 'Advertising and marketing', *The Times* (18 October 1972).

131 O'Connor, 'Yorkshire's new dynamic outlook', 66.

132 *Ibid.*, 64.

133 'Progress of Italy's wool textile industry', *Wool Record*, 103 (17 May 1963), 33.

134 O'Connor, 'Yorkshire's new dynamic outlook', 59.

135 Beckett interview.

136 *Ibid.*; Norman Renton, interview by author, Guiseley, West Yorkshire (17 March 2015).

137 'Looms without shuttles', *Manchester Guardian* (18 February 1949); 'Weaving machinery by Sulzer for £1m', *Financial Times* (2 April 1968); 'Build-up of output at new works', *Guardian* (22 May 1968).

138 'Projectile weaves fine fabrics', *Financial Times* (2 February 1977).

139 O'Connor, 'Yorkshire's new dynamic outlook', 59.

140 A. J. P. Walsh and J. P. T. Walsh interview.

141 AM–AF, Minutes, 24 June 1983.

142 Gerald Long, Guiseley, West Yorkshire, Papers related to James Ives & Company, clippings, 'Yeadon mills founded 125 years ago', *Wharfedale and Airedale Observer* (30 March 1973) and 'Happy birthday James Ives', *Bradford Telegraph and Argus* (29 March 1973).

143 A. J. P. Walsh interview (29 May 2015).

144 A. J. P. Walsh and J. P. T. Walsh interview.

145 'New looms in Switzerland', *Manchester Guardian* (22 October 1945); 'The Sulzer automatic loom', *Manchester Guardian* (28 January 1947); 'The new automatic loom', *Manchester Guardian* (3 February 1947).

146 D. Brunnschweiler, 'Quicker cloth-making', *Manchester Guardian* (3 May 1955); P. Abbenheim, 'Textile machinery survey: (iv) Weaving', *Financial Times* (11 February 1969).

147 Beckett interview.

148 Renton interview.

149 E. Tenner, *Why Things Bite Back: Technology and the Revenge of Unintended Consequences* (New York: Vintage Book, 1997), chap. 1.

150 A. J. P. Walsh and J. P. T. Walsh interview.

151 A. J. P. Walsh interview (29 May 2015).

152 O'Connor, 'Yorkshire's new dynamic outlook', 59.

153 *Ibid.*, 61.

154 *Ibid.*, 62.

155 *Ibid.*, 63.

6 Adjustments

1 Abraham Moon and Sons Ltd, Guiseley, West Yorkshire, Archival files (hereafter cited as AM–AF), Minutes of the Board of Directors (hereafter cited as Minutes), 15 December 1978.

2 G. Lockwood, interview by author, Guiseley, West Yorkshire (17 March 2015).

3 National Economic Development Office, *The Strategic Future of the Wool Textile Industry: A Report Prepared by W S Atkins & Partners for the Marketing Study Steering*

Group of the Economic Development Committee for the Wool Textile Industry (London: HMSO, 1969).

4   *Ibid.*, pp. xi–xii.

5   H. O'Neill, 'A time for reappraisal', *Financial Times* (13 January 1970).

6   *Ibid.*

7   P. Long, 'Knitted fabrics find buyers' approval', *Wool Record*, 113 (26 January 1968), 33.

8   H. O'Neill, 'Fashion favours Yorkshire', *Financial Times* (21 August 1970).

9   H. O'Neill, 'Clothing trade pattern in the 1970's', *Financial Times* (20 January 1970).

10 *Ibid.*

11 '30% profits increase reflects Coats Patons geographical strength', *Financial Times* (31 May 1972).

12 H. O'Neill, 'How Coats Patons bought a future in textiles', *Financial Times* (24 July 1970); 'J. & P. Coats, Patons & Baldwins Limited', *Financial Times* (3 June 1965); 'Coats Patons', *Financial Times* (1 June 1967); 'Coats Patons Limited', *Financial Times* (17 November 1967).

13 H. O'Neill, 'Textile trends', *Financial Times* (27 July 1970).

14 AM–AF, Minutes, 16 June 1970.

15 *Post Office London Directory for 1962* (London: Kelly's Directories, 1962), pp. 1,845, 1,908; 'The next steps ahead: The *Financial Times* Review of British Industry', *Financial Times* (4 July 1966).

16 Trevor Brann, interview by author, London (17 April 2015); A. J. P. Walsh, interview by author, Guiseley, West Yorkshire (21 June 2016).

17 A. J. P. Walsh, interview by author, Guiseley, West Yorkshire (28 April 2015).

18 G. M. Smith, interview by author, Guiseley, West Yorkshire (5 May 2015).

19 Leeds Central Library, Local and Family History Library, Leeds City Council, *Aireborough, Horsforth and Bramhope Local Plan* (Leeds: Leeds City Council, Department of Planning, 1989), p. 21; S. Burt and K. Grady, *The Illustrated History of Leeds*, 2nd edn (Derby: Breedon Books, 2002), p. 229.

20 A. Laurence, *Murgatroyd: The Yeadon Legends* (n.p.: no publisher, [after 2005]), pp. 3, 12, 14.

21 'Factory bought', *Manchester Guardian* (24 June 1972).

22 '30% profits'.

23 L. F. Gray and J. Love (eds), *Jane's Major Companies of Europe* (London: Sampson Low, Marston & Company, 1974), p. C67.

24 'WR Fabrics', *Guardian* (17 December 1974); J. Love (ed.), *Jane's Major Companies of Europe* (London: Jane's Yearbooks, 1976), p. C46.

25 A. J. P. Walsh, interview by author, Burnsall, North Yorkshire (3 May 2014)

26 'Japan will continue to buy steadily', *Wool Trend*, 31 (June 1974), 4–5.

27 'Wool consumption lowest ever as crisis bites', *Wool Record*, 125 (8 March 1974), 18.

28 'Woollen manufacturers to close one of their mills', *Wool Record*, 125 (6 September 1974), 27.

29 L. Elliott, 'British recessions: A short history', *Guardian* (7 December 2012).

30 National Economic Development Council, *Wool Textile EDC: Progress Report 1980* (London: National Economic Development Office, 1980), p. 2; R. David, 'Fears about future for wool textiles', *Financial Times* (12 March 1979).

31 J. Richmond, interview by author, Guiseley, West Yorkshire, 7 May 2015.

32 AM–AF, Minutes, 3 January 1967, and 10 June 1969; *Kelly's Post Office London Directory for 1970* (London: Kelly's Directories, 1970), p. 1,236.

33 Brann interview (17 April 2015); *Post Office London Directory for 1960* (London: Kelly's Directories, 1960), p. 3,186.

34 Brann interview (17 April 2015); P. Long, 'Huddersfield survey: The relationship with Golden Square', *Wool Record*, 114 (20 September 1968), 29.

35 Brann interview (17 April 2015); *Post Office London Directory for 1960*, pp. 1,277, 1,438, 1,671, 1,927; S. Stemp, 'Lachasse', in A. de la Haye and E. Ehrman (eds), *London Couture, 1923–1975: British Luxury* (London: V&A Publishing, 2015), pp. 60–5; P. Golbin (ed.), *Balenciaga Paris* (New York: Thames & Hudson, 2006), pp. 86, 98, 111, 135.

36 Brann interview (17 April 2015); T. Brann, interview by author, London (6 June 2016); *The Yorkshire Textile Industry, 1970–71*, 85th edn (Croydon: Thomas Skinner & Company, 1970), pp. 65, 105, 107, 112, 118, 133.

37 Brann interview (17 April 2015).

38 *Ibid.*; *Post Office London Directory for 1941* (London: Kelly's Directories, 1941), p. 1,999; *Post Office London Directory for 1942* (London: Kelly's Directories, 1942), p. 1,678; *Post Office London Directory for 1962*, p. 1,964.

39 *Post Office London Directory for 1962*, p. 1,743; Brann interviews (17 April 2015 and 6 June 2016).

40 Brann interview (17 April 2015).

41 'Calderdale writer Jean Illingworth sparks nostalgia for Huddersfield workers penning book about life in Harella clothing factory in the 1960s', *Huddersfield Daily Examiner* (18 November 2015).

42 'Windsmoor PLC', *Financial Times* (7 July 1986); R. Tomkins, 'Offer values Windsmoor at £23m', *Financial Times* (7 July 1986); *Kelly's Post Office London Directory 1976* (Kingston-upon-Thames, Surrey: Kelly's Directories, 1976), p. 1,440.

43 Brann interview (17 April 2015); T. Brann, interview by author, London (27 June 2016); *Kelly's Post Office London Directory 1976*, p. 1,194.

44 H. Riches, 'The making of Mansfield', *Drapers' Record* (22 February 1986), 15; K. Whitehorn, 'Top dressing time', *Observer* (10 May 1987); 'The big chance', *Guardian* (24 October 1979).

45 *Kelly's Post Office London Directory 1976*, p. 1016.

46 'Short particulars: Ellis & Goldstein, Limited', *Financial Times* (2 November 1936); 'Ellis & Goldstein', *Financial Times* (10 March 1939); 'Ellis & Goldstein', *Financial Times* (26 March 1940).

47 'Ellis & Goldstein acquisition', *Financial Times* (14 December 1946).

48 'Ellis & Goldstein Limited', *Financial Times* (12 April 1951).

49 'Ellis & Goldstein', *Financial Times* (20 June 1955).

50 'Ellis & Goldstein Ltd', *Financial Times* (27 June 1957).

51 Brann interview (6 June 2016); D. Ritter, advertisement, *Times (London)*, (24 March 1945); Deréta of London, advertisement, *Sunday Times (London)*, (15 April 1956).

52 'Ellis & Goldstein (Holdings) Limited', *Financial Times* (28 June 1967).

53 'Ellis & Goldstein setback', *Financial Times* (30 March 1968).

54 'Ellis & Goldstein (Holdings) Limited', *Financial Times* (19 April 1972); 'Ellis & Goldstein forecasts £1.35m', *Financial Times* (25 August 1972); 'Ellis & Goldstein ahead', *Financial Times* (29 March 1973); 'Ellis & Goldstein record', *Financial Times* (22 August 1973); '£3.1m. by Ellis & Goldstein', *Financial Times* (24 April 1974), 'Ellis & Goldstein overseas', *Financial Times* (13 May 1974).

55 'Taking shops in shops abroad', *Financial Times* (1 May 1974).

56 'Ellis & Goldstein (Holdings) Limited', *Financial Times* (2 May 1973).

57 'Ellis & Goldstein prospects', *Financial Times* (19 May 1977).

58 'Ellis & Goldstein (Holdings) Limited', *Financial Times* (18 May 1978).

59 Brann interviews (6 June 2016 and 27 June 2016).

60 S. Brompton and R. Tyler, 'Everything Ted Heath ought to know about Margaret Thatcher', *Daily Mail* (24 January 1975).

61 'Country Casuals', *Financial Times* (3 November 1973); 'Country Casuals', *Financial Times* (7 September 1974); 'Co-ordinates cut a dash', *Financial Times* (28 September 1985).

62 'Country Casuals', *Financial Times* (7 September 1974).

63 Rosalind Coward, *Diana: The Portrait* (Kansas City, MO: Andrews McMeel Publishing, 2004), pp. 106–7.

64 Brann interview (27 June 2016).

65 A. J. P. Walsh and J. P. T. Walsh, interview by author, Guiseley, West Yorkshire (5 May 2014).

66 J. Zeitlin, 'The clothing industry in transition: International trends and British response', in S. D. Chapman (ed.), *The Textile Industries*, vol. 4: *Twentieth-Century Developments* (London: I. B. Tauris, 1997), pp. 142–3.

67 'Long term investment the way to retail supremacy', *The Times)* (17 July 1970); M. Corina, 'High street battle with the multiples', *The Times* (12 January 1971); 'Change

over the counter', *The Times* (6 June 1971); B. Polan and A. Chubb, 'Cheap chic and snappy suits that helped the 1960s swing', *Daily Mail* (16 June 2000).

68 A. J. P. Walsh and J. P. T. Walsh interview.

69 L. van der Post, 'What ever happened to the traditional winter coat?', *Financial Times* (23 October 1976).

70 'Cloth designers and buyers call for "closer liaison"', *Wool Record*, 114 (20 December 1968), 14.

71 'Producing a menswear collection', *Wool Record*, 125 (22 March 1974), 12.

72 J. Richmond, interview by author, Guiseley, West Yorkshire (7 May 2015).

73 A. J. P. Walsh interview (21 June 2016).

74 M. Aveyard, interview by author, Guiseley, West Yorkshire (22 April 2015).

75 P. Long, 'Strong British contingent for Paris shows', *Wool Record*, 103 (23 February 1963), 36; P. Long, 'Exporters disappointed by the new budget', *Wool Record*, 103 (12 April 1963), 25; P. Long, 'British wool garments top the bill in Paris', *Wool Record*, 103 (24 May 1963), 36.

76 P. Long, 'Golden opportunities for British cloth makers', *Wool Record*, 104 (22 November 1963), 30, 40.

77 'Milan Samples Fair of world-wide importance', *International Textiles*, 302:4 (1958), 119.

78 'Tenth industries fair at Dornbirn, Austria', *International Textiles*, 301:3 (1958), 85.

79 B. Wubs and T. Maillet, 'Building competing fashion textile fairs in Europe, 1970–2010: Première Vision (Paris) vs. Interstoff (Frankfurt)', *Journal of Macromarketing*, 37 (March 2017), 25–39.

80 *Ibid.*

81 '12 British firms at Frankfurt Interstoff', *Wool Record*, 104 (6 December 1963), 7.

82 'Frankfurt's rag time', *Guardian* (26 November 1974).

83 Aveyard interview (22 April 2015).

84 Peter Ackroyd, Saltaire, West Yorkshire, Records of the National Wool Textile Export Corporation (hereafter cited as PA–NWTEC), *British Wool Textile Exports 1966–67* (Bradford: National Wool Textile Executive and National Wool Textile Export Corporation, 1967), p. 6.

85 PA–NWTEC, *British Wool Textile Exports 1963–64* (Bradford: National Wool Textile Executive and National Wool Textile Export Corporation, 1964), p. 26.

86 'British wool cloth does well at Interstoff', *Wool Record*, 103 (31 May 1963), 3.

87 PA–NWTEC, *British Wool Textile Exports 1968–69* (Bradford: National Wool Textile Executive and National Wool Textile Export Corporation, [1969]), p. 21, and PA–NWTEC, *British Wool Textile Exports 1969–70* (Bradford: National Wool Textile Executive and National Wool Textile Export Corporation, [1970]), p. 28.

88 'British world textile fair suggested', *Wool Record*, 126 (13 December 1974), 6.

89 'Bonus for men's wear at 33rd Interstoff', *Wool Record*, 127 (30 May 1975), 20.

90 'World-wide Woolmark fashion textiles sustain natural look for Interstoff', *Wool Record*, 127 (2 May 1975), 28.

91 PA–NWTEC, *British Wool Textile Exports: Annual Report of the National Wool Textile Export Corporation 1977–78* (Bradford: National Wool Textile Export Corporation, [1978]), pp. 18–20.

92 P. Kerwien, Historisches Arhiv, Messe Frankfurt GmBH, email to author, 4 November 2016.

93 M. Aveyard, interview by author, Guiseley, West Yorkshire (21 June 2016).

94 Aveyard interview (22 April 2015).

95 Westminster City Archives, London, 1327: Jaeger Archives, 1327/414: Editorial press book, vol. 21, January–December 1974, clipping, A. Chubb, 'Why the girls of Paris are buying terribly British', *Evening News* (28 January 1974).

96 National Economic Development Council, *Wool Textile EDC: Progress Report 1980*, p. 10.

97 'Dutch newsletter: How trade with Common Market partners has developed', *Wool Record*, 103 (3 May 1963), 39; 'Italian imports causing difficulties in Holland', *Textile Recorder*, 85 (July 1967), 43.

98 'Marked rise in Italian wool cloth shipments to Britain', *Wool Record*, 127 (24 January 1975), 27.

99 R. David, 'British textile mills facing an uphill struggle', *Financial Times* (4 December 1979); 'Little firms that loom large', *Financial Times* (29 June 1982).

100 'An uphill stretch for textiles', *Financial Times* (11 May 1976).

101 Z. A. Silberston, *The Future of the Multi-Fibre Arrangement: Implications for the UK Economy* (London: HMSO, 1989), 1–3.

102 David, 'British textile mills facing an uphill struggle'.

103 *Ibid.*

104 G. Portland, telephone interview by author (8 October 2015); Aveyard interview (22 April 2015); T. Brann, email to author, 10 November 2016.

105 National Economic Development Council, *Wool Textile EDC: Progress Report 1980*, p. 16.

106 Portland interview; J. P. T. Walsh, interview by author, Guiseley, West Yorkshire, 22 April 2015; Brann email.

107 AM–AF, G. Portland, Purley, Surrey to J. P. T. Walsh, 24 January 2000.

108 Smith interview; *Kelly's Post Office London Directory 1981* (East Grinstead, West Sussex: Kelly's Directories, 1981), p. 1,779.

109 A. J. P. Walsh interview (21 June 2016).

110 Smith interview.

111 *Ibid.*; Federal Trade Commission, Commission Decision Volumes: N, Complaint in the matter of Norlic Import Company, Inc., et al., Decision 22 October 1974, 1173, available

at www.ftc.gov/enforcement/cases-proceedings/commission-decision-volumes/n (accessed 2 November 2016).

112 Smith interview; J. Barrett, 'House panel warns U.S. stores on Marianas' goods', *Women's Wear Daily* (31 July 1992); P. Shenon, 'Made in the U.S.A.?—hard labor on a Pacific island', *New York Times* (18 July 1983).

113 J. Ramey, 'U.S. seeking to reform Mariana's apparel industry', *Women's Wear Daily* (23 July 1997).

114 Aveyard interview (22 April 2015).

115 Aveyard interview (21 June 2016).

116 *Ibid.*

117 P. Ackroyd, interview by author, Saltaire, West Yorkshire (12 May 2015).

118 Aveyard interview (21 June 2016); P. Ackroyd, telephone interview by author, 21 October 2016.

119 Aveyard interview (21 June 2016).

120 *Ibid.*

121 *Ibid.*

122 *Ibid.*

123 AM–AF, Minutes, 23 February 1979.

124 *Ibid.*

125 Aveyard interview (22 April 2015).

126 'Facing up to the future', *Financial Times* (20 September 1980).

127 *Ibid.*

128 AM–AF, Minutes, 18 April 1979.

129 AM–AF, Minutes, 30 November 1979.

130 I. Owen, 'Problems of textiles industry "exaggerated"', *Financial Times* (14 November 1979).

131 R. David, 'Textile import controls to stay', *Financial Times* (1 February 1980).

132 AM–AF, Minutes, 24 November 1978.

133 *Ibid.*

7 What's next?

1 Abraham Moon and Sons Ltd, Guiseley, West Yorkshire (hereafter cited as AM), Archival files, Minutes of the Board of Directors (hereafter cited as AM–AF, Minutes), 19 February 1982.

2 'Britain's Fabrex '79 ends on upbeat', *Women's Wear Daily* (2 May 1979).

3 AM, Executive files (hereafter cited as AM–EF), P. Long, 'Fabric, a certain taste in fashion', in *Fashion Fabrex '79, National Hall Olympia October 30th–November 2nd*, not paginated.

4 International Wool Secretariat, 'Wool comes to town', advertisement in *Fashion Fabrex '79* not paginated.

5 T. Brann, interview by author, London (27 June 2016).

6 L. Robbins, 'Bulk orders spark Fabrex despite a slow opening day', *Women's Wear Daily* (22 March 1984).

7 Fabrex, 'Fashion Fabrex', advertisement in *Women's Wear Daily* (28 July 1981); Fabrex, 'Around the world in one day', advertisement in *Women's Wear Daily* (8 March 1984).

8 L. Robbins, 'Sales strong but traffic softer at '84 Fabrex fair', *Women's Wear Daily* (26 March 1984).

9 National Economic Development Council, *Wool Textile EDC: Progress Report 1980* (London: National Economic Development Office, 1980), pp. 9–10, 16–18, 20, 25.

10 *Ibid.*, 20; R. David, 'Persuading the textile trade to think Italian', *Financial Times* (13 March 1980).

11 AM–AF, Minutes, 22 October 1980.

12 M. Monden, 'Ivy in Japan: A regalia of non-conformity and privilege', in P. Mears (ed.), *Ivy Style: Radical Conformists* (New Haven: Yale University Press; New York: Fashion Institute of Technology, 2012), pp. 176, 179.

13 M. Aveyard, interview by author, Guiseley, West Yorkshire (22 April 2015).

14 G. M. Smith, interview by author, Guiseley, West Yorkshire (21 June 2016).

15 'Deaths', *The Times* (30 September 1967); 'Business appointments: New chairman for Switchgear', *The Times)* (28 October 1967); 'Leafield Mills', advertisement in *Guardian* (4 October 1980); D. Hildrew, 'Foreign buyers claim bargains from wool mills they helped close', *Guardian* (20 August 1980); G. Long, interview by author, Yeadon, West Yorkshire (19 April 2016).

16 Aireborough Historical Society, images for James Ives & Company, at www. aireboroughhistoricalsociety.com (accessed 31 October 2016).

17 West Yorkshire Archive Service, Leeds (hereafter cited as WYAS–L), WYL2139: Records of A. W. Hainsworth and Sons Ltd (hereafter cited as WYL2139), box 36, D. Gaunt, Reuben Gaunt & Sons Ltd, Pudsey, 'Chairman's statement', 1 April 1982.

18 AM–AF, Minutes, 12 December 1980.

19 AM–EF, folder: Analysis of export, 'London district sales' (September 1980–February 1981); T. Brann, interview by author, London (6 June 2016).

20 Brann interview (6 June 2016); *Post Office London Directory for 1960* (London: Kelly's Directories, 1960), p. 223.

21 J. Richmond, interview by author, Guiseley, West Yorkshire (7 May 2015); S. Chapman, 'The decline and rise of textile merchanting, 1880–1990', *Business History*, 32:4 (November 1990), 183.

22 AM–EF, R. A. Hammond, 'Report for business potential for next year in the U.K. excluding the protected London accounts', 4 December 1981.

23 *Kelly's Post Office London Directory 1981* (East Grinstead, West Sussex: Kelly's Directories, 1981), p. 1,603.

24 Hammond, 'Report for business potential'.

25 AM–EF, folder: Analysis of export, 'Monthly analysis of sales, 1982/83'.

26 AM–EF, folder: Analysis of export, 'Comparison of exports by turnover', 1980–83.

27 *Kelly's Post Office London Directory 1981*, p. 1,747; *Kelly's Post Office London Directory 1982* (East Grinstead, West Sussex: Kelly's Directories, 1982), p. 1,469.

28 Aveyard interview (22 April 2015).

29 G. M. Smith, interview by author, Guiseley, West Yorkshire (5 May 2015); G. Portland, telephone interview by author (8 October 2015).

30 M. Aveyard, interview by author, Guiseley, West Yorkshire (21 June 2016).

31 M. L. Gavenas, 'Who decides the color of the season? How a trade show called Première Vision changed fashion culture', in R. L. Blaszczyk and U. Spiekermann (eds), *Bright Modernity: Color, Commerce, and Consumer Culture* (New York: Palgrave Macmillan, 2017), pp. 251–69.

32 'Changes in wool export promotion', *Guardian* (18 July 1967); Peter Ackroyd, Saltaire, West Yorkshire, Records of the National Wool Textile Export Corporation (hereafter cited as PA–NWTEC), *British Wool Textile Exports 1968–69* (Bradford: National Wool Textile Executive and National Wool Textile Export Corporation, [1969]), pp. 16, 20–1.

33 'Car prizes to promote wool', *Guardian* (18 September 1969); *British Wool Textile Exports 1968–69*, pp. 22–6.

34 PA–NWTEC, *British Wool Textile Exports: Annual Report of the National Wool Textile Export Corporation for 1983–84* (Bradford: National Wool Textile Export Corporation, 1984), pp. 9–16.

35 Gavenas, 'Who decides the color of the season?', pp. 251–69.

36 AM–EF, British Wool Textile Export Corporation, 'The British wool textile industry, visit of HRH the Duke of York to Premiere Vision, 13th February 2003', 21 January 2003, 11; AM–EF, *National Wool Textile Export Corporation Annual Report for 1996/1997* (Bradford: British Wool Textile Export Corporation, 1996), p. 8; 'Textiles show the way says Sir Digby', *West Yorkshire and North Yorkshire Counties Publications* (14 March 2005).

37 P. Ackroyd, interview by author, Saltaire, West Yorkshire (12 May 2015); 'Founder of Première Vision dies in Lyon', *Wool Record*, 165 (October 2006), 15.

38 AM–EF, 'Minutes of a meeting of the council of the National Wool Textile Export Corporation', 7 April 1981.

39 'Paris exhibitions', *Wool Record*, 139 (April 1981), 15; 'British business at Paris shows', *Wool Record*, 139 (May 1981), 49.

40 Aveyard interview (21 June 2016).

41 'British business at Paris shows', p. 49.

42 AM–EF, 'Minutes of a meeting of the council of the National Wool Textile Export Corporation', 5 January 1982.

43 AM–EF, 'Minutes of a meeting of the council of the National Wool Textile Export Corporation', 23 March 1982; AM–EF, National Wool Textile Export Corporation, Weekly letter no. 1643, 26 March 1982.

44 AM–EF, National Wool Textile Export Corporation, Weekly letter no. 1644, 2 April 1982.

45 'We invite you to discover British Woollens at the Waldorf', advertisement in *Women's Wear Daily* (13 August 1980).

46 AM–EF, 'Minutes of a meeting of the council of the National Wool Textile Export Corporation', 15 September 1981.

47 E. B. Brill and O. Wilde, 'British Woollens show off to rosy start', *Women's Wear Daily* (1 September 1982).

48 'British woolen, worsted show slated for June 22–23 in New York', *Women's Wear Daily* (25 May 1993).

49 The Dorchester show was launched by the Wool Textile Manufacturers' Federation of Bradford in 1981. The National Wool Textile Export Corporation assumed responsibility for the show in October 1982. P. Ackroyd, telephone interview by author (21 October 2016).

50 'Good response to Dorchester show', *Wool Record*, 140 (September 1981), 19; T. Brann interview by author, London (27 June 2016); Ackroyd interview (21 October 2016).

51 AM–EF, National Wool Textile Export Corporation, Weekly letter no. 1951, 19 August 1988.

52 Gerald Long, Guiseley, West Yorkshire, Papers related to James Ives & Company, James Ives & Company Ltd, '125th Anniversary (1848–1973)' and 'Reply by Mrs. E. Kenneth Ives', [both March 1973].

53 Long interview.

54 AM–AF, Minutes, 26 June 1981.

55 AM–AF, Minutes, 7 December 1981.

56 AM–AF, Minutes, 15 January 1982.

57 AM–AF, Minutes, 19 February 1982.

58 AM–AF, Minutes, 14 May 1982.

59 AM–AF, Minutes, 21 June 1982.

60 AM–AF, Minutes, 14 May 1982.

61 'Ellis & Goldstein cuts payout as profits fall', *Financial Times* (14 May 1981); 'Ellis & Goldstein profits slide midway', *Financial Times* (3 November 1982).

62 'Ellis & Goldstein moves ahead to £1.4m for year', *Financial Times* (13 May 1982).

63 M. Keighley, 'Better prospects for Colne Valley woollen manufacturers', *Wool Record*, 139 (June 1981), 54; *Kelly's Post Office London Directory 1981*, p. 2,358.

64 AM–AF, Minutes, 19 February 1982.

65 'Windsmoor PLC', *Financial Times* (7 July 1986).

66 'Facing up to the future', *Financial Times* (20 September 1980).

67 *Ibid.*

68 A. Moreton, 'Export buoyancy aids woven cloth', *Financial Times* (26 January 1982).

69 R. David, 'British textile mills facing an uphill struggle', *Financial Times* (4 December 1979); J. Buxton, 'Little firms that loom large', *Financial Times* (29 June 1982).

70 AM–AF, Minutes, 22 June 1981.

71 AM–AF, Minutes, 7 December 1981.

72 G. Davies and J. Davies, *What's Next?* (London: Century, 1989), p. 63; D. Churchill, 'Clothes: How the big empires are striking back', *Financial Times* (4 May 1984); 'A double-quick creation', *Financial Times* (10 August 1984); 'Next man', *Financial Times* (28 December 1984); *The UK Fashion Report* ([Great Britain]: EMAP Fashion, [1997]), p. 353.

73 E. Musgrave, 'The Next move aims at a largely untapped market', *Drapers' Record* (13 February 1982), 47.

74 Churchill, 'Clothes: How the big empires are striking back'; D. Churchill, 'The Next collection of developments', *Financial Times* (21 August 1986).

75 AM–AF, Minutes, 19 February 1982.

76 *Ibid.*

77 Davies and Davies, *What's Next?*, p. 55.

78 *Ibid.*, p. 56; 'A double-quick creation'.

79 AM–AF, Minutes, 19 February 1982.

80 AM–AF, Minutes, 6 January 1983.

81 *Ibid.*

82 AM–AF, Minutes, 24 June 1983.

83 Linked In, resumé for Rona Stean, available at www.linkedin.com/in/rona-stean-81a12770 (accessed 27 October 2016).

84 Aveyard interview (22 April 2015).

85 AM–AF, Minutes, 19 July 1983.

86 Smith interview (5 May 2015).

87 AM–EF, folder: Analysis of export, 'London district sales [and] sundry district sales', September 1979–February 1980, and 'London district sales [and] sundry district sales', March 1980–August 1980.

88 AM–EF, folder: Analysis of export, 'Monthly analysis of sales, 1982/83'.

89 AM–AF, Minutes, 19 July 1983; AM–EF, V. S. Smith, Fowler & Orr, London, to Abraham Moon and Sons, 12 July 1983.

90 J. P. T. Walsh, interview by author, Weeton, North Yorkshire (23 May 2015); J. P. T. Walsh, email to author (5 July 2016).

91 J. P. T. Walsh, interview by author, Guiseley, West Yorkshire (25 October 2016).

92 AM–AF, Minutes, 5 July 1984, 5 December 1984.

93 AM–AF, Minutes, 23 August 1985.

94 J. P. T. Walsh interview (25 October 2016).

95 AM–AF, Minutes, 19 July 1983.

96 AM–EF, 'Analysis of home sales, ½ to 30.9.84'; G. M. Smith, email to author, 21 December 2015; A. Moreton, 'End of a long courtship', *Financial Times* (26 June 1985).

97 Classiq, 'Style in film: Richard Gere in *American Gigolo*', 23 July 2014, at http://classiq. me/style-in-film-richard-gere-american-gigolo (accessed 28 October 2016).

98 A. Stanley, 'Fighting crime, setting trends', *New York Times* (6 January 2006); G. Trebay, 'Roll up your sleeves and indulge in a Miami vice', *New York Times* (20 July 2006); J. Serwer, '"The sky started raining panties": Don Johnson on 30 years of "Miami Vice",'*Rolling Stone* (9 October 2014), at www.rollingstone.com/tv/ features/don-johnson-on-30-years-of-miami-vice-20141009 (accessed 30 October 2016).

99 'Ellis & Goldstein down year end', *Financial Times* (11 May 1983); 'Ellis & Goldstein recovers', *Financial Times* (3 November 1983); 'Ellis & Goldstein's Dash to £1.3m', *Financial Times* (1 November 1984); 'Ellis profits reach £3.6m as Dash growth continues', *Financial Times* (25 April 1985); 'Ellis & Goldstein profits increase to over £4m', *Financial Times* (23 April 1986); 'Lower interest helps Ellis & Goldstein profits to £1.53m', *Financial Times* (31 October 1986).

100 A. Rawsthorn, 'Berkertex attacks Ellis for allowing brands to "languish"', *Financial Times* (10 June 1988); Ellis & Goldstein (Holdings) plc.,'Ellis & Goldstein: Strength from specialisation', advertisement in *Financial Times* (5 July 1988).

101 'Ellis & Goldstein downturn to £3.7m', *Financial Times* (23 April 1987).

102 AM–EF, J. Morris, MEAD (Manufacturing Eastex Alexon Division), Luton, to Abraham Moon and Sons, 19 June 1989.

103 AM–EF, Agenda and appendices for directors' meeting, 30 June 1988, 'Schedule 10'.

104 AM–EF, Agenda and appendices for directors' meeting, 30 June 1988, 'Schedule 1'.

105 J. P. T. Walsh, email to author (11 November 2016).

106 AM–EF, folder: Analysis of export, 'Comparison of exports—By percentage, share of export turnover, [1982–86]'.

107 AM–EF, Agenda and appendices for directors' meeting, 30 June 1988, 'Schedule 6. Comparison of exports by % share of export turnover'.

108 Paul Stuart, 'Our story', at www.paulstuart.com (accessed 10 November 2016).

109 P. Smith, D. Sudjic, and D. Loveday, *Hello, My Name is Paul Smith: Fashion and Other Stories* (New York: Rizzoli, 2013), 88–9.

110 Ackroyd interview (12 May 2015); Stuart, 'Our story'.

111 AM–EF, National Wool Textile Export Corporation, *British Wool Textile Exports: Annual Report for 1988/89* (Bradford: National Wool Textile Export Corporation, 1989), not paginated.

112 J. P. T. Walsh, email to author, 7 November 2016.

113 AM–AF, Minutes, 29 January 1987; 26 June 1987.

114 AM–AF, Minutes, 19 October 1987.

115 WYAS–L, WYL2139, box 36, D. Gaunt, 'Chairman's statement', 10 April 1981, in Reuben Gaunt & Sons Ltd, 'Report and accounts statement, 3rd October 1980'.

116 Aveyard interview (22 April 2015).

117 Aveyard interviews (22 April 2015 and 21 June 2016).

118 AM–AF, Minutes, 23 March 1988; AM–EF, 'Present structure', [ca. 1987]; Linked in, resumé for Rona Stean; J. L. Coates, interview by author, Guiseley, West Yorkshire (5 May 2015).

119 Coates interview; AM–EF, National Wool Textile Export Corporation, Weekly letter no. 1955, 30 September 1988.

120 'St. Andrews Textile to move', *Women's Wear Daily* (25 January 1926); 'Monotones of unusual weave distinguish dressy coatings in Picardie New York line', *Women's Wear Daily* (2 May 1929); 'Bright Irish green with white cited among new vivid shades for spring', *Women's Wear Daily* (15 August 1929); 'A. H. Campbell joins St. Andrews Textile Company', *Women's Wear Daily* (21 September 1933); 'English quality shirtings make renewed appeal in woven stripes and fancy Jacquards', *Women's Wear Daily* (17 October 1929).

121 'A. H. Campbell joins St. Andrews Textile Company'; 'Colorful nubbed tweeds considered promising for fall', *Women's Wear Daily* (20 February 1930).

122 'Fashions from the Scotch tweeds for fall', *Women's Wear Daily* (18 April 1938).

123 'Dreschel resigns post with Carson's', *Women's Wear Daily* (15 December 1948); 'Dreschel leaves Wilson Bros.', *Women's Wear Daily* (16 August 1950); 'Dressy tweeds, three-piece costume scheme', *Women's Wear Daily* (17 December 1957).

124 Coates interview; David Hudson, telephone interview by author, 11 November 2016. Hudson was the main designer at the St. Andrews Textile Company from 1986 to 2003.

125 Hudson interview.

126 'Milan and Florence report', *International Textiles*, 688 (February 1988), 104–19.

127 Hudson interview; Coates interview; J. P. T. Walsh interview (25 October 2016).

128 Hudson interview; Coates interview.

129 Government of Canada, 'Canada–United States Free Trade Agreement (FTA)', 19 May 2016, at www.international.gc.ca/trade-agreements-accords-commerciaux/agr-acc/us-eu.aspx?lang=eng (accessed 30 October 2016); J. Romalis, 'NAFTA's and CUSFTA's impact on international trade', NBER Working Paper No. 11059, January 2005, at www.nber.org/papers/W11059 (accessed 30 October 2016).

130 Hudson interview.

131 'Windsmoor PLC'.

132 'Marriage of Giants', *Drapers' Record* (12 April 1986), 6; A. Rawsthorn, 'Coats Viyella falls 36% to £135m', *Financial Times* (11 March 1989); 'Coats Viyella sells Country Casuals chain', *Women's Wear Daily* (21 March 1989).

133 Aireborough Historical Society, images for Nunroyd Mills, at www. aireboroughhistoricalsociety.com (accessed 31 October 2016).

134 AM–AF, Minutes, 3 October 1985.

135 AM–AF, Minutes, 5 December 1985.

136 AM–EF, 'Comparative performance, Spring '90/Winter '89, Pieces sold by market'.

137 AM–AF, Minutes, 17 March 1989 and 23 March 1989.

138 J. P. T. Walsh interview (23 May 2015).

8 Reinvention

1 A. Bounds and C. Tighe, 'High-end demand revives Yorkshire's mills', *Financial Times* (3 November 2013).

2 Première Vision, 'Historique', at www.premierevision.com/fr/historique/?lang=fr (accessed 12 November 2016).

3 J. P. T. Walsh, interview by author, Weeton, West Yorkshire (23 May 2015).

4 *Ibid.*

5 *Ibid.*

6 Abraham Moon and Sons Ltd, Guiseley, West Yorkshire (hereafter cited as AM), Executive files (hereafter cited as AM–EF), Confederation of British Wool Textiles, 'Wool Textile Manufacturers' Federation, Meeting 30th November 1988'.

7 AM–EF, Confederation of British Wool Textiles, 'Wool Textile Manufacturers' Federation: chairman's report for the year 1987/88', 23 November 1988.

8 AM–EF, Confederation of British Wool Textiles, 'Note of a meeting of the IWTO Cloth Committee held in Paris on Thursday, 8th December, 1988'.

9 Parliamentary Business, House of Commons, 'The future of Multi-Fibre Arrangement', 12 January 1990, column 1240, available www.parliament.uk (accessed 12 November 2016).

10 *Ibid.*, column 1244.

11 *Ibid.*, column 1243.

12 'Czech the winter scene', *International Textiles*, 692 (1988), 66–7.

13 'The future of the Multi-Fibre Arrangement', column 1243.

14 *Ibid.*

15 *Ibid.*, column 1244.

16 J. Sewell, 'Performing masculinity through objects in postwar America: The playboy's pipe', in A. Moran and S. O'Brien (eds), *Love Objects: Emotion, Design and Material Culture* (London: Bloomsbury, 2014), pp. 63–71.

17 M. Kielmas, 'Questions over trade weave through Britain's wool revival', *Christian Science Monitor* (23 September 1988).

18 J. P. T. Walsh, interview by author, Weeton, North Yorkshire (23 May 2015).

19 Kielmas, 'Questions over trade'.

20 A. Rawsthorn, 'No brass for the Yorkshire mills', *Financial Times* (27 June 1989).

21 G. Jackson-Stops (ed.), *The Treasure Houses of Britain: Five Hundred Years of Private Patronage and Art Collecting* (Washington, DC: National Gallery of Art; New Haven: Yale University Press, 1985).

22 T. Graham and T. Blanchard, *Dressing Diana* (Princeton, NJ: Benford Books; New York: Welcome Rain, 1998), pp. 146–7.

23 J. A. Trachtenberg, *Ralph Lauren: The Man Behind the Mystique* (New York: Little, Brown and Company, 1988), pp. 140, 205–11, 221–3, 266–7, 270; L. Birnbach, *The Official Preppy Handbook* (New York: Workman, 1980).

24 'Textile workers' village wears the crown of World Heritage status', *Financial Times* (5 August 2002); 'Breathing life into an old mill', *Financial Times* (6 March 1984).

25 'Laura Ashley', *Financial Times* (25 November 1985).

26 M. Aveyard, interview by author, Guiseley, West Yorkshire, 21 June 2016; AM, Design department files (hereafter cited as AM–DD), Derek Harvey and Associates, press pack, The GB Clothing Company, Autumn 85/Winter 86.

27 S. Roberts, 'Elliot Gant, marketer of the button-down shirt, dies at 89', *New York Times* (18 March 2016).

28 Aveyard interview (21 June 2016); Gant Heritage, at www.gant.Companyuk/heritage/the-heritage (accessed 4 November 2016); 'Gant Company', *Real Deals*, 1 October 2004, at http://realdeals.eu.com (accessed 4 November 2016); AM–DD, *Gant Martha's Vineyard Fall Collection 1989*; *Fall in Connecticut Valley, Gant American Sportswear* (Autumn 1990); and *Gant in the Adirondacks, Fall 1991*.

29 AM–EF, National Wool Textile Export Corporation, Weekly letter no. 1643, 26 March 1982; AM–EF, National Wool Textile Export Corporation, Weekly letter no. 1990, 23 June 1989; M. Mazzaraco, 'British wool show returns to New York after eight years', *Women's Wear Daily* (29 June 1993).

30 J. P. T. Walsh interview (23 May 2015); J. P. T. Walsh, interview by author, Guiseley, West Yorkshire (21 June 2016).

31 J. Simms, 'A corporate image of some substance', *Independent* (5 September 1989).

32 AM–EF, Tom Clarke, Department of Trade and Industry, Leeds, 'Business review: Report by the enterprise counsellor' (23 December 1988), [p. 10].

33   AM, Archival files (hereafter cited as AM–AF), Minutes of the Board of Directors
     (hereafter cited as Minutes), 8 February 1989; Aveyard interview (21 June 2016).

34   C. Dowdy, 'Designers' creative flair fails to draw the money men', *Financial Times*
     (3 August 2004); B. Ginns, 'Elmwood boss', *Yorkshire Post* (26 August 2014).

35   Aveyard interview.

36   J. P. T. Walsh interview (21 June 2016); AM–EF, *Creating the cloth*, promotional
     brochure designed by Haluk Gurer, ca. 1989.

37   AM–AF, Minutes, 11 February 1993.

38   West Yorkshire Archive Service, Leeds (hereafter cited as WYAS–L), WYL2139: Records
     of A. W. Hainsworth and Sons Ltd (hereafter cited as WYL2139), box 36, R. Gaunt &
     Sons (Holdings) Ltd, *Report and Accounts*, 30 September 1995, 'Chairman's speech given
     at the A. G. M. 1996'.

39   WYAS–L, WYL2139, box 36, A. Turner, chairman, R. Gaunt & Sons (Holdings) Ltd,
     'Exit route from textiles', 7 October 1998.

40   AM–EF, 'Phase 2' postcards, October 1996; 'A trend to tweed and towards typical
     "English" look', *Wool Record*, 155 (November 1996), 66.

41   J. L. Coates, interview by author, Guiseley, West Yorkshire, 5 May 2015; M. Aveyard,
     interview by author, Guiseley, West Yorkshire, 22 April 2015; 'A story behind every
     cloth', *Wool Record*, 167 (July 2008), 52.

42   AM–EF, J. P. T. Walsh, Abraham Moon and Sons Ltd, Guiseley, to G. Portland, Purley,
     Surrey, 4 March 1997.

43   J. P. T. Walsh, interview by author, Guiseley, West Yorkshire, 25 October 2016; AM-EF,
     'Analysis of Export Turnover on a Monthly Basis Year to March '94'.

44   J. P. T. Walsh interview (23 May 2015).

45   R. Negrini, email to author, 7 November 2016; Essevi archive, Milan, J. Walsh to
     Ennetex s.a.s. di R. Negrini & C., Milan, 30 March 1987.

46   J. P. T. Walsh, email to author, 7 November 2016.

47   J. P. T. Walsh interview (23 May 2015).

48   'New patterns of production in the Prato textile trade', *Wool Record*, 153 (July 1994), 37.

49   AM–EF, 'UK customers, winter 92/93', 21 November 1991.

50   J. P. T. Walsh, interview by author, Guiseley, West Yorkshire (26 May 2016); 'Italians
     beaten at their own game', *Yorkshire Post* (22 April 1996).

51   World Trade Organization, 'Understanding the WTO: who we are', at www.wto.org/
     english/thewto_e/whatis_e/who_we_are_e.htm (accessed 12 November 2016).

52   'Dormeuil give an added meaning to Entente Cordiale', *Wool Record*, 151 (March 1992),
     55; D. E. and J. Levy, 'Dormeuil House: The most spectacular new office building in the
     West End', advertisement in *Financial Times* (23 September 1994).

53   S. Roberts, 'Dormeuil see bright future for high-quality wool suits: Joint ventures in the
     Far East', *Wool Record*, 155 (January 1996), 12.

54 P. Ackroyd, telephone interview by author (21 October 2016); AM–EF, *National Wool Textile Export Corporation Report for 1996/1997* (Bradford: British Wool Textile Export Corporation, 1996), p. 8; AM–EF, British Wool Textile Export Corporation, *British Wool Textile Exports 1997/98* (Bradford: British Wool Textile Export Corporation, 1997), p. 2.

55 P. Ackroyd, interview by author, Saltaire, West Yorkshire, 12 May 2015; AM–EF, British Wool Textile Export Corporation, *National Wool Textile Export Corporation Annual Report for 1996/97*, pp. 4–9; AM–EF, British Wool Textile Export Corporation, 'Chairman's briefing note, joint meeting of the council of the corporation and the promotion committee of NWTEC', 12 December 2007.

56 A. Garrett, 'Handing out the gongs for industry', *Observer* (21 April 1996); 'The 1996 winners of the Queen's Awards', *Independent* (21 April 1996).

57 N. Renton, interview by author, Guiseley, West Yorkshire, 17 March 2015.

58 J. Luesby, 'The Queen's Awards: Designs on global markets', *Financial Times* (22 April 1996).

59 T. L. Friedman, 'Big Mac I', *New York Times* (8 December 1996); T. L. Friedman, 'Big Mac II', *New York Times* (11 December 1996).

60 J. Luesby, 'Forget the width—feel the quality', *Financial Times* (8 May 1996).

61 P. Brown, 'When cloth is cut to suit the market', *The Times* (22 April 1996).

62 Luesby, 'The Queen's Awards'.

63 AM–EF, John P. T. Walsh to Richard Bruce, Dept. T16, Marks and Spencer, London, 8 October 1998.

64 AM–EF, Ashley Portland, 'A critical evaluation of the production techniques adopted by Moon & Sons Ltd as compared with Neill Johnstone Ltd' (autumn 1997), p. 3; AM–EF, Konen Herrenkleiderfabrik KG to Abraham Moon and Sons, 21 February 1989; AM–EF, 'Seasonal statistics report—summary as of 27/4/97'; J. P. T. Walsh interview (21 June 2016).

65 AM–EF, Textile and Clothing Strategy Group, *A National Strategy for the UK Textile and Clothing Industry* [2000], pp. 7, 22.

66 'C&A to close all 109 UK stores', *Financial Times* (16 June 2000); P. Hollinger and C. Tighe, 'C&A was forced down-market and now out', *Financial Times* (16 June 2000).

67 'Interstoff opens new trade doors in Asia', *Wool Record*, 151 (January 1992), 10.

68 The dates of the first Intertextile shows are documented in the Messe Frankfurt archive; P. Kerwien, Historisches Archiv, Messe Frankfurt, Frankfurt am Main, Germany, email to author, 9 December 2016; AM–EF, British Wool Textile Export Corporation, *National Wool Textile Export Corporation Annual Report for 1996/97*, p. 10.

69 J. P. T. Walsh, email to author, 14 November 2016; J. P. T. Walsh interview (21 June 2016); AM–EF, British Wool Textile Export Corporation, *National Wool Textile Export Corporation Annual Report for 1996/97*, p. 10; AM–EF, British Wool Textile Export

Corporation, *British Wool Textile Exports 1998/99: Annual Report of the National Wool Textile Export Corporation* (Bradford: British Wool Textile Export Corporation, 1999), n.p.; AM–EF, National Wool Textile Export Corporation, Weekly letter no. 2778, 4 May 2007.

70 'Consumer confidence severely shaken since September 11 attacks', *Wool Record*, 160 (January 2002), 7; 'United States downturn hurts Europe', *Wool Record*, 160 (January 2002), 62; 'Wool popular in fancies for summer 2003', *Wool Record*, 160 (February 2002), 16–17; H. Williams, 'Doubts over early shows', *Wool Record*, 160 (April 2002), 53.

71 H. Williams, 'Positive signs after a tough year in luxury markets', *Wool Record*, 161 (September 2002), 40.

72 H. Williams, 'Industry leaders define keys to recovery', *Wool Record*, 161 (November 2002), 53.

73 H. Williams, 'Bond between Italy and Britain', *Wool Record*, 161 (January 2003), 11.

74 'Another hard year for luxury apparel', *Wool Record*, 162 (September 2003), 73.

75 H. Williams, 'Première Vision to look beyond Europe', *Wool Record*, 161 (April 2002), 7; H. Williams, 'Stylish return to the 1940s', *Wool Record*, 161 (November 2002), 43.

76 AM–EF, British Wool Textile Export Corporation, 'The British wool textile industry: Visit of HRH the Duke of York to Première Vision, 13th February 2003', 21 January 2003; 'Royal visit boosts British weaving sector', *Wool Record*, 162 (April 2003), 11.

77 Founded by entrepreneur Sidney Kimmel in 1970 as a division of W. R. Grace, Jones New York took inspiration from Cacharel Paris, producing clothes for the 26-year-old career girl who wanted a good fit and a slightly edgy look. Kimmel made Jones New York into one of Seventh Avenue's top women's wear designer-manufacturers using a multi-brand strategy that included the eponymous Jones label along with Evan-Picone, Rena Rowan and Lauren by Ralph Lauren.

78 Jones Apparel Group, *1996 Annual Report*, pp. 5, 13.

79 J. P. T. Walsh interview (21 June 2016).

80 A. D'Innocenzio, 'Jones's new take on Evan-Picone', *Women's Wear Daily* (17 February 1999).

81 E. Wilson and T. J. Ryan, 'Polo-Jones new deal: A global presence for Lauren, Ralph lines', *Women's Wear Daily* (16 November 2000).

82 Jones Apparel Group, *2002 Annual report*, pp. 9–11; L. Lockwood, 'Sidney Kimmel: The quiet giant tells his story', *Women's Wear Daily* (21 April 2014).

83 J. P. T. Walsh interview (21 June 2016).

84 AM–EF, S. S. Markowitz, Todtman, Nachamie, Spizz & Johns, New York, to creditors of the St. Andrews Textile Company, Inc., 9 April 2003; 'John Dreschel: Obituary', *NorthJersey.com*, 26 May 2013, at www.legacy.com/obituaries/northjersey/obituary.aspx?pid=165010007 (accessed 5 November 2016).

85 David Hudson, telephone interview by author, 11 November 2016; AM–EF, list of customers with appointments at trade fairs, autumn 2004.

86 AM, Minutes, 19 July 1996 and 30 July 1997.

87 AM–EF, 'Management meeting', 19 April 1999.

88 AM–EF, G. Strange, Fabric Brokers UK, Bradford, to J. P. T. Walsh, 15 April 1999; A. Morton, KPMG, Huddersfield, to J. P. T. Walsh, 30 September 1996.

89 J. P. T. Walsh interview (23 May 2015).

90 Minimalism dominated *Elle Decoration* in September and October 2003. The astute reader, however, might anticipate the return of bold colour and textured embellishments from features such as 'Just hanging around', *Elle Decoration* (September 2003), 128–35, which paired modern and vintage styles.

91 'Things we love', *Country Homes & Interiors* (October 2004), 13; 'City charm', *Country Homes & Interiors* (October 2004), 51–7; 'A history lesson', *Country Homes & Interiors* (October 2004), 43–6; 'Mix and match pastel tweeds', *Country Homes & Interiors* (October 2004), 65–73.

92 J. Liddle, 'Rapid growth in the United States', *Wool Record*, 160 (August 2001), 28.

93 J. P. T. Walsh interviews (23 May 2015 and 25 October 2016).

94 J. P. T. Walsh interview (23 May 2015); AM–EF, confidential reports by the home furnishings consultant, 2003–2005.

95 AM–EF, press release, 'Heimtextil 2004'; AM–EF, *Moon Established 1837*, brochure for furnishings collection, ca. 2004.

96 AM–EF, *Design and Decoration Awards 2004*, p. 8.

97 'Hainsworth launches new interiors business', *Wool Record*, 165 (June 2006), 33; 'Study urges re-launch for wool in interior textiles', *Wool Record*, 165 (July 2006), 21.

98 J. Carracher, 'British fabrics go high-end', *Daily News Record* (19 July 2004).

99 T. Wyatt, 'Textiles show the way says Sir Digby', *West Yorkshire and North Yorkshire Counties Publications* (14 March 2005).

100 AM–EF, 'U.S. visit 11th October', [2002].

101 Minutes of the management meeting, 19 April 1999; AM–EF, 'Abraham Moon, Marketing Plan Proposal', 3 May 2000.

102 J. P. T. Walsh interview (23 May 2015).

103 'Desire for fashion as prosperity spreads', *Wool Record*, 160 (July 2001), 24.

104 G. de Jonquières, 'Clothes on the line', *Financial Times* (19 July 2004).

105 M. Keighley, 'China's textile engine moves into a higher gear', *Wool Record*, 162 (April 2003), 1.

106 '"Surrendering without a fight" on Chinese imports', *Wool Record*, 164 (May 2005), 1.

107 'Intense competition in the UK apparel market', *Wool Record*, 162 (January 2004), 15; S. Bain, 'High street stores move to new pricing structures', *Wool Record*, 165 (February 2006), 32.

108 'Jaeger and Viyella businesses have new owners', *Wool Record*, 162 (April 2003), 6.

109 S. Bain, 'How high street stores source clothing', *Wool Record*, 164 (October 2005), 44; Bain, 'High street stores move to new price structures'.

110 J. P. T. Walsh interview (25 October 2016); AM–EF, 'Sales meeting', 20 October 2005.

111 'Luxury market is ripe for product evolution', *Wool Record*, 162 (December 2003), 82–3; J. Sugden, telephone interview by author, 21 October 2016.

112 'British mills advised to aim at the top end', *Wool Record*, 163 (July 2004), 21.

113 'Boho chick meets luxury pup', *Elle Decoration* (October 2005), 173.

114 J. P. T. Walsh interview (23 May 2015); J. P. T. Walsh, email to author (14 March 2017). Tempest Bailey was subsequently folded into Abraham Moon and Sons Ltd.

115 H. Williams, 'Men and women abandon dressing down', *Wool Record*, 160 (May 2001), 4; 'Return to formal dress', *Wool Record,* 160 (May 2001), 37; 'Smartness back in vogue', *Wool Record*, 160 (July 2001), 43.

116 J. Liddle, 'Dormeuil continues to support British mills', *Wool Record*, 161 (April 2002), 60–1.

117 S. Hoppough, 'The Sophisticate', *Daily News Record* (21 July 2008).

118 J. P. T. Walsh interview (23 May 2015).

119 S. Bain, 'Women thinking twice before spending on fashion', *Wool Record,* 165 (July 2006), 31.

120 J. P. T. Walsh interview (23 May 2015).

121 AM–EF, 'Analysis of export turnover on a monthly basis year to March 2006'.

122 J. P. T. Walsh interview (21 June 2016).

123 J. P. T. Walsh interview (23 May 2015).

124 'Lifetime's creativity, *Wool Record*, 162 (September 2003), 77.

125 'Renewed optimism at Neill Johnstone', *Wool Record*, 166 (October 2007), 43.

126 G. Lockwood, interview by author, Guiseley, West Yorkshire (17 March 2015); J. P. T. Walsh interview (23 May 2015).

127 AM–EF, British/National Wool Textile Export Corporation, 'Minutes of the joint meeting of the council and the promotion committee of the British/National Wool Textile Export Corporation', 12 December 2007.

128 AM–EF, 'Sales plan/review', 6 July 2006.

129 'Chance for quality as people seek to escape empty lives', *Wool Record*, 164 (November 2005), 13.

130 J. P. T. Walsh interview (23 May 2015); 'Vertical mill's new horizons', *Wool Record*, 161 (January 2003), 25; AM–EF, J. P T. Walsh, 'Purchase of the assets, stock and business of Wallass & Company Ltd', 2007; 'Companies get together to save jobs', *Yorkshire Post* (13 September 2007); 'Abraham Moon saves Bradford worsted firm', *Wool Record*, 166 (November 2007), 6.

131 A. McIntyre, 'The big dilemma: Green fields of the survival of a local

company?', *Wharfedale Observer* (23 October 2007); 'Guiseley group opposes company bid to build houses', *Wharfedale Observer* (14 February 2008).

132 R. E. Wilkinson, interview by author, Guiseley, West Yorkshire (23 June 2016); J. P. T. Walsh interview (23 May 2016).

133 'Johnstons install new dyehouse', *Wool Record*, 160 (September 2001), 19–21.

134 Wilkinson interview; 'Tweed production is consolidated', *Wool Record*, 149 (September 1990), 15.

135 AM–EF, J. P. T. Walsh, 'Moon announcement to all employees of J. D. Matthewman based at Morley', [2009]; AM–EF, 'Bronte Tweeds sales order list', 12 December 2009; J. P. T. Walsh interview (23 May 2015).

136 'Be inspired by modern rustic style', *Country Homes & Interiors* (October 2009), 72–5.

137 Wilkinson interview.

138 *Ibid.*

139 J. P. T. Walsh interview (23 May 2015).

140 D. Thomas, *Deluxe: How Luxury Lost Its Luster* (New York: Penguin, 2007).

141 AM–EF, British Wool Textile Export Corporation, Weekly letter no. 2802, 1 February 2008.

142 J. Dyson, 'Meeting the demands of today's consumer', *Wool Record*, 167 (January 2008), 3.

143 AM–DD, promotional materials for Heritage Collection, 2007; S. O'Grady, 'Minor British institutions: Prince of Wales check', *Independent* (1 October 2010).

144 J. P. T. Walsh interview (21 June 2016).

145 AM–EF, 'Abraham Moon & Sons Limited: P&L forecast based on client information', 18 October 2007; AM–EF, 'New York 2007'; J. P. T. Walsh interview (23 May 2015).

146 J. P. T. Walsh interview (23 May 2015).

147 Marsh, 'Men's designers see allure in fabrics from Britain'.

148 Ackroyd interview (12 May 2015); AM–EF, B. Greenwood, Department for Business Enterprise and Regulatory Reform, London, to G. Lockwood, Abraham Moon and Sons, 25 January 2008; AM–EF, British Wool Textile Export Corporation, Weekly letter no. 2802, 1 February 2008; AM–EF, 'Minutes of the joint meeting of the council and the promotion committee of the British/National Wool Textile Export Corporation', 29 April 2008; AM–EF, Geoffrey Martin & Company, Leeds, to J. Walsh, Leeds, 30 April 2010.

149 AM–EF, Malcolm Jarvis, President, Confederation of British Wool Textiles Ltd, Huddersfield, to All Member Firms, 29 June 2009.

150 F. Britten, 'Made in Britain—manufacturing in the UK?', *Sunday Times* (22 January 2012).

151 E. Marsh, 'Men's designers see allure in fabrics from Britain', *Women's Wear Daily* (9 April 2009).

152 'Turning history into heritage', *Daily Telegraph* (28 November 2011).

153 AM–EF, John P.T. Walsh, Memo re: Jon Wall, 3 January 2011.

154 AM–EF, 'Yorkshire furnishings firm Moon boosts sales & profits', *The Furnishing Report* (23 October 2012).

155 Britten, 'Made in Britain—manufacturing in the UK?'

156 'Turning history into heritage'.

157 J. Warren, 'Why wool is spinning back into fashion', *Express* (25 March 2013); G. Ruddick, 'M&S turns to "Best of British" for clothing revival', *Telegraph* (19 February 2013); B. Barrow, 'Would you go to M&S for an £800 suit?', *DailyMail.com* (19 July 2013); University of Leeds, Marks and Spencer Company Archive, press release, 'M&S Collection, Best of British, M&S Menswear to show at London Collections: Men', June 2013, and booklet, 'Marks & Spencer, Best of British, Autumn Winter 13'.

158 D. Nicholls, 'Men's hotlist', *Telegraph Magazine* (24 August 2013); 'M&S Best of British menswear range', *Guardian* (11 October 2013).

159 'Quintessentially British collection launching for Autumn/Winter 2014', *Country Homes & Interiors* (October 2014), 15, 83–90.

160 'Turning history into heritage'.

161 'Boom time as Moon balloons from its Guiseley mill', *Yorkshire Post* (24 June 2013); 'Guiseley woollen mill is expanded', *Bradford Telegraph and Argue* (20 July 2013).

162 J. P. T. Walsh interview (23 May 2015).

163 *Ibid.*

164 'Gripping yarn of mill success', *Yorkshire Post* (5 July 2015).

165 'Textile jobs to boost Yorkshire', *Yorkshire Post* (10 February 2015).

9 Fashionability: the way forward

1 Author's observations, Top Drawer, 18–19 January 2016; Olympia London, 'Our story', at http://olympia.london/about-us/our-story (accessed 20 November 2016); Top Drawer, 'About Top Drawer', at www.topdrawer.co.uk/about (accessed 20 November 2016).

2 Author's observations, Top Drawer.

3 *Ibid.*

4 K. Anderson, telephone interview by author, 8 July 2016.

5 Author's observations, Top Drawer.

6 P. Birchenall, interview by author, Guiseley, West Yorkshire, 22 June 2016.

7 A. Seal, interview by author, Bradford, West Yorkshire, 21 October 2016.

8 A. Dougill, interview by author, Guiseley, West Yorkshire, 22 June 2016.

9 C. Pearson, interview by author, Guiseley, West Yorkshire, 22 June 2016.

10 Birchenall interview.

11 J. Crew, 'Ludlow blazer in herringbone English tweed', comments on 'Terribly Tasty Tweed' by a consumer from Pittsburgh, PA, 4 December 2015, at www.jcrew.com/uk/p/C8778 (accessed 19 November 2016).

12 Crew, 'Ludlow blazer in herringbone English tweed'.

13 Abraham Moon and Sons Ltd, Guiseley, West Yorkshire, Executive files (AM–EF), B. Northcote, Clarence House, London, to J. P. T. Walsh, 21 December 2009; S. Conti, 'Prince Charles touts wool', *Women's Wear Daily* (28 January 2010); Australian Wool Innovation, 'AWI's History', at www.wool.com/about-awi/who-we-are/awis-history/ (accessed 19 November 2016).

14 'HRH, Prince of Wales attends global Campaign for Wool event', *Wireless News*, 17 November 2012; 'UK Wool Week', *Twist*, 47 (December 2012), 12.

15 'Campaign for Wool launches in China', *Twist*, 41 (May 2012), 7; C. Rogers, 'Optimistic outlook', *Twist*, 43 (July/August 2012), 5; 'C. Rogers, 'Campaign catch up', *Twist*, 49 (February/March 2013), 48–9.

16 AM–EF, Campaign for Wool, 'The Dumfries House Wool Declaration', issued at the Dumfries House Conference, 9 September 2016.

17 J. Sugden, telephone interview by author, 21 October 2016.

18 P. Ackroyd, telephone interview by author, 21 October 2016.

19 C. Rogers, 'Getting it right', *Twist*, 45 (October 2012), 4; 'Bangladesh fire reverberations continue', *Twist*, 48 (January 2013), 7; C. Rogers, 'Too high a price to pay', *Twist*, 52 (June 2013), 6; 'Taking responsibility', Twist, 52 (June 2013), 12–13.

20 L. Siegle, 'Am I a fool to expect more than corporate greenwashing?', *Guardian* (3 April 2016); R. L. Blaszczyk, *American Consumer Society, 1865–2005: From Hearth to HDTV* (Hoboken, NJ: Wiley, 2009).

21 J. Crew, 'Social Responsibility', at www.jcrew.com/uk/flatpages/social_res_april1.jsp?bmUID=lxSQ3i_&bmLocale=en_GB (accessed 19 November 2016).

22 C. Rogers, 'Best of British', *Twist*, 49 (February/March 2013), 21–2.

23 'Sugden "profoundly optimistic" for UK textiles industry', *Twist*, 46 (November 2012), 7.

Select bibliography

Archives

NB: abbreviations are used in the Notes.

Abraham Moon and Sons Ltd, Guiseley, West Yorkshire
    Archival files (AM–AF)
    Executive files (AM–EF)
    Design department files (AM–DD)

Aireborough Historical Society, Yeadon, West Yorkshire (AHS)

Boston Public Library, Boston, MA, USA
    Filene's marketing archive (BPL–FA)

Bradford College, Bradford, West Yorkshire
    Bradford Textile Archive

Worshipful Company of Clothworkers, London (CC)
    Clothworkers' Company Archive

Gerald Long, Guiseley, West Yorkshire
    Papers related to James Ives & Company

Jane Blake, Guiseley, West Yorkshire
    Papers related to Crooklands

Leeds Central Library, Local and Family History Library (LCL)

Peter Ackroyd, Saltaire, West Yorkshire
    Records of the National Wool Textile Export Corporation (PA–NWTEC)

The National Archives, Kew (TNA)
    TNA–BT43 Records of the Board of Trade and successors, Design Registry
    TNA–BT64/855 Records of the Board of Trade and successors, Wool Concentration
    TNA–WO372 Records of the War Office, Service Medal and Award Rolls Index, First
        World War
    TNA–WO374 Records of the War Office, Officers' Services, First World War,
        Personal files

University of Glasgow Archive Services
    UG–C, GB 248 UGD 199/1 J & P Coats Ltd Archive

University of Leeds

    Marks and Spencer Company Archive (UL–M&S)

    Brotherton Library, Special Collections

        BUS/Boyd: Records of Thomas Boyd

        BUS/Crowther: W. & E. Crowther Ltd, Business Archive

        BUS/Clay: J. T. Clay and Sons Ltd, Business Archive

        LAVC/NSP/38: Leeds Tailoring Industry Papers

    An Archive of International Textiles, University of Leeds (ULITA)

    University Archive (UL–UA)

    Yorkshire Fashion Archive, School of Design

Westminster City Archives, London (WCA)

    1327: Jaeger Archives

    2268: S. Addington & Company Ltd, Business Records

West Yorkshire Archive Service, Leeds (WYAS–L)

    BDP29: Records of Guiseley Parish

    GB–GAU: Diary of Reuben Gaunt, Pudsey, 1841–54, transcription, 1975

    WYL434: Records of John Barran & Sons Ltd

    WYL1008: Records of Heatons of Leeds Ltd

    WYL2139: Records of A. W. Hainsworth and Sons Ltd

    WYL2142: Records of Fred Armitage Lodge and Sons

    Microfiche: Records of Guiseley Parish

West Yorkshire Archive Service, Wakefield (WYAS–W)

    West Yorkshire Registry of Deeds (WYRD)

Books and articles

Aldcroft, D. H. (ed.), *The Development of British Industry and Foreign Competition, 1875–1914* (London: George Allen & Unwin, 1968).

Anderson, F., 'Spinning the ephemeral with the sublime: Modernity and landscape in men's fashion textiles, 1860–1900', *Fashion Theory*, vol. 9, no. 3, 2005.

Anderson, F., 'This sporting cloth: Tweed, gender and fashion, 1860–1900', *Textile History*, vol. 37, no. 2, 2006.

Anderson, F., *Tweed* (London: Bloomsbury Academic, 2016).

Bathelt, H., F. Golfetto, and D. Rinallo (eds), *Trade Shows in the Globalizing Knowledge Economy* (Cambridge: Cambridge University Press, 2014).

Bathelt, H., and G. Zeng (eds), *Temporary Knowledge Ecologies: The Rise of Trade Fairs in the Asia-Pacific Region* (Cheltenham: Edward Elgar, 2015).

Bentley, P., *Colne Valley Cloth: From the Earliest Times to the Present Day* (London: Curwen Press, 1947).

Beresford, M. W., and R. Unsworth, 'Locating the early service sector of Leeds: The origins of an office district', *Northern History*, vol. 44, no. 1, March 2007.

Blaszczyk, R. L., 'Styling synthetics: DuPont's marketing of fabrics and fashions in postwar America', *Business History Review*, vol. 80, no. 3, autumn 2006.

Blaszczyk, R. L., *American Consumer Society, 1865–2005: From Hearth to HDTV* (Hoboken, NJ: Wiley, 2009).

Blaszczyk, R. L., *The Color Revolution* (Cambridge, MA: The MIT Press, 2012).

Blaszczyk, R.L., and B. Wubs (eds), *The Fashion Forecasters: A Hidden History of Color and Trend Prediction* (London: Bloomsbury Academic, forthcoming).

Breward, C., *The Suit: Form, Function and Style* (London: Reaktion Books, 2016).

Burt, S., and K. Grady, *The Illustrated History of Leeds*, 2nd edn (Derby: Breedon Books, 2002).

Caunce, S. A., 'Complexity, community structure and competitive advantage within the Yorkshire woollen industry, c. 1700–1850', *Business History*, vol. 39, no. 4, October 1997.

Caunce, S. A., 'Houses as museums: The case of the Yorkshire wool textile industry', *Transactions of the Royal Historical Society*, vol. 13, 2003.

Chapman, S., 'The decline and rise of textile merchanting, 1880–1990', *Business History*, vol. 32, no. 4, November 1990.

Chapman, S., *Merchant Enterprise in Britain: From the Industrial Revolution to World War I* (Cambridge: Cambridge University Press, 1992).

Church, R. A. (ed.), *The Dynamics of Victorian Business: Problems and Perspectives to the 1870s* (London: Allen & Unwin, 1980).

Clapham, J. H., *The Woollen and Worsted Industries* (London: Methuen & Company, 1907).

Cooper, W., *Bygone Guiseley* (Guiseley: M. T. D. Rigg, 1995).

Crump, W. B., and G. Ghorbal, *History of the Huddersfield Woollen Industry* (Huddersfield: Alfred Jubb & Son, 1935).

Daly, S., 'Kashmir shawls in mid-Victorian novels', *Victorian Literature and Culture*, vol. 30, no. 1, 2002.

Davies, G., and J. Davies, *What's Next?* (London: Century, 1989).

Dobson, E. P., and J. B. Ives, *A Century of Achievement: The History of James Ives & Company Limited, 1848–1948* (London: William Sessions, 1948).

Farnie, D. A., 'John Rylands of Manchester', *Bulletin of the John Rylands University Library of Manchester*, vol. 56, no. 1, autumn 1973.

Fraser, D. (ed.), *A History of Modern Leeds* (Manchester: Manchester University Press, 1980).

Gavenas, M. L., 'Who decides the color of the season? How a trade show called Première Vision changed fashion culture', in R. L. Blaszczyk and U. Spiekermann (eds), *Bright Modernity: Color, Commerce, and Consumer Culture* (New York: Palgrave Macmillan, 2017).

Godley, A., *Jewish Immigrant Entrepreneurship in New York and London, 1880–1914: Enterprise and Culture* (New York: Palgrave, 2001).

Gosden, P., 'From county college to civic university, Leeds, 1904', *Northern History*, vol. 42, no. 2, September 2005.

Gregory, D., *Regional Transformation and Industrial Revolution: A Geography of the Yorkshire Woollen Industry* (London: Macmillan Press, 1982).

Green, N. L., *Ready-to-Wear and Ready-to-Work: A Century of Industry and Immigrants in Paris and New York* (Durham, NC: Duke University Press, 1997).

Greysmith, D., 'Patterns, piracy and protection in the textile printing industry, 1787–1850', *Textile History*, vol. 14, no. 2, 1983.

Gulvin, C., *The Tweedmakers: A History of the Scottish Fancy Woollen Industry, 1600–1914* (Newton Abbott: David & Charles, 1973).

Halls, J., 'Questions of attribution: Registered designs at the National Archives', *Journal of Design History*, vol. 26, no. 4, 2013.

Harrison, E. P., *Scottish Estate Tweeds* (Elgin, Scotland: Johnstons of Elgin, 1995).

Hartley, W. C. E., *Banking in Yorkshire* (Clapham, North Yorkshire: Dalesman, 1975).

Hatcher, C. J., *The Industrial Architecture of Yorkshire* (Chichester: Phillimore & Co., 1985).

Hitchon, P. M., *Chanel and the Tweedmaker: Weavers of Dreams* (Carlisle: P3 Publications, 2013).

Honeyman, K., *Well Suited: A History of the Leeds Clothing Industry, 1850–1900* (Oxford: Oxford University Press, 2000).

Honeyman, K., 'Style monotony and the business of fashion: The marketing of menswear in inter-war England', *Textile History*, no. 34, no. 2, 2003.

Howe, A., *Free Trade and Liberal England, 1846–1946* (Oxford: Oxford University Press, 1997).

Hudson, P., *The Genesis of Industrial Capital: A Study of the West Riding Wool Textile Industry, c. 1750–1850* (Cambridge: Cambridge University Press, 1986).

Hughes, K., *Great War Britain: Bradford Remembering 1914–18* (Stroud: History Press, 2015).

Jeffreys, J. B., *Retail Trading in Britain, 1850–1950* (Cambridge: Cambridge University Press, 1954).

Jenkins, D. T., 'The response of the European wool textile manufacturers to the opening of the Japanese market', *Textile History*, vol. 19, no. 2, 1988.

Jenkins, D. T., and K. G. Ponting, *The British Wool Textile Industry, 1770–1914* (London: Heinemann Educational Books, 1982).

Keighley, M., *Wool City: A History of the Bradford Textile Industry in the 20th Century* (Ilkley: G. Whitaker & Co., 2007).

Kindleberger, C. P., 'The rise of free trade in Western Europe, 1820–1875', *Journal of Economic History*, 35, no. 1, March 1975.

Kriegel, L., 'Culture and the copy: Calico, capitalism, and design copyright in early Victorian Britain', *Journal of British Studies*, vol. 43, no. 2, April 2004.

Lampe, M., 'Explaining nineteenth-century bilateralism: Economic and political determinants of the Cobden-Chevalier network', *Economic History Review*, vol. 64, no. 2, 2011.

Lazer, D., 'The free trade epidemic of the 1860s and other outbreaks of economic discrimination', *World Politics*, vol. 51, no. 4, July 1999.

Leavitt, T. W., 'Fashion, commerce and technology in the nineteenth century: The shawl trade', *Textile History*, vol. 3, no. 1, 1972.

Levitt, S., 'Cheap mass-produced men's clothing in the nineteenth and early twentieth centuries', *Textile History*, vol. 22, no. 2, 1991.

Lorin, P., *Dormeuil: The History of Fabric Is Woven into the Fabric of History* (Paris: Dormeuil Frères, 1992).

Lyons, A. M. M., 'The textile fabrics of India and [the] Huddersfield cloth industry', *Textile Industry*, vol. 27, no. 2, 1996.

Marsh, P. T., *Bargaining on Europe: Britain and the First Common Market, 1860–92* (New Haven: Yale University Press, 1999).

Mitchell, M. R., *A History of Leeds* (Bath: Phillimore & Co., 2000).

National Institute of Economic and Social Research, *Trade Regulations and Commercial Policy of the United Kingdom* (Cambridge: Cambridge University Press, 1943).

Pasold, Eric W., *Ladybird, Ladybird: A Story of Private Enterprise* (Manchester: Manchester University Press, 1977).

Philpott, W. J., *The Organisation of Wholesale Textile Distribution* (London: MacDonald, 1959).

O'Byrne, R., *Style City: How London Became a Fashion Capital* (London: Frances Lincoln, 2009).

Owen, G, *The Rise and Fall of Great Companies: Courtaulds and the Reshaping of the Man-Made Fibres Industry* (Oxford and New York: Oxford University Press, 2010).

Prescott, J., *Fashion Textiles Now* (London: Vivays Publishing, 2013).

Rees, G., *St Michael: A History of Marks and Spencer* (London: Weidenfeld and Nicolson, 1969).

Ritaine, E., 'Prato: An extreme case of diffuse industrialization', *International Studies of Management and Organization*, vol. 20, no. 4, 1990.

Rothstein, N., 'The introduction of the Jacquard loom to Great Britain', in V. Gervers (ed.) *Studies in Textile History in Memory of Harold B. Burnham* (Toronto: Royal Ontario Museum, 1977).

Schoeser, M., and C. Rufey, *English and American Textiles, from 1790 to the Present* (London: Thames and Hudson, 1989).

Sigsworth, E. M., *Montague Burton: The Tailor of Taste* (Manchester: Manchester University Press, 1990).

Smail, J., *The Origins of Middle-Class Culture: Halifax, Yorkshire, 1660–1780* (Ithaca, NY: Cornell University Press, 1994).

Smail, J., *Merchants, Markets and Manufacture: The English Wool Textile Industry in the Eighteenth Century* (New York: St. Martin's Press, 1999).

Smail, J., 'The sources of innovation in the woollen and worsted industry of eighteenth-century Yorkshire', *Business History*, vol. 41, no. 1, January 1999.

Smith, P., D. Sudjic, and D. Loveday, *Hello, My Name Is Paul Smith: Fashion and Other Stories* (New York: Rizzoli, 2013).

Spoerer, M., *C&A: A Family Business in Germany, the Netherlands and the United Kingdom, 1911–1961* (Munich: Verlag C. H. Beck, 2016).

Stillie, T. A., 'The evolution of pattern design in the Scottish woollen textile industry in the nineteenth century', *Textile History*, vol. 1, no. 3, 1970.

Sykas, P. A., 'The public require spots: Modernism and the nineteenth century calico designer', *Journal of the Textile Institute*, vol. 89, no. 3, 1998.

Taylor, L., 'Wool cloth and gender: The use of woollen cloth in women's dress in Britain, 1865-85', in A. de la Haye and E. Wilson (eds), *Defining Dress: Dress as Object, Meaning and Identity* (Manchester: Manchester University Press, 1999).

Thornton, D., *The Story of Leeds* (Stroud: The History Press, 2013).

Toms, S., and Q. Zhang, 'Marks & Spencer and the decline of the British textile industry, 1950–2000', *Business History Review*, vol. 90, no.1, March 2016.

Trentmann, F., *Free Trade Nation: Commerce, Consumption, and Civil Society in Modern Britain* (Oxford: Oxford University Press, 2008).

Tynan, J., 'Military dress and men's outdoor leisurewear: Burberry's trench coat in First World War Britain', *Journal of Design History*, vol. 24, no. 2, 2011.

Tynan, J., *British Army Uniform and the First World War: Men in Khaki* (Basingstoke: Palgrave Macmillan, 2013).

Webster, C. (ed.), *Building a Great Victorian City: Leeds Architects and Architecture, 1790–1914* (England: Northern Heritage Publications, 2011).

Wilson, R. G., *Gentleman Merchants: The Merchant Community in Leeds, 1700–1830* (Manchester: Manchester University Press, 1971).

Worth, R., *Fashion for the People: A History of Clothing at Marks & Spencer* (New York: Berg, 2007).

Wrathmell, S., *Leeds* (New Haven: Yale University Press, 2005).

Young, C., and A. Martin, *Tartan and Tweed* (London: Frances Lincoln, 2017).

Zeitlin, J., 'The clothing industry in transition: International trends and British response', in S. D. Chapman (ed.), *The Textile Industries*, vol. 4: *Twentieth-Century Developments* (London: I. B. Tauris, 1997).

Index

Note: trading names are given with first name first; italics indicate an illustration